1 test.
2 ways.
The choice is yours.

The GMAT™ exam is available everyday. Online & in-person.

 gmat.com

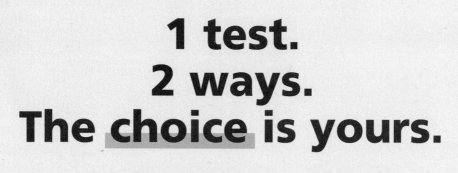

Compare.

Download the **free comparison grid** to see which format is best for you.

ONLINE **&** TEST CENTER

gmat.com/compare

Learn.

Listen to **Inside the GMAT™** official podcast to become a GMAT insider.

insidethegmat.com

Graduate Management Admission Council

GMAT™

GMAT™ Official Guide Quantitative Review 2022

Add over 370 quantitative practice questions to your prep.

 Book +  Online + Mobile

What's included

Book:

- ✓ Over 370 practice questions not included in the main Official Guide
- ✓ Answer explanations
- ✓ Review chapter with 25 practice questions
- ✓ Quick reference sheets of common formulas and concepts

The ONLY source of real GMAT™ questions from past exams

Online tools:

- ✓ Question Bank
- ✓ Flash cards
- ✓ Mobile app

GMAT™ Official Prep

GMAT™ Official Guide Quantitative Review 2022

For general information on our other products and services or to obtain technical support please contact our Customer Care Department within the U.S. at (877) 762-2974, outside the U.S. at (317) 572-3993 or fax (317) 572-4002.

Wiley also publishes its books in a variety of electronic formats. Some content that appears in print may not be available in electronic books. For more information about Wiley products, please visit our Web site at www.wiley.com.

ISBN 978-1-119-79378-6 (pbk); ISBN 978-1-119-79387-8 (ePub)

Printed in the United States of America

SKY10024664_041221

Table of Contents

Dear GMAT™ Test-Taker,

Thank you for your interest in graduate management education. Today more than 7,000 graduate programs around the world use the GMAT exam to establish their MBA, business master's, and other graduate-level management degree programs as hallmarks of excellence. Nine out of ten new MBA enrollments globally are made using a GMAT score.*

By using the *GMAT™ Official Guide* to prepare for the GMAT™ exam, you're taking a very important step toward achieving your goals and pursuing admission to the MBA or business master's program that is the best fit for you.

This book, *GMAT™ Official Guide Quantitative Review 2022*, is designed to help you prepare for and build confidence to do your best on exam day. It's the only guide that features real questions from past exams published by the Graduate Management Admission Council (GMAC), the makers of the GMAT exam.

For more than 60 years, the GMAT exam has helped candidates like you demonstrate their command of the skills needed for success in the classroom and showcase to schools their commitment to pursuing a graduate business degree. Schools use and trust the GMAT exam as part of their admissions process because it's a proven predictor of classroom success and your ability to excel in your chosen program.

The mission of GMAC is to ensure no talent goes undiscovered. We are driven to continue improving the GMAT exam as well as helping you find and connect with the best-fit schools and programs for you. I applaud your commitment to educational success. This guide and the other GMAT™ Official Prep products available at mba.com will give you the confidence to achieve your personal best on the GMAT exam and launch or reinvigorate a rewarding career.

I wish you the best success on all your future educational and professional endeavors.

Sincerely,

Sangeet Chowfla
President & CEO of the Graduate Management Admission Council

---

*Top 100 *Financial Times* full-time MBA programs

GMAT™ Official Guide
Quantitative Review 2022

1.0 What Is the GMAT™ Exam?

1.0 What Is the GMAT™ Exam?

The Graduate Management Admission Test™ (GMAT™) exam is a standardized exam used in admissions decisions by more than 7,000 graduate management programs, at approximately 2,300 graduate business schools worldwide. It helps you gauge, and demonstrate to schools, your academic potential for success in graduate-level management studies.

The four-part exam measures your Analytical Writing, Integrated Reasoning, Verbal Reasoning, and Quantitative Reasoning skills—higher-order reasoning skills that management faculty, admissions professionals, and employers worldwide have identified as important for incoming students to have. "Higher-order" reasoning skills involve complex judgments, and include critical thinking, analysis, and problem solving. Unlike undergraduate grades and curricula, which vary in their meaning across regions and institutions, your GMAT scores provide a standardized, statistically valid and reliable measure of how you are likely to perform academically in the core curriculum of a graduate management program. The GMAT exam's validity, fairness, and value in admissions have been well-established through numerous academic studies.

The GMAT exam is delivered online or at a test center, entirely in English, and solely on a computer. It is not a test of business knowledge, subject-matter mastery, English vocabulary, or advanced computational skills. The GMAT exam also does not measure other factors related to success in graduate management study, such as job experience, leadership ability, motivation, and interpersonal skills. Your GMAT score is intended to be used as one admissions criterion among other, more subjective, criteria, such as admissions essays and interviews.

1.1 Why Take the GMAT™ Exam?

Taking the GMAT exam helps you stand out in the admissions process and demonstrate your readiness and commitment to pursuing graduate management education. Schools use GMAT scores to help them select the most qualified applicants—because they know that candidates who take the GMAT exam are serious about earning a graduate business degree, and it's a proven predictor of a student's ability to succeed in his or her chosen program. When you consider which programs to apply to, you can look at a school's use of the GMAT exam as one indicator of quality. Schools that use the GMAT exam typically list score ranges or average scores in their class profiles, so you may also find these profiles helpful in gauging the academic competitiveness of a program you are considering and how well your performance on the exam compares with that of the students enrolled in the program.

No matter how you perform on the GMAT exam, you should contact the schools that interest you to learn more and to ask how they use GMAT scores and other criteria (such as your undergraduate grades, essays, and letters of recommendation) in their admissions processes. School admissions offices, websites, and materials published by schools are the key sources of information when you are doing research about where you might want to go to business school.

> *Myth* -vs- **FACT**
>
> *M* – **If I don't achieve a high score on the GMAT exam, I won't get into my top choice schools.**
>
> F – **There are great schools available for candidates at any GMAT score range.**
>
> Fewer than 50 of the ~200,000 people taking the GMAT exam each year get a perfect score of 800; and many more get into top business school programs around the world each year. Admissions Officers use GMAT scores as one component in their admissions decisions, in conjunction with undergraduate records, application essays, interviews, letters of recommendation, and other information when deciding whom to accept into their programs. Visit School Finder on mba.com to learn about schools that are the best fit for you.

For more information on the GMAT exam, test preparation materials, registration, how to use and send your GMAT scores to schools, and applying to business school, please visit mba.com/gmat.

1.2 GMAT™ Exam Format

The GMAT exam consists of four separately timed sections (see the table on the next page). The Analytical Writing Assessment (AWA) section consists of one essay. The Integrated Reasoning section consists of graphical and data analysis questions in multiple response formats. The Quantitative and Verbal Reasoning sections consist of multiple-choice questions.

The Quantitative and Verbal Reasoning sections of the GMAT exam are computer adaptive, which means that the test draws from a large bank of questions to tailor itself to your ability level, and you won't get many questions that are too hard or too easy for you. The first question will be of medium difficulty. As you answer each question, the computer scores your answer and uses it—as well as your responses to all preceding questions—to select the next question.

Computer-adaptive tests become more difficult the more questions you answer correctly, but if you get a question that seems easier than the last one, it does not necessarily mean you answered the last question incorrectly. The test must cover a range of content, both in the type of question asked and the subject matter presented.

Myth -vs- FACT

M – **Getting an easier question means I answered the last one wrong.**

F – **You should not become distracted by the difficulty level of a question.**

Many different factors contribute to the difficulty of a question, so don't worry when taking the test or waste valuable time trying to determine the difficulty of the question you are answering.

To ensure that everyone receives the same content, the test selects a specific number of questions of each type. The test may call for your next problem to be a relatively hard data sufficiency question involving arithmetic operations. But, if there are no more relatively difficult data sufficiency questions involving arithmetic, you might be given an easier question.

Because the computer uses your answers to select your next questions, you may not skip questions or go back and change your answer to a previous question. If you don't know the answer to a question, try to eliminate as many choices as possible, then select the answer you think is best.

Though the individual questions are different, the mix of question types is the same for every GMAT exam. Your score is determined by the difficulty and statistical characteristics of the questions you answer as well as the number of questions you answer correctly. By adapting to each test-taker, the GMAT exam is able to accurately and efficiently gauge skill levels over a full range of abilities, from very high to very low.

The test includes the types of questions found in this book and in the online question bank found at gmat.wiley.com, but the format and presentation of the GMAT exam questions are different.

Five things to know about GMAT exam questions:

- Only one question or question prompt at a time is presented on the computer screen.
- The answer choices for the multiple-choice questions will be preceded by radio buttons, rather than by letters.
- Different question types appear in random order in the multiple-choice and Integrated Reasoning sections.
- You must choose an answer and confirm your choice before moving on to the next question.
- You may not go back to previous screens to change answers to previous questions.

Format of the GMAT™ Exam		
	Questions	Timing
Analytical Writing Assessment	1	30 min.

Integrated Reasoning
    Multi-Source Reasoning
    Table Analysis
    Graphics Interpretation
    Two-Part Analysis
	12	30 min.

Quantitative Reasoning
    Problem Solving
    Data Sufficiency
	31	62 min.

Verbal Reasoning
    Reading Comprehension
    Critical Reasoning
    Sentence Correction
	36	65 min.

	Total Time:	187 min.

On exam day, immediately prior to the start of the first exam section, you will have the flexibility to select your section order for the GMAT exam from three order combinations.

Order #1	Order #2	Order #3
Analytical Writing Assessment	Verbal Reasoning	Quantitative Reasoning
Integrated Reasoning		
Optional 8-minute break		
Quantitative Reasoning	Quantitative Reasoning	Verbal Reasoning
Optional 8-minute break		
Verbal Reasoning	Integrated Reasoning	Integrated Reasoning
	Analytical Writing Assessment	Analytical Writing Assessment

1.3 What Will the Test Experience Be Like?

The GMAT exam offers the flexibility to take the exam either online or at a test center—wherever you feel most comfortable. You may feel more comfortable at home with the online delivery format or prefer the structure and environment of a test center. The choice and flexibility is yours. Both delivery options include the exact same content, structure, two optional 8-minute breaks, scores & score scales, and scores are uniformly accepted by schools worldwide, so you can choose the option that works best for you.

At the Test Center: The GMAT exam is administered under standardized conditions at over 700 test centers worldwide. Each test center has a proctored testing room with individual computer workstations that allow you to take the exam under quiet conditions and with some privacy. You may not take notes or scratch paper with you into the testing room, but an erasable notepad and marker will be provided for you to use during the test. For more information about exam day visit mba.com/gmat.

Online: The GMAT Online exam is a remote proctored experience in the comfort of your home or office. You will need a quiet workspace with a desktop or laptop computer that meets minimum system requirements, a webcam, and a reliable internet connection. During your exam you will be able to use a physical whiteboard with up to two dry-erase markers and an eraser and/or an online whiteboard to work through the exam questions (no scratch paper is allowed). For more information about exam day visit mba.com/gmatonline.

To learn more about accommodations options for the GMAT exam, visit mba.com/accommodations.

1.4 What Is the Content of the GMAT™ Exam Like?

The GMAT exam measures higher-order analytical skills encompassing several types of reasoning. The Analytical Writing Assessment asks you to analyze the reasoning behind an argument and respond in writing; the Integrated Reasoning section asks you to interpret and synthesize information from multiple sources and in different formats to make reasoned conclusions; the Quantitative Reasoning section includes basic arithmetic, algebra, and geometry; and the Verbal Reasoning section asks you to read and comprehend written material and to reason and evaluate arguments.

Test questions may address a variety of subjects, but all the information you need to answer the questions will be included on the exam, with no outside knowledge of the subject matter necessary. The GMAT exam is not a test of business knowledge, English vocabulary, or advanced computational skills. You will need to read and write in English and have basic math and English skills to perform well on the test, but its difficulty comes from analytical and critical thinking abilities.

> ### *Myth* -vs- **FACT**
>
> *M* – **My success in business school is not predicted by the GMAT exam.**
>
> F – **False. The GMAT exam measures your critical thinking and reasoning skills, the ones used in business school and beyond in your career.**
>
> The exam measures your ability to make inferences, problem-solve, and analyze data. In fact, some employers even use the GMAT exam to determine your skill sets in these areas. If your program does not require the GMAT exam, you can stand out from the crowd with your performance on the exam and show that you have skills that it takes to succeed in business school.

The questions in this book are organized by question type and from easiest to most difficult, but keep in mind that when you take the test, you may see different types of questions in any order within each section.

1.5 Analytical Writing Assessment Section

The GMAT Analytical Writing Assessment (AWA) section consists of one 30-minute writing task: Analysis of an Argument. The AWA measures your ability to think critically, communicate your ideas, and formulate an appropriate and constructive critique. You will type your essay on a computer keyboard.

1.6 Integrated Reasoning Section

The GMAT Integrated Reasoning section highlights the relevant skills that business managers in today's data-driven world need in order to analyze sophisticated streams of data and solve complex problems. It measures your ability to understand and evaluate multiple sources and types of information—graphic, numeric, and verbal—as they relate to one another. This section will require you to use both quantitative and verbal reasoning to solve complex problems and solve multiple problems in relation to one another.

Four types of questions are used in the Integrated Reasoning section:

- Multi-Source Reasoning
- Table Analysis
- Graphics Interpretation
- Two-Part Analysis

Integrated Reasoning questions may require quantitative or verbal reasoning skills, or a combination of both. You will have to interpret graphics and sort tables to extract meaning from data, but advanced statistical knowledge and spreadsheet manipulation skills are not necessary. For both online and test center exams you will have access to an onscreen calculator with basic functions for the Integrated Reasoning section but note that the calculator is ***not*** available on the Quantitative Reasoning section.

1.7 Quantitative Reasoning Section

The GMAT Quantitative Reasoning section measures your ability to solve quantitative problems and interpret graphic data.

Two types of multiple-choice questions are used in the Quantitative Reasoning section:

- Problem Solving
- Data Sufficiency

Both are intermingled throughout the Quantitative Reasoning section, and require basic knowledge of arithmetic, elementary algebra, and commonly known concepts of geometry.

To review the basic mathematical concepts that you will need to answer Quantitative Reasoning questions, see the math review in Chapter 3. For test-taking tips specific to the question types in the Quantitative Reasoning section, practice questions, and answer explanations, see Chapters 4 and 5.

1.8 Verbal Reasoning Section

The GMAT Verbal Reasoning section measures your ability to read and comprehend written material and to reason and evaluate arguments. The Verbal Reasoning section includes reading sections from several different content areas. Although you may be generally familiar with some of the material, neither the reading passages nor the questions assume detailed knowledge of the topics discussed.

Three types of multiple-choice questions are intermingled throughout the Verbal Reasoning section:

- Reading Comprehension
- Critical Reasoning
- Sentence Correction

1.9 How Are Scores Calculated?

Verbal Reasoning and Quantitative Reasoning sections are scored on a scale of 6 to 51, in one-point increments. The Total GMAT score ranges from 200 to 800 and is based on your performance in these two sections. Your score is determined by:

- The number of questions you answer
- The number of questions you answer correctly or incorrectly
- The level of difficulty and other statistical characteristics of each question

Your Verbal Reasoning, Quantitative Reasoning, and Total GMAT scores are determined by an algorithm that takes into account the difficulty of the questions that were presented to you and how you answered them. When you answer the easier questions correctly, you get a chance to answer harder questions, making it possible to earn a higher score. After you have completed all the questions on the exam, or when your time is expired, the computer will calculate your scores.

You will receive five scores: Total Score (which is based on your Quantitative Reasoning and Verbal Reasoning scores), Integrated Reasoning Score, and Analytical Writing Assessment Score. The following table summarizes the different types of scores, the scales, and the increments.

Type of Score	Scale	Increments
Total (based on Quantitative Reasoning and Verbal Reasoning)	200–800	10
Quantitative Reasoning	6–51	1
Verbal Reasoning	6–51	1
Integrated Reasoning	1–8	1
Analytical Writing Assessment	0–6	0.5

Your GMAT scores are valid for five years from the date of the exam.

Your GMAT score includes a percentile ranking that compares your skill level with other test-takers from the past three years. The percentile rank of your score shows the percentage of tests taken with scores lower than your score. Every July, percentile ranking tables are updated. Visit mba.com to view the most recent percentile rankings tables.

2.0   How to Prepare

2.0 How to Prepare

2.1 How Should I Prepare to Take the Test?

The GMAT™ exam is designed specifically to measure reasoning skills needed for management education, and the test contains several question formats unique to the GMAT exam. At a minimum, you should be familiar with the test format and the question formats before you sit for the test. Because the GMAT exam is a timed exam, you should practice answering test questions, not only to better understand the question formats and the skills they require, but also to help you learn to pace yourself so you can finish each section when you sit for the exam.

Because the exam measures reasoning rather than subject-matter knowledge, you most likely will not find it helpful to memorize facts. You do not need to study advanced mathematical concepts, but you should be sure your grasp of basic arithmetic, algebra, and geometry is sound enough that you can use these skills in quantitative problem solving. Likewise, you do not need to study advanced vocabulary words, but you should have a firm understanding of basic English vocabulary and grammar for reading, writing, and reasoning.

Myth -vs- FACT

M – **You need very advanced math skills to get a high GMAT score.**

F – **The GMAT exam measures your reasoning and critical thinking abilities, rather than your advanced math skills.**

The GMAT exam only requires basic quantitative skills. You should review the math skills (algebra, geometry, basic arithmetic) presented in this guide (Chapter 3) and the *GMAT™ Official Guide Quantitative Review 2022*. The difficulty of GMAT Quantitative Reasoning questions stems from the logic and analysis used to solve the problems and not the underlying math skills.

2.2 Getting Ready for Exam Day

Whether you are testing online or in a test center, it is important to know what to expect to have a successful and worry-free testing experience.

Test Center

While checking into a test center be prepared to:

- Present appropriate identification.
- Provide your palm vein scan (where permitted by law).
- Provide your digital signature stating that you understand and agree to the Test-Taker Rules and Agreement.
- Have a digital photograph taken.

For more information visit mba.com/gmat.

Online

Preparing to take your exam online:

- Check your computer—before your exam day, ensure that your computer meets the minimum system requirements to run the exam.
- Prepare your workspace—identify a quiet place to take your exam and prepare your workspace by ensuring it is clean and all objects are removed except for your computer and whiteboard.

- Whiteboard—if you plan to use a physical whiteboard during your exam, make sure your whiteboard fits the approved dimensions, and you have up to two dry-erase markers, and an eraser.

- Plan ahead—you should plan to begin your check-in process 30 minutes before your scheduled exam time.

For more information visit mba.com/gmatonline.

2.3 How to Use the *GMAT™ Official Guide Quantitative Review*

The *GMAT™ Official Guide Quantitative Review* is designed for those who have completed the Quantitative Reasoning questions in the *GMAT™ Official Guide* and are looking for additional practice questions, as well as those who are interested in practicing only Quantitative Reasoning questions. Questions in each chapter are organized by difficulty level from easy to hard, so if you are new to studying, we recommend starting at the beginning of each chapter and working your way through the questions sequentially. You may find certain "easy" questions to be hard and some "hard" questions to be easy; this is not unusual and reflects the fact that different people will often have different perceptions of a question's difficulty level.

You may also find questions in the *GMAT™ Official Guide Quantitative Review* to be easier or harder than questions you see on the GMAT™ Official Practice Exams and/or the actual GMAT exam. This is expected because, unlike the Official Practice Exams, the *GMAT™ Official Guide Quantitative Review* is not computer-adaptive and does not adjust to your ability. If you were to complete all of the questions in this book, you will encounter roughly one-third easy questions, one-third medium questions, and one-third hard questions, whereas on the actual exam, you will not likely see such an even mix of questions across difficulty levels.

To find questions of a specific type and difficulty level (e.g., easy arithmetic questions), use the index of questions in Chapter 6. Note that the ratio of questions across different content areas in the *GMAT™ Official Guide Quantitative Review* in no way reflects the ratio of questions across different content areas on the actual GMAT exam.

Finally, because the GMAT exam is administered on a computer, we encourage you to practice the questions in the *GMAT™ Official Guide Quantitative Review* using the Online Question Bank at gmat.wiley.com. All of the questions in this book are available there, and you'll be able to create practice sets and track your progress more easily. The Online Question Bank is also available on your mobile device through the Wiley Efficient Learning mobile app. To access the Online Question Bank on your mobile device, first create an account at gmat.wiley.com and then sign in to your account on the mobile app.

2.4 How to Use Other GMAT™ Official Prep Products

In addition to the *GMAT™ Official Guide*, we recommend using our other GMAT™ Official Prep products.

- **For those who want a realistic simulation of the GMAT exam:** GMAT™ Official Practice Exams 1–6 are the only practice exams that use questions from past GMAT exams and feature the same scoring algorithm and user interface as the real exam, including the online whiteboard tool that is used in the online version of the GMAT exam. The first two practice exams are free to all test-takers and available at mba.com/exam-prep.

- **For those who want more practice questions:** GMAT™ Official Practice Questions 1 and 2 offer additional questions that are not available in the *GMAT™ Official Guide* series.

- **For those who are looking for additional practice with challenging questions:** *GMAT™ Official Advanced Questions* is a compilation of 300 hard Quantitative Reasoning and Verbal Reasoning questions, similar in difficulty level to hard questions found in the *GMAT™ Official Guide* series.

To maximize your studying efforts:

1. Start by learning about the GMAT exam and the question types in the *GMAT™ Official Guide*.

2. Take GMAT™ Official Practice Exam 1 to become familiar with the exam and get a baseline score. Don't worry about your score on the first practice exam! The goal is to become familiar with the exam and set a baseline for measuring your progress.

3. Go to gmat.wiley.com and practice the questions in the *GMAT™ Official Guide*, focusing on areas that require your attention. As you continue to practice, take additional GMAT™ Official Practice Exams to gauge your progress.

4. Before your actual GMAT exam, take a final Official Practice Exam to simulate the real test-taking experience and see how you score.

Remember: The first two GMAT™ Official Practice Exams are part of the free GMAT™ Official Starter Kit, which includes 90 free practice questions and is available to everyone with an mba.com account. GMAT™ Official Practice Exams 3 to 6, additional GMAT™ Official Practice Questions, and other Official Prep products are available for purchase through mba.com/prep.

2.5 General Test-Taking Suggestions

Specific test-taking strategies for individual question types are presented later in this book. The following are general suggestions to help you perform your best on the test.

1. **Use your time wisely.**
   Although the GMAT exam stresses accuracy more than speed, it is important to use your time wisely.

   On average, you will have about $1\frac{3}{4}$ minutes for each Verbal Reasoning question, about 2 minutes for each Quantitative Reasoning question, and about $2\frac{1}{2}$ minutes for each Integrated Reasoning question, some of which have multiple questions. Once you start the test, an onscreen clock will show the time you have left. You can hide this display if you want, but it is a good idea to check the clock periodically to monitor your progress. The clock will automatically alert you when 5 minutes remain for the section you are working on.

Myth -vs- **FACT**

$\mathbb{M}$ – **It is more important to respond correctly to the test questions than it is to finish the test.**

F – **There is a significant penalty for not completing the GMAT™ exam.**

Pacing is important. If you are stumped by a question, give it your best guess and move on. If you guess incorrectly, the computer program will likely give you an easier question, which you are likely to answer correctly, and the computer will rapidly return to giving you questions matched to your ability. If you don't finish the test, your score will be reduced. Failing to answer five verbal questions, for example, could reduce your score from the 91st percentile to the 77th percentile.

---

2. Determine your preferred section order before the actual exam.

The GMAT exam allows you to select the order in which to take the sections. Use the GMAT™ Official Practice Exams as an opportunity to practice and determine your preferred order. Remember: There is no "right" order in which to take the exam; you can practice each order and see which one works best for you.

3. Answer practice questions ahead of time.

After you become generally familiar with all question types, use the practice questions in this book and online at gmat.wiley.com to prepare for the actual test (note that Integrated Reasoning questions are only available online). It may be useful to time yourself as you answer the practice questions to get an idea of how long you will have for each question when you sit for the actual test, as well as to determine whether you are answering quickly enough to finish the test in the allotted time.

4. Read all test directions carefully.

The directions explain exactly what is required to answer each question type. If you read hastily, you may miss important instructions and impact your ability to answer correctly. To review directions during the test, click on the Help icon. But be aware that the time you spend reviewing directions will count against your time allotment for that section of the test.

5. Read each question carefully and thoroughly.

Before you answer a question, determine exactly what is being asked and then select the best choice. Never skim a question or the possible answers; skimming may cause you to miss important information or nuances.

6. Do not spend too much time on any one question.

If you do not know the correct answer, or if the question is too time-consuming, try to eliminate answer choices you know are wrong, select the best of the remaining answer choices, and move on to the next question.

Not completing sections and randomly guessing answers to questions at the end of each test section can significantly lower your score. As long as you have worked on each section, you will receive a score even if you do not finish one or more sections in the allotted time. You will not earn points for questions you never get to see.

7. Confirm your answers ONLY when you are ready to move on.

On the Quantitative Reasoning and Verbal Reasoning sections, once you have selected your answer to a multiple-choice question, you will be asked to confirm it. Once you confirm your response, you cannot go back and change it. You may not skip questions. In the Integrated Reasoning section, there may be several questions based on information provided in the same question prompt. When there is more than one response on a single screen, you can change your response to any of the questions on the screen before moving on to the next screen. However, you may not navigate back to a previous screen to change any responses.

Myth -vs- FACT

M – **The first 10 questions are critical and you should invest the most time on those.**

F – **All questions count.**

The computer-adaptive testing algorithm uses each answered question to obtain an *initial* estimate. However, as you continue to answer questions, the algorithm self-corrects by computing an updated estimate on the basis of all the questions you have answered, and then administers questions that are closely matched to this new estimate of your ability. Your final score is based on all your responses and considers the difficulty of all the questions you answered. Taking additional time on the first 10 questions will not game the system and can hurt your ability to finish the test.

8. **Plan your essay answer before you begin to write.**

    The best way to approach the Analytical Writing Assessment (AWA) section is to read the directions carefully, take a few minutes to think about the question, and plan a response before you begin writing. Take time to organize your ideas and develop them fully but leave time to reread your response and make any revisions that you think would improve it.

    This book and other study materials released by the Graduate Management Admission Council (GMAC) are the ONLY source of real questions that have been used on the GMAT exam. All questions that appear or have appeared on the GMAT exam are copyrighted and owned by GMAC, which does not license them to be reprinted elsewhere. Accessing live Integrated Reasoning, Quantitative Reasoning, and/or Verbal Reasoning test questions in advance or sharing test content during or after you take the test is a serious violation, which could cause your scores to be canceled and schools to be notified. In cases of a serious violation, you may be banned from future testing and other legal remedies may be pursued.

To register for the GMAT™ exam go to www.mba.com/gmat

3.0 Math Review

3.0 Math Review

This chapter reviews the basic mathematical concepts, terms, and formulas you should be familiar with in order to answer Quantitative Reasoning questions on the GMAT™ exam. Only a high-level overview is provided, so if you find unfamiliar terms or concepts, consult other resources for a more detailed discussion and explanation.

Knowledge of basic math, while necessary, is seldom sufficient for answering GMAT questions. Unlike traditional math problems you may have encountered in school, GMAT Quantitative Reasoning questions require you to *apply* your knowledge of math. For example, rather than asking you to demonstrate your knowledge of prime factorization by listing a number's prime factors, a GMAT question may require you to *apply* your knowledge of prime factorization and exponents to simplify an algebraic expression with a radical.

To prepare for the GMAT Quantitative Reasoning section, we recommend first reviewing basic mathematical concepts and formulas to ensure you have the foundational knowledge needed to answer the questions before moving on to practicing this knowledge on real GMAT questions from past exams.

Section 3.1, "Value, Order, and Factors," includes the following topics:

1. Numbers and the Number Line
2. Factors, Multiples, Divisibility, and Remainders
3. Exponents
4. Decimals and Place Value
5. Properties of Operations

Section 3.2, "Algebra, Equalities, and Inequalities," includes the following topics:

1. Algebraic Expressions and Equations
2. Linear Equations
3. Factoring and Quadratic Equations
4. Inequalities
5. Functions
6. Formulas and Measurement Conversion

Section 3.3, "Rates, Ratios, and Percents," includes the following topics:

1. Ratio and Proportion
2. Fractions
3. Percents
4. Converting Decimals, Fractions, and Percents
5. Working with Decimals, Fractions, and Percents
6. Rate, Work, and Mixture Problems

Section 3.4, "Statistics, Sets, Counting, Probability, Estimation, and Series," includes the following topics:

1. Statistics
2. Sets
3. Counting Methods
4. Probability
5. Estimation
6. Sequences and Series

Section 3.5, "Geometry," includes the following topics:

1. Lines and Angles
2. Polygons
3. Triangles
4. Quadrilaterals
5. Circles
6. Rectangular Solids and Cylinders
7. Coordinate Geometry

Section 3.6, "Reference Sheets"

3.1 Value, Order, and Factors

1. Numbers and the Number Line

A. All *real numbers* correspond to points on *the number line*, and all points on the number line correspond to real numbers.

An illustration of the number line below, shows points corresponding to the real numbers $-\frac{3}{2}$, 0.2, and $\sqrt{2}$.

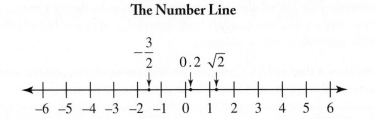

The Number Line

B. On a number line, numbers corresponding to points to the left of zero are *negative* and numbers corresponding to points to the right of zero are *positive*. All real numbers except zero are either positive or negative.

C. For any two numbers on the number line, the number to the left is less than the number to the right. So as shown in the figure above, $-4 < -3 < -\frac{3}{2} < -1$, and $1 < \sqrt{2} < 2$.

D. To say that a number n is between 1 and 4 on the number line means that $n > 1$ and $n < 4$; that is, $1 < n < 4$. If n is "between 1 and 4, inclusive," then $1 \leq n \leq 4$.

E. The *absolute value* of a real number x, denoted $|x|$, is defined to be x if $x \geq 0$ and $-x$ if $x < 0$. A number's absolute value is the distance between that number and zero on the number line. Thus -3 and 3 have the same absolute value, since they are both three units from zero on the number line. The absolute value of any nonzero number is positive.

Examples:

$|-5| = |5| = 5$, $|0| = 0$, and

$\left|\frac{-7}{2}\right| = \frac{7}{2}$.

For any real numbers x and y, $|x + y| \leq |x| + |y|$.

Examples:

If $x = 10$ and $y = 2$, then $|x + y| = |12| = 12 = |x| + |y|$.

If $x = 10$ and $y = -2$, then $|x + y| = |8| = 8 < 12 = |x| + |y|$.

2. Factors, Multiples, Divisibility, and Remainders

A. An *integer* is any number in the set $\{\ldots -3, -2, -1, 0, 1, 2, 3, \ldots\}$. For any integer n, the numbers in the set $\{n, n + 1, n + 2, n + 3, \ldots\}$ are *consecutive integers.*

B. If x and y are integers and $x \neq 0$, then x is a *divisor* or *factor* of y if $y = xn$ for some integer n. In this case, y is said to be *divisible* by x or to be a *multiple* of x.

> *Example:*
>
> Since $28 = (7)(4)$, both 4 and 7 are divisors or factors of 28.
>
> But 8 is not a divisor or factor of 28, since there is no integer n such that $28 = 8n$.

C. Dividing a positive integer y by a positive integer x, and then rounding down to the nearest nonnegative integer, yields the *quotient* of the division.

The *remainder* is calculated by multiplying x by the quotient, and then subtracting the result from y. That is, the quotient and the remainder are the unique positive integers q and r, respectively, such that

$y = xq + r$ and $0 \leq r < x$.

> *Example:*
>
> When 28 is divided by 8, the quotient is 3 and the remainder is 4, because $28 = (8)(3) + 4$.

The remainder r is 0 if and only if y is *divisible* by x. In that case, x is a divisor or factor of y, and y is a multiple of x.

> *Example:*
>
> Since 32 divided by 8 yields a remainder of 0, 32 is divisible by 8. So 8 is a divisor or factor of 32, and 32 is a multiple of 8.

When a smaller integer is divided by a larger integer, the quotient is 0 and the remainder is the smaller integer.

> *Example:*
>
> When 5 is divided by 7, the quotient is 0 and the remainder is 5, since $5 = (7)(0) + 5$.

D. Any integer divisible by 2 is an *even integer;* the set of even integers is $\{\ldots -4, -2, 0, 2, 4, 6, 8, \ldots\}$. Integers that are not divisible by 2 are *odd integers,* so $\{\ldots -3, -1, 1, 3, 5, \ldots\}$ is the set of odd integers. For any integer n, the numbers in the set $\{2n, 2n + 2, 2n + 4, \ldots\}$ are *consecutive even integers,* and the numbers in the set $\{2n + 1, 2n + 3, 2n + 5, \ldots\}$ are *consecutive odd integers.*

If at least one factor of a product of integers is even, then the product is even; otherwise the product is odd. If two integers are both even or both odd, then their sum and their difference are even. Otherwise, their sum and their difference are odd.

E. A *prime* number is a positive integer that has exactly two different positive divisors, 1 and itself. In other words, a prime number is not divisible by any integer other than itself and 1.

> *Example:*
>
> The first six prime numbers are 2, 3, 5, 7, 11, and 13.
>
> But 15 is not a prime number, because it has four different positive divisors: 1, 3, 5, and 15.
>
> And 1 is not a prime number either, because it has only one positive divisor: itself.

Every integer greater than 1 either is prime or can be uniquely expressed as a product of prime factors. An integer greater than 1 that is not prime is called a *composite number*.

> *Example:*
>
> $14 = (2)(7)$, $81 = (3)(3)(3)(3)$, and
>
> $484 = (2)(2)(11)(11)$ are composite numbers.

3. Exponents

A. An expression of the form k^n means the nth *power* of k, or k raised to the nth power, where n is the *exponent* and k is the *base*.

B. A positive integer exponent on a number or a variable indicates how many instances of the number or variable are multiplied together. In other words, when the exponent n is a positive integer, k^n is the product of n instances of k.

> *Examples:*
>
> x^5 means $(x)(x)(x)(x)(x)$; that is, the product in which x is a factor 5 times and there are no other factors. In this example, x^5 is the 5th power of x, or x raised to the 5th power.
>
> The second power of 2, also known as 2 *squared*, is $2^2 = 2 \times 2 = 4$. The third power of 2, also known as 2 *cubed*, is $2^3 = 2 \times 2 \times 2 = 8$.

Squaring a number greater than 1, or raising it to any power greater than 1, results in a larger number.

Squaring a number between 0 and 1 results in a smaller number.

> *Examples:*
>
> $3^2 = 9$, and $9 > 3$.
>
> $(0.1)^2 = 0.01$, and $0.01 < 0.1$.

C. A *square root* of a number n is a number x such that $x^2 = n$. Every positive number has two real square roots, one positive and the other negative. The positive square root of n is denoted by $\sqrt{n}$ or by $n^{\frac{1}{2}}$.

> *Example:*
>
> The two square roots of 9 are $\sqrt{9} = 3$ and $-\sqrt{9} = -3$.

Note that for any x, the nonnegative square root of x^2 equals the absolute value of x; that is, $\sqrt{x^2} = |x|$.

The square root of a negative number is not a real number and is called an ***imaginary number***.

D. Every real number r has exactly one real ***cube root***, which is the number s such that $s^3 = r$. The real cube root of r is denoted by $\sqrt[3]{r}$ or by $r^{\frac{1}{3}}$.

> *Examples:*
>
> Since $2^3 = 8$, $\sqrt[3]{8} = 2$.
>
> Similarly, $\sqrt[3]{-8} = -2$ because $(-2)^3 = -8$.

4. Decimals and Place Value

A. In the decimal system, the position of the period or ***decimal point*** determines the ***place values*** of the digits.

> *Example:*
>
> The digits in the number 7,654.321 have the following place values:
>
> | Thousands | | Hundreds | Tens | Ones or units | | Tenths | Hundredths | Thousandths |
> |:---:|:---:|:---:|:---:|:---:|:---:|:---:|:---:|:---:|
> | 7 | , | 6 | 5 | 4 | . | 3 | 2 | 1 |

B. In ***scientific notation***, a decimal is expressed as a number with only one nonzero digit to the left of the decimal point, multiplied by a power of 10. To convert a number expressed in scientific notation to regular decimal notation, move the decimal point by the number of places equal to the absolute value of the exponent on the 10. Move the decimal point to the right if the exponent is positive and to the left if the exponent is negative.

Examples:

In scientific notation, 231 is written as 2.31×10^2, and 0.0231 is written as 2.31×10^{-2}.

You can convert the expression 2.013×10^4 to regular decimal notation by moving the decimal point 4 places to the right, yielding the result 20,130.

Similarly, you can convert the expression 1.91×10^{-4} to regular decimal notation by moving the decimal point 4 places to the left, yielding the result 0.000191.

C. To add or subtract decimals, line up their decimal points. If one of the numbers has fewer digits to the right of its decimal point than another, insert zeros to the right of the last digit.

Examples:

To add 17.6512 and 653.27, insert zeroes to the right of the last digit in 653.27 so that the decimal points line up when the numbers are arranged in a column:

$$
\begin{array}{r}
17.6512 \\
+\ 653.2700 \\
\hline
670.9212
\end{array}
$$

Likewise for 653.27 minus 17.6512:

$$
\begin{array}{r}
653.2700 \\
-17.6512 \\
\hline
635.6188
\end{array}
$$

D. To multiply decimals, multiply the numbers as if they were integers and then insert the decimal point in the product so that the number of digits to the right of the decimal point equals the sum of the numbers of digits to the right of the decimal points in the numbers being multiplied, the *multiplicands*.

Example:

To multiply 2.09 by 1.3, first multiply the integers 209 and 13 to obtain 2,717. Since there are $2 + 1 = 3$ digits to the right of the decimal points in the numbers 2.09 and 1.3, put 3 digits in 2,717 to the right of the decimal point to obtain the product:

$$
\begin{array}{r}
2.09 \quad \text{(2 digits to the right)} \\
\times\ 1.3 \quad \text{(1 digit to the right)} \\
\hline
627 \qquad\qquad\qquad\quad \\
2090 \qquad\qquad\qquad\ \\
\hline
2.717 \quad (2+1=3 \text{ digits to the right})
\end{array}
$$

E. To divide a number (the ***dividend***) by a decimal (the ***divisor***), move the decimal point of the divisor to the right until the divisor is an integer. Then move the decimal point of the dividend the same number of places to the right and divide as you would integers. The decimal point in the quotient will be directly above the decimal point in the new dividend.

Example:

To divide 698.12 by 12.4, first move the decimal points in both the divisor 12.4 and the dividend 698.12 one place to the right to make the divisor an integer. In other words, replace 698.12/12.4 with 6981.2/124. Then proceed normally with the long division:

$$
\begin{array}{r}
56.3 \\
124\overline{)6981.2} \\
\underline{620} \\
781 \\
\underline{744} \\
372 \\
\underline{372} \\
0
\end{array}
$$

5. Properties of Operations

Here are some basic properties of arithmetical operations for any real numbers x, y, and z.

A. Addition and Subtraction

$x + 0 = x = x - 0$

$x - x = 0$

$x + y = y + x$

$x - y = -(y - x) = x + (-y)$

$(x + y) + z = x + (y + z)$

If x and y are both positive, then $x + y$ is also positive.

If x and y are both negative, then $x + y$ is negative.

B. Multiplication and Division

$x \times 1 = x = \dfrac{x}{1}$

$x \times 0 = 0$

If $x \neq 0$, then $\dfrac{x}{x} = 1$.

$\dfrac{x}{0}$ is undefined.

$xy = yx$

If $x \neq 0$ and $y \neq 0$, then $\dfrac{x}{y} = \dfrac{1}{\left(\frac{y}{x}\right)}$.

$(xy)z = x(yz)$

$xy + xz = x(y + z)$

If $y \neq 0$, then $\left(\dfrac{x}{y}\right) + \left(\dfrac{z}{y}\right) = \dfrac{(x + z)}{y}$.

If x and y are both positive, then xy is also positive.

If x and y are both negative, then xy is positive.

If x is positive and y is negative, then xy is negative.

If $xy = 0$, then $x = 0$ or $y = 0$, or both.

C. Exponentiation

$x^1 = x$

$x^0 = 1$

If $x \neq 0$, then $x^{-1} = \dfrac{1}{x}$

$(x^y)^z = x^{yz} = (x^z)^y$

$x^{y + z} = x^y x^z$

If $x \neq 0$, then $x^{y - z} = \dfrac{x^y}{x^z}$.

$(xz)^y = x^y z^y$

If $z \neq 0$, then $\left(\dfrac{x}{z}\right)^y = \dfrac{x^y}{z^y}$.

If $z \neq 0$, then $x^{\frac{y}{z}} = (x^y)^{\frac{1}{z}} = \left(x^{\frac{1}{z}}\right)^y$.

All the practice questions that appear in this chapter are real questions from past GMAT exams and will test the concepts you have just reviewed. The full answer explanations follow the practice question(s) and outline the reasoning for why each answer choice is correct, or incorrect.

PS87710.03*

Practice Question 1

The average distance between the Sun and a certain planet is approximately 2.3×10^{14} inches. Which of the following is closest to the average distance between the Sun and the planet, in kilometers? (1 kilometer is approximately 3.9×10^4 inches.)

   (A) 7.1×10^8

   (B) 5.9×10^9

   (C) 1.6×10^{10}

   (D) 1.6×10^{11}

   (E) 5.9×10^{11}

DS38350.03

Practice Question 2

If x and y are positive, is $x < 10 < y$?

(1) $x < y$ and $xy = 100$

(2) $x^2 < 100 < y^2$

   (A)   Statement (1) ALONE is sufficient, but statement (2) alone is not sufficient.

   (B)   Statement (2) ALONE is sufficient, but statement (1) alone is not sufficient.

   (C)   BOTH statements TOGETHER are sufficient, but NEITHER statement ALONE is sufficient.

   (D)   EACH statement ALONE is sufficient.

   (E)   Statements (1) and (2) TOGETHER are NOT sufficient.

*These numbers correlate with the online test bank question number. See the GMAT™ Official Guide Quantitative Review Question Index in the back of this book.

DS75160.03
Practice Question 3

Which of the positive numbers x or y is greater?

(1) $y = 2x$

(2) $2x + 5y = 12$

    (A)   Statement (1) ALONE is sufficient, but statement (2) alone is not sufficient.

    (B)   Statement (2) ALONE is sufficient, but statement (1) alone is not sufficient.

    (C)   BOTH statements TOGETHER are sufficient, but NEITHER statement ALONE is sufficient.

    (D)   EACH statement ALONE is sufficient.

    (E)   Statements (1) and (2) TOGETHER are NOT sufficient.

PS10241.03
Practice Question 4

Judy bought a quantity of pens in packages of 5 for $0.80 per package. She sold all of the pens in packages of 3 for $0.60 per package. If Judy's profit from the pens was $8.00, how many pens did she buy and sell?

    (A)   40

    (B)   80

    (C)   100

    (D)   200

    (E)   400

DS10680.03
Practice Question 5

For any positive integer x, the 2-height of x is defined to be the greatest nonnegative integer n such that 2^n is a factor of x. If k and m are positive integers, is the 2-height of k greater than the 2-height of m?

(1) $k > m$

(2) $\dfrac{k}{m}$ is an even integer.

    (A)   Statement (1) ALONE is sufficient, but statement (2) alone is not sufficient.

    (B)   Statement (2) ALONE is sufficient, but statement (1) alone is not sufficient.

    (C)   BOTH statements TOGETHER are sufficient, but NEITHER statement ALONE is sufficient.

    (D)   EACH statement ALONE is sufficient.

    (E)   Statements (1) and (2) TOGETHER are NOT sufficient.

PS87710.03
Answer Explanation 1

The average distance between the Sun and a certain planet is approximately 2.3×10^{14} inches. Which of the following is closest to the average distance between the Sun and the planet, in kilometers? (1 kilometer is approximately 3.9×10^4 inches.)

    (A) 7.1×10^8

    (B) 5.9×10^9

    (C) 1.6×10^{10}

    (D) 1.6×10^{11}

    (E) 5.9×10^{11}

Arithmetic Measurement Conversion

Convert to kilometers and then estimate.

$$(2.3 \times 10^{14} \text{ in})\left(\frac{1 \text{ km}}{3.9 \times 10^{4} \text{ in}}\right) = \frac{2.3 \times 10^{14}}{3.9 \times 10^{4}} \text{ km}$$

$$= \frac{2.3}{3.9} \times 10^{14-4} \text{ km}$$

$$\approx \frac{2}{4} \times 10^{10}$$

$$= 0.5 \times 10^{10}$$

$$= 5 \times 10^{9}$$

The correct answer is B.

DS38350.03
Answer Explanation 2

If x and y are positive, is $x < 10 < y$?

(1) $x < y$ and $xy = 100$
(2) $x^2 < 100 < y^2$

Algebra Inequalities

(1)   Given that $x < y$, multiply both sides by x, which is positive, to get $x^2 < xy$. Then, since $xy = 100$, it follows that $x^2 < 100$. Similarly, multiply both sides of $x < y$ by y, which is positive, to get $xy < y^2$. Again, since $xy = 100$, it follows that $100 < y^2$.

Combining $x^2 < 100$ and $100 < y^2$ gives $x^2 < 100 < y^2$, from which it follows that $\sqrt{x^2} < \sqrt{100} < \sqrt{y^2}$ and, therefore, $x < 10 < y$, since x and y are both positive; SUFFICIENT.

(2)   Given that $x^2 < 100 < y^2$, it follows that $x < 10 < y$ as shown in (1) above; SUFFICIENT.

The correct answer is D; each statement alone is sufficient.

DS75160.03
Answer Explanation 3

Which of the positive numbers x or y is greater?

(1) $y = 2x$
(2) $2x + 5y = 12$

Algebra Order

(1)   Given that x is positive and y is twice the value of x, it follows that y is the greater number. This can be seen algebraically by adding x to both sides of $x > 0$ to get $x + x > x$, or $2x > x$, or $y > x$; SUFFICIENT.

(2)   Given that $2x + 5y = 12$, then it is possible that $x = 1$ and $y = 2$, and thus it is possible that y is greater than x. However, it is also possible that $x = 2$ and $y = \frac{8}{5}$, and thus it is possible that x is greater than y; NOT sufficient.

The correct answer is A; statement 1 alone is sufficient.

PS10241.03
Answer Explanation 4

Judy bought a quantity of pens in packages of 5 for $0.80 per package. She sold all of the pens in packages of 3 for $0.60 per package. If Judy's profit from the pens was $8.00, how many pens did she buy and sell?

- (A) 40
- (B) 80
- (C) 100
- (D) 200
- (E) 400

Arithmetic Applied Problems; Operations With Decimals

Judy purchased the pens for $\frac{\$0.80}{5} = \$0.16$ each and sold them for $\frac{\$0.60}{3} = \$0.20$ each. Therefore, her profit on each pen was $\$0.20 - \$0.16 = \$0.04$. If her total profit was $8.00, then she bought and sold $\frac{\$8.00}{\$0.04} = 200$ pens.

The correct answer is D.

DS10680.03
Answer Explanation 5

For any positive integer x, the 2-height of x is defined to be the greatest nonnegative integer n such that 2^n is a factor of x. If k and m are positive integers, is the 2-height of k greater than the 2-height of m?

(1) $k > m$

(2) $\frac{k}{m}$ is an even integer.

Arithmetic Properties of Numbers

(1) Given that $k > m$, the 2-height of k can be greater than m (choose $k = 4$, which has a 2-height of 2, and choose $m = 2$, which has a 2-height of 1) and the 2-height of k can fail to be greater than m (choose $k = 3$, which has a 2-height of 0, and choose $m = 2$, which has a 2-height of 1); NOT sufficient.

(2) Given that $\frac{k}{m}$ is an even integer, it follows that $\frac{k}{m} = 2n$ for some integer n, or $k = 2mn$. This implies that the 2-height of k is at least one more than the 2-height of m; SUFFICIENT.

The correct answer is B; statement 2 alone is sufficient.

3.2 Algebra, Equalities, and Inequalities

1. Algebraic Expressions and Equations

A. Algebra is based on the operations of arithmetic and on the concept of an ***unknown quantity,*** or ***variable.*** Letters such as x or n are used to represent unknown quantities. Numerical expressions are used to represent known quantities called ***constants***. A combination of variables, constants, and arithmetical operations is called an ***algebraic expression.***

Solving word problems often requires translating verbal expressions into algebraic expressions. The following table lists words and phrases that can be translated as mathematical operations used in algebraic expressions:

3.2 Translating Words into Mathematical Operations

$x + y$	$x - y$	xy	$\dfrac{x}{y}$	x^y
x added to y *x increased by y* *x more than y* *x plus y* *the sum of x and y* *the total of x and y*	*x decreased by y* *difference of x and y* *y fewer than x* *y less than x* *x minus y* *x reduced by y* *y subtracted from x*	*x multiplied by y* *the product of x and y* *x times y*	*x divided by y* *x over y* *the quotient of x and y* *the ratio of x to y*	*x to the power of y* *x to the yth power*
		If $y = 2$: *double x* *twice x*	If $y = 2$: *half of x* *x halved*	If $y = 2$: *x squared*
		If $y = 3$: *triple x*		If $y = 3$: *x cubed*

B. In an algebraic expression, a ***term*** is either a constant, a variable, or the product of one or more constants and/or variables. The variables in a term may be raised to exponents. A term with no variables is called a ***constant term***. The constant in a term that includes one or more variables is called a ***coefficient***.

> *Example:*
>
> Suppose Pam has 5 more pencils than Fred has. If F represents the number of pencils Fred has, then the number of pencils Pam has is $F + 5$. This algebraic expression includes two terms: the variable F and the constant term 5.

C. A ***polynomial*** is an algebraic expression that is a sum of terms and contains exactly one variable. Each term in a polynomial consists of a variable raised to some power and multiplied by some coefficient. If the highest power to which the variable is raised is 1, the expression is called a ***first degree*** (or ***linear***) ***polynomial*** in that variable. If the highest power to which the variable is raised is 2, the expression is called a ***second degree*** (or ***quadratic***) ***polynomial*** in that variable.

> *Examples:*
>
> The expression $F + 5$ is a linear polynomial in F, since the highest power of F is 1.
>
> The expression $19x^2 - 6x + 3$ is a quadratic polynomial in x, since the highest power of x is 2.
>
> The expression $\dfrac{3x^2}{(2x - 5)}$ is not a polynomial, because it is not a sum of terms that are each a power of x multiplied by a coefficient.

D. Often when working with algebraic expressions, it is necessary to simplify them by factoring or combining ***like*** terms.

> *Examples:*
>
> The expression $6x + 5x$ is equivalent to $(6 + 5)x$, or $11x$.
>
> In the expression $9x - 3y$, 3 is a factor common to both terms: $9x - 3y = 3(3x - y)$.
>
> In the expression $5x^2 + 6y$, there are no like terms and no common factors.

E. In a fraction $\frac{n}{d}$, n is the **numerator** and d is the **denominator.** If there are common factors in the numerator and denominator of an algebraic expression, they can be divided out, provided they are not equal to zero.

> *Example:*
>
> If $x \neq 3$, then $\frac{(x - 3)}{(x - 3)} = 1$.
>
> Therefore, $\frac{(3xy - 9y)}{(x - 3)} = \frac{3y(x - 3)}{(x - 3)} = 3y(1) = 3y$.

F. To multiply two algebraic expressions, multiply each term of one expression by each term of the other expression.

> *Example:*
>
> $(3x - 4)(9y + x) = 3x(9y + x) - 4(9y + x)$
>
> $\qquad\qquad = 3x(9y) + 3x(x) - 4(9y) - 4(x)$
>
> $\qquad\qquad = 27xy + 3x^2 - 36y - 4x$

G. An algebraic expression can be evaluated by substituting constants for the variables in the expression.

> *Example:*
>
> If $x = 3$ and $y = -2$, then $3xy - x^2 + y$ can be evaluated as
>
> $3(3)(-2) - (3)^2 + (-2) = -18 - 9 - 2 = -29$.

H. A major focus of algebra is to solve equations involving algebraic expressions. The **solutions** of such an equation are those sets of assignments of constant values to the equation's variables that make the equation true, or "satisfy the equation." An equation may have no solution or one or more solutions. If two or more equations are to be solved together, the solutions must satisfy all the equations simultaneously. The solutions of an equation are also called the **roots** of the equation. These roots can be checked by substituting them into the original equation to determine whether they satisfy the equation.

I. Two equations with the same solution or solutions are **equivalent equations.**

Examples:

The equations $2 + x = 3$ and $4 + 2x = 6$ are equivalent because each has the unique solution $x = 1$. Note that the second equation is the first equation multiplied by 2.

Similarly, the equations $3x - y = 6$ and $6x - 2y = 12$ are equivalent, although in this case each equation has infinitely many solutions. If any value is assigned to x, then $3x - 6$ is a corresponding value for y that will satisfy both equations. For example, $x = 2$ and $y = 0$ is a solution to both equations, and so is $x = 5$ and $y = 9$.

2. Linear Equations

A. A *linear equation* is an equation with a linear polynomial on one side of the equals sign and either a linear polynomial or a constant on the other side, or an equation that can be converted into that form. A linear equation with only one variable is a *linear equation with one unknown.* A linear equation with two variables is *a linear equation with two unknowns*.

Examples:

$5x - 2 = 9 - x$ is a linear equation with one unknown.

$3x + 1 = y - 2$ is a linear equation with two unknowns.

B. To solve a linear equation with one unknown (that is, to find the value of the unknown that satisfies the equation), the unknown should be isolated on one side of the equation. This can be done by performing the same mathematical operations on both sides of the equation. Remember that if the same number is added to or subtracted from both sides of the equation, this does not change the equality; likewise, multiplying or dividing both sides by the same nonzero number does not change the equality.

Example:

To solve the equation $\dfrac{5x - 6}{3} = 4$, isolate the variable x using the following steps:

$$5x - 6 = 12 \quad \text{(multiplying by 3)}$$
$$5x = 18 \quad \text{(adding 6)}$$
$$x = \frac{18}{5} \quad \text{(dividing by 5)}$$

The result, $\dfrac{18}{5}$, can be checked by substituting it for x in the original equation to determine whether it satisfies that equation:

$$\frac{\left(5\left(\frac{18}{5}\right) - 6\right)}{3} = \frac{(18 - 6)}{3} = \frac{12}{3} = 4$$

Therefore, $x = \dfrac{18}{5}$ is the solution.

C. If two linear equations with the same two unknowns are equivalent, then they have infinitely many solutions, as illustrated in the second example in 3.2.1.I above. But if two linear equations with the same two unknowns are not equivalent, then they have at most one solution.

There are several methods of solving two linear equations with two unknowns. With any method, if a trivial equation such as $0 = 0$ is reached, then the equations are equivalent and have infinitely many solutions. But if a contradiction is reached, the equations have no solution.

Example:

Consider the two equations: $3x + 4y = 17$ and $6x + 8y = 35$. Note that $3x + 4y = 17$ implies $6x + 8y = 34$, which contradicts the second equation. Thus, no values of x and y can simultaneously satisfy both equations.

If neither a trivial equation nor a contradiction is reached, then a unique solution can be found.

D. One way to solve two linear equations with two unknowns is to express one of the unknowns in terms of the other using one of the equations, then substitute the expression into the remaining equation to obtain an equation with only one unknown. This equation can be solved and the value of the unknown substituted into either of the original equations to find the value of the other unknown.

Example:

The following two equations can be solved for x and y:

$$(1) \quad 3x + 2y = 11$$

$$(2) \quad x - y = 2$$

In equation (2), $x = 2 + y$. So in equation (1), substitute $2 + y$ for x:

$$3(2 + y) + 2y = 11$$
$$6 + 3y + 2y = 11$$
$$6 + 5y = 11$$
$$5y = 5$$
$$y = 1$$

Since $y = 1$, it follows that $x - 1 = 2$ and $x = 2 + 1 = 3$.

E. Another way to eliminate one of the unknowns and solve for x and y is by making the coefficients of one of the unknowns the same (disregarding the sign) in both equations and either adding the equations or subtracting one equation from the other.

Example:

Use this method to solve the equations:

(1) $6x + 5y = 29$ and

(2) $4x - 3y = -6$

Multiply equation (1) by 3 and equation (2) by 5 to get

$18x + 15\ y = 87$ and

$20x - 15\ y = -30$

Adding the two equations eliminates y, yielding $38x = 57$, or $x = \dfrac{3}{2}$.

Finally, substituting $\dfrac{3}{2}$ for x in one of the equations gives $y = 4$. These answers can be checked by substituting both values into both of the original equations.

3. Factoring and Quadratic Equations

A. Some equations can be solved by *factoring*. To do this, first add or subtract expressions to bring all the expressions to one side of the equation, with 0 on the other side. Then try to express the nonzero side as a product of factors that are algebraic expressions. If this is possible, setting any one of the factors equal to 0 will yield a simpler equation, because for any factors x and y, if $xy = 0$, then $x = 0$ or $y = 0$, or both. The solutions of the simpler equations produced in this way will be solutions of the factored equation.

Example:

Factor to find the solutions of the equation $x^3 - 2x^2 + x = -5(x-1)^2$:

$$x^3 - 2x^2 + x + 5(x-1)^2 = 0$$
$$x(x^2 - 2x + 1) + 5(x-1)^2 = 0$$
$$x(x-1)^2 + 5(x-1)^2 = 0$$
$$(x+5)(x-1)^2 = 0$$
$$x + 5 = 0 \text{ or } x - 1 = 0$$
$$x = -5 \text{ or } x = 1.$$

Therefore $x = -5$ or $x = 1$.

B. To use factoring to find solutions to equations with algebraic fractions, note that a fraction equals 0 if and only if its numerator equals 0 and its denominator does not.

Example:

Find the solutions of the equation $\dfrac{x(x-3)(x^2+5)}{x-4}=0$

First note that the numerator must equal 0: $x(x-3)(x^2+5)=0$.

Therefore, $x=0$ or $x-3=0$ or $x^2+5=0$, so $x=0$ or $x=3$ or $x^2+5=0$.

But $x^2+5=0$ has no real solution because $x+5>0$ for every real number. Thus, the solutions are 0 and 3.

C. The standard form for a ***quadratic equation*** is $ax^2+bx+c=0$, where a, b, and c are real numbers and $a \neq 0$.

Examples:

$$x^2+6x+5=0$$

$$3x^2-2x=0, \text{ and}$$

$$x^2+4=0$$

D. Some quadratic equations can easily be solved by factoring.

Example (1):

$$x^2+6x+5=0$$
$$(x+5)(x+1)=0$$
$$x+5=0 \text{ or } x+1=0$$
$$x=-5 \text{ or } x=-1$$

Example (2):

$$3x^2-3=8x$$
$$3x^2-8x-3=0$$
$$(3x+1)(x-3)=0$$
$$3x+1=0 \text{ or } x-3=0$$
$$x=-\frac{1}{3} \text{ or } x=3$$

E. A quadratic equation has at most two real roots and may have just one or even no real root.

Examples:

The equation $x^2-6x+9=0$ can be expressed as $(x-3)^2=0$, or $(x-3)(x-3)=0$; thus its only root is 3.

The equation $x^2+4=0$ has no real root. Since the square of any real number is greater than or equal to zero, x^2+4 must be greater than zero if x is a real number.

F. An expression of the form a^2-b^2 can be factored as $(a-b)(a+b)$.

Example:

The quadratic equation $9x^2 - 25 = 0$ can be solved as follows:

$$(3x - 5)(3x + 5) = 0$$
$$3x - 5 = 0 \text{ or } 3x + 5 = 0$$
$$x = \frac{5}{3} \text{ or } x = -\frac{5}{3}$$

G. If a quadratic expression is not easily factored, then its roots can always be found using the **quadratic formula:** If $ax^2 + bx + c = 0$ and $a \neq 0$, then the roots are

$$x = \frac{-b + \sqrt{b^2 - 4ac}}{2a} \text{ and } x = \frac{-b - \sqrt{b^2 - 4ac}}{2a}$$

These roots are two distinct real numbers unless $b^2 - 4ac \leq 0$.

If $b^2 - 4ac = 0$, then these two expressions both equal $-\dfrac{b}{2a}$, so the equation has only one root.

If $b^2 - 4ac < 0$, then $\sqrt{b^2 - 4ac}$ is not a real number, so the equation has no real roots.

4. Inequalities

A. An *inequality* is a statement that uses one of the following symbols:

$\neq$ is not equal to

$>$ is greater than

$\geq$ is greater than or equal to

$<$ is less than

$\leq$ is less than or equal to

Example:

$5x - 3 < 9$ and $6x \geq y$

B. Solving a linear inequality with one unknown is similar to solving a linear equation; the unknown is isolated on one side of the inequality. As in solving an equation, the same number can be added to or subtracted from both sides of the inequality, or both sides of an inequality can be multiplied or divided by a positive number without changing the order of the inequality. However, multiplying or dividing an inequality by a negative number reverses the order of the inequality. Thus, $6 > 2$, but $(-1)(6) < (-1)(2)$.

Example (1):

To solve the inequality $3x - 2 > 5$ for x, isolate x:

$$3x - 2 > 5$$
$$3x > 7 \quad \text{(adding 2 to both sides)}$$
$$x > \frac{7}{3} \quad \text{(dividing both sides by 3)}$$

Example (2):

To solve the inequality $\dfrac{5x-1}{-2} < 3$ for x, isolate x:

$$\frac{5x-1}{-2} < 3$$
$$5x - 1 > -6 \quad \text{(multiplying both sides by } -2)$$
$$5x > -5 \quad \text{(adding 1 to both sides)}$$
$$x > -1 \quad \text{(dividing both sides by 5)}$$

5. Functions

A. An algebraic expression in one variable can be used to define a *function* of that variable. A function is denoted by a letter such as f or g along with the variable in the expression. Function notation provides a short way of writing the result of substituting a value for a variable.

Examples:

(1) The expression $x^3 - 5x^2 + 2$ defines a function f that can be denoted by $f(x) = x^3 - 5x^2 + 2$.

(2) The expression $\dfrac{2z+7}{\sqrt{z+1}}$ defines a function g that can be denoted by $g(z) = \dfrac{2z+7}{\sqrt{z+1}}$

In these examples, the symbols "$f(x)$" and "$g(z)$" do not represent products. Each is merely the symbol for an algebraic expression, and is read "f of x" or "g of z."

If $x = 1$ is substituted in the first expression, the result can be written $f(1) = -2$, and $f(1)$ is called the "value of f at $x = 1$."

Similarly, if $z = 0$ is substituted in the second expression, then the value of g at $z = 0$ is $g(0) = 7$.

B. Once a function $f(x)$ is defined, it is useful to think of the variable x as an input and $f(x)$ as the corresponding output. In any function there can be at most one output for any given input. However, different inputs can give the same output.

Example:

If $h(x) = |x + 3|$, then $h(-4) = 1 = h(-2)$.

C. The set of all allowable inputs for a function is called the ***domain*** of the function. For f and g as defined in the examples in 3.2.5.A above, the domain of f is the set of all real numbers and the domain of g is the set of all numbers greater than -1.

The domain of any function can be arbitrarily specified, as in the function defined by "$a(x) = 9x - 5$ for $0 \le x \le 10$." Without such a restriction, the domain is assumed to be all values of x that result in a real number when substituted into the function.

D. The set of all outputs for a function is called the ***range*** of the function.

Examples:

(i) For the function $h(x) = |x + 3|$ considered in the example in 3.2.5.B above, the range is the set of all numbers greater than or equal to 0.

(ii) For the function $a(x) = 9x - 5$ for $0 \leq x \leq 10$ considered in 3.2.5.C above, the range is the set including every value y such that $-5 \leq y \leq 85$.

6. Formulas and Measurement Conversion

A. A *formula* is an algebraic equation with specific meanings associated with its variables. To apply a formula in a particular context, find quantities that can be assigned to the formula's variables to match the meanings associated with those variables.

Example:

In the physics formula $F = ma$, the variable F stands for force, the variable m stands for mass, and the variable a stands for acceleration. The standard metric measure of force, the newton, is a force sufficient to accelerate a mass of 1 kilogram by 1 meter/second^2.

So if we are told that a rock with a mass of 2 kilograms is accelerating at 5 meters/second^2, we can apply the formula $F = ma$ by substituting 2 kilograms for the variable m and 5 meters/second^2 for the variable a, allowing us to calculate the force applied to the rock as 10 newtons.

Note: you do not need to learn physics formulas or terminology used in this example to prepare for the GMAT, but some formulas and terminology may be introduced within specific questions on the exam.

B. Any quantitative relationship between units of measure may be represented as a formula.

Examples:

(i) Since 1 kilometer is 1000 meters, the relationship between kilometers (k) and meters (m) may be represented by the formula $m = 1000k$.

(ii) The formula $C = \dfrac{5}{9}(F - 32)$ may be used to represent the relationship between measurements of temperature in degrees Celsius (C) and degrees Fahrenheit (F).

C. Except for units of time, if a GMAT question requires converting one unit of measure to another, the relationship between those units will be given.

Example:

A train travels at a constant rate of 25 meters per second. How many kilometers does it travel in 5 minutes? (1 kilometer = 1,000 meters)

Solution: In 1 minute the train travels $(25)(60) = 1,500$ meters, so in 5 minutes it travels 7,500 meters. Since 1 kilometer = 1,000 meters, it follows that 7,500 meters = 7.5 kilometers.

D. In some cases the relationship between units to be converted may be indicated in a table or graph.

Example:

Population by Age Group (in thousands)	
Age	Population
17 years and under	63,376
18–44 years	86,738
45–64 years	43,845
65 years and over	24,051

According to the table above, how many people are 44 years old or younger?

Solution: The table header states that the population figures are given in *thousands*. The answer in thousands can be obtained by adding 63,376 thousand and 86,738 thousand. The result is 150,114 thousand, which is 150,114,000.

PS21840.03

Practice Question 6

Number of Solid-Colored Marbles in Three Jars			
Jar	Number of red marbles	Number of green marbles	Total number of red and green marbles
P	x	y	80
Q	y	z	120
R	x	z	160

In the table above, what is the number of green marbles in Jar R ?

(A) 70

(B) 80

(C) 90

(D) 100

(E) 110

DS71210.03

Practice Question 7

In Mr. Smith's class, what is the ratio of the number of boys to the number of girls?

(1) There are 3 times as many girls as boys in Mr. Smith's class.

(2) The number of boys is $\frac{1}{4}$ of the total number of boys and girls in Mr. Smith's class.

(A) Statement (1) ALONE is sufficient, but statement (2) alone is not sufficient.

(B) Statement (2) ALONE is sufficient, but statement (1) alone is not sufficient.

(C) BOTH statements TOGETHER are sufficient, but NEITHER statement ALONE is sufficient.

(D) EACH statement ALONE is sufficient.

(E) Statements (1) and (2) TOGETHER are NOT sufficient.

DS84820.03

Practice Question 8

If x is an integer, is $9^x + 9^{-x} = b$?

(1) $3^x + 3^{-x} = \sqrt{b + 2}$

(2) $x > 0$

    (A)   Statement (1) ALONE is sufficient, but statement (2) alone is not sufficient.

    (B)   Statement (2) ALONE is sufficient, but statement (1) alone is not sufficient.

    (C)   BOTH statements TOGETHER are sufficient, but NEITHER statement ALONE is sufficient.

    (D)   EACH statement ALONE is sufficient.

    (E)   Statements (1) and (2) TOGETHER are NOT sufficient.

DS67730.03

Practice Question 9

What is the total number of executives at Company P?

(1)   The number of male executives is $\frac{3}{5}$ the number of female executives.

(2)   There are 4 more female executives than male executives.

    (A)   Statement (1) ALONE is sufficient, but statement (2) alone is not sufficient.

    (B)   Statement (2) ALONE is sufficient, but statement (1) alone is not sufficient.

    (C)   BOTH statements TOGETHER are sufficient, but NEITHER statement ALONE is sufficient.

    (D)   EACH statement ALONE is sufficient.

    (E)   Statements (1) and (2) TOGETHER are NOT sufficient.

DS53060.02

Practice Question 10

Is $x > y$?

(1) $x = y + 2$

(2) $\dfrac{x}{2} = y - 1$

    (A)   Statement (1) ALONE is sufficient, but statement (2) alone is not sufficient.

    (B)   Statement (2) ALONE is sufficient, but statement (1) alone is not sufficient.

    (C)   BOTH statements TOGETHER are sufficient, but NEITHER statement ALONE is sufficient.

    (D)   EACH statement ALONE is sufficient.

    (E)   Statements (1) and (2) TOGETHER are NOT sufficient.

PS21840.03

Answer Explanation 6

Number of Solid-Colored Marbles in Three Jars			
Jar	Number of red marbles	Number of green marbles	Total number of red and green marbles
P	x	y	80
Q	y	z	120
R	x	z	160

In the table above, what is the number of green marbles in Jar R?

(A) 70
(B) 80
(C) 90
(D) 100
(E) 110

Arithmetic; Algebra Interpretation of Tables; Applied Problems

First, set up an equation to find the total number of marbles in the three jars as follows:

$x + y + y + z + x + z = 80 + 120 + 160$

$\quad\quad 2x + 2y + 2z = 360$ combine the like terms

$\quad\quad\quad x + y + z = 180$ divide both sides by 2

Then, since it can be seen from the table that the number of green marbles in Jar R is z, solve for z to answer the problem. To do this most efficiently, use the information from the table for Jar P, which is that $x + y = 80$.

$x + y + z = 180$

$\quad 80 + z = 180$ substitute 80 for $x + y$

$\quad\quad\quad z = 100$

The correct answer is D.

DS71210.03
Answer Explanation 7

In Mr. Smith's class, what is the ratio of the number of boys to the number of girls?

(1) There are 3 times as many girls as boys in Mr. Smith's class.
(2) The number of boys is $\frac{1}{4}$ of the total number of boys and girls in Mr. Smith's class.

Algebra Ratio and Proportion

Letting B be the number of boys and G be the number of girls, determine the value of $\frac{B}{G}$.

(1) It is given that $G = 3B$, so $\frac{1}{3} = \frac{B}{G}$; SUFFICIENT.

(2) It is given that $B = \frac{1}{4}(B+G)$. Therefore, $4B = B + G$, or $3B = G$, or $\frac{B}{G} = \frac{1}{3}$; SUFFICIENT.

The correct answer is D; each statement alone is sufficient.

DS84820.03
Answer Explanation 8

If x is an integer, is $9^x + 9^{-x} = b$?

(1) $3^x + 3^{-x} = \sqrt{b+2}$
(2) $x > 0$

Algebra Exponents

When solving this problem it is helpful to note that $(x^r)(x^{-s}) = x^{r-s}$ and that $(x^r)^2 = x^{2r}$. Note also that $x^0 = 1$.

(1)   From this, $3^x + 3^{-x} = \sqrt{b+2}$. Squaring both sides gives:

$$(3^x + 3^{-x})^2 = b + 2$$
$$3^{2x} + 2(3^x)(3^{-x}) + 3^{-2x} = b + 2$$
$$9^x + 2(3^0) + 9^{-x} = b + 2 \text{ property of exponents}$$
$$9^x + 2 + 9^{-x} = b + 2 \text{ property of exponents}$$
$$9^x + 9^{-x} = b \quad \text{subtract 2 from both sides; SUFFICIENT.}$$

(2)   This gives no information about the relationship between x and b; NOT sufficient.

The correct answer is A; statement 1 alone is sufficient.

DS67730.03
Answer Explanation 9

What is the total number of executives at Company P ?

(1)   The number of male executives is $\frac{3}{5}$ the number of female executives.

(2)   There are 4 more female executives than male executives.

Algebra Simultaneous Equations

Let M be the number of male executives at Company P and let F be the number of female executives at Company P. Determine the value of $M + F$.

(1)   Given that $M = \frac{3}{5}F$, it is not possible to determine the value of $M + F$. For example, if $M = 3$ and $F = 5$, then $M = \frac{3}{5}F$ and $M + F = 8$. However, if $M = 6$ and $F = 10$, then $M = \frac{3}{5}F$ and $M + F = 16$; NOT sufficient.

(2)   Given that $F = M + 4$, it is not possible to determine the value of $M + F$. For example, if $M = 3$ and $F = 7$, then $F = M + 4$ and $M + F = 10$. However, if $M = 4$ and $F = 8$, then $F = M + 4$ and $M + F = 12$; NOT sufficient.

Taking (1) and (2) together, then $F = M + 4$ and $M = \frac{3}{5}F + 4$, so $F = \frac{3}{5}F + 4$. Now solve for F to get $\frac{2}{5}F = 4$ and $F = 10$. Therefore, using $F = 10$ and $F = M + 4$, it follows that $M = 6$, and hence $M + F = 6 + 10 = 16$.

The correct answer is C; both statements together are sufficient.

DS53060.02
Answer Explanation 10

Is $x > y$?

(1) $x = y + 2$

(2) $\frac{x}{2} = y - 1$

Algebra Inequalities

(1) $x = y + 2$ so $x - y = 2$ and since $2 > 0$,
$x - y > 0$ and $x > y$; SUFFICIENT.

(2) The equation given is equivalent to $x = 2y - 2$, which is satisfied both by $x = 0$ and $y = 1$ ($x > y$ is false) and by $x = 4$ and $y = 3$ ($x > y$ is true); NOT sufficient.

The correct answer is A; statement 1 alone is sufficient.

3.3 Rates, Ratios, and Percents

1. Ratio and Proportion

    A. The *ratio* of the number x to a nonzero number y may be expressed as $x : y$, or $\frac{x}{y}$, or x to y. The order of the terms is important in a ratio. Unless the absolute values of x and y are equal, $\frac{x}{y} \neq \frac{y}{x}$.

> *Examples:*
>
> The ratio of 2 to 3 may be written as 2:3, or $\frac{2}{3}$, or 2 to 3.
>
> The ratio of the number of months with exactly 30 days to the number with exactly 31 days is 4:7, not 7:4.

    B. A *proportion* is a statement that two ratios are equal.

> *Example:*
>
> 2:3 = 8:12 is a proportion.

    C. One way to find the value of an unknown variable in a proportion is to cross multiply, then solve the resulting equation.

> *Example:*
>
> To solve for n in the proportion $\frac{2}{3} = \frac{n}{12}$, cross multiply to obtain $3n = 24$, then divide both sides by 3 to find $n = 8$.

    D. Some word problems can be solved using ratios.

> *Example:*
>
> If 5 shirts cost a total of \$44, then what is the total cost of 8 shirts at the same cost per shirt?
>
> *Solution:* If c is the cost of the 8 shirts, then $\frac{5}{44} = \frac{8}{c}$. Cross multiplication yields $5c = 8 \times 44 = 352$, so $c = \frac{352}{5} = 70.4$. Thus, the 8 shirts cost a total of \$70.40.

2. Fractions

A. In a fraction $\frac{n}{d}$, n is the **numerator** and d is the **denominator.** The denominator of a fraction can never be 0, because division by 0 is not defined.

B. Two fractions are **equivalent** if they represent the same number. To determine whether two fractions are equivalent, divide each fraction's numerator and denominator by the largest factor the numerator and the denominator have in common, which is called their **greatest common divisor** (gcd). This process is called **reducing each fraction to its lowest terms.** The two fractions are equivalent if and only if reducing each to its lowest terms yields identical results.

Example:

To determine whether $\frac{8}{36}$ and $\frac{14}{63}$ are equivalent, first reduce each to its lowest terms. In the first fraction, the gcd of the numerator 8 and the denominator 36 is 4. Dividing both the numerator and the denominator of $\frac{8}{36}$ by 4 yields $\frac{2}{9}$. In the second fraction, the gcd of the numerator 14 and the denominator 63 is 7. Dividing both the numerator and the denominator of $\frac{14}{63}$ by 7 also yields $\frac{2}{9}$. Since reducing each fraction to its lowest terms yields the same result, $\frac{8}{36}$ and $\frac{14}{63}$ are equivalent.

C. Two fractions with the same denominator can be added or subtracted by performing the required operation with the numerators, leaving the denominators the same.

Example:

$$\frac{3}{5} + \frac{4}{5} = \frac{3+4}{5} = \frac{7}{5} \text{ and}$$

$$\frac{5}{7} - \frac{2}{7} = \frac{5-2}{7} = \frac{3}{7}$$

D. If two fractions do not have the same denominator, you can add or subtract them by first expressing them as fractions with the same denominator.

Examples:

To add $\frac{3}{5}$ and $\frac{4}{7}$, multiply the numerator and denominator of $\frac{3}{5}$ by 7 to obtain $\frac{21}{35}$. Then multiply the numerator and denominator of $\frac{4}{7}$ by 5 to obtain $\frac{20}{35}$. Since both fractions are now expressed with the same denominator 35, you can easily add them: $\frac{3}{5} + \frac{4}{7} = \frac{21}{35} + \frac{20}{35} = \frac{41}{35}$

E. To multiply two fractions, simply multiply the two numerators and also multiply the two denominators.

Example:

$$\frac{2}{3} \times \frac{4}{7} = \frac{2 \times 4}{3 \times 7} = \frac{8}{21}$$

F. In general, the *reciprocal* of a fraction $\frac{n}{d}$ is $\frac{d}{n}$, when n and d are not 0.

Example:

The reciprocal of $\frac{4}{7}$ is $\frac{7}{4}$

G. To divide by a fraction, multiply by the reciprocal of the divisor.

Example:

$$\frac{2}{3} \div \frac{4}{7} = \frac{2}{3} \times \frac{7}{4} = \frac{14}{12} = \frac{7}{6}$$

H. A *mixed number* is written as an integer together with a fraction and equals the sum of the integer and the fraction.

Example:

The mixed number $7\frac{2}{3} = 7 + \frac{2}{3}$

I. To express a mixed number as a fraction, multiply the integer portion of the mixed number by the denominator of the fraction portion of the mixed number. Add this product to the numerator. Then put this sum over the denominator.

Example:

$$7\frac{2}{3} = \frac{(7 \times 3) + 2}{3} = \frac{23}{3}$$

3. Percents

A. The term *percent* means *per hundred* or *number out of 100*.

Example:

The statement that 37 percent, or 37%, of the houses in a city are painted blue means that 37 out of every 100 houses in the city are painted blue.

B. A percent may be greater than 100.

Example:

The statement that the number of blue houses in a city is 150% of the number of red houses means that the city has 150 blue houses for every 100 red houses. Since 150:100 = 3:2, this is equivalent to saying that the city has 3 blue houses for every 2 red houses.

C. A percent need not be an integer.

Example:

The statement that the number of pink houses in a city is 0.5% of the number of blue houses means that the city has 0.5 of a pink house for every 100 blue houses. Since 0.5:100 = 1:200, this is equivalent to saying that the city has 1 pink house for every 200 blue houses.

Similarly, the statement that the number of orange houses is 12.5% of the number of blue houses means that the ratio of orange houses to blue houses is 12.5:100 = 1:8, so there is 1 orange house for every 8 blue houses.

---

4. Converting Decimals, Fractions, and Percents

A. Decimal numbers may be represented as fractions or sums of fractions.

Example:

$$0.321 = \frac{3}{10} + \frac{2}{100} + \frac{1}{1,000} = \frac{321}{1,000}$$

$$0.0321 = \frac{0}{10} + \frac{3}{100} + \frac{2}{1,000} + \frac{1}{10,000} = \frac{321}{10,000}$$

$$1.56 = 1 + \frac{5}{10} + \frac{6}{100} = \frac{156}{100}$$

B. A percent may be represented as a fraction in which the percent number is the numerator over a denominator of 100. A percent may also be represented as a decimal by moving the decimal point in the percent two places to the left. Conversely, a decimal may be represented as a percent by moving the decimal point two places to the right, then adding a percent sign (%).

Examples:

$$37\% = \frac{37}{100} = 0.37$$

$$300\% = \frac{300}{100} = 3$$

$$0.5\% = \frac{0.5}{100} = 0.005$$

C. To find a certain percent of a number, multiply the number by the percent expressed as a fraction or as a decimal.

Examples:

20% of $90 = 90\left(\dfrac{20}{100}\right) = 90\left(\dfrac{1}{5}\right) = \dfrac{90}{5} = 18$

20% of $90 = 90(0.2) = 18$

250% of $80 = 80\left(\dfrac{250}{100}\right) = 80(2.5) = 200$

0.5% of $12 = 12\left(\dfrac{0.5}{100}\right) = 12(0.005) = 0.06$

5. Working with Decimals, Fractions, and Percents

A. To find the percent increase or decrease from one quantity to another quantity, first find the amount of the increase or decrease. Then divide this amount by the original quantity, and express this quotient as a percent.

Examples:

Suppose the price of an item increases from $24 to $30. To find the percent increase, first note that the amount of the increase is $30 − $24 = $6. Therefore, the percent increase is $\dfrac{6}{24}$ = 0.25 = 25%.

Now suppose the price decreases from $30 to $24. The amount of the decrease is $30 − $24 = $6. Therefore, the percent decrease is $\dfrac{6}{30}$ = 0.20 = 20%.

Note that the percent **increase** from 24 to 30 (25%) does not equal the percent **decrease** from 30 to 24 (20%).

A percent increase and a percent decrease may be greater than 100%.

Example:

Suppose the price of a certain house in 2018 was 300% of its price in 2003. By what percent did the price increase?

Solution: If n is the price in 2003, then the percent increase is $\left|\dfrac{(3n - n)}{n}\right| = \left|\dfrac{2n}{n}\right| = 2$, or 200%.

B. If a price is discounted by n percent, then the discounted price is $(100 - n)$ percent of the original price.

Example:

A customer paid $24 for a dress. If that price reflected a 25% discount off the original price of the dress, what was the original price before the discount?

Solution: If p is the original price of the dress, then $0.75p$ is the discounted price, so $0.75p = \$24$. Thus, $p = \$32$, the original price before the discount.

Two discounts may be combined to yield a larger discount.

Example:

A price is discounted by 20%, and then this reduced price is discounted by an additional 30%. These two discounts combined yield an overall discount of what percent?

Solution: If p is the original price of the item, then $0.8p$ is the price after the first discount. The price after the second discount is $(0.7)(0.8)\,p = 0.56p$. This represents an overall discount of 44% $(100\% - 56\%)$.

C. Gross profit equals revenues minus expenses, or selling price minus cost.

Example:

A certain appliance costs a merchant $30. At what price should the merchant sell the appliance in order to make a gross profit of 50% of the cost of the appliance?

Solution: If s is the selling price of the appliance, then $s - 30 = (0.5)(30)$, or $s = \$45$. Thus, the merchant should sell the appliance for $45.

D. *Simple annual interest* on a loan or investment is computed based only on the original loan or investment amount (the ***principal***), and equals (principal) × (interest rate) × (time).

Example:

If $8,000 is invested at 6% simple annual interest, how much interest is earned after 3 months?

Solution: Since the annual interest rate is 6%, the interest for 1 year is $(0.06)(\$8{,}000) = \$480$. There are 12 months in a year, so the interest earned in 3 months is $\left(\dfrac{3}{12}\right)(\$480) = \$120$.

E. *Compound interest* is computed on the principal as well as on any interest already earned.

compound interest over n periods = (principal) × (1 + interest per period)^n − principal.

Example:

If $10,000 is invested at 10% annual interest, compounded semiannually, what is the balance after 1 year?

Solution: Since the interest is compounded semiannually (every 6 months), the interest rate for each 6-month period is 5%, which is half of the 10% annual rate. Thus, the balance after the first 6 months would be $10,000 + (10,000)(0.05) = \$10,500$.

For the second 6-month period, the interest is calculated on the $10,500 balance at the end of the first 6-month period. Thus, the balance after 1 year would be $10,500 + (10,500)(0.05) = \$11,025$.

The balance after one year can also be expressed as $10,000 \times \left(1 + \dfrac{0.10}{2}\right)^2$ dollars.

F. Some GMAT questions require working with decimals, fractions, and percents in graphs.

Example:

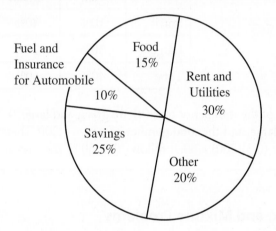

DISTRIBUTION OF AL'S WEEKLY NET SALARY

Al's weekly net salary is $350. How many of the categories shown in the chart above were each individually allocated at least $80 of Al's weekly net salary?

Solution: In the circle graph, the relative sizes of the sectors are proportional to their corresponding values, and the sum of the percents given is 100%. Note that $\dfrac{\$80}{\$350}$ is approximately 23%, so $80 or more of Al's salary was allocated to a category if and only if at least 23% of his salary was allocated to that category. Thus, according to the graph, there were exactly two categories to each of which at least $80 of Al's salary was allocated—the category **Savings** was allocated 25% of his salary, and the category **Rent and Utilities** was allocated 30%.

G. To solve some word problems involving percents and fractions, it can be helpful to organize the given information in a table.

Example:

In a certain production lot, 40% of the toys are red and the remaining toys are green. Half of the toys are small and half are large. If 10% of the toys are red and small, and 40 toys are green and large, how many of the toys are red and large?

Solution: First create a table to organize the information provided:

	Red	Green	Total
Small	10%		50%
Large			50%
Total	40%	60%	100%

Then fill in the missing percents so that the "Red" and "Green" percents in each row add up to the total in that row, and the "Small" and "Large" percents in each column add up to the total in that column:

	Red	Green	Total
Small	10%	40%	50%
Large	30%	20%	50%
Total	40%	60%	100%

Since 20% of the number of toys (n) are green and large, $0.20n = 40$. That is, 40 of the toys are green and large, and the total number of toys $n = 200$. Therefore, 30% of the 200 toys are red and large. Since $(0.3)(200) = 60$, it follows that 60 of the toys are red and large.

6. Rate, Work, and Mixture Problems

A. The distance an object travels equals the average speed at which it travels multiplied by the amount of time it takes to travel that distance. That is, ***distance = rate × time.***

Example:

If a car travels at an average speed of 70 kilometers per hour for 4 hours, how many kilometers does it travel?

Solution: Since distance = rate × time, simply multiply 70 km/hour × 4 hours. Thus, the car travels 280 kilometers in 4 hours.

B. To determine the average rate at which an object travels, divide the total distance traveled by the total amount of traveling time.

Example:

On a 600-kilometer trip, a car traveled half the distance at an average speed of 60 kilometers per hour (kph) and the other half at an average speed of 100 kph. The car did not stop between the two halves of the trip. What was the car's average speed during the trip as a whole?

Solution: First determine the total amount of traveling time. During the first 300 kilometers, the car travelled at 60 kph, so it took $\dfrac{300}{60} = 5$ hours to travel the first 300 kilometers. During the second 300 kilometers, the car travelled at 100 kph, so it took $\dfrac{300}{100} = 3$ hours to travel the second 300 kilometers. Thus, the total amount of traveling time was 5 + 3 = 8 hours, and the car's average speed was $\dfrac{600 \text{ kilometers}}{8 \text{ hours}} = 75$ kph.

Note that the average speed is **not** $\dfrac{(60 + 100)}{2} = 80$ kph.

C. In a *work problem*, the rates at which certain persons or machines work alone are usually given, and it is necessary to compute the rate at which they work together (or vice versa).

The basic formula for solving work problems is $\dfrac{1}{r} + \dfrac{1}{s} = \dfrac{1}{h}$, where r is the length of time it takes the first person or machine to complete an amount of work when working alone, s is the length of time it takes the second person or machine to complete that same amount of work when working alone, and h is the length of time it takes them to complete that amount of work when they are both working simultaneously.

Example:

Suppose one machine can produce 1,000 bolts in 4 hours, whereas a second machine can produce 1,000 bolts in 5 hours. Then in how many hours can the two machines, working simultaneously at these constant rates, produce 1,000 bolts?

Solution:

$$\frac{1}{4} + \frac{1}{5} = \frac{1}{h}$$

$$\frac{5}{20} + \frac{4}{20} = \frac{1}{h}$$

$$\frac{9}{20} = \frac{1}{h}$$

$$9h = 20$$

$$h = \frac{20}{9} = 2\frac{2}{9}$$

Working together, the two machines can produce 1,000 bolts in $2\dfrac{2}{9}$ hours.

The same formula can be applied to determine how long it would take one of the people or machines to do a given amount of work alone.

Example:

Suppose that Art and Rita can complete an amount of work in 4 hours when working simultaneously at their respective constant rates, and that Art can complete the same amount of work in 6 hours working alone. Then in how many hours can Rita complete that amount of work working alone?

Solution:

$$\frac{1}{6} + \frac{1}{R} = \frac{1}{4}$$

$$\frac{1}{R} = \frac{1}{4} - \frac{1}{6} = \frac{1}{12}$$

$$R = 12$$

Working alone, Rita can complete the work in 12 hours.

D. In *mixture problems,* substances with different characteristics are combined, and it is necessary to determine the characteristics of the resulting mixture.

Example:

If 6 kilograms of nuts that cost $1.20 per kilogram are mixed with 2 kilograms of nuts that cost $1.60 per kilogram, then how much does the mixture cost per kilogram?

Solution: The total cost of the 8 kilograms of nuts is 6($1.20) + 2($1.60) = $10.40. Thus, the cost per kilogram is $\frac{\$10.40}{8}$ = $1.30.

More complex mixture problems may involve calculating percents.

Example:

How many liters of a solution that is 15% salt must be added to 5 liters of a solution that is 8% salt so that the resulting solution is 10% salt?

Solution: Let *n* represent the number of liters of the 15% solution. The amount of salt in the 15% solution [0.15*n*] plus the amount of salt in the 8% solution [(0.08)(5)] must equal the amount of salt in the 10% mixture [0.10(*n* + 5)]. Therefore,

$$0.15n + 0.08(5) = 0.10(n + 5)$$

$$15n + 40 = 10n + 50$$

$$5n = 10$$

$$n = 2 \text{ liters}$$

Two liters of the 15% salt solution must be added to the 8% solution to obtain the 10% solution.

PS51061.03

Practice Question 11

As a salesperson, Phyllis can choose one of two methods of annual payment: either an annual salary of $35,000 with no commission or an annual salary of $10,000 plus a 20% commission on her total annual sales. What must her total annual sales be to give her the same annual pay with either method?

- (A) $100,000
- (B) $120,000
- (C) $125,000
- (D) $130,000
- (E) $132,000

DS15161.03

Practice Question 12

For which type of investment, J or K, is the annual rate of return greater?

(1) Type J returns $115 per $1,000 invested for any one-year period and type K returns $300 per $2,500 invested for any one-year period.

(2) The annual rate of return for an investment of type K is 12%.

- (A) Statement (1) ALONE is sufficient, but statement (2) alone is not sufficient.
- (B) Statement (2) ALONE is sufficient, but statement (1) alone is not sufficient.
- (C) BOTH statements TOGETHER are sufficient, but NEITHER statement ALONE is sufficient.
- (D) EACH statement ALONE is sufficient.
- (E) Statements (1) and (2) TOGETHER are NOT sufficient.

DS07061.03

Practice Question 13

If Car X followed Car Y across a certain bridge that is a $\frac{1}{2}$ mile long, how many seconds did it take Car X to travel across the bridge?

(1) Car X drove onto the bridge exactly 3 seconds after Car Y drove onto the bridge and drove off the bridge exactly 2 seconds after Car Y drove off the bridge.

(2) Car Y traveled across the bridge at a constant speed of 30 miles per hour.

- (A) Statement (1) ALONE is sufficient, but statement (2) alone is not sufficient.
- (B) Statement (2) ALONE is sufficient, but statement (1) alone is not sufficient.
- (C) BOTH statements TOGETHER are sufficient, but NEITHER statement ALONE is sufficient.
- (D) EACH statement ALONE is sufficient.
- (E) Statements (1) and (2) TOGETHER are NOT sufficient.

PS23461.03

Practice Question 14

If $x > 0$, $\dfrac{x}{50} + \dfrac{x}{25}$ is what percent of x?

- (A) 6%
- (B) 25%
- (C) 37%
- (D) 60%
- (E) 75%

PS61361.03
Practice Question 15

The cost to rent a small bus for a trip is x dollars, which is to be shared equally among the people taking the trip. If 10 people take the trip rather than 16, how many more dollars, in terms of x, will it cost per person?

(A) $\dfrac{x}{6}$

(B) $\dfrac{x}{10}$

(C) $\dfrac{x}{16}$

(D) $\dfrac{3x}{40}$

(E) $\dfrac{3x}{80}$

PS51061.03
Answer Explanation 11

As a salesperson, Phyllis can choose one of two methods of annual payment: either an annual salary of $35,000 with no commission or an annual salary of $10,000 plus a 20% commission on her total annual sales. What must her total annual sales be to give her the same annual pay with either method?

(A) $100,000
(B) $120,000
(C) $125,000
(D) $130,000
(E) $132,000

Algebra Applied Problems

Letting *s* be Phyllis's total annual sales needed to generate the same annual pay with either method, the given information can be expressed as $35,000 = $10,000 + 0.2*s*. Solve this equation for *s*.

$35,000 = $10,000 + 0.2*s*

$25,000 = 0.2*s*

$125,000 = *s*

The correct answer is C.

DS15161.03
Answer Explanation 12

For which type of investment, J or K, is the annual rate of return greater?

(1) Type J returns $115 per $1,000 invested for any one-year period and type K returns $300 per $2,500 invested for any one-year period.

(2) The annual rate of return for an investment of type K is 12%.

Arithmetic Percents

Compare the annual rates of return for Investments J and K.

(1) For Investment J, the annual rate of return is $115 per $1,000 for any one-year period, which can be converted to a percent. For Investment K, the annual rate of return is $300 per $2,500 for any one-year period, which can also be converted to a percent. These two percents can be compared to determine which is greater; SUFFICIENT

(2) Investment K has an annual rate of return of 12%, but no information is given about the annual rate of return for Investment J; NOT sufficient.

The correct answer is A; statement 1 alone is sufficient.

DS07061.03
Answer Explanation 13

If Car X followed Car Y across a certain bridge that is a $\frac{1}{2}$ mile long, how many seconds did it take Car X to travel across the bridge?

(1) Car X drove onto the bridge exactly 3 seconds after Car Y drove onto the bridge and drove off the bridge exactly 2 seconds after Car Y drove off the bridge.

(2) Car Y traveled across the bridge at a constant speed of 30 miles per hour.
  - (A) Statement (1) ALONE is sufficient, but statement (2) alone is not sufficient.
  - (B) Statement (2) ALONE is sufficient, but statement (1) alone is not sufficient.
  - (C) BOTH statements TOGETHER are sufficient, but NEITHER statement ALONE is sufficient.
  - (D) EACH statement ALONE is sufficient.
  - (E) Statements (1) and (2) TOGETHER are NOT sufficient.

Arithmetic Rate Problem

Find the number of seconds that it took Car X to cross the $\frac{1}{2}$-mile bridge.

(1) If Car X drove onto the bridge 3 seconds after Car Y and drove off the bridge 2 seconds after Car Y, then Car X took 1 second less to cross the bridge than Car Y. Since there is no information on how long Car Y took to cross the bridge, there is no way to determine how long Car X took to cross the bridge; NOT sufficient.

(2) If the speed of Car Y was 30 miles per hour, it took Car Y $\frac{1}{60}$ hour = 1 minute = 60 seconds to cross the bridge. However, there is no information on how long Car X took to cross the bridge; NOT sufficient.

Taking (1) and (2) together, Car X took 1 second less than Car Y to cross the bridge and Car Y took 60 seconds to cross the bridge, so Car X took 60 − 1 = 59 seconds to cross the bridge.

The correct answer is C; both statements together are sufficient.

PS23461.03
Answer Explanation 14

If $x > 0$, $\frac{x}{50} + \frac{x}{25}$ is what percent of x ?

  - (A) 6%
  - (B) 25%
  - (C) 37%
  - (D) 60%
  - (E) 75%

Algebra Arithmetic; Simplifying Algebraic Expressions; Percents

Because we want a percent, use a common denominator of 100 to combine the two terms.

$\frac{x}{50} + \frac{x}{25} = \frac{2x}{100} + \frac{4x}{100} = \frac{6x}{100} = \left(\frac{6}{100}\right)x$, which is 6% of x.

The correct answer is A.

PS61361.03
Answer Explanation 15

The cost to rent a small bus for a trip is x dollars, which is to be shared equally among the people taking the trip. If 10 people take the trip rather than 16, how many more dollars, in terms of x, will it cost per person?

(A) $\frac{x}{6}$

(B) $\frac{x}{10}$

(C) $\frac{x}{16}$

(D) $\frac{3x}{40}$

(E) $\frac{3x}{80}$

Algebra Applied Problems

If 16 take the trip, the cost per person would be $\frac{x}{16}$ dollars. If 10 take the trip, the cost would be $\frac{x}{10}$ dollars. (Note that the lowest common multiple of 10 and 16 is 80.) Thus, if 10 take the trip, the increase in dollars per person would be $\frac{x}{10} - \frac{x}{16} = \frac{8x}{80} - \frac{5x}{80} = \frac{3x}{80}$.

The correct answer is E.

3.4 Statistics, Sets, Counting, Probability, Estimation, and Series

1. Statistics

A. One of the most common statistical measures is the **average,** or **(arithmetic) mean,** which locates a type of "center" for the numbers in a set of data. The average or mean of n numbers is defined as the sum of the n numbers divided by n.

Example:

The average of the 5 numbers 6, 4, 7, 10, and 4 is $\frac{(6+4+7+10+4)}{5} = \frac{31}{5} = 6.2$

B. The *median* is another type of center for a set of numbers. To determine the median of a set of n numbers, first order the numbers from least to greatest. If n is odd, the median is defined as the middle number in the list, whereas if n is even, the median is defined as the average of the two middle numbers. The median may be less than, equal to, or greater than the mean of the same set of numbers.

> *Example:*
>
> To find the median of the 5 numbers 6, 4, 7, 10, and 4, first order them from least to greatest:
>
> 4, 4, 6, 7, 10. The median is 6, the middle number in this list.
>
> The median of the 6 numbers 4, 6, 6, 8, 9, 12 is $\dfrac{(6+8)}{2} = 7$. Note that the mean of these 6 numbers is
>
> $\dfrac{(4+6+6+8+9+12)}{6} = \dfrac{45}{6} = 7.5$.

Often about half of the data in a set is less than the median and about half is greater than the median, but not always.

> *Example:*
>
> For the 15 numbers 3, 5, 7, 7, 7, 7, 7, 7, 8, 9, 9, 9, 9, 10, and 10, the median is 7, but only $\dfrac{2}{15}$ of the numbers are less than the median.

C. The *mode* of a list of numbers is the number that occurs most frequently in the list.

> *Example:*
>
> The mode of the list of numbers 1, 3, 6, 4, 3, 5 is 3, since 3 is the only number that occurs more than once in the list.

A list of numbers may have more than one mode.

> *Example:*
>
> The list of numbers 1, 2, 3, 3, 3, 5, 7, 10, 10, 10, 20 has two modes, 3 and 10.

D. The degree to which numerical data are spread out or dispersed can be measured in many ways. The simplest measure of dispersion is the *range,* which is defined as the greatest value in the numerical data minus the least value.

> *Example:*
>
> The range of the 5 numbers 11, 10, 5, 13, 21 is $21 - 5 = 16$. Note how the range depends on only two values in the data.

E. Another common measure of dispersion is the ***standard deviation.*** Generally speaking, the more the data are spread away from the mean, the greater the standard deviation. The standard deviation of n numbers can be calculated as follows:

(1) Find the arithmetic mean,

(2) Find the differences between the mean and each of the n numbers,

(3) Square each of the differences,

(4) Find the average of the squared differences, and

(5) Take the nonnegative square root of this average.

Example:

The table below is used in calculating the standard deviation of the 5 numbers 0, 7, 8, 10, 10, which have the mean 7.

x	$x-7$	$(x-7)^2$
0	−7	49
7	0	0
8	1	1
10	3	9
10	3	9
	Total	68

Standard deviation $\sqrt{\dfrac{68}{5}} \approx 3.7$

Notice that the standard deviation depends on every data value, although it depends most on values farthest from the mean. This is why a data set whose data is grouped closely around the mean will have a smaller standard deviation than will a data set whose data is spread far from the mean.

Consider as a second example the data 6, 6, 6.5, 7.5, 9, which also have mean 7. Note that the numbers in this second example are grouped more closely around the mean of 7 than the numbers in the first example are. As a result, the standard deviation of the numbers in this second example is only about 1.1, significantly lower than the standard deviation of 3.7 in the first example above.

F. There are many ways to display numerical data in order to show how the data are distributed. One simple way is with a ***frequency distribution,*** which is useful for data in which values occur with varying frequencies.

Example:

Consider the following data set of 20 numbers:

$$
\begin{array}{cccccccccc}
-4 & 0 & 0 & -3 & -2 & -1 & -1 & 0 & -1 & -4 \\
-1 & -5 & 0 & -2 & 0 & -5 & -2 & 0 & 0 & -1
\end{array}
$$

The data set's frequency distribution can be displayed in a table by listing each different data value x and the frequency f with which x occurs:

Data Value x	Frequency f
−5	2
−4	2
−3	1
−2	3
−1	5
0	7
Total	20

This frequency distribution table can be used to easily compute statistical measures of the data set:

Mean: $= \dfrac{(-5)(2)+(-4)(2)+(-3)(1)+(-2)(3)+(-1)(5)+(0)(7)}{20} = -1.6$

Median: −1 (the average of the 10th and 11th numbers)

Mode: 0 (the number that occurs most frequently)

Range: $0 - (-5) = 5$

Standard deviation: $\sqrt{\dfrac{(-5+1.6)^2(2)+(-4+1.6)^2(2)+\ldots+(0+1.6)^2(7)}{20}} \approx 1.7$

G. Some GMAT questions require identifying or computing statistical measures for data displayed in graphs.

Example:

AVERAGE TEMPERATURE AND PRECIPITATION IN CITY X

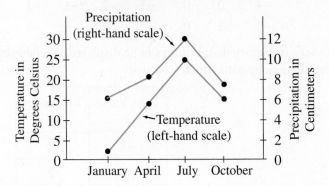

What are the average temperature and precipitation in City X during April?

Solution: Note that the scale on the left applies to the temperature line graph and the one on the right applies to the precipitation line graph. According to the graph, during April the average temperature is approximately 14° Celsius and the average precipitation is approximately 8 centimeters. Since the question is about only the averages during April, the data points shown for January, July, and October are irrelevant.

2. Sets

A. In mathematics a ***set*** is a collection of numbers or other objects. The objects are called the ***elements*** of the set. A set with a finite number of elements may be denoted by listing its elements within a pair of braces. The order in which the elements are listed does not matter.

Example:

$\{-5, 0, 1\}$ is the same set as $\{0, 1, -5\}$; that is, $\{-5, 0, 1\} = \{0, 1, -5\}$.

B. If S is a set with a finite number of elements, then the number of elements is denoted by $|S|$.

Example:

$S = \{-5, 0, 1\}$ is a set with $|S| = 3$.

C. If all the elements of a set S are also elements of a set T, then S is a ***subset*** of T. This relationship is expressed by $S \subseteq T$ or by $T \supseteq S$.

Example:

$\{-5, 0, 1\}$ is a subset of $\{-5, 0, 1, 4, 10\}$; that is, $\{-5, 0, 1\} \subseteq \{-5, 0, 1, 4, 10\}$.

D. The *union* of two sets A and B is the set of all elements that are in A or in B or in both. The union is denoted by $A \cup B$.

> *Example:*
>
> $\{3, 4\} \cup \{4, 5, 6\} = \{3, 4, 5, 6\}$

E. The *intersection* of two sets A and B is the set of all elements that are **both** in A and in B. The intersection is denoted by $A \cap B$.

> *Example:*
>
> $\{3, 4\} \cap \{4, 5, 6\} = \{4\}$

F. Two sets that have no elements in common are said to be *disjoint* or *mutually exclusive.*

> *Example:*
>
> $\{-5, 0, 1\}$ and $\{4, 10\}$ are disjoint.

G. The relationship between sets may be illustrated with a *Venn diagram* in which the sets are represented as regions in a plane. If two sets S and T are not disjoint, and neither is a subset of the other, their intersection $S \cap T$ is represented by the shaded region of the Venn diagram in the figure below.

> **A Venn Diagram of the Intersection of Two Sets**
>
>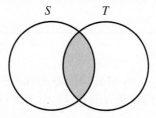
>
> A Venn diagram showing two sets S and T, with their intersection $S \cap T$ shaded.

H. The number of elements in the union of any two finite sets S and T equals the sum of their individual numbers of elements minus the number of elements in their intersection. More concisely, $|S \cup T| = |S| + |T| - |S \cap T|$. This counting method is called the *general addition rule for two sets.*

> *Example:*
>
> $$|\{3, 4\} \cup \{4, 5, 6\}| = |\{3, 4\}| + |\{4, 5, 6\}| - |\{3, 4\} \cap \{4, 5, 6\}| =$$
> $$|\{3, 4\}| + |\{4, 5, 6\}| - |\{4\}| = 2 + 3 - 1 = 4.$$

As a special case, if S and T are disjoint, then $|S \cup T| = |S| + |T|$, since $|S \cap T| = 0$.

I. Word problems involving sets can often be solved using Venn diagrams and the general addition rule.

Example:

Each of 25 people is enrolled in history, mathematics, or both. If 20 of them are enrolled in history and 18 are enrolled in mathematics, how many are enrolled in both history and mathematics?

Solution: The 25 people can be divided into three sets: those enrolled in history only, those enrolled in mathematics only, and those enrolled in both history and mathematics. Thus, a Venn diagram may be drawn as follows, where n is the number of people enrolled in both courses, $20 - n$ is the number enrolled in history only, and $18 - n$ is the number enrolled in mathematics only.

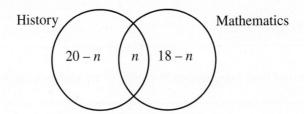

Since there are 25 people total, $(20 - n) + n + (18 - n) = 25$, or $n = 13$. Therefore, 13 people are enrolled in both history and mathematics. Note that $20 + 18 - 13 = 25$, which is an instance of the general addition rule for two sets.

---

3. Counting Methods

A. To count objects and sets of objects without actually listing the elements to be counted, the following ***multiplication principle*** is essential:

If an object is to be chosen from a set of m objects and a second object is to be chosen from a different set of n objects, then there are mn different possible choices.

Example:

If a meal consists of 1 entree and 1 dessert, and there are 5 entrees and 3 desserts on the menu, then there are $5 \times 3 = 15$ different meals that can be ordered from the menu.

B. A more general version of the multiplication principle is that the number of possible choices of 1 object apiece out of each of any number of sets is the product of the numbers of objects contained in those sets. So if 1 object apiece is to be chosen out of each of 3 sets that contain x, y, and z elements respectively, there are xyz possible choices. And if 1 object apiece is to be chosen out of each of n different sets that each contain exactly m objects apiece, there are mn possible choices.

Example:

Each time a coin is flipped, there are 2 possible results, heads and tails. If there are 8 consecutive coin flips, then each flip may be mathematically treated as a set containing those 2 possible results. Since there are 8 flips, there are 8 of these sets. Thus, the set of 8 flips has a total of 2^8 possible results.

C. A concept often used with the multiplication principle is the ***factorial.*** If n is an integer greater than 1, then n factorial, denoted by $n!$, is defined as the product of all the integers from 1 through n.

Example:

$2! = \times 2 \times 1 = 2$

$3! = 3 \times 2 \times 1 = 6$

$4! = 4 \times 3 \times 2 \times 1 = 24$, etc.

Also, by definition, $0! = 1! = 1$. Two additional equations that may be useful when working with factorials are $n! = (n-1)!(n)$ and $(n+1)! = (n!)(n+1)$.

D. Each possible sequential ordering of the objects in a set is called a ***permutation*** of the set. A permutation can be thought of as a selection process in which objects are selected one by one in a certain order.

The factorial is useful for finding the number of permutations of a given set. If a set of n objects is to be ordered from 1st to n^{th}, then there are n choices for the 1st object, $n-1$ choices remaining for the 2nd object, $n-2$ choices remaining for the 3rd object, and so on, until there is only 1 choice remaining for the nth object. Thus, by the multiplication principle, the number of permutations of a set of n objects is $n(n-1)(n-2) \ldots (3)(2)(1) = n!$.

Example:

The number of permutations of the set of letters A, B, and C is 3!, or 6. The 6 permutations are ABC, ACB, BAC, BCA, CAB, and CBA.

E. Consider a set of n objects from which k objects are to be selected without regard to order, where $0 \le k \le n$. The number of possible complete selections of k objects is denoted by $\binom{n}{k}$ and is called the number of ***combinations*** of n objects taken k at a time. Its numerical value may be calculated as $\binom{n}{k} = \frac{n!}{k!(n-k)!}$. Note that $\binom{n}{k}$ is the number of k-element subsets of a set with n elements. Note also that $\binom{n}{k} = \binom{n}{n-k}$.

Example:

Suppose that $S = \{A, B, C, D, E\}$. The number of 2-element subsets of S, or the number of combinations of the 5 letters in S taken 2 at a time, may be calculated as $\binom{5}{2} = \dfrac{5!}{2!3!} = \dfrac{120}{(2)(6)} = 10$. The 10 subsets are $\{A, B\}, \{A, C\}, \{A, D\}, \{A, E\}, \{B, C\}, \{B, D\}, \{B, E\}, \{C, D\}, \{C, E\}$, and $\{D, E\}$.

Note that $\binom{5}{2} = 10 = \binom{5}{3}$ because every 2-element subset chosen from a set of 5 elements corresponds to a unique 3-element subset consisting of the elements *not* chosen.

4. Probability

A. Many of the ideas discussed above about sets and counting methods are important to the study of ***discrete probability***. Discrete probability is concerned with ***experiments*** that have a finite number of possible ***outcomes***. Given such an experiment, an ***event*** is a particular set of outcomes.

Example:

Rolling a 6-sided die with faces numbered 1 to 6 is an experiment with 6 possible outcomes that may be denoted as 1, 2, 3, 4, 5, and 6, with each number representing the side of the die facing up after the roll. One event in this experiment is that the outcome is 4. This event is denoted $\{4\}$.

Another event in the experiment is that the outcome is an odd number. This event is denoted $\{1, 3, 5\}$.

B. The probability that an event E occurs is a number between 0 and 1, inclusive, and is denoted by $P(E)$. If E is an empty set containing no possible outcomes, then E is ***impossible*** and $P(E) = 0$. If E is the set of all possible outcomes of the experiment, then E is ***certain*** to occur and $P(E) = 1$. Otherwise, E is possible but uncertain, and $0 < P(E) < 1$. If F is a subset of E, then $P(F) \leq P(E)$.

C. If the probabilities of any two outcomes of an experiment are identical, those outcomes are said to be ***equally likely***. For experiments in which all the individual outcomes are equally likely, the probability of an event E is $P(E) = \dfrac{\text{the number of outcomes in } E}{\text{the total number of possible outcomes}}$.

Example:

Returning to the previous example in which a 6-sided die is rolled once, if the 6 outcomes are equally likely (that is, if the die is fair), then the probability of each outcome is $\dfrac{1}{6}$. The probability that the outcome is an odd number is $P(\{1, 3, 5\}) = \dfrac{|\{1, 3, 5\}|}{6} = \dfrac{3}{6} = \dfrac{1}{2}$.

D. Given two events E and F in an experiment, the following additional events can be defined:

(i) "not E" is the set of outcomes that are not outcomes in E;

(ii) "E or F" is the set of outcomes in E or F or both, that is, $E \cup F$;

(iii) "E and F" is the set of outcomes in both E and F, that is, $E \cap F$.

The probability that E does not occur is $P(\text{not } E) = 1 - P(E)$.

The probability that "E or F" occurs is $P(E \text{ or } F) = P(E) + P(F) - P(E \text{ and } F)$. This is derived using the general addition rule for two sets presented above in 3.4.2.H.

Example:

Consider again the example above in which a 6-sided die is rolled once. Let E be the event $\{1, 3, 5\}$ that the outcome is an odd number. Let F be the event $\{2, 3, 5\}$ that the outcome is a prime number. Then

$$P(E \text{ and } F) = P(E \cap F) = P(\{3,5\}) = \frac{|\{3,5\}|}{6} = \frac{2}{6} = \frac{1}{3}. \text{ Therefore}$$

$$P(E \text{ or } F) = P(E) + P(F) - P(E \text{ and } F) = \frac{3}{6} + \frac{3}{6} - \frac{2}{6} = \frac{4}{6} = \frac{2}{3}.$$

Note that the event "E or F" is $E \cup F = \{1, 2, 3, 5\}$, and hence $P(E \text{ or } F) = \frac{|\{1,2,3,5\}|}{6} = \frac{4}{6} = \frac{2}{3}$.

If the event "E and F" is impossible (that is, $E \cap F$ has no outcomes), then E and F are said to be ***mutually exclusive*** events, and $P(E \text{ and } F) = 0$. In that case $P(E \text{ or } F) = P(E) + P(F)$. This is the special addition rule for the probability of two mutually exclusive events.

E. Two events A and B are said to be ***independent*** if the occurrence of either event does not alter the probability that the other event occurs. The following multiplication rule holds for any independent events E and F:

$$P(E \text{ and } F) = P(E)P(F).$$

Example:

Returning again to the example of the 6-sided die rolled once, let A be the event $\{2, 4, 6\}$ and B be the event $\{5, 6\}$. Then the probability that A occurs is $P(A) = \frac{|A|}{6} = \frac{3}{6} = \frac{1}{2}$. And **presuming B occurs**, the probability that A occurs is $\frac{|A \cap B|}{|B|} = \frac{|\{6\}|}{|\{5,6\}|} = \frac{1}{2}$, the same as $P(A)$.

Similarly, the probability that B occurs is $P(B) = \frac{|B|}{6} = \frac{2}{6} = \frac{1}{3}$. And **presuming A occurs**, the probability that B occurs is $\frac{|B \cap A|}{|A|} = \frac{\{6\}}{|\{2,4,6\}|} = \frac{1}{3}$, the same as $P(B)$.

Thus, the occurrence of either event does not affect the probability that the other event occurs. Therefore, A and B are independent. So by the multiplication rule for independent events,

$$P(A \text{ and } B) = P(A) P(B) = \left(\frac{1}{2}\right)\left(\frac{1}{3}\right) = \frac{1}{6}.$$

Note that the event "A and B" is $A \cap B = \{6\}$, so $P(A \text{ and } B) = P(\{6\}) = \frac{1}{6}$.

It follows from the general addition rule and the multiplication rule above that if E and F are independent, then $P(E \text{ or } F) = P(E) + P(F) - P(E)P(F)$.

F. An event A is said to be *dependent* on an event B if the occurrence of B alters the probability that A occurs.

The probability of A occurring if B occurs is represented as $P(A \mid B)$. So the statement that A is dependent on B may be represented as $P(A \mid B) \neq P(A)$.

The following general multiplication rule holds for any dependent or independent events A and B:

$P(A \text{ and } B) = P(A \mid B) P(B)$.

Example:

Returning to the example of the 6-sided die rolled once, let A be the event $\{4, 6\}$ and B be the event $\{4, 5, 6\}$. Then the probability that A occurs is $P(A) = \dfrac{|A|}{6} = \dfrac{2}{6} = \dfrac{1}{3}$. But **presuming B occurs**, the probability that A occurs is $P(A \mid B) = \dfrac{|A \cap B|}{|B|} = \dfrac{|\{4, 6\}|}{|\{4, 5, 6\}|} = \dfrac{2}{3}$. Thus, $P(A \mid B) \neq P(A)$, so A is dependent on B.

Similarly, the probability that B occurs is $P(B) = \dfrac{|B|}{6} = \dfrac{3}{6} = \dfrac{1}{2}$. But **presuming A occurs**, the probability that B occurs is $P(B \mid A) = \dfrac{|B \cap A|}{|A|} = \dfrac{|\{4,6\}|}{|\{4,6\}|} = 1$. Thus, $P(B \mid A) \neq P(B)$, so B is dependent on A.

By the general multiplication rule for events,

$P(A \text{ and } B) = P(A \mid B)P(B) = \left(\dfrac{2}{3}\right)\left(\dfrac{1}{2}\right) = \dfrac{1}{3}$. Similarly, $P(A \text{ and } B) = P(B \mid A)P(A) = (1)\left(\dfrac{1}{3}\right) = \dfrac{1}{3}$.

Note that the event "A and B" is $A \cap B = \{4, 6\} = A$, so $P(A \text{ and } B) = P(\{4, 6\}) = \dfrac{1}{3} = P(A)$.

G. The rules above may be used together for more complex probability calculations.

Example:

Consider an experiment with events A, B, and C for which $P(A) = 0.23$, $P(B) = 0.40$, and $P(C) = 0.85$. Suppose that events A and B are mutually exclusive, and that events B and C are independent. Since A and B are mutually exclusive, $P(A \text{ or } B) = P(A) + P(B) = 0.23 + 0.40 = 0.63$.

Since B and C are independent, $P(B \text{ or } C) = P(B) + P(C) - P(B) P(C) = 0.40 + 0.85 - (0.40)(0.85) = 0.91$.

Note that $P(A \text{ or } C)$ and $P(A \text{ and } C)$ cannot be determined using the information given. But since $P(A) + P(C) = 1.08$, which is greater than 1, it cannot equal $P(A \text{ or } C)$, which like any probability must be less than or equal to 1. It follows that A and C cannot be mutually exclusive and that $P(A \text{ and } C) \geq 0.08$.

Since $A \cap B$ is a subset of A, one can also deduce that $P(A \text{ and } C) \leq P(A) = 0.23$.

And since C is a subset of $A \cup C$, it follows that $P(A \text{ or } C) \geq P(C) = 0.85$.

Thus, one can conclude that $0.85 \leq P(A \text{ or } C) \leq 1$ and $0.08 \leq P(A \text{ and } C) \leq 0.23$.

---

5. Estimation

A. Often it is too difficult or time-consuming to calculate an exact numerical answer to a complex mathematical question. In these cases, it may be faster and easier to estimate the answer by simplifying the question.

One such estimation technique is to **round** the numbers in the original question: replace each number in the question with a nearby number that has fewer digits. Commonly, a number is rounded to a nearby multiple of some specific power of 10.

For any integer n and real number m, to **round m down** to a multiple of 10^n, simply delete all of m's digits to the right of the one representing multiples of 10^n.

To **round m up** to a multiple of 10^n, first add 10^n to m, then round the result down.

To **round m to the nearest** 10^n, first identify the digit in m that represents a multiple of 10^{n-1}. If this digit is 5 or higher, round m up to a multiple of 10^n. Otherwise, round m down to a multiple of 10^n.

Example:

(i) To round 7651.4 to the nearest hundred (multiple of 10^2), first note that the digit representing tens (multiples of 10^1) is 5.

Since this digit is 5 or higher, round up:

Add 100 to the original number: 7651.4 + 100 = 7751.4.

Then delete all the digits to the right of the one representing multiples of 100 to obtain 7700.

A simple way of thinking of this is that 7700 is closer to 7651.4 than 7600 is, so 7700 is the nearest 100.

(ii) To round 0.43248 to the nearest thousandth (multiple of 10^{-3}), first note that the digit representing ten-thousandths (multiples of 10^{-4}) is 4. Since 4 < 5, round down: simply delete all the digits to the right of the one representing thousandths to obtain 0.432.

B. Rounding can be used to simplify complex arithmetical calculations and produce approximate solutions. The solutions will likely be more accurate, but the calculations more time-consuming, if you retain more digits of the original numbers.

Example:

You can roughly estimate the value of $\dfrac{(298.534 + 58.296)}{1.4822 + 0.937 + 0.014679}$ by rounding the numbers in the dividend to the nearest 10 and the numbers in the divisor to the nearest 0.1:

$$\frac{(298.534 + 58.296)}{1.4822 + 0.937 + 0.014679} \approx \frac{300 + 60}{1.5 + 0.9 + 0} = \frac{360}{2.4} = 150$$

C. In some cases, an estimate can be produced more effectively by rounding to a multiple of a number other than 10, or by rounding to the nearest number that is the square or cube of an integer.

Example:

(i) You can roughly estimate the value of $\dfrac{2447.16}{11.9}$ by noting first that both the dividend and the divisor are close to multiples of 12: 2448 and 12. Thus, $\dfrac{2447.16}{11.9} \approx \dfrac{2448}{12} = 204$.

(ii) You can roughly estimate the value of $\sqrt{\dfrac{8.96}{24.82 \times 4.057}}$ by noting first that each decimal number in the expression is close to the square of an integer: $8.96 \approx 9 = 3^2$, $24.82 \approx 25 = 5^2$, and $4.057 \approx 4 = 2^2$. Thus $\sqrt{\dfrac{8.96}{24.82 \times 4.057}} \approx \sqrt{\dfrac{3^2}{5^2 \times 2^2}} = \sqrt{\dfrac{3^2}{10^2}} = \dfrac{3}{10}$.

D. In some cases, rather than producing a single number as the estimated value of a complex expression, it is more helpful to determine a **range** of possible values for the expression. The **upper bound** of such a range is the smallest number that has been determined to be greater than (or greater than or equal to) the expression's value. The **lower bound** of the range is the largest number that has been determined to be less than (or less than or equal to) the expression's value.

Example:

Consider the equation $x = \dfrac{2.32^2 - 2.536}{2.68^2 + 2.79}$. Note that each decimal in this expression is greater than 2 and less than 3. Therefore, $\dfrac{2^2 - 3}{3^2 + 3} < x < \dfrac{3^2 - 2}{2^2 + 2}$. Simplifying these fractions, we can determine that x is in the range $\dfrac{1}{12} < x < \dfrac{7}{6}$. The lower bound of this range is $\dfrac{1}{12}$, and the upper bound is $\dfrac{7}{6}$.

6. Sequences and Series

A. A *sequence* is any algebraic function whose domain consists of only positive integers. If a function $a(n)$ is a sequence, it may be denoted as an. The domain of an *infinite sequence* includes all the positive integers. For any positive integer n, the domain of a *finite sequence of length n* includes only the first n positive integers.

Example:

(i) The function $a(n) = n^2 + \left(\dfrac{n}{5}\right)$ with the domain of all positive integers $n = 1, 2, 3, \ldots$ is an infinite sequence a_n. Its value at $n = 3$ is $a_3 = 3^2 + \dfrac{3}{5} = 9.6$.

(ii) The same function $a(n) = n^2 + \left(\dfrac{n}{5}\right)$ restricted to the domain $\{1, 2, 3\}$ is a finite sequence of length 3 whose range is $\{1.2, 3.4, 9.6\}$.

(iii) Consider the infinite sequence defined by $b_n = (-1)^n(n!)$. A sequence like this may be indicated by listing its values in the order $b_1, b_2, b_3, \ldots, b_n, \ldots$ as follows: $-1, 2, -6, \ldots,$ $(-1)^n(n!), \ldots$.

The value $(-1)^n(n!)$ is called the nth term of the sequence.

B. A *series* is the sum of the terms in a sequence.

For an infinite sequence $a(n)$, the corresponding *infinite series* is denoted $\sum_{n=1}^{\infty} a(n)$ and is the sum of the infinitely many terms in the sequence, $a_1 + a_2 + a_3 + \dots$

The sum of the first k terms of series a_n is called a *partial sum* of the series and is denoted $\sum_{i=1}^{k} a_i$, or $a_1 + \dots + a_k$.

Example:

The infinite series corresponding to the function $a(n) = n^2 + \left(\frac{n}{5}\right)$ is $\sum_{i=1}^{\infty} n^2 + \left(\frac{n}{5}\right)$ and is the sum of the infinitely many terms $\left(1^2 + \frac{1}{5}\right) + \left(2^2 + \frac{2}{5}\right) + \left(3^2 + \frac{3}{5}\right) + \dots$

For this same function $a(n) = n^2 + \left(\frac{n}{5}\right)$, the partial sum of the first three terms is

$$\sum_{i=1}^{3} a_i = \left(1^2 + \frac{1}{5}\right) + \left(2^2 + \frac{2}{5}\right) + \left(3^2 + \frac{3}{5}\right) = 1.2 + 4.4 + 9.6 = 15.2.$$

PS07310.03

Practice Question 16

The numbers of cars sold at a certain dealership on six of the last seven business days were 4, 7, 2, 8, 3, and 6, respectively. If the number of cars sold on the seventh business day was either 2, 4, or 5, for which of the three values does the average (arithmetic mean) number of cars sold per business day for the seven business days equal the median number of cars sold per day for the seven days?

I. 2

II. 4

III. 5

    (A)   II only

    (B)   III only

    (C)   I and II only

    (D)   II and III only

    (E)   I, II, and III

PS02775.03

Practice Question 17

List S consists of 10 consecutive odd integers, and list T consists of 5 consecutive even integers. If the least integer in S is 7 more than the least integer in T, how much greater is the average (arithmetic mean) of the integers in S than the average of the integers in T?

    (A)   2

    (B)   7

    (C)   8

    (D)   12

    (E)   22

PS97920.03
Practice Question 18

If *m* is the average (arithmetic mean) of the first 10 positive multiples of 5 and if *M* is the median of the first 10 positive multiples of 5, what is the value of *M – m*?

(A) –5
(B) 0
(C) 5
(D) 25
(E) 27.5

DS22030.03
Practice Question 19

In a survey of 200 college graduates, 30% said they had received student loans during their college careers, and 40% said they had received scholarships. What percent of those surveyed said that they had received neither student loans nor scholarships during their college careers?

(1) 25% of those surveyed said that they had received scholarships but no loans.
(2) 50% of those surveyed who said that they had received loans also said that they had received scholarships.

(A) Statement (1) ALONE is sufficient, but statement (2) alone is not sufficient.
(B) Statement (2) ALONE is sufficient, but statement (1) alone is not sufficient.
(C) BOTH statements TOGETHER are sufficient, but NEITHER statement ALONE is sufficient.
(D) EACH statement ALONE is sufficient.
(E) Statements (1) and (2) TOGETHER are NOT sufficient.

DS11040.03
Practice Question 20

A box contains only red chips, white chips, and blue chips. If a chip is randomly selected from the box, what is the probability that the chip will be either white or blue?

(1) The probability that the chip will be blue is $\frac{1}{5}$.

(2) The probability that the chip will be red is $\frac{1}{3}$.

(A) Statement (1) ALONE is sufficient, but statement (2) alone is not sufficient.
(B) Statement (2) ALONE is sufficient, but statement (1) alone is not sufficient.
(C) BOTH statements TOGETHER are sufficient, but NEITHER statement ALONE is sufficient.
(D) EACH statement ALONE is sufficient.
(E) Statements (1) and (2) TOGETHER are NOT sufficient.

PS07310.03
Answer Explanation 16

The numbers of cars sold at a certain dealership on six of the last seven business days were 4, 7, 2, 8, 3, and 6, respectively. If the number of cars sold on the seventh business day was either 2, 4, or 5, for which of the three values does the average (arithmetic mean) number of cars sold per business day for the seven business days equal the median number of cars sold per day for the seven days?

I.   2

II.   4

III. 5

    (A)   II only

    (B)   III only

    (C)   I and II only

    (D)   II and III only

    (E)   I, II, and III

Arithmetic Statistics

Listed in numerical order, the given numbers are 2, 3, 4, 6, 7, and 8. If the 7th number were 2 or 4, then the numbers in numerical order would be 2, 2, 3, 4, 6, 7, and 8 or 2, 3, 4, 4, 6, 7, and 8. In either case the median would be 4 and the average would be $\frac{2 + 2 + 3 + 4 + 6 + 7 + 8}{7} = \frac{32}{7}$ or $\frac{2 + 3 + 4 + 4 + 6 + 7 + 8}{7} = \frac{34}{7}$, neither of which equals 4. So, for neither of the values in I or II does the average equal the median. If the 7th number were 5, then the numbers in numerical order would be 2, 3, 4, 5, 6, 7, and 8. The median would be 5 and the average would be $\frac{2 + 3 + 4 + 5 + 6 + 7 + 8}{7} = \frac{35}{7} = 5.$ Thus, for the value in III, the average equals the mean.

The correct answer is B.

PS57720.03
Answer Explanation 17

List S consists of 10 consecutive odd integers, and list T consists of 5 consecutive even integers. If the least integer in S is 7 more than the least integer in T, how much greater is the average (arithmetic mean) of the integers in S than the average of the integers in T?

    (A)   2

    (B)   7

    (C)   8

    (D)   12

    (E)   22

Arithmetic Statistics

Let the integers in S be $s, s + 2, s + 4, \ldots, s + 18$, where s is odd. Let the integers in T be $t, t + 2, t + 4, t + 6, t + 8$, where t is even. Given that $s = t + 7$, it follows that $s - t = 7$. The average of the integers in S is $\dfrac{10s + 90}{10} = s + 9$, and, similarly, the average of the integers in T is $\dfrac{5t + 20}{5} = t + 4$. The difference in these averages is $(s + 9) - (t + 4) = (s - t) + (9 - 4) + 7 + 5 = 12$. Thus, the average of the integers in S is 12 greater than the average of the integers in T.

The correct answer is D.

PS97920.03
Answer Explanation 18

If m is the average (arithmetic mean) of the first 10 positive multiples of 5 and if M is the median of the first 10 positive multiples of 5, what is the value of $M - m$?

(A) −5
(B) 0
(C) 5
(D) 25
(E) 27.5

Arithmetic Statistics

The first 10 positive multiples of 5 are 5, 10, 15, 20, 25, 30, 35, 40, 45, and 50. From this, the average of the 10 multiples, that is, $\dfrac{\text{sum of values}}{\text{number of values}}$, can be calculated:

$$m = \frac{5 + 10 + 15 + 20 + 25 + 30 + 35 + 40 + 45 + 50}{10} = \frac{275}{10} = 27.5.$$

Since there is an even number of multiples, the median, M, is the average of the middle two numbers, 25 and 30:

$$M = \frac{25 + 30}{2} = 27.5.$$

Therefore, the median minus the average is:

$$M - m = 27.5 - 27.5 = 0.$$

This problem can also be solved as follows. Since the values can be grouped in pairs (i.e., 5 and 50, 10 and 45, 15 and 40, etc.), each of which is symmetric with respect to the median, it follows that the mean and median are equal.

The correct answer is B.

DS22030.03

Answer Explanation 19

In a survey of 200 college graduates, 30% said they had received student loans during their college careers, and 40% said they had received scholarships. What percent of those surveyed said that they had received neither student loans nor scholarships during their college careers?

(1)   25% of those surveyed said that they had received scholarships but no loans.

(2)   50% of those surveyed who said that they had received loans also said that they had received scholarships.

Arithmetic Sets

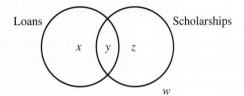

Using the variables shown on the Venn diagram above, determine the value of w. According to the information given, 30% had received student loans, so $x + y = 0.3(200) = 60$ and $x = 60 - y$. Also, 40% had received scholarships, so $y + z = 0.4(200) = 80$ and $z = 80 - y$. Then, since $x + y + z + w = 200$, $w = 200 - x - y - z = 200 - (60 - y) - y - (80 - y) = 60 + y$. Thus, if the value of y can be determined, then the value of w can be determined.

(1)   Since 25% received scholarships but no loans, $z = 80 - y = 0.25(200) = 50$ and $y = 30$; SUFFICIENT.

(2)   Since 50% of those who had received loans had also received scholarships, $0.5(x + y) = y$ and so $0.5(60) = 30 = y$; SUFFICIENT.

The correct answer is D; each statement alone is sufficient.

DS11040.03

Answer Explanation 20

A box contains only red chips, white chips, and blue chips. If a chip is randomly selected from the box, what is the probability that the chip will be either white or blue?

(1)   The probability that the chip will be blue is $\frac{1}{5}$.

(2)   The probability that the chip will be red is $\frac{1}{3}$.

Arithmetic Probability

(1)   Since the probability of drawing a blue chip is known, the probability of drawing a chip that is not blue (in other words, a red or white chip) can also be found. However, the probability of drawing a white or blue chip cannot be determined from this information; NOT sufficient.

(2)   The probability that the chip will be either white or blue is the same as the probability that it will NOT be red. Thus, the probability is $1 - \left(\frac{1}{3}\right) = \left(\frac{2}{3}\right)$; SUFFICIENT.

The correct answer is B; statement 2 alone is sufficient.

3.5 Geometry

1. Lines and Angles

A. In geometry, a *line* is straight and extends without end in both directions. A *line segment* is the part of a line between two points on the line. Those two points are the *endpoints* of the segment.

A Line and a Line Segment

The line above can be referred to as line PQ or line l. The line segment with endpoints P and Q is denoted by $\overline{PQ}$. The length of segment $\overline{PQ}$ is denoted by PQ.

B. If two line segments $\overline{DE}$ and $\overline{FG}$ intersect at a point H, then $\overline{DE}$ is said to *bisect* $\overline{FG}$ if $FH = HG$.

C. The angle at a point B between two line segments $\overline{AB}$ and $\overline{BC}$ is denoted by $\angle ABC$. The angle can be measured as a number n of *degrees* between 0 and 360, and denoted by $n°$. If $\overline{AB}$ and $\overline{BC}$ are segments of the same line AC and have no point other than B in common, then the measure of $\angle ABC$ is 180°.

D. Two angles opposite each other, formed by the intersection of two lines, are called *vertical angles* and are equal in measure.

Vertical Angles

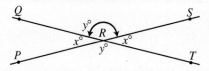

In this figure, $\angle PRQ$ and $\angle SRT$ are one pair of vertical angles, and $\angle QRS$ and $\angle PRT$ are the second pair of vertical angles. Note that $x° + y° = 180°$, since PR and RS are segments of the same line PS.

E. An angle with a measure of 90° is a *right angle.* Two lines intersecting at a right angle are *perpendicular.* The statement that lines l_1 and l_2 are perpendicular is represented as $l_1 \perp l_2$.

Perpendicular Lines Forming a Right Angle

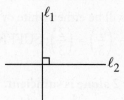

In this figure, perpendicular lines l_1 and l_2 form a right angle, so $l_1 \perp l_2$. The small square at their intersection is a right angle symbol indicating that the lines are perpendicular.

F. Two lines in the same plane that do not intersect are *parallel.* The statement that lines l_1 and l_2 are parallel is represented as $l_1 \parallel l_2$.

Parallel Lines

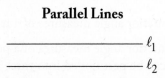

In this figure, lines l_1 and l_2 are parallel, so $l_1 \parallel l_2$.

G. If two parallel lines are intersected by a third line, then the angle measures are related as indicated in the figure below, where $x° + y° = 180°$.

Angles Formed by a Line Intersecting Two Parallel Lines

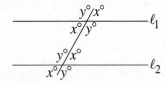

---

2. Polygons

A. A *polygon* is a closed plane figure formed by three or more line segments, called the *sides* of the polygon. Each side intersects exactly two other sides at their endpoints. The points of intersection of the sides are *vertices.* This chapter will use the term "polygon" to mean a *convex* polygon, that is, a polygon in which each interior angle has a measure of less than 180°. A polygon with three sides is a *triangle*; with four sides, a *quadrilateral*; with five sides, a *pentagon*; and with six sides, a *hexagon.*

Examples:

(i) The following two figures are both polygons. The one on the left is a quadrilateral, and the one on the right is a hexagon.

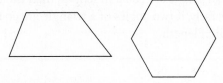

(ii) The three figures below are not polygons.

B. The sum of the interior angle measures of a polygon with *n* sides is $(n-2)180°$.

Examples:

(i) The sum of the interior angle measures of a triangle is 180°.

(ii) The sum of the interior angle measures of a pentagon is $(5-2)180° = (3)180° = 540°$. Note that a pentagon can be partitioned into three triangles, as illustrated below. Therefore, the sum of the angle measures of a pentagon equals the sum of the angle measures of three triangles.

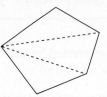

C. The *perimeter* of a polygon is the sum of the lengths of the polygon's sides.

3. Triangles

A. The sum of the lengths of any two sides of any triangle is greater than the length of the third side, as illustrated in the figure below.

Lengths of the Sides of a Triangle

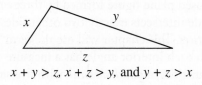

$x + y > z,\ x + z > y,$ and $y + z > x$

In this figure, the variables x, y, and z represent the lengths of the triangle's three sides.

B. An *equilateral* triangle is one whose sides are all the same length. All the angles of an equilateral triangle have equal measure. An *isosceles* triangle is one with at least two sides of equal length.

If two sides of a triangle are equal in length, then the two angles opposite those sides are equal in measure. Conversely, if two angles of a triangle are equal in measure, then the sides opposite those angles are equal in length.

Example:

In isosceles triangle ΔPQR below, $x = y$ since $PQ = QR$.

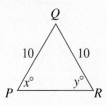

C. A triangle that has a right angle is a ***right*** triangle. In a right triangle, the side opposite the right angle is the ***hypotenuse,*** and the other two sides are the ***legs.*** Any triangle in which the lengths of the sides are in the ratio 3:4:5 is a right triangle.

An important theorem about right triangles is the ***Pythagorean theorem,*** which states:

In a right triangle, the square of the length of the hypotenuse equals the sum of the squares of the lengths of the legs.

That is, the Pythagorean theorem states that if a and b are the lengths of the legs of a right triangle, and c is the length of the hypotenuse, then $a^2 + b^2 = c^2$.

Example:

In right triangle $\triangle RST$ below, by the Pythagorean theorem $(RS)^2 + (RT)^2 = (ST)^2$.

Note that $RS = 6$ and $RT = 8$. Therefore, since $6^2 + 8^2 = 36 + 64 = 100 = (ST)^2$ and $ST = \sqrt{100}$, it follows that $ST = 10$.

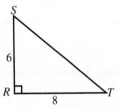

D. In $45°- 45°- 90°$ triangles, the lengths of the sides are in the ratio $1:1:\sqrt{2}$. In $30°- 60°- 90°$ triangles, the lengths of the sides are in the ratio $1:\sqrt{3}: 2$.

Examples:

(i) In $45°- 45°- 90°$ triangle $\triangle JKL$ below, $JK = JL = 2$, and $KL = 2\sqrt{2}$.

(ii) In $30°- 60°- 90°$ triangle $\triangle XYZ$ below, $XZ = 3$, $XY = 3\sqrt{3}$, and $YZ = 6$.

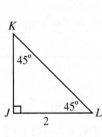 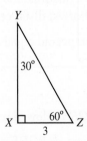

E. The ***altitude*** of a triangle is the segment drawn from a vertex perpendicular to the side opposite that vertex. Relative to that vertex and altitude, the opposite side is called the ***base.***

The area of a triangle equals $\dfrac{(\text{the length of the altitude}) \times (\text{the length of the base})}{2}$.

Example:

In triangle $\triangle ABC$ below, $\overline{BD}$ is the altitude to base $\overline{AC}$, and $\overline{AE}$ is the altitude to base $\overline{BC}$.

The area of $\triangle ABC$ is $\dfrac{BD \times AC}{2} = \dfrac{5 \times 8}{2} = 20$. The area also equals $\dfrac{AE \times BC}{2}$.

If $\triangle ABC$ is isosceles and $AB = BC$, then altitude $\overline{BD}$ bisects the base; that is, $AD = DC = 4$.

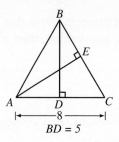

$BD = 5$

F. Any altitude of an equilateral triangle bisects the side to which it is drawn.

Example:

In equilateral triangle $\triangle DEF$ below, $DE = 6$, so $DG = 3$ and $EG = 3\sqrt{3}$.

The area of $\triangle DEF$ is $\dfrac{3\sqrt{3} \times 6}{2} = 9\sqrt{3}$.

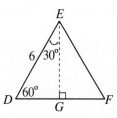

4. Quadrilaterals

A. A *trapezoid* is a quadrilateral with exactly two parallel sides, which are called its *bases.* A trapezoid's *height* is the shortest distance between its bases.

The area of a trapezoid equals $\dfrac{\text{(the sum of the lengths of the bases)} \times \text{(the height)}}{2}$.

Example:

In trapezoid $PQRS$ below, the bases are $\overline{QR}$ and $\overline{PS}$, and the height is 8.

Therefore, the area of $PQRS$ is $(QR + PS) \times \dfrac{8}{2} = (12 + 16) \times \dfrac{8}{2} = 28 \times 4 = 112$.

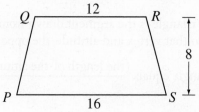

B. A *parallelogram* is a quadrilateral in which both pairs of opposite sides are parallel.

The opposite sides of a parallelogram are equal in length. When one side is taken as the base, the height is the shortest distance between that side and its opposite side.

The *diagonals* of a parallelogram are the two-line segments between its opposite vertices. A parallelogram's diagonals bisect each other.

The area of a parallelogram equals (the length of the base) × (the height).

Example:

In parallelogram $JKLM$ below, $\overline{JK} \parallel \overline{LM}$, and $JK = LM$. Also, $\overline{KL} \parallel \overline{JM}$, and $KL = JM$.

Since the diagonals $\overline{JL}$ and $\overline{KM}$ bisect each other, $KN = NM$ and $JN = NL$.

The area of $JKLM$ is $JM \times 4 = 6 \times 4 = 24$.

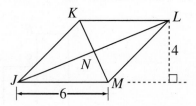

C. A parallelogram with right angles is a *rectangle,* and a rectangle with all sides of equal length is a *square.*

The diagonals of a rectangle are equal in length.

The perimeter of a rectangle equals 2 × (the height + the length of the base).

Example:

In rectangle $WXYZ$ below, the perimeter equals $2(3 + 7) = 20$.

The area of $WXYZ$ is $3 \times 7 = 21$.

Since the diagonals of $WXYZ$ are equal in length, by the Pythagorean theorem $WY = XZ = \sqrt{9 + 49} = \sqrt{58}$.

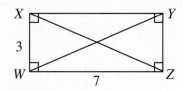

D. On the GMAT exam you may encounter problems involving shapes composed of conjoined polygons.

Example:

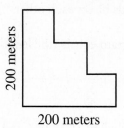

The figure above shows an aerial view of a piece of land. If all angles shown are right angles, what is the perimeter of the piece of land?

Solution: For reference, label the figure as

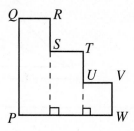

Since all the angles are right angles, $QR + ST + UV = PW$, and $RS + TU + VW = PQ$. Hence, the perimeter of the land is $2PW + 2PQ = 2 \times 200 + 2 \times 200 = 800$ meters.

5. Circles

A. A *circle* is a set of points in a plane that are all located the same distance from a fixed point, the circle's *center*.

A *chord* of a circle is a line segment whose endpoints are on the circle. A chord that passes through the center of the circle is a *diameter* of the circle. A *radius* of a circle is a segment from the center of the circle to a point on the circle. The words "diameter" and "radius" are also used to refer to the lengths of these segments.

The *circumference* of a circle is the distance around the circle. The circumference of a circle of radius r is $2\pi r$, where π is approximately $\frac{22}{7}$ or 3.14.

The area of a circle of radius r is πr^2.

Example:

In the circle below, O is the center, and $\overline{JK}$ and $\overline{PR}$ are chords. $\overline{PR}$ is a diameter and $\overline{OR}$ is a radius. Since $OR = 7$, the circle's circumference is $2\pi(7) = 14\pi$. The circle's area is $\pi(7)^2 = 49\pi$.

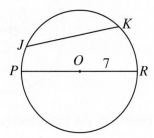

B. An *arc* of a circle is a part of the circle sharing endpoints with a chord of the circle. Any chord defines two arcs with the same endpoints, and the circle is the union of those two arcs. The number of degrees of arc in a circle (that is, the number of degrees in a complete revolution) is 360. If C is the circle's center, m is the circle's circumference, and B and D are points on the circle, an angle $\angle BCD$ of $n°$ defines an arc of length $\frac{nm}{360}$ with endpoints B and D.

Example:

In the circle below, O is the center. Suppose the circle's circumference is m.

Since angle $\angle ROT$ has a measure of 60°, the length of arc RST is $\frac{60m}{360} = \frac{m}{6}$.

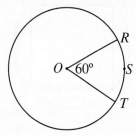

C. A line that has exactly one point in common with a circle is said to be *tangent* to the circle. That common point is called the *point of tangency.*

A radius or diameter with an endpoint at the point of tangency is perpendicular to the tangent line. Conversely, a line that is perpendicular to a radius or diameter at one of its endpoints on the circle is tangent to the circle at that endpoint.

A Tangent to a Circle

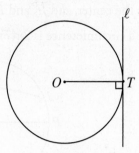

In this figure, line *l* is tangent to the circle, and radius $\overline{OT}$ is perpendicular to *l*.

D. If each vertex of a polygon lies on a circle, then the polygon is ***inscribed*** in the circle and the circle is ***circumscribed*** about the polygon.

If each side of a polygon is tangent to a circle, then the polygon is circumscribed about the circle and the circle is inscribed in the polygon.

Examples:

In the figures below, quadrilateral *PQRS* is inscribed in a circle, and hexagon *ABCDEF* is circumscribed about a circle.

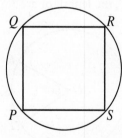 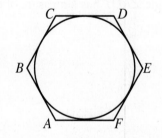

E. A triangle inscribed in a circle so that one of its sides is a diameter of the circle is a right triangle.

Example:

In the circle below with center O, $\overline{XZ}$ is a diameter. Angle ∠*XYZ* has a measure of 90°.

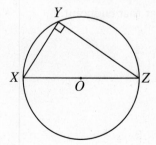

6. Rectangular Solids and Cylinders

A. A *rectangular solid* is a three-dimensional figure formed by 6 rectangular surfaces. Each rectangular surface is a *face.* Each line segment where two faces meet is an *edge,* and each point at which the edges meet is a *vertex.*

A rectangular solid has 6 faces, 12 edges, and 8 vertices. Its opposite faces are parallel rectangles with the same dimensions.

A rectangular solid whose edges are all of equal length is a *cube.*

The *surface area* of a rectangular solid is the sum of the areas of all the faces.

The *volume* of a rectangular solid equals (length) × (width) × (height).

Example:

In the rectangular solid below, the dimensions are 3, 4, and 8.

The surface area is 2(3 × 4) + 2(3 × 8) + 2(4 × 8) = 136.

The volume is 3 × 8 × 4 = 96.

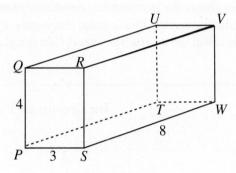

B. A *right circular cylinder* is a three-dimensional figure whose *bases* are two circles equal in size aligned so that a line segment called the *axis* or the *altitude,* with endpoints at the centers of the circles, is perpendicular to the diameters of both circles. The length of the axis is the cylinder's *height.*

A Right Circular Cylinder

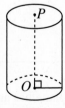

In this figure, points O and P are the centers of the two bases of a right circular cylinder, so $\overline{OP}$ is the cylinder's axis or altitude, and OP is the height.

The surface area of a right circular cylinder with height h and a base of radius r is $2(\pi r^2) + 2\pi rh$ (the sum of the areas of the two bases plus the area of the curved surface).

The volume of a right circular cylinder is $\pi r^2 h$, that is, (area of base) × (height).

Example:

In the right circular cylinder below, the surface area is $2(25\pi) + 2\pi\,(5)(8) = 130\pi$, and the volume is $25\pi\,(8) = 200\pi$.

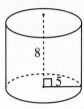

7. Coordinate Geometry

A. The figure below shows the (rectangular) *coordinate plane.* The horizontal line is called the *x-axis* and the perpendicular vertical line is called the *y-axis.* The point at which these two axes intersect, designated O, is called the *origin.* The axes divide the plane into four quadrants, I, II, III, and IV, as shown.

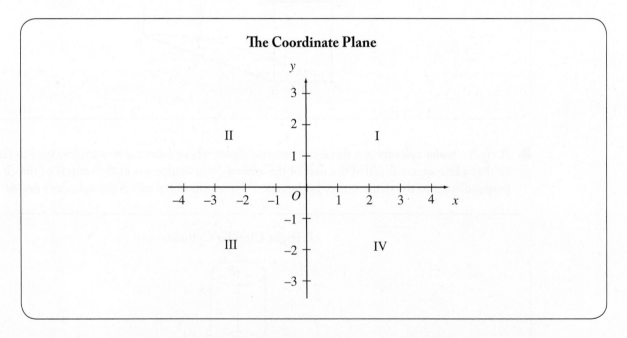

B. Each point in the coordinate plane has an *x-coordinate* and a *y-coordinate.* A point is identified by an ordered pair (x,y) of numbers in which the x-coordinate is the first number and the y-coordinate is the second number.

Example:

In the graph below, the (x,y) coordinates of point P are $(2,3)$ since P is 2 units to the right of the y-axis (that is, $x = 2$) and 3 units above the x-axis (that is, $y = 3$).

Similarly, the (x,y) coordinates of point Q are $(-4,-3)$. The origin O has coordinates $(0,0)$.

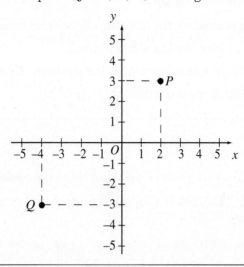

C. One way to find the distance between two points in the coordinate plane is to use the Pythagorean theorem.

Example:

To find the distance between points R and S using the Pythagorean theorem, draw the triangle as shown in the figure below. Note that Z has (x,y) coordinates $(-2,-3)$, $RZ = 7$, and $ZS = 5$. Therefore, the distance between R and S is $\sqrt{7^2 + 5^2} = \sqrt{74}$.

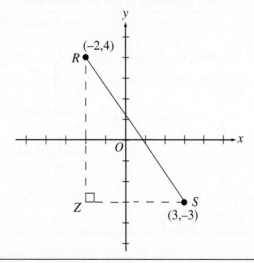

D. For a line in the coordinate plane, the coordinates of each point on the line satisfy a linear equation of the form $y = mx + b$ (or the form $x = a$ if the line is vertical).

In this equation $y = mx + b$, the coefficient m is the line's **slope,** and the constant term b is the line's **y-intercept.**

The y-intercept is the y-coordinate of the point at which the line intersects the y-axis. Similarly, the **x-intercept** is the x-coordinate of the point at which the line intersects the x-axis.

For any two points on the line, the slope is the ratio of the difference in the y-coordinates to the difference in the x-coordinates. Note that after you subtract the y-coordinate of one point from that of the other, it is important to also subtract the x-coordinate of the former point from that of the latter, not the other way around.

If a line's slope is negative, the line slants downward from left to right.

If the slope is positive, the line slants upward.

If the slope is 0, the line is horizontal. The equation of such a line is of the form $y = b$ since $m = 0$.

For a vertical line, slope is not defined.

Example:

In the graph below, each point on the line satisfies the equation $y = -\dfrac{1}{2}x + 1$. One can verify this for the points $(-2,2)$, $(2,0)$, and $(0,1)$ by substituting the respective coordinates for x and y in the equation.

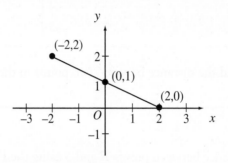

Using the points $(-2, 2)$ and $(2, 0)$, the line's slope may be calculated as:

$$\frac{\text{the difference in the } y\text{-coordinates}}{\text{the difference in the } x\text{-coordinates}} = \frac{0-2}{2-(-2)} = \frac{-2}{4} = -\frac{1}{2}.$$

The y-intercept is 1, which is the value of y when x is set equal to 0 in $y = -\dfrac{1}{2}x + 1$.

Similarly, the x-intercept may be calculated by setting y equal to 0 in the same equation:

$$-\frac{1}{2}x + 1 = 0$$

$$-\frac{1}{2}x = -1$$

$$x = 2.$$

Thus, the x-intercept is 2.

E. Given any two points (x_1, y_1) and (x_2, y_2) with $x_1 \neq x_2$, the equation of the line passing through these points can be found by applying the definition of slope. The slope is $m = \dfrac{y_2 - y_1}{x_2 - x_1}$. So using the known point (x_1, y_1) and the same slope m, any other point (x, y) on the line must satisfy the equation $\dfrac{y - y_1}{x - x_1} = m$, or equivalently $(y - y_1) = m(x - x_1)$. Using (x_2, y_2) instead of (x_1, y_1) as the known point would yield an equivalent equation.

Example:

In the graph below, consider the points $(-2,4)$ and $(3,-3)$.

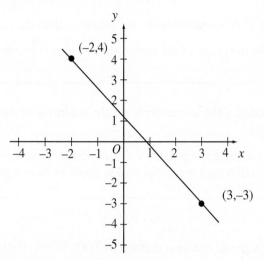

The line's slope is $\dfrac{(-3-4)}{(3-(-2))} = \dfrac{-7}{5}$. So an equation of this line can be found using the point $(3,-3)$ as follows:

$$y - (-3) = \left(-\frac{7}{5}\right)(x-3)$$

$$y + 3 = \left(-\frac{7}{5}\right)x + \frac{21}{5}$$

$$y = \left(-\frac{7}{5}\right)x + \frac{6}{5}$$

Thus, the y-intercept is $\dfrac{6}{5}$.

The x-intercept can be found as follows:

$$0 = -\frac{7}{5}x + \frac{6}{5}$$

$$\frac{7}{5}x = \frac{6}{5}$$

$$x = \frac{6}{7}$$

Both of these intercepts can be seen on the graph.

F. If two linear equations with unknowns x and y have a unique solution, then the graphs of the equations are two lines that intersect in one point, which is the solution.

If the equations are equivalent, then they represent the same line with infinitely many points or solutions.

If the equations have no solution, then they represent parallel lines, which do not intersect.

G. Any function $f(x)$ can be graphed in the coordinate plane by equating y with the value of the function: $y = f(x)$. So for any x in the domain of the function f, the point with coordinates $(x, f(x))$ is on the graph of f, and the graph consists entirely of these points.

Example:

Consider the function $f(x) = -\dfrac{7}{5}x + \dfrac{6}{5}$.

If the value of $f(x)$ is equated with the variable y, then the graph of the function in the xy-coordinate plane is simply the graph of the equation $y = -\dfrac{7}{5}x + \dfrac{6}{5}$ considered in the example above.

H. For any function f, the x-intercepts are the solutions of the equation $f(x) = 0$ and the y-intercept is the value $f(0)$.

The graph of a quadratic polynomial function is called a ***parabola*** and always has a characteristic curved shape, although it may be upside down or have a greater or lesser width.

Example:

Consider a quadratic function defined by $f(x) = x^2 - 1$. One can plot several points $(x, f(x))$ in the coordinate plane to understand the connection between the function and its graph:

x	$f(x)$
-2	3
-1	0
0	-1
1	0
2	3

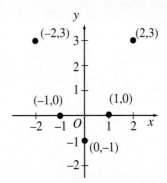

If all the points were graphed for $-2 \le x \le 2$, the graph would appear as follows:

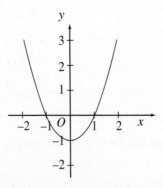

Note that the roots of the equation $f(x) = x^2 - 1 = 0$ are $x = 1$ and $x = -1$; these coincide with the x-intercepts since x-intercepts are found by setting $y = 0$ and solving for x.

Also, the y-intercept is $f(0) = -1$ because this is the value of y corresponding to $x = 0$.

PS22061.03

Practice Question 21

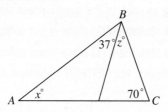

In △ABC above, what is x in terms of z?

(A) z + 73

(B) z − 73

(C) 70 − z

(D) z − 70

(E) 73 − z

DS17061.03

Practice Question 22

What is the maximum number of rectangular blocks, each with dimensions 12 centimeters by 6 centimeters by 4 centimeters, that will fit inside rectangular box X ?

(1) When box X is filled with the blocks and rests on a certain side, there are 25 blocks in the bottom layer.

(2) The inside dimensions of box X are 60 centimeters by 30 centimeters by 20 centimeters.

(A) Statement (1) ALONE is sufficient, but statement (2) alone is not sufficient.

(B) Statement (2) ALONE is sufficient, but statement (1) alone is not sufficient.

(C) BOTH statements TOGETHER are sufficient, but NEITHER statement ALONE is sufficient.

(D) EACH statement ALONE is sufficient.

(E) Statements (1) and (2) TOGETHER are NOT sufficient.

PS29261.03

Practice Question 23

The annual budget of a certain college is to be shown on a circle graph. If the size of each sector of the graph is to be proportional to the amount of the budget it represents, how many degrees of the circle should be used to represent an item that is 15% of the budget?

(A) 15°

(B) 36°

(C) 54°

(D) 90°

(E) 150°

DS48061.03

Practice Question 24

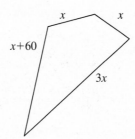

The figure above shows the number of meters in the lengths of the four sides of a jogging path. What is the total distance around the path?

(1)   One of the sides of the path is 120 meters long.

(2)   One of the sides of the path is twice as long as each of the two shortest sides.

    (A)   Statement (1) ALONE is sufficient, but statement (2) alone is not sufficient.

    (B)   Statement (2) ALONE is sufficient, but statement (1) alone is not sufficient.

    (C)   BOTH statements TOGETHER are sufficient, but NEITHER statement ALONE is sufficient.

    (D)   EACH statement ALONE is sufficient.

    (E)   Statements (1) and (2) TOGETHER are NOT sufficient.

DS39161.03

Practice Question 25

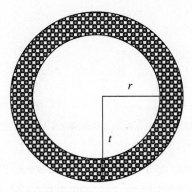

The figure above shows the circular cross section of a concrete water pipe. If the inside radius of the pipe is r feet and the outside radius of the pipe is t feet, what is the value of r?

(1)   The ratio of $t - r$ to r is 0.15 and $t - r$ is equal to 0.3 feet.

(2)   The area of the concrete in the cross section is 1.29π square feet.

    (A)   Statement (1) ALONE is sufficient, but statement (2) alone is not sufficient.

    (B)   Statement (2) ALONE is sufficient, but statement (1) alone is not sufficient.

    (C)   BOTH statements TOGETHER are sufficient, but NEITHER statement ALONE is sufficient.

    (D)   EACH statement ALONE is sufficient.

    (E)   Statements (1) and (2) TOGETHER are NOT sufficient.

PS22061.03

Answer Explanation 21

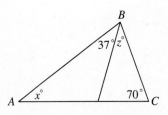

In $\triangle ABC$ above, what is x in terms of z?

    (A) $z + 73$

    (B) $z - 73$

    (C) $70 - z$

    (D) $z - 70$

    (E) $73 - z$

Geometry Angle Measure in Degrees

Since the sum of the degree measures of the angles in a triangle equals 180°,

$x + 37 + z + 70 = 180$. Solve this equation for x.

$$x + 37 + z + 70 = 180$$
$$x + z + 107 = 180$$
$$x + z = 73$$
$$x = 73 - z$$

The correct answer is E.

DS17061.03

Answer Explanation 22

What is the maximum number of rectangular blocks, each with dimensions 12 centimeters by 6 centimeters by 4 centimeters, that will fit inside rectangular box X ?

(1)   When box X is filled with the blocks and rests on a certain side, there are 25 blocks in the bottom layer.

(2)   The inside dimensions of box X are 60 centimeters by 30 centimeters by 20 centimeters.

    (A)   Statement (1) ALONE is sufficient, but statement (2) alone is not sufficient.

    (B)   Statement (2) ALONE is sufficient, but statement (1) alone is not sufficient.

    (C)   BOTH statements TOGETHER are sufficient, but NEITHER statement ALONE is sufficient.

    (D)   EACH statement ALONE is sufficient.

    (E)   Statements (1) and (2) TOGETHER are NOT sufficient.

Geometry Volume

Determine how many rectangular blocks will fit in a rectangular box.

(1)   The side on which the box is resting could be 30 cm by 20 cm. If the blocks are resting on the side that is 6 cm by 4 cm, there would be $\dfrac{30}{6} \times \dfrac{20}{4} = 5 \times 5 = 25$ blocks on the bottom layer. If the box is 12 cm tall, a maximum of 25 blocks would fit inside the box. However, if the box is 48 cm tall, a maximum of 100 blocks would fit inside the box; NOT sufficient.

(2)   If the box is resting on a side that is 30 cm by 20 cm, then $\dfrac{30}{6} \times \dfrac{20}{4} = 5 \times 5 = 25$ blocks will fit on the bottom layer. In this case, the height of the box is 60 cm and $\dfrac{60}{12} = 5$ layers will fit inside the box. If the box is resting on a side that is 60 cm by 30 cm, then $\dfrac{60}{12} \times \dfrac{30}{6} = 5 \times 5 = 25$ blocks will fit on the bottom layer. In this case, the height of the box is 20 cm and $\dfrac{20}{4} = 5$ layers will fit inside the box. If the box is resting on a side that is 60 cm by 20 cm, then $\dfrac{60}{12} \times \dfrac{20}{4} = 5 \times 5 = 25$ blocks will fit on the bottom layer. In this case, the height of the box is 30 cm and $\dfrac{30}{6} = 5$ layers will fit inside the box. In all cases, the maximum number of blocks that will fit inside the box is $5 \times 25 = 125$; SUFFICIENT.

The correct answer is B; statement 2 alone is sufficient.

PS29261.03
Answer Explanation 23

The annual budget of a certain college is to be shown on a circle graph. If the size of each sector of the graph is to be proportional to the amount of the budget it represents, how many degrees of the circle should be used to represent an item that is 15% of the budget?

- (A) 15°
- (B) 36°
- (C) 54°
- (D) 90°
- (E) 150°

Geometry; Arithmetic Percents; Interpretation of Graphs

Since there are 360 degrees in a circle, the measure of the central angle in the circle should be $0.15(360°) = 54°$.

The correct answer is C.

DS48061.03
Answer Explanation 24

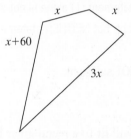

The figure above shows the number of meters in the lengths of the four sides of a jogging path. What is the total distance around the path?

(1) One of the sides of the path is 120 meters long.
(2) One of the sides of the path is twice as long as each of the two shortest sides.

- (A) Statement (1) ALONE is sufficient, but statement (2) alone is not sufficient.
- (B) Statement (2) ALONE is sufficient, but statement (1) alone is not sufficient.
- (C) BOTH statements TOGETHER are sufficient, but NEITHER statement ALONE is sufficient.
- (D) EACH statement ALONE is sufficient.
- (E) Statements (1) and (2) TOGETHER are NOT sufficient.

Algebra; Geometry Quadrilaterals

Determine the value of $6x + 60$, which can be determined exactly when the value of x can be determined.

(1) Given that one of the sides has length 120, it is possible that $x = 120$, that $3x = 120$, or $x + 60 = 120$. These possibilities generate more than one value for x; NOT sufficient.
(2) Since $x < x + 60$ and $x < 3x$ (the latter because x is positive), the two shortest side lengths are x. One of the two other side lengths is twice this, so it follows that $x + 60 = 2x$, or $x = 60$; SUFFICIENT.

The correct answer is B; statement 2 alone is sufficient.

DS39161.03
Answer Explanation 25

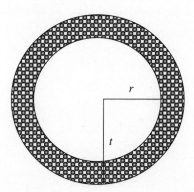

The figure above shows the circular cross section of a concrete water pipe. If the inside radius of the pipe is r feet and the outside radius of the pipe is t feet, what is the value of r?

(1)   The ratio of $t - r$ to r is 0.15 and $t - r$ is equal to 0.3 feet.

(2)   The area of the concrete in the cross section is 1.29π square feet.

   (A)   Statement (1) ALONE is sufficient, but statement (2) alone is not sufficient.

   (B)   Statement (2) ALONE is sufficient, but statement (1) alone is not sufficient.

   (C)   BOTH statements TOGETHER are sufficient, but NEITHER statement ALONE is sufficient.

   (D)   EACH statement ALONE is sufficient.

   (E)   Statements (1) and (2) TOGETHER are NOT sufficient.

Geometry Circles; Area

Determine the value of r.

(1)   Since $\dfrac{t - r}{r} = 0.15$ and $t - r = 0.3$, then $\dfrac{0.3}{r} = 0.15$ and $r = \dfrac{0.3}{0.15} = 2$; SUFFICIENT.

(2)   The area of the concrete in the cross section is the area of the circular region with radius t minus the area of the circular region with radius r. The area of a circular region with radius R is πR^2, so the area of the concrete in the cross section is $\pi t^2 - \pi r^2$. This area is 1.29π, so $\pi t^2 - \pi r^2 = 1.29\pi$, and $t^2 - r^2 = 1.29$, from which it is impossible to determine a unique value for r. For example, if $t = \sqrt{2.29}$, then $r = 1$, but if $t = \sqrt{5.29}$, then $r = 2$; NOT sufficient.

The correct answer is A; statement 1 alone is sufficient.

3.6   Reference Sheets

Arithmetic and Decimals

ABSOLUTE VALUE:

$|x|$ is x if $x \geq 0$ and $-x$ if $x < 0$.

For any x and y, $|x + y| \leq |x| + |y|$.

$\sqrt{x^2} = |x|$.

EVEN AND ODD NUMBERS:

Even × Even = Even	Even × Odd = Even
Odd × Odd = Odd	Even + Even = Even
Even + Odd = Odd	Odd + Odd = Even

ADDITION AND SUBTRACTION:

$x + 0 = x = x - 0$

$x - x = 0$

$x + y = y + x$

$x - y = -(y - x) = -y + x$

$(x + y) + z = x + (y + z)$

If x and y are both positive, then $x + y$ is also positive.

If x and y are both negative, then $x + y$ is negative.

DECIMALS:

Add or subtract decimals by lining up their decimal points:

17.6512	653.2700
+ 653.2700	−17.6512
670.9212	635.6188

To multiply decimal A by decimal B:

First, disregard the decimal points, and multiply A and B as if they were integers.

Next, if decimal A has n digits to the right of its decimal point, and decimal B has m digits to the right of its decimal point, place the decimal point so that $A \times B$ has $m + n$ digits to the right of the decimal point.

To divide decimal A by decimal B, first move the decimal points of A and B equally many digits to the right until B is an integer, then divide as you would integers.

QUOTIENTS AND REMAINDERS:

The quotient q and the remainder r of dividing positive integer x by positive integer y are unique positive integers such that

$y = xq + r$ and $0 \leq r < x$.

The remainder r is 0 if and only if y is divisible by x. In that case, x is a factor of y.

MULTIPLICATION AND DIVISION:

$x \times 1 = x = \dfrac{x}{1}$

$x \times 0 = 0$

If $x \neq 0$, then $\dfrac{x}{x} = 1$.

$\dfrac{x}{0}$ is undefined.

$xy = yx$

If $x \neq 0$ and $y \neq 0$, then $\dfrac{x}{y} = \dfrac{1}{\left(\frac{y}{x}\right)}$.

$(xy)z = x(yz)$

$xy + xz = x(y + z)$

If $y \neq 0$, then $\left(\dfrac{x}{y}\right) + \left(\dfrac{z}{y}\right) = \dfrac{(x + z)}{y}$

If x and y are both positive, then xy is also positive.

If x and y are both negative, then xy is positive.

If x is positive and y is negative, then xy is negative.

If $xy = 0$, then $x = 0$ or $y = 0$, or both.

SCIENTIFIC NOTATION:

To convert a number in the scientific notation $A \times 10^n$ into regular decimal notation, move the decimal point in A to the right by n places if n is positive, or to the left by $|n|$ places if n is negative.

To convert a number B from decimal notation to scientific notation, move the decimal point n spaces so that exactly one nonzero digit is to its left. Multiply the result by 10^n if you moved the decimal point to the left or by 10^{-n} if you moved it to the right.

Exponents

SQUARES, CUBES, AND SQUARE ROOTS:

Every positive number has two real square roots, one positive and the other negative. The table below shows the positive square roots rounded to the nearest hundredth.

n	n^2	n^3	$\sqrt{n}$
1	1	1	1
2	4	8	1.41
3	9	27	1.73
4	16	64	2
5	25	125	2.24
6	36	216	2.45
7	49	343	2.65
8	64	512	2.83
9	81	729	3
10	100	1,000	3.16

EXPONENTIATION:

Formula	Example
$x^1 = x$	$2^1 = 2$
$x^0 = 1$	$2^0 = 1$
If $x \neq 0$, then $x^{-1} = \dfrac{1}{x}$.	$2^{-1} = \dfrac{1}{2}$
If $x > 1$ and $y > 1$, then $x^y > x$.	$2^3 = 8 > 2$
If $0 < x < 1$ and $y > 1$, then $x^y < x$.	$0.2^3 = 0.008 < 0.2$
$(x^y)^z = x^{yz} = (x^z)^y$	$(2^3)^4 = 2^{12} = (2^4)^3$
$x^{y+z} = x^y x^z$	$2^7 = 2^3 2^4$
If $x \neq 0$, then $x^{y-z} = \dfrac{x^y}{x^z}$.	$2^{5-3} = \dfrac{2^5}{2^3}$
$(xz)^y = x^y z^y$	$6^4 = 2^4 3^4$
If $z \neq 0$, then $\left(\dfrac{x}{z}\right)^y = \dfrac{x^y}{z^y}$	$\left(\dfrac{3}{4}\right)^2 = \dfrac{3^2}{4^2} = \dfrac{9}{16}$
If $z \neq 0$, then $x^{\frac{y}{z}} = (x^y)^{\frac{1}{z}} = (x^{\frac{1}{z}})^y$.	$4^{\frac{2}{3}} = (4^2)^{\frac{1}{3}} = (4^{\frac{1}{3}})^2$

Algebraic Expressions and Linear Equations

TRANSLATING WORDS INTO MATHEMATICAL OPERATIONS:

$x + y$	$x - y$	xy	$\dfrac{x}{y}$	x^y
x added to y x increased by y x more than y x plus y the sum of x and y the total of x and y	x decreased by y difference of x and y y fewer than x y less than x x minus y x reduced by y y subtracted from x	x multiplied by y the product of x and y x times y If $y = 2$: double x twice x If $y = 3$: triple x	x divided by y x over y the quotient of x and y the ratio of x to y If $y = 2$: half of x x halved	x to the power of y x to the yth power If $y = 2$: x squared If $y = 3$: x cubed

MANIPULATING ALGEBRAIC EXPRESSIONS:

Technique	Example
Factor to combine like terms	$3xy - 9y = 3y(x - 3)$
Divide out common factors	$\dfrac{(3xy - 9y)}{(x - 3)} = \dfrac{3y(x - 3)}{(x - 3)} = 3y(1) = 3y$
Multiply two expressions by multiplying each term of one expression by each term of the other	$(3x - 4)(9y + x) = 3x(9y + x) - 4(9y + x)$ $= 3x(9y) + 3x(x) + -4(9y) + -4(x)$ $= 27xy + 3x^2 - 36y - 4x$
Substitute constants for variables	If $x = 3$ and $y = -2$, then $3xy - x^2 + y$ can be evaluated as $3(3)(-2) - (3)^2 + (-2) = -18 - 9 - 2 = -29$.

SOLVING LINEAR EQUATIONS:

Technique	Example
Isolate a variable on one side of an equation by performing the same operations on both sides of the equation	Solve the equation $\frac{(5x-6)}{3} = 4$ using the following steps: (1) Multiply both sides by 3 to obtain $5x - 6 = 12$. (2) Add 6 to both sides to obtain $5x = 18$. (3) Divide both sides by 5 to obtain $x = \frac{18}{5}$.
To solve two equations with two variables x and y: (1) Express x in terms of y using one of the equations. (2) Substitute the expression for x to make the second equation have only the variable y. (3) Solve the second equation for y. (4) Substitute the solution for y into the first equation to find the value of x.	Solve the equations A: $x - y = 2$ and B: $3x + 2y = 11$: (1) From A, $x = 2 + y$. (2) In B, substitute $2 + y$ for x to obtain $3(2 + y) + 2y = 11$. (3) Solve B for y: $6 + 3y + 2y = 11$ $\qquad 6 + 5y = 11$ $\qquad\quad 5y = 5$ $\qquad\quad\ y = 1.$ (4) Since $y = 1$, it follows from A that $x = 2 + 1 = 3$.
Alternative technique: (1) Multiply both sides of one equation or both equations so that the coefficients on y have the same absolute value in both equations. (2) Add or subtract the two equations to eliminate y and solve for x. (3) Substitute the solution for x into the first equation to find the value of y.	Solve the equations A: $x - y = 2$ and B: $3x + 2y = 11$: (1) Multiply both sides of A by 2 to obtain $2x - 2y = 4$. (2) Add this result to equation B: $2x - 2y + 3x + 2y = 4 + 11$ $\qquad 5x = 15$ $\qquad\ x = 3.$ (3) Since $x = 3$, it follows from A that $3 - y = 2$, so $y = 1$.

Factoring, Quadratic Equations, and Inequalities

SOLVING EQUATIONS BY FACTORING:

Techniques	Example
(1) Start with a polynomial equation. (2) Add or subtract expressions until 0 is on one side of the equation. (3) Express the nonzero side as a product of factors. (4) Set each factor equal to 0 to find a simple equation yielding a solution to the original equation.	$x^3 - 2x^2 + x = -5(x-1)^2$ $x^3 - 2x^2 + x + 5(x-1)^2 = 0$ (i) $x(x^2 - 2x + 1) + 5(x-1)^2 = 0$ (ii) $x(x-1)^2 + 5(x-1)^2 = 0$ (iii) $(x+5)(x-1)^2 = 0$ $x + 5 = 0$ or $x - 1 = 0$. Therefore $x = -5$ or $x = 1$.

FORMULAS FOR FACTORING:

$a^2 - b^2 = (a-b)(a+b)$

$a^2 + 2ab + b^2 = (a+b)(a+b)$

$a^2 - 2ab + b^2 = (a-b)(a-b)$

THE QUADRATIC FORMULA:

For any quadratic equation $ax^2 + bx + c = 0$ with $a \neq 0$, the roots are

$$x = \frac{-b + \sqrt{b^2 - 4ac}}{2a} \text{ and } x = \frac{-b - \sqrt{b^2 - 4ac}}{2a}$$

These roots are two distinct real numbers unless $b^2 - 4ac \leq 0$.

If $b^2 - 4ac = 0$, the equation has only one root: $\frac{-b}{2a}$.

If $b^2 - 4ac < 0$, the equation has no real roots.

SOLVING INEQUALITIES:

Explanation	Example
As in solving an equation, the same number can be added to or subtracted from both sides of the inequality, or both sides can be multiplied or divided by a positive number without changing the order of the inequality. But multiplying or dividing an inequality by a negative number reverses the order of the inequality. Thus, $6 > 2$, but $(-1)(6) < (-1)(2)$.	To solve the inequality $\frac{(5x-1)}{-2} < 3$ for x, isolate x as follows: (1) $5x - 1 > -6$ (multiplying both sides by -2, reverse the order of the inequality) (2) $5x > -5$ (add 1 to both sides) (3) $x > -1$ (divide both sides by 5)

Rates, Ratios, and Percentages

FRACTIONS:

Equivalent or Equal Fractions:

Two fractions represent the same number if dividing each fraction's numerator and denominator by their greatest common divisor yields identical results for both fractions.

Adding, Subtracting, Multiplying, and Dividing Fractions:

$$\frac{a}{b} + \frac{c}{d} = \frac{ad}{bd} + \frac{bc}{bd}; \frac{a}{b} - \frac{c}{d} = \frac{ad}{bd} - \frac{bc}{bd}$$

$$\frac{a}{b} \times \frac{c}{d} = \frac{ac}{bd}; \frac{a}{b} \div \frac{c}{d} = \frac{ad}{bc}$$

MIXED NUMBERS:

A mixed number of the form $a\frac{b}{c}$ is equivalent to the fraction $\frac{ac+b}{c}$.

RATE:

distance = rate × time

PROFIT:

Gross profit = revenues − expenses, or

Gross profit = selling price − cost.

INTEREST:

Simple annual interest =

(principal) × (interest rate) × (time)

Compound interest over n periods =

(principal) × (1 + interest per period)^n − principal

PERCENTS:

$x\% = \dfrac{x}{100}$.

$x\%$ of y equals $\dfrac{xy}{100}$.

To convert a percent to a decimal, drop the percent sign, then move the decimal point two digits left.

To convert a decimal to a percent, add a percent sign, then move the decimal point two digits right.

PERCENT INCREASE OR DECREASE:

The percent increase from x to y is $100\left(\dfrac{y-x}{x}\right)\%$.

The percent decrease from x to y is $100\left(\dfrac{x-y}{x}\right)\%$.

DISCOUNTS:

A price discounted by n percent becomes $(100 − n)$ percent of the original price.

A price discounted by n percent and then by m percent becomes $(100 − n)(100 − m)$ percent of the original price.

WORK:

$\dfrac{1}{r} + \dfrac{1}{s} = \dfrac{1}{h}$, where r is the length of time it takes one person or machine to complete an amount of work when working alone, s is the length of time it takes a second person or machine to complete that same amount of work when working alone, and h is the length of time it takes them to complete that amount of work when they are both working simultaneously.

MIXTURES:

	Number of units of a substance or mixture	Quantity of an ingredient per unit of the substance or mixture	Total quantity of that ingredient in the substance or mixture
Substance A	X	M	X × M
Substance B	Y	N	Y × N
Mixture of A and B	X + Y	$\dfrac{(X \times M) + (Y \times N)}{X + Y}$	(X × M) + (Y × N)

Statistics, Sets, and Counting Methods

STATISTICS:

Concept	Definition for a set of n numbers ordered from least to greatest	Example with data set $\{4, 4, 5, 7, 10\}$
Mean	The sum of the n numbers, divided by n	$\dfrac{(4 + 4 + 5 + 7 + 10)}{5} = \dfrac{30}{5} = 6$
Median	The middle number if n is odd; The mean of the two middle numbers if n is even	5 is the middle number in $\{4, 4, 5, 7, 10\}$.
Mode	The number that appears most frequently in the set	4 is the only number that appears more than once in $\{4, 4, 5, 7, 10\}$.
Range	The largest number in the set minus the smallest	$10 - 4 = 6$
Standard Deviation	Calculated as follows: (1) Find the arithmetic mean, (2) Find the differences between each of the n numbers and the mean. (3) Square each of the differences, (4) Find the average of the squared differences, and (5) Take the nonnegative square root of this average.	(1) The mean is 6. (2) $-2, -2, -1, 1, 4$ (3) $4, 4, 1, 1, 16$ (4) $\dfrac{26}{5} = 5.2$ (5) $\sqrt{5.2}$

SETS:

Concept	Notation for finite sets S and T	Example
Number of elements	$|S|$	$S = \{-5, 0, 1\}$ is a set with $|S| = 3$.
Subset	$S \subseteq T$ (S is a subset of T); $S \supseteq T$ (T is a subset of S)	$\{-5, 0, 1\}$ is a subset of $\{-5, 0, 1, 4, 10\}$.
Union	$S \cup T$	$\{3, 4\} \cup \{4, 5, 6\} = \{3, 4, 5, 6\}$
Intersection	$S \cap T$	$\{3, 4\} \cap \{4, 5, 6\} = \{4\}$
The general addition rule for two sets	$|S \cup T| = |S| + |T| - |S \cap T|$	$|\{3, 4\} \cup \{4, 5, 6\}| =$ $|\{3, 4\}| + |\{4, 5, 6\}| - |\{3, 4\} \cap \{4, 5, 6\}| =$ $|\{3, 4\}| + |\{4, 5, 6\}| - |\{4\}| = 2 + 3 - 1 = 4.$

COUNTING METHODS:

Concept and Equations	Examples
Multiplication Principle: The number of possible choices of 1 element apiece from each of the sets $A_1, A_2, ..., A_n$ is $|A_1| \times |A_2| \times ... \times |A_n|$.	The number of possible choices of 1 element apiece from each of the sets $S = \{-5, 0, 1\}$, $T = \{3, 4\}$, and $U = \{3, 4, 5, 6\}$ is $|S| \times |T| \times |U| = 3 \times 2 \times 4 = 24$.
Factorial: $n! = n \times (n - 1) \times ... \times 1$ $0! = 1! = 1$ $n! = (n - 1)!(n)$	$4! = 4 \times 3 \times 2 \times 1 = 24$ $4! = 3! \times 4$
Permutations: The number of permutations of a set of n objects is $n!$.	The number of permutations of the set of letters A, B, and C is 3!, or 6: ABC, ACB, BAC, BCA, CAB, and CBA.
Combinations: The number of possible complete selections of k objects from a set of n objects is $\binom{n}{k} = \dfrac{n!}{k!(n-k)!}$.	The number of 2-element subsets of set {A, B, C, D, E} is $$\binom{5}{2} = \frac{5!}{2!3!} = \frac{120}{(2)(6)} = 10.$$ The 10 subsets are: {A, B}, {A, C}, {A, D}, {A, E}, {B, C}, {B, D}, {B, E}, {C, D}, {C, E}, and {D, E}.

Probability, Sequences, and Partial Sums

PROBABILITY:

Concept	Definition, Notation, and Equations	Example: Rolling a die with 6 numbered sides once
Event	A set of outcomes of an experiment	The event of the outcome being an odd number is the set $\{1, 3, 5\}$.
Probability	The probability of an event E is a number between 0 and 1, inclusive, and is denoted $P(E)$. If each outcome is equally likely, $P(E) = \dfrac{\text{(the number of possible outcomes in E)}}{\text{(the total number of possible outcomes)}}$.	If the 6 outcomes are equally likely, then the probability of each outcome is $\dfrac{1}{6}$. The probability that the outcome is an odd number is $P(\{1, 3, 5\}) = \dfrac{|\{1,3,5\}|}{6} = \dfrac{3}{6} = \dfrac{1}{2}$.
Conditional Probability	The probability that E occurs if F occurs is $P(E\|F) = \dfrac{|E \cap F|}{|F|}$.	$P(\{1, 3, 5\}\|\{1, 2\}) = \dfrac{|\{1\}|}{|\{1,2\}|} = \dfrac{1}{2}$
Not E	The set of outcomes that are not in event E: $P(\text{not } E) = 1 - P(E)$.	$P(\text{not } \{3\}) = \dfrac{6-1}{6} = \dfrac{5}{6}$
E and F	The set of outcomes in both E and F, that is, $E \cap F$; $P(E \text{ and } F) = P(E \cap F) = P(E\|F)P(F)$.	For $E = \{1, 3, 5\}$ and $F = \{2, 3, 5\}$: $P(E \text{ and } F) = P(E \cap F) = P(\{3, 5\}) = \dfrac{|\{3,5\}|}{6} = \dfrac{3}{6} = \dfrac{1}{3}$.
E or F	The set of outcomes in E or F or both, that is, $E \cup F$; $P(E \text{ or } F) = P(E) + P(F) - P(E \text{ and } F)$.	For $E = \{1, 3, 5\}$ and $F = \{2, 3, 5\}$: $P(E \text{ or } F) = P(E) + P(F) - P(E \text{ and } F) =$ $\dfrac{3}{6} + \dfrac{3}{6} - \dfrac{2}{6} = \dfrac{4}{6} = \dfrac{2}{3}$.
Dependent and Independent Events	E is dependent on F if $P(E\|F) \neq P(E)$. E and F are independent if neither is dependent on the other. If E and F are independent, $P(E \text{ and } F) = P(E)P(F)$.	For $E = \{2, 4, 6\}$ and $F = \{5, 6\}$: $P(E\|F) = P(E) = \dfrac{1}{2}$, and $P(F\|E) = P(F) = \dfrac{1}{3}$, so E and F are independent. Thus $P(E \text{ and } F) = P(E)P(F) = \left(\dfrac{1}{2}\right)\left(\dfrac{1}{3}\right) = \dfrac{1}{6}$.

SEQUENCE:

An algebraic function whose domain consists of only positive integers.

Example: Function $a(n) = n^2 + \left(\dfrac{n}{5}\right)$ with the domain of all positive integers $n = 1, 2, 3, \dots$ is an infinite sequence a_n.

PARTIAL SUM:

The sum of the first k terms of series a_n is called a partial sum of the series and is denoted $\displaystyle\sum_{i=1}^{k} a_i$

Example: For this same function $a(n) = n^2 + \left(\dfrac{n}{5}\right)$, the partial sum of the first three terms is

$$\sum_{i=1}^{3} a_i = \left(1^2 + \frac{1}{5}\right) + \left(2^2 + \frac{2}{5}\right) + \left(3^2 + \frac{3}{5}\right).$$

Angles and Polygons

VERTICAL ANGLES:

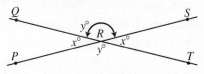

$\angle PRQ$ and $\angle SRT$ are a pair of vertical angles, and so are $\angle QRS$ and $\angle PRT$. Note that $x° + y° = 180°$.

ANGLES FORMED BY A LINE INTERSECTING TWO PARALLEL LINES:

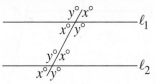

If two parallel lines are intersected by a third line, then the angle measures are related as indicated in the figure above, where $x° + y° = 180°$.

INTERIOR ANGLES OF A POLYGON:

The sum of the interior angle measures of a polygon with n sides is $(n-2)180°$. For example, the sum of the interior angle measures of a pentagon is $(5-2)180° = (3)180° = 540°$.

EQUILATERAL AND ISOSCELES TRIANGLES:

An equilateral triangle's sides are all the same length. An isosceles triangle has at least two sides of equal length.

AREA OF A TRIANGLE:

Area of a triangle $= \dfrac{(\text{length of altitude})(\text{length of base})}{2}$

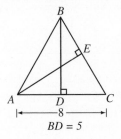

$BD = 5$

The area of $\triangle ABC$ is $\dfrac{(BD \times AC)}{2} = \dfrac{5 \times 8}{2} = 20$.

If $AB = BC$, then $AD = DC = 4$.

If two sides of a triangle are equal in length, the two angles opposite those sides are equal in measure, and vice versa.

Any altitude of an equilateral triangle bisects the side to which it is drawn.

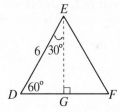

In equilateral triangle $\triangle DEF$, $DE = 6$, so $DG = 3$ and $EG = 3\sqrt{3}$.

AREA OF A TRAPEZOID:

Area of a trapezoid = $\dfrac{\text{(sum of lengths of bases)(height)}}{2}$

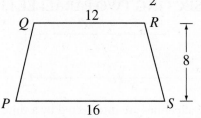

The area of $PQRS$ is $(QR + PS) \times \dfrac{8}{2} = (12 + 16) \times \dfrac{8}{2} = 28 \times 4 = 112$.

AREA OF A PARALLELOGRAM:

The area of a rectangle or other parallelogram = (length of base)(height)

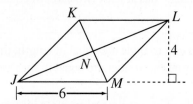

Since the diagonals bisect each other, $KN = NM$ and $JN = NL$. The area of $JKLM$ is $JM \times 4 = 6 \times 4 = 24$.

RIGHT TRIANGLES:

In a right triangle, the side opposite the right angle is the hypotenuse, and the other two sides are the legs.

Any triangle in which the lengths of the sides are in the ratio 3:4:5 is a right triangle.

In 45°– 45° – 90° triangles, the lengths of the sides are in the ratio $1:1:\sqrt{2}$. In 30° – 60° – 90° triangles, the lengths of the sides are in the ratio $1:\sqrt{3}:2$.

The Pythagorean theorem:

If a and b, are the lengths of the bases of a right triangle, and c is the length of the hypotenuse, then $a^2 + b^2 = c^2$.

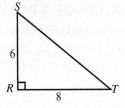

In right triangle $\triangle RST$, $RS = 6$ and $RT = 8$. Since $6^2 + 8^2 = 36 + 64 = 100 = (ST)^2$ and $ST = \sqrt{100}$, it follows that $ST = 10$.

Circles, Solids, and Coordinates

CIRCLES:

The circumference of a circle of radius r is $2\pi r$, where π is approximately $\frac{22}{7}$ or 3.14.

The area of a circle of radius r is πr^2.

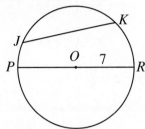

In the circle above, O is the center, and $\overline{JK}$ and $\overline{PR}$ are chords. $\overline{PR}$ is a diameter and $\overline{OR}$ is a radius.

Since $OR = 7$, the circumference is $2\pi(7) = 14\pi$.

The area is $\pi(7)^2 = 49\pi$.

RECTANGULAR SOLIDS:

Surface area of a rectangular solid = the sum of the areas of all the faces.

Volume of a rectangular solid = (length)(width)(height).

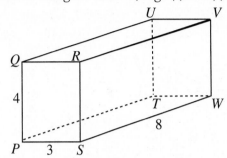

The dimensions of the rectangular solid above are 8, 3, and 4.

The surface area is $2(3 \times 4) + 2(3 \times 8) + 2(4 \times 8) = 136$.

The volume is $8 \times 3 \times 4 = 96$.

RIGHT CIRCULAR CYLINDERS:

The surface area of a right circular cylinder with height h and a base of radius r is $2(\pi r^2) + 2\pi rh$.

The volume is $\pi r^2 h$, that is, (area of base) × (height).

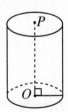

In the right circular cylinder above, where $r = 5$ and $h = 8$, the surface area is $2(25\pi) + 2\pi(5)(8) = 130\pi$.

The volume is $25\pi (8) = 200\pi$.

LINES IN THE COORDINATE PLANE:

An equation $y = mx + b$ determines a line whose slope is m and whose y-intercept is b.

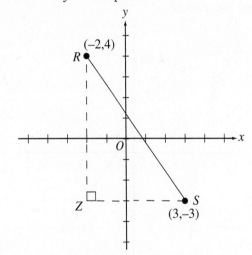

Given any two points (x_1, y_1) and (x_2, y_2) with $x_1 \neq x_2$, the slope is $m = \dfrac{(y_2 - y_1)}{(x_2 - x_1)}$. So using the known point (x_1, y_1) and the same slope m, any other point (x, y) on the line must satisfy the equation $m = \dfrac{(y - y_1)}{(x - x_1)}$.

Above, the line's slope is $\dfrac{(-3-4)}{(3-(-2))} = \dfrac{7}{5}$. So an equation of the line can be found using the point $(3,-3)$:

$$y - (-3) = \left(-\tfrac{7}{5}\right)(x - 3)$$

$$y + 3 = \left(-\tfrac{7}{5}\right)x + \tfrac{21}{5}$$

$$y = \left(-\tfrac{7}{5}\right)x + \tfrac{6}{5}$$

Thus, the y-intercept is $\tfrac{6}{5}$.

The x-intercept can be found as follows:

$$0 = \left(-\tfrac{7}{5}\right)x + \tfrac{6}{5}$$

$$\left(\tfrac{7}{5}\right)x = \tfrac{6}{5}$$

$$x = \tfrac{6}{7}$$

Both of these intercepts can be seen on the graph.

DISTANCES ON THE COORDINATE PLANE:

Use the Pythagorean theorem to find the distance between two points:

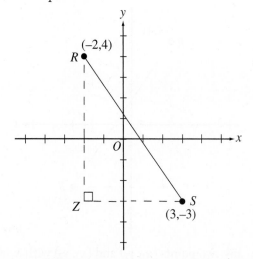

To find the distance between points R and S, draw the triangle as shown. Note that Z has (x,y) coordinates $(-2,-3)$, $RZ = 7$, and $ZS = 5$. Therefore, the distance between R and S is $\sqrt{7^2 + 5^2} = \sqrt{74}$.

PARABOLAS:

The graph of a quadratic polynomial function is a parabola.

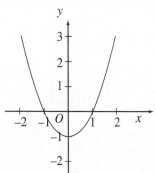

Above is the graph of the quadratic function $f(x) = x^2 - 1$.

4.0 Problem Solving

4.0 Problem Solving

The Quantitative Reasoning section of the GMAT exam uses Problem Solving and Data Sufficiency questions to gauge your skill level. This chapter focuses on problem solving questions. Remember that quantitative questions require knowledge of the following:

- Arithmetic
- Elementary algebra
- Commonly known concepts of geometry.

Problem Solving questions are designed to test your basic mathematical skills and understanding of elementary mathematical concepts, as well as your ability to reason quantitatively, solve quantitative problems, and interpret graphic data. The mathematics knowledge required to answer the questions is no more advanced than what is generally taught in secondary school (or high school) mathematics classes.

In these questions, you are asked to solve each problem and select the best of the five answer choices given. Begin by reading the question thoroughly to determine exactly what information is given and to make sure you understand what is being asked. Scan the answer choices to understand your options. If the problem seems simple, take a few moments to see whether you can determine the answer. Then, check your answer against the choices provided.

If you do not see your answer among the choices, or if the problem is complicated, take a closer look at the answer choices and think again about what the problem is asking. See whether you can eliminate some of the answer choices and narrow down your options. If you are still unable to narrow the answer down to a single choice, reread the question. Keep in mind that the answer will be based solely on the information provided in the question—don't allow your own experience and assumptions to interfere with your ability to find the correct answer to the question.

If you find yourself stuck on a question or unable to select the single correct answer, keep in mind that you have about 2 minutes to answer each quantitative question. You may run out of time if you take too long to answer any one question; you may simply need to pick the answer that seems to make the most sense. Although guessing is generally not the best way to achieve a high GMAT score, making an educated guess is a good strategy for answering questions you are unsure of. Even if your answer to a particular question is incorrect, your answers to other questions will allow the test to accurately gauge your ability level.

The following pages include test-taking strategies, directions that will apply to questions of this type, sample questions, an answer key, and explanations for all the problems. These explanations present problem solving strategies that could be helpful in answering the questions.

4.1 Test-Taking Strategies

1. **Pace yourself.**

    Consult the on-screen timer periodically. Work as carefully as possible, but do not spend valuable time checking answers or pondering problems that you find difficult.

2. **Use the erasable notepad provided.**

    Working a problem out may help you avoid errors in solving the problem. If diagrams or figures are not presented, it may help to draw your own.

3. **Read each question carefully to determine what is being asked.**

    For word problems, take one step at a time, reading each sentence carefully and translating the information into equations or other useful mathematical representations.

4. **Scan the answer choices before attempting to answer a question.**

    Scanning the answers can prevent you from putting answers in a form that is not given (e.g., finding the answer in decimal form, such as 0.25, when the choices are given in fractional form, such as $\frac{1}{4}$). Also, if the question requires approximations, a shortcut could serve well (e.g., you may be able to approximate 48 percent of a number by using half).

5. **Don't waste time trying to solve a problem that is too difficult for you.**

    Make your best guess and then move on to the next question.

4.2 Section Instructions

Go to www.mba.com/tutorial to view instructions for the section and get a feel for what the test center screens will look like on the actual GMAT exam.

4.3 Practice Questions

Solve the problem and indicate the best of the answer choices given.

Numbers: All numbers used are real numbers.

Figures: A figure accompanying a Problem Solving question is intended to provide information useful in solving the problem. Figures are drawn as accurately as possible. Exceptions will be clearly noted. Lines shown as straight are straight, and lines that appear jagged are also straight. The positions of points, angles, regions, etc., exist in the order shown, and angle measures are greater than zero. All figures lie in a plane unless otherwise indicated.

Questions 1 to 81 - Difficulty: Easy

*PS03439

1. Working at a constant rate, a copy machine makes 20 copies of a one-page document per minute. If the machine works at this constant rate, how many hours does it take to make 4,800 copies of a one-page document?

    (A) 4
    (B) 5
    (C) 6
    (D) 7
    (E) 8

PS11042

2. If $x + y = 2$ and $x^2 + y^2 = 2$, what is the value of xy?

    (A) −2
    (B) −1
    (C) 0
    (D) 1
    (E) 2

PS02978

3. The sum S of the first n consecutive positive even integers is given by $S = n(n + 1)$. For what value of n is this sum equal to 110?

    (A) 10
    (B) 11
    (C) 12
    (D) 13
    (E) 14

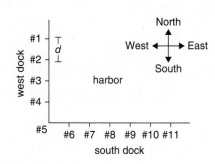

PS08375

4. A certain harbor has docking stations along its west and south docks, as shown in the figure; any two adjacent docking stations are separated by a uniform distance d. A certain boat left the west dock from docking station #2 and moved in a straight line diagonally until it reached the south dock. If the boat was at one time directly east of docking station #4 and directly north of docking station #7, at which docking station on the south dock did the boat arrive?

    (A) #7
    (B) #8
    (C) #9
    (D) #10
    (E) #11

PS03887

5. $6(87.30 + 0.65) - 5(87.30) =$

    (A)   3.90
    (B) 39.00
    (C) 90.90
    (D) 91.20
    (E) 91.85

---

*These numbers correlate with the online test bank question number. See the GMAT™ Official Guide Quantitative Review Question Index in the back of this book.

112

PS13800

6. Points *A*, *B*, *C*, and *D*, in that order, lie on a line. If *AB* = 3 cm, *AC* = 4 cm, and *BD* = 6 cm, what is *CD*, in centimeters?

   (A) 1
   (B) 2
   (C) 3
   (D) 4
   (E) 5

PS05292

7. What is the value of $x^2yz - xyz^2$, if $x = -2$, $y = 1$, and $z = 3$?

   (A) 20
   (B) 24
   (C) 30
   (D) 32
   (E) 48

PS11468

8. A souvenir vendor purchased 1,000 shirts for a special event at a price of $5 each. The vendor sold 600 of the shirts on the day of the event for $12 each and 300 of the shirts in the week following the event for $4 each. The vendor was unable to sell the remaining shirts. What was the vendor's gross profit on the sale of these shirts?

   (A) $1,000
   (B) $2,200
   (C) $2,700
   (D) $3,000
   (E) $3,400

PS06937

9. If *x* > *y* and *y* > *z*, which of the following represents the greatest number?

   (A) *x* − *z*
   (B) *x* − *y*
   (C) *y* − *x*
   (D) *z* − *y*
   (E) *z* − *x*

PS12926

10. To order certain plants from a catalog, it costs $3.00 per plant, plus a 5 percent sales tax, plus $6.95 for shipping and handling regardless of the number of plants ordered. If Company C ordered these plants from the catalog at the total cost of $69.95, how many plants did Company C order?

    (A) 22
    (B) 21
    (C) 20
    (D) 19
    (E) 18

PS00812

11. A rug manufacturer produces rugs at a cost of $75 per rug. What is the manufacturer's gross profit from the sale of 150 rugs if $\frac{2}{3}$ of the rugs are sold for $150 per rug and the rest are sold for $200 per rug?

    (A) $10,350
    (B) $11,250
    (C) $13,750
    (D) $16,250
    (E) $17,800

PS07793

12. The value of Maureen's investment portfolio has decreased by 5.8 percent since her initial investment in the portfolio. If her initial investment was $16,800, what is the current value of the portfolio?

    (A) $7,056.00
    (B) $14,280.00
    (C) $15,825.60
    (D) $16,702.56
    (E) $17,774.40

PS03036

13. Company C produces toy trucks at a cost of $5.00 each for the first 100 trucks and $3.50 for each additional truck. If 500 toy trucks were produced by Company C and sold for $10.00 each, what was Company C's gross profit?

    (A) $2,250
    (B) $2,500
    (C) $3,100
    (D) $3,250
    (E) $3,500

	Profit or Loss (in millions of dollars)				
Division	1991	1992	1993	1994	1995
A	1.1	(3.4)	1.9	2.0	0.6
B	(2.3)	5.5	(4.5)	3.9	(2.9)
C	10.0	(6.6)	5.3	1.1	(3.0)

PS02019

14. The annual profit or loss for the three divisions of Company T for the years 1991 through 1995 are summarized in the table shown, where losses are enclosed in parentheses. For which division and which three consecutive years shown was the division's profit or loss for the three-year period closest to $0 ?

   (A) Division A for 1991–1993
   (B) Division A for 1992–1994
   (C) Division B for 1991–1993
   (D) Division B for 1993–1995
   (E) Division C for 1992–1994

PS13583

15. Of the following, which is least?

   (A) $\dfrac{0.03}{0.00071}$

   (B) $\dfrac{0.03}{0.0071}$

   (C) $\dfrac{0.03}{0.071}$

   (D) $\dfrac{0.03}{0.71}$

   (E) $\dfrac{0.03}{7.1}$

PS08011

16. If the average (arithmetic mean) of 5 numbers j, $j + 5$, $2j - 1$, $4j - 2$, and $5j - 1$ is 8, what is the value of j?

   (A) $\dfrac{1}{3}$

   (B) $\dfrac{7}{13}$

   (C) 1

   (D) 3

   (E) 8

PS14037

17. Guadalupe owns 2 rectangular tracts of land. One is 300 m by 500 m and the other is 250 m by 630 m. The combined area of these 2 tracts is how many square meters?

   (A)   3,360
   (B)   307,500
   (C)   621,500
   (D)   704,000
   (E) 2,816,000

PS03918

18. There are five sales agents in a certain real estate office. One month Andy sold twice as many properties as Ellen, Bob sold 3 more than Ellen, Cary sold twice as many as Bob, and Dora sold as many as Bob and Ellen together. Who sold the most properties that month?

   (A) Andy
   (B) Bob
   (C) Cary
   (D) Dora
   (E) Ellen

PS10862

19. In a field day at a school, each child who competed in n events and scored a total of p points was given an overall score of $\dfrac{p}{n} + n$. Andrew competed in 1 event and scored 9 points. Jason competed in 3 events and scored 5, 6, and 7 points, respectively. What was the ratio of Andrew's overall score to Jason's overall score?

   (A) $\dfrac{10}{23}$

   (B) $\dfrac{7}{10}$

   (C) $\dfrac{4}{5}$

   (D) $\dfrac{10}{9}$

   (E) $\dfrac{12}{7}$

PS06719
20. A certain work plan for September requires that a work team, working every day, produce an average of 200 items per day. For the first half of the month, the team produced an average of 150 items per day. How many items per day must the team average during the second half of the month if it is to attain the average daily production rate required by the work plan?

   (A) 225
   (B) 250
   (C) 275
   (D) 300
   (E) 350

PS01949
21. A company sells radios for $15.00 each. It costs the company $14.00 per radio to produce 1,000 radios and $13.50 per radio to produce 2,000 radios. How much greater will the company's gross profit be from the production and sale of 2,000 radios than from the production and sale of 1,000 radios?

   (A) $500
   (B) $1,000
   (C) $1,500
   (D) $2,000
   (E) $2,500

PS06555
22. Which of the following represent positive numbers?

   I. $-3 - (-5)$
   II. $(-3)(-5)$
   III. $-5 - (-3)$

   (A) I only
   (B) II only
   (C) III only
   (D) I and II
   (E) II and III

PS09983
23. Point X lies on side BC of rectangle ABCD, which has length 12 and width 8. What is the area of triangular region AXD ?

   (A) 96
   (B) 48
   (C) 32
   (D) 24
   (E) 20

PS07659
24. A grocer has 400 pounds of coffee in stock, 20 percent of which is decaffeinated. If the grocer buys another 100 pounds of coffee of which 60 percent is decaffeinated, what percent, by weight, of the grocer's stock of coffee is decaffeinated?

   (A) 28%
   (B) 30%
   (C) 32%
   (D) 34%
   (E) 40%

PS05129
25. The toll T, in dollars, for a truck using a certain bridge is given by the formula $T = 1.50 + 0.50(x - 2)$, where x is the number of axles on the truck. What is the toll for an 18-wheel truck that has 2 wheels on its front axle and 4 wheels on each of its other axles?

   (A) $2.50
   (B) $3.00
   (C) $3.50
   (D) $4.00
   (E) $5.00

PS13917
26. For what value of x between −4 and 4, inclusive, is the value of $x^2 - 10x + 16$ the greatest?

   (A) −4
   (B) −2
   (C)   0
   (D)   2
   (E)   4

PS15994
27. If $x = -\dfrac{5}{8}$ and $y = -\dfrac{1}{2}$, what is the value of the expression $-2x - y^2$?

   (A) $-\dfrac{3}{2}$
   (B) −1
   (C) 1
   (D) $\dfrac{3}{2}$
   (E) $\dfrac{7}{4}$

PS13686

28. If $x - y = R$ and $xy = S$, then $(x - 2)(y + 2) =$
   (A) $R + S - 4$
   (B) $R + 2S - 4$
   (C) $2R - S - 4$
   (D) $2R + S - 4$
   (E) $2R + S$

PS01466

29. For positive integers a and b, the remainder when a is divided by b is equal to the remainder when b is divided by a. Which of the following could be a value of ab?

   I.   24
   II. 30
   III. 36

   (A)   II only
   (B)   III only
   (C)   I and II only
   (D)   II and III only
   (E)   I, II, and III

PS01867

30. List S consists of the positive integers that are multiples of 9 and are less than 100. What is the median of the integers in S?

   (A)   36
   (B)   45
   (C)   49
   (D)   54
   (E)   63

PS07380

31. A rope 20.6 meters long is cut into two pieces. If the length of one piece of rope is 2.8 meters shorter than the length of the other, what is the length, in meters, of the longer piece of rope?

   (A)   7.5
   (B)   8.9
   (C)   9.9
   (D)   10.3
   (E)   11.7

PS01120

32. If x and y are integers and $x - y$ is odd, which of the following must be true?

   I. xy is even.
   II. $x^2 + y^2$ is odd.
   III. $(x + y)^2$ is even.

   (A)   I only
   (B)   II only
   (C)   III only
   (D)   I and II only
   (E)   I, II, and III

PS00335

33. On Monday, the opening price of a certain stock was $100 per share and its closing price was $110 per share. On Tuesday the closing price of the stock was 10 percent less than its closing price on Monday, and on Wednesday the closing price of the stock was 4 percent greater than its closing price on Tuesday. What was the approximate percent change in the price of the stock from its opening price on Monday to its closing price on Wednesday?

   (A)   A decrease of 6%
   (B)   A decrease of 4%
   (C)   A decrease of 1%
   (D)   An increase of 3%
   (E)   An increase of 4%

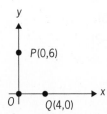

PS05109

34. In the rectangular coordinate system shown above, points O, P, and Q represent the sites of three proposed housing developments. If a fire station can be built at any point in the coordinate system, at which point would it be equidistant from all three developments?

   (A)   (3,1)
   (B)   (1,3)
   (C)   (3,2)
   (D)   (2,2)
   (E)   (2,3)

PS05008
35. What is the perimeter, in meters, of a rectangular garden 6 meters wide that has the same area as a rectangular playground 16 meters long and 12 meters wide?

(A)   48
(B)   56
(C)   60
(D)   76
(E)   192

PS00918
36. $1 - 0.000001 =$

(A) $(1.01)(0.99)$
(B) $(1.11)(0.99)$
(C) $(1.001)(0.999)$
(D) $(1.111)(0.999)$
(E) $(1.0101)(0.0909)$

PS57330.02
37. In a certain history class of 17 juniors and seniors, each junior has written 2 book reports and each senior has written 3 book reports. If the 17 students have written a total of 44 book reports, how many juniors are in the class?

(A)   7
(B)   8
(C)   9
(D)   10
(E)   11

PS04362
38. $|-4|(|-20|-|5|) =$

(A)   −100
(B)   −60
(C)   60
(D)   75
(E)   100

PS12934
39. Of the total amount that Jill spent on a shopping trip, excluding taxes, she spent 50 percent on clothing, 20 percent on food, and 30 percent on other items. If Jill paid a 4 percent tax on the clothing, no tax on the food, and an 8 percent tax on all other items, then the total tax that she paid was what percent of the total amount that she spent, excluding taxes?

(A)   2.8%
(B)   3.6%
(C)   4.4%
(D)   5.2%
(E)   6.0%

PS15469
40. How many integers x satisfy both $2 < x \le 4$ and $0 \le x \le 3$?

(A)   5
(B)   4
(C)   3
(D)   2
(E)   1

PS09322
41. At the opening of a trading day at a certain stock exchange, the price per share of stock K was $8. If the price per share of stock K was $9 at the closing of the day, what was the percent increase in the price per share of stock K for that day?

(A)   1.4%
(B)   5.9%
(C)   11.1%
(D)   12.5%
(E)   23.6%

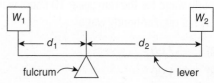

PS14237
42. As shown in the diagram above, a lever resting on a fulcrum has weights of w_1 pounds and w_2 pounds, located d_1 feet and d_2 feet from the fulcrum. The lever is balanced and $w_1 d_1 = w_2 d_2$. Suppose w_1 is 50 pounds and w_2 is 30 pounds. If d_1 is 4 feet less than d_2, what is d_2, in feet?

(A)   1.5
(B)   2.5
(C)   6
(D)   10
(E)   20

PS01650
43. If r and s are positive integers such that $(2^r)(4^s) = 16$, then $2r + s =$

(A)   2
(B)   3
(C)   4
(D)   5
(E)   6

PS06726

44. Three people each contributed x dollars toward the purchase of a car. They then bought the car for y dollars, an amount less than the total number of dollars contributed. If the excess amount is to be refunded to the three people in equal amounts, each person should receive a refund of how many dollars?

(A) $\dfrac{3x - y}{3}$

(B) $\dfrac{x - y}{3}$

(C) $\dfrac{x - 3y}{3}$

(D) $\dfrac{y - 3x}{3}$

(E) $3(x - y)$

PS07080

45. Last week Jack worked 70 hours and earned $1,260. If he earned his regular hourly wage for the first 40 hours worked, $1\frac{1}{2}$ times his regular hourly wage for the next 20 hours worked, and 2 times his regular hourly wage for the remaining 10 hours worked, what was his regular hourly wage?

(A) $7.00
(B) $14.00
(C) $18.00
(D) $22.00
(E) $31.50

PS13426

46. If a and b are positive integers and $(2^a)^b = 2^3$, what is the value of $2^a\, 2^b$?

(A) 6
(B) 8
(C) 16
(D) 32
(E) 64

PS01099

47. Five machines at a certain factory operate at the same constant rate. If four of these machines, operating simultaneously, take 30 hours to fill a certain production order, how many <u>fewer</u> hours does it take all five machines, operating simultaneously, to fill the same production order?

(A) 3
(B) 5
(C) 6
(D) 16
(E) 24

PS01443

48. A certain toll station on a highway has 7 tollbooths, and each tollbooth collects $0.75 from each vehicle that passes it. From 6 o'clock yesterday morning to 12 o'clock midnight, vehicles passed each of the tollbooths at the average rate of 4 vehicles per minute. Approximately how much money did the toll station collect during that time period?

(A) $1,500
(B) $3,000
(C) $11,500
(D) $23,000
(E) $30,000

PS13829

49. How many integers between 1 and 16, inclusive, have exactly 3 different positive integer factors? (Note: 6 is NOT such an integer because 6 has 4 different positive integer factors: 1, 2, 3, and 6.)

(A) 1
(B) 2
(C) 3
(D) 4
(E) 6

PS14063

50. Stephanie has $2\frac{1}{4}$ cups of milk on hand and makes 2 batches of cookies, using $\frac{2}{3}$ cup of milk for each batch of cookies. Which of the following describes the amount of milk remaining after she makes the cookies?

(A) Less than $\frac{1}{2}$ cup

(B) Between $\frac{1}{2}$ cup and $\frac{3}{4}$ cup

(C) Between $\frac{3}{4}$ cup and 1 cup

(D) Between 1 cup and $1\frac{1}{2}$ cups

(E) More than $1\frac{1}{2}$ cups

PS01656

51. The expression $n!$ is defined as the product of the integers from 1 through n. If p is the product of the integers from 100 through 299 and q is the product of the integers from 200 through 299, which of the following is equal to $\frac{p}{q}$?

(A) 99!

(B) 199!

(C) $\frac{199!}{99!}$

(D) $\frac{299!}{99!}$

(E) $\frac{299!}{199!}$

PS15753

52. A school club plans to package and sell dried fruit to raise money. The club purchased 12 containers of dried fruit, each containing $16\frac{3}{4}$ pounds. What is the maximum number of individual bags of dried fruit, each containing $\frac{1}{4}$ pounds, that can be sold from the dried fruit the club purchased?

(A) 50

(B) 64

(C) 67

(D) 768

(E) 804

Height	Price
Less than 5 ft	$14.95
5 ft to 6 ft	$17.95
Over 6 ft	$21.95

PS02498

53. A nursery sells fruit trees priced as shown in the chart above. In its inventory 54 trees are less than 5 feet in height. If the expected revenue from the sale of its entire stock is estimated at $2,450, approximately how much of this will come from the sale of trees that are at least 5 feet tall?

(A) $1,730

(B) $1,640

(C) $1,410

(D) $1,080

(E) $810

PS04971

54. A certain bridge is 4,024 feet long. Approximately how many minutes does it take to cross this bridge at a constant speed of 20 miles per hour? (1 mile = 5,280 feet)

(A) 1

(B) 2

(C) 4

(D) 6

(E) 7

PS25440.02

55. A purse contains 57 coins, all of which are nickels, dimes, or quarters. If the purse contains x dimes and 8 more nickels than dimes, which of the following gives the number of quarters the purse contains in terms of x ?

(A) 2x − 49

(B) 2x + 49

(C) 2x − 65

(D) 49 − 2x

(E) 65 − 2x

PS12657

56. The annual interest rate earned by an investment increased by 10 percent from last year to this year. If the annual interest rate earned by the investment this year was 11 percent, what was the annual interest rate last year?

(A) 1%
(B) 1.1%
(C) 9.1%
(D) 10%
(E) 10.8%

PS07394

57. A total of 5 liters of gasoline is to be poured into two empty containers with capacities of 2 liters and 6 liters, respectively, such that both containers will be filled to the same percent of their respective capacities. What amount of gasoline, in liters, must be poured into the 6-liter container?

(A) $4\frac{1}{2}$
(B) 4
(C) $3\frac{3}{4}$
(D) 3
(E) $1\frac{1}{4}$

PS13882

58. What is the larger of the 2 solutions of the equation $x^2 - 4x = 96$?

(A) 8
(B) 12
(C) 16
(D) 32
(E) 100

$$x = \frac{1}{6}gt^2$$

PS89821.02

59. In the formula shown, if g is a constant and $x = -6$ when $t = 2$, what is the value of x when $t = 4$?

(A) −24
(B) −20
(C) −15
(D) 20
(E) 24

PS10921

60. $\dfrac{(39,897)(0.0096)}{198.76}$ is approximately

(A) 0.02
(B) 0.2
(C) 2
(D) 20
(E) 200

PS13205

61. If a square region has area n, what is the length of the diagonal of the square in terms of n ?

(A) $\sqrt{2n}$
(B) $\sqrt{n}$
(C) $2\sqrt{n}$
(D) $2n$
(E) $2n^2$

PS00817

62. The "prime sum" of an integer n greater than 1 is the sum of all the prime factors of n, including repetitions. For example, the prime sum of 12 is 7, since $12 = 2 \times 2 \times 3$ and $2 + 2 + 3 = 7$. For which of the following integers is the prime sum greater than 35 ?

(A) 440
(B) 512
(C) 620
(D) 700
(E) 750

PS02256

63. Each machine at a toy factory assembles a certain kind of toy at a constant rate of one toy every 3 minutes. If 40 percent of the machines at the factory are to be replaced by new machines that assemble this kind of toy at a constant rate of one toy every 2 minutes, what will be the percent increase in the number of toys assembled in one hour by all the machines at the factory, working at their constant rates?

(A) 20%
(B) 25%
(C) 30%
(D) 40%
(E) 50%

PS10339
64. When a subscription to a new magazine was purchased for m months, the publisher offered a discount of 75 percent off the regular monthly price of the magazine. If the total value of the discount was equivalent to buying the magazine at its regular monthly price for 27 months, what was the value of m ?

   (A)   18
   (B)   24
   (C)   30
   (D)   36
   (E)   48

PS10422
65. At a garage sale, all of the prices of the items sold were different. If the price of a radio sold at the garage sale was both the 15th highest price and the 20th lowest price among the prices of the items sold, how many items were sold at the garage sale?

   (A)   33
   (B)   34
   (C)   35
   (D)   36
   (E)   37

PS11738
66. Half of a large pizza is cut into 4 equal-sized pieces, and the other half is cut into 6 equal-sized pieces. If a person were to eat 1 of the larger pieces and 2 of the smaller pieces, what fraction of the pizza would remain <u>uneaten</u>?

   (A) $\dfrac{5}{12}$

   (B) $\dfrac{13}{24}$

   (C) $\dfrac{7}{12}$

   (D) $\dfrac{2}{3}$

   (E) $\dfrac{17}{24}$

PS14293
67. If $a = 1 + \dfrac{1}{4} + \dfrac{1}{16} + \dfrac{1}{64}$ and $b = 1 + \dfrac{1}{4}a$, then what is the value of $a - b$?

   (A) $-\dfrac{85}{256}$

   (B) $-\dfrac{1}{256}$

   (C) $-\dfrac{1}{4}$

   (D) $\dfrac{125}{256}$

   (E) $\dfrac{169}{256}$

PS10174
68. In a certain learning experiment, each participant had three trials and was assigned, for each trial, a score of either –2, –1, 0, 1, or 2. The participant's final score consisted of the sum of the first trial score, 2 times the second trial score, and 3 times the third trial score. If Anne received scores of 1 and –1 for her first two trials, not necessarily in that order, which of the following could NOT be her final score?

   (A)   –4
   (B)   –2
   (C)   1
   (D)   5
   (E)   6

PS00111
69. For all positive integers m and v, the expression $m \ominus v$ represents the remainder when m is divided by v. What is the value of $((98 \ominus 33) \ominus 17) - (98 \ominus (33 \ominus 17))$?

   (A)   –10
   (B)   –2
   (C)   8
   (D)   13
   (E)   17

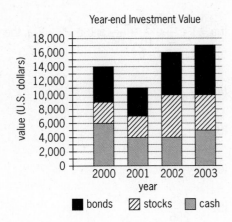

Year-end Investment Value

■ bonds   ▨ stocks   ▨ cash

PS13841

70. The chart above shows year-end values for Darnella's investments. For just the stocks, what was the increase in value from year-end 2000 to year-end 2003 ?

(A) $1,000
(B) $2,000
(C) $3,000
(D) $4,000
(E) $5,000

PS05775

71. If the sum of the reciprocals of two consecutive odd integers is $\frac{12}{35}$, then the greater of the two integers is

(A) 3
(B) 5
(C) 7
(D) 9
(E) 11

PS05916

72. What is the sum of the odd integers from 35 to 85, inclusive?

(A) 1,560
(B) 1,500
(C) 1,240
(D) 1,120
(E) 1,100

PS21080.02

73. For all numbers a, b, c, and d, $\begin{vmatrix} a & b \\ c & d \end{vmatrix}$ is defined by the equation $\begin{vmatrix} a & b \\ c & d \end{vmatrix} = ad - cb$. Which of the following is equal to $\begin{vmatrix} s & t \\ 1 & 3 \end{vmatrix} - \begin{vmatrix} -t & 2 \\ s & 4 \end{vmatrix} + \begin{vmatrix} 2 & 2 \\ t & s \end{vmatrix}$?

(A) $\begin{vmatrix} s & t \\ 1 & 5 \end{vmatrix}$

(B) $\begin{vmatrix} s & t \\ 7 & 1 \end{vmatrix}$

(C) $\begin{vmatrix} s & t \\ 5 & 7 \end{vmatrix}$

(D) $\begin{vmatrix} s & -t \\ 1 & 5 \end{vmatrix}$

(E) $\begin{vmatrix} s & -t \\ 1 & 7 \end{vmatrix}$

PS00777

74. In a certain sequence, each term after the first term is one-half the previous term. If the tenth term of the sequence is between 0.0001 and 0.001, then the twelfth term of the sequence is between

(A) 0.0025 and 0.025
(B) 0.00025 and 0.0025
(C) 0.000025 and 0.00025
(D) 0.0000025 and 0.000025
(E) 0.00000025 and 0.0000025

PS04765

75. A certain drive-in movie theater has a total of 17 rows of parking spaces. There are 20 parking spaces in the first row and 21 parking spaces in the second row. In each subsequent row there are 2 more parking spaces than in the previous row. What is the total number of parking spaces in the movie theater?

(A) 412
(B) 544
(C) 596
(D) 632
(E) 692

PS10810

76. Ada and Paul received their scores on three tests. On the first test, Ada's score was 10 points higher than Paul's score. On the second test, Ada's score was 4 points higher than Paul's score. If Paul's average (arithmetic mean) score on the three tests was 3 points higher than Ada's average score on the three tests, then Paul's score on the third test was how many points higher than Ada's score?

(A)   9
(B)   14
(C)   17
(D)   23
(E)   25

PS06180

77. The price of a certain stock increased by 0.25 of 1 percent on a certain day. By what fraction did the price of the stock increase that day?

(A) $\dfrac{1}{2,500}$

(B) $\dfrac{1}{400}$

(C) $\dfrac{1}{40}$

(D) $\dfrac{1}{25}$

(E) $\dfrac{1}{4}$

PS03831

78. For each trip, a taxicab company charges $4.25 for the first mile and $2.65 for each additional mile or fraction thereof. If the total charge for a certain trip was $62.55, how many miles at most was the trip?

(A)   21
(B)   22
(C)   23
(D)   24
(E)   25

PS12857

79. When 24 is divided by the positive integer n, the remainder is 4. Which of the following statements about n must be true?

   I. n is even.

   II. n is a multiple of 5.

   III. n is a factor of 20.

(A)   III only
(B)   I and II only
(C)   I and III only
(D)   II and III only
(E)   I, II, and III

PS80871.02

80. Terry needs to purchase some pipe for a plumbing job that requires pipes with lengths of 1 ft 4 in, 2 ft 8 in, 3 ft 4 in, 3 ft 8 in, 4 ft 8 in, 5 ft 8 in, and 9 ft 4 in. The store from which Terry will purchase the pipe sells pipe only in 10-ft lengths. If each 10-ft length can be cut into shorter pieces, what is the minimum number of 10-ft pipe lengths that Terry needs to purchase for the plumbing job?

(Note: 1 ft = 12 in)

(A)   3
(B)   4
(C)   5
(D)   6
(E)   7

PS12759

81. What is the thousandths digit in the decimal equivalent of $\dfrac{53}{5,000}$?

(A)   0
(B)   1
(C)   3
(D)   5
(E)   6

Questions 82 to 158 - Difficulty: Medium

PS67502.01

82. If $\frac{1}{2}$ the result obtained when 2 is subtracted from $5x$ is equal to the sum of 10 and $3x$, what is the value of x?

(A) −22
(B) −4
(C) 4
(D) 18
(E) 22

PS48502.01

83. In a rectangular coordinate system, straight line k passes through points $(0, 0)$ and $(3, 2)$. Which of the following are coordinates of a point on k?

(A) $(9, 4)$
(B) $(4, 9)$
(C) $(-4, 6)$
(D) $(-6, -9)$
(E) $(-6, -4)$

PS87502.01

84. If Car A took n hours to travel 2 miles and Car B took m hours to travel 3 miles, which of the following expresses the time it would take Car C, traveling at the average (arithmetic mean) of those rates, to travel 5 miles?

(A) $\dfrac{10nm}{3n+2m}$

(B) $\dfrac{3n+2m}{10(n+m)}$

(C) $\dfrac{2n+3m}{5nm}$

(D) $\dfrac{10(n+m)}{2n+3m}$

(E) $\dfrac{5(n+m)}{2n+3m}$

PS78502.01

85. If x, y, and k are positive and x is less than y, then $\dfrac{x+k}{y+k}$ is

(A) 1

(B) greater than $\dfrac{x}{y}$

(C) equal to $\dfrac{x}{y}$

(D) less than $\dfrac{x}{y}$

(E) less than $\dfrac{x}{y}$ or greater than $\dfrac{x}{y}$, depending on the value of k

PS09502.01

86. Consider the following set of inequalities: $p > q$, $s > r$, $q > t$, $s > p$, and $r > q$. Between which two quantities is no relationship established?

(A) p and r
(B) s and t
(C) s and q
(D) p and t
(E) r and t

PS68502.01

87. Carl averaged $2m$ miles per hour on a trip that took him h hours. If Ruth made the same trip in $\frac{2}{3}h$ hours, what was her average speed in miles per hour?

(A) $\dfrac{1}{3}mh$

(B) $\dfrac{2}{3}mh$

(C) m

(D) $\dfrac{3}{2}m$

(E) $3m$

PS29502.01

88. Of three persons, two take relish, two take pepper, and two take salt. The one who takes no salt takes no pepper, and the one who takes no pepper takes no relish. Which of the following statements must be true?

    I. The person who takes no salt also takes no relish.

    II. Any of the three persons who takes pepper also takes relish and salt.

    III. The person who takes no relish is not one of those who takes salt.

    (A) I only
    (B) II only
    (C) III only
    (D) I and II only
    (E) I, II, and III

PS88502.01

89. If a rectangle of area 24 can be partitioned into exactly 3 nonoverlapping squares of equal area, what is the length of the longest side of the rectangle?

    (A) $2\sqrt{2}$
    (B) 6
    (C) 8
    (D) $6\sqrt{2}$
    (E) $12\sqrt{2}$

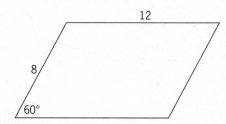

PS50602.01

90. In the figure above, the area of the parallelogram is

    (A) 40
    (B) $24\sqrt{3}$
    (C) 72
    (D) $48\sqrt{3}$
    (E) 96

PS91602.01

91. If the smaller of 2 consecutive odd integers is a multiple of 5, which of the following could NOT be the sum of these 2 integers?

    (A) −8
    (B) 12
    (C) 22
    (D) 52
    (E) 252

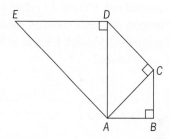

PS73602.01

92. In the figure above, if triangles ABC, ACD, and ADE are isosceles right triangles and the area of $\triangle ABC$ is 6, then the area of $\triangle ADE$ is

    (A) 18
    (B) 24
    (C) 36
    (D) $12\sqrt{2}$
    (E) $24\sqrt{2}$

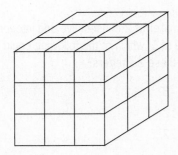

PS93602.01

93. Each of 27 white 1-centimeter cubes will have exactly one face painted red. If these 27 cubes are joined together to form one large cube, as shown above, what is the greatest possible fraction of the surface area that could be red?

(A) $\dfrac{11}{27}$

(B) $\dfrac{13}{27}$

(C) $\dfrac{1}{2}$

(D) $\dfrac{5}{9}$

(E) $\dfrac{19}{27}$

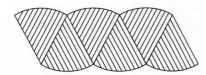

PS44602.01

94. The figure above is constructed by separating a circular region into 6 equal parts and rearranging the parts as shown. If the diameter of the circle is d, what is the perimeter of the figure above?

(A) πd

(B) $2\pi d$

(C) $\pi d + 2$

(D) $\pi d + d$

(E) $2\pi d + d$

PS54602.01

95. On a scale drawing of a triangular piece of land, the sides of the triangle have lengths 5, 12, and 13 centimeters. If 1 centimeter on the drawing represents 3 meters, what is the area, in square meters, of the piece of land?

(A) 90

(B) 180

(C) 240

(D) 270

(E) 540

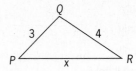

Note: Figure not drawn to scale.

PS05602.01

96. Which of the following gives all possible values of x in the figure above?

(A) $1 < x < 4$

(B) $1 < x < 7$

(C) $3 < x < 5$

(D) $4 < x < 7$

(E) $5 < x < 12$

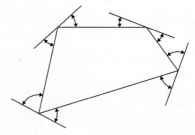

PS15602.01

97. In the figure above, lines are drawn at the vertices of the quadrilateral as shown. What is the sum of the degree measures of the marked angles?

(A) 450

(B) 360

(C) 270

(D) 240

(E) 180

PS25602.01

98. The dimensions of a ream of paper are $8\frac{1}{2}$ inches by 11 inches by $2\frac{1}{2}$ inches. The inside dimensions of a carton that will hold exactly 12 reams of paper could be

(A) $8\frac{1}{2}$ in by 11 in by 12 in

(B) 17 in by 11 in by 15 in

(C) 17 in by 22 in by 3 in

(D) 51 in by 66 in by 15 in

(E) 102 in by 132 in by 30 in

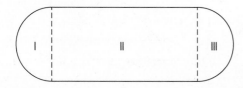

PS35602.01

99. In the racetrack shown above, regions I and III are semicircular with radius r. If region II is rectangular and its length is twice its width, what is the perimeter of the track in terms of r?

(A) $2r(\pi + 2)$

(B) $2r(\pi + 4)$

(C) $2r(\pi + 8)$

(D) $4r(\pi + 2)$

(E) $4r(\pi + 4)$

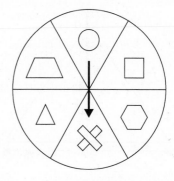

PS85602.01

100. The figure above, which is divided into 6 sectors of equal area, contains an arrow representing a spinner. If the spinner is rotated 3,840 degrees in a clockwise direction from the position shown, which of the following indicates the sector to which the arrow on the spinner will point?

(A) △

(B) □

(C) ○

(D) ⏢

(E) ⬡

PS95602.01

101. When a rectangular vat that is 3 feet deep is filled to $\frac{2}{3}$ of its capacity, it contains 60 gallons of water. If $7\frac{1}{2}$ gallons of water occupies 1 cubic foot of space, what is the area, in square feet, of the base of the vat?

(A) 4

(B) 8

(C) 12

(D) 150

(E) 225

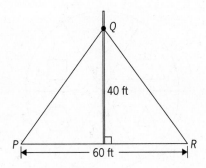

PS06602.01

102. The figure above represents an antenna tower with two guy wires that extend from point Q, 40 feet above the ground, to points P and R as shown. If the two wires have equal length, approximately what is the total length, in feet, of the two wires?

(A)   60
(B)   80
(C)   100
(D)   120
(E)   180

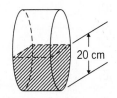

PS16602.01

103. The figures above show a sealed container that is a right circular cylinder filled with liquid to $\frac{1}{2}$ its capacity. If the container is placed on its base, the depth of the liquid in the container is 10 centimeters and if the container is placed on its side, the depth of the liquid is 20 centimeters. How many cubic centimeters of liquid are in the container?

(A) $4{,}000\pi$
(B) $2{,}000\pi$
(C) $1{,}000\pi$
(D) 400π
(E) 200π

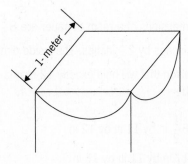

PS26602.01

104. The figure above shows a drop-leaf table. With all four leaves down the tabletop is a square, and with all four leaves up the tabletop is a circle. What is the radius, in meters, of the tabletop when all four leaves are up?

(A) $\frac{1}{2}$
(B) $\frac{\sqrt{2}}{2}$
(C) 1
(D) $\sqrt{2}$
(E) 2

PS36602.01

105. If the diameter of a circular skating rink is 60 meters, the area of the rink is approximately how many square meters?

(A)   90
(B)   180
(C)   900
(D)   2,800
(E)   10,800

PS46602.01

106. What is the greatest number of blocks 8 centimeters by 6 centimeters by 9 centimeters that will fit into a storage space that is 60 centimeters by 72 centimeters by 96 centimeters?

(A)   60
(B)   840
(C)   896
(D)   960
(E)   1,080

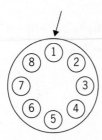

PS56602.01

107. Eight light bulbs numbered 1 through 8 are arranged in a circle as shown above. The bulbs are wired so that every third bulb, counting in a clockwise direction, flashes until all bulbs have flashed once. If the bulb numbered 1 flashes first, which numbered bulb will flash last?

(A) 2

(B) 3

(C) 4

(D) 6

(E) 7

Closing Prices of Stock X
During a Certain Week
(in dollars)

Monday	Tuesday	Wednesday	Thursday	Friday
21	19	22	$24\frac{1}{2}$	23

PS28580.02

108. A certain financial analyst defines the "volatility" of a stock during a given week to be the result of the following procedure: find the absolute value of the difference in the stock's closing price for each pair of consecutive days in the week and then find the average (arithmetic mean) of these 4 values. What is the volatility of Stock X during the week shown in the table?

(A) 0.50

(B) 1.80

(C) 2.00

(D) 2.25

(E) 2.50

PS29580.02

109. If $y = \dfrac{|3x - 5|}{-x^2 - 3}$, for what value of x will the value of y be greatest?

(A) −5

(B) $-\dfrac{3}{5}$

(C) 0

(D) $\dfrac{3}{5}$

(E) $\dfrac{5}{3}$

PS22680.02

110. What values of x have a corresponding value of y that satisfies both $xy > 0$ and $xy = x + y$?

(A) $x \le -1$

(B) $-1 < x \le 0$

(C) $0 < x \le 1$

(D) $x > 1$

(E) All real numbers

PS17680.02

111. Employee X's annual salary is $12,000 more than half of Employee Y's annual salary. Employee Z's annual salary is $15,000 more than half of Employee X's annual salary. If Employee X's annual salary is $27,500, which of the following lists these three people in order of increasing annual salary?

(A) Y, Z, X

(B) Y, X, Z

(C) Z, X, Y

(D) X, Y, Z

(E) X, Z, Y

$$C = \begin{cases} 0.10s, \text{ if } s \le 60{,}000 \\ 0.10s + 0.04(s - 60{,}000), \text{ if } s > 60{,}000 \end{cases}$$

PS27680.02

112. The formula above gives the contribution C, in dollars, to a certain profit-sharing plan for a participant with a salary of s dollars. How many more dollars is the contribution for a participant with a salary of $70,000 than for a participant with a salary of $50,000?

(A) $800

(B) $1,400

(C) $2,000

(D) $2,400

(E) $2,800

PS39680.02

113. Next month, Ron and Cathy will each begin working part-time at $\frac{3}{5}$ of their respective current salaries.

If the sum of their reduced salaries will be equal to Cathy's current salary, then Ron's current salary is what fraction of Cathy's current salary?

(A) $\frac{1}{3}$

(B) $\frac{2}{5}$

(C) $\frac{1}{2}$

(D) $\frac{3}{5}$

(E) $\frac{2}{3}$

PS84780.02

114. David and Ron are ordering food for a business lunch. David thinks that there should be twice as many sandwiches as there are pastries, but Ron thinks the number of pastries should be 12 more than one-fourth of the number of sandwiches. How many sandwiches should be ordered so that David and Ron can agree on the number of pastries to order?

(A) 12

(B) 16

(C) 20

(D) 24

(E) 48

PS34880.02

115. The cost of purchasing each box of candy from a certain mail order catalog is v dollars per pound of candy, plus a shipping charge of h dollars. How many dollars does it cost to purchase 2 boxes of candy, one containing s pounds of candy and the other containing t pounds of candy, from this catalog?

(A) $h + stv$

(B) $2h + stv$

(C) $2hstv$

(D) $2h + s + t + v$

(E) $2h + v(s + t)$

PS16980.02

116. If $x \neq -\frac{1}{2}$, then $\dfrac{6x^3 + 3x^2 - 8x - 4}{2x + 1} =$

(A) $3x^2 + \frac{3}{2}x - 8$

(B) $3x^2 + \frac{3}{2}x - 4$

(C) $3x^2 - 4$

(D) $3x - 4$

(E) $3x + 4$

PS29980.02

117. If $x^2 + bx + 5 = (x + c)^2$ for all numbers x, where b and c are positive constants, what is the value of b ?

(A) $\sqrt{5}$

(B) $\sqrt{10}$

(C) $2\sqrt{5}$

(D) $2\sqrt{10}$

(E) 10

PS08090.02

118. Last year Shannon listened to a certain public radio station 10 hours per week and contributed $35 to the station. Of the following, which is closest to Shannon's contribution per minute of listening time last year?

(A) $0.001

(B) $0.010

(C) $0.025

(D) $0.058

(E) $0.067

PS97190.02

119. Each of the 20 employees at Company J is to receive an end-of-year bonus this year. Agnes will receive a larger bonus than any other employee, but only $500 more than Cheryl will receive. None of the employees will receive a smaller bonus than Cheryl. If the amount of money to be distributed in bonuses at Company J this year totals $60,000, what is the largest bonus Agnes can receive?

(A) $3,250

(B) $3,325

(C) $3,400

(D) $3,475

(E) $3,500

PS90731.02
120. Beth, Naomi, and Juan raised a total of $55 for charity. Naomi raised $5 less than Juan, and Juan raised twice as much as Beth. How much did Beth raise?

    (A) $9
    (B) $10
    (C) $12
    (D) $13
    (E) $15

PS16731.02
121. The set of solutions for the equation $(x^2 - 25)^2 = x^2 - 10x + 25$ contains how many real numbers?

    (A)   0
    (B)   1
    (C)   2
    (D)   3
    (E)   4

PS67941.02
122. An aerosol can is designed so that its bursting pressure, B, in pounds per square inch, is 120% of the pressure, F, in pounds per square inch, to which it is initially filled. Which of the following formulas expresses the relationship between B and F?

    (A) $B = 1.2F$
    (B) $B = 120F$
    (C) $B = 1 + 0.2F$
    (D) $B = \dfrac{F}{1.2}$
    (E) $B = \dfrac{1.2}{F}$

PS00986
123. The average (arithmetic mean) of the positive integers x, y, and z is 3. If $x < y < z$, what is the greatest possible value of z?

    (A)   5
    (B)   6
    (C)   7
    (D)   8
    (E)   9

PS14087
124. The product of 3,305 and the 1-digit integer x is a 5-digit integer. The units (ones) digit of the product is 5 and the hundreds digit is y. If A is the set of all possible values of x and B is the set of all possible values of y, then which of the following gives the members of A and B?

	A	B
(A)	{1, 3, 5, 7, 9}	{0, 1, 2, 3, 4, 5, 6, 7, 8, 9}
(B)	{1, 3, 5, 7, 9}	{1, 3, 5, 7, 9}
(C)	{3, 5, 7, 9}	{1, 5, 7, 9}
(D)	{5, 7, 9}	{1, 5, 7}
(E)	{5, 7, 9}	{1, 5, 9}

PS07001
125. If x and y are integers such that $2 < x \le 8$ and $2 < y \le 9$, what is the maximum value of $\dfrac{1}{x} - \dfrac{x}{y}$?

    (A) $-3\dfrac{1}{8}$
    (B)   0
    (C) $\dfrac{1}{4}$
    (D) $\dfrac{5}{18}$
    (E)   2

PS01875
126. Items that are purchased together at a certain discount store are priced at $3 for the first item purchased and $1 for each additional item purchased. What is the maximum number of items that could be purchased together for a total price that is less than $30?

    (A)   25
    (B)   26
    (C)   27
    (D)   28
    (E)   29

PS00774
127. What is the least integer z for which $(0.000125)(0.0025)(0.00000125) \times 10^z$ is an integer?

    (A)   18
    (B)   10
    (C)   0
    (D)   −10
    (E)   −18

PS08407
128. The average (arithmetic mean) length per film for a group of 21 films is t minutes. If a film that runs for 66 minutes is removed from the group and replaced by one that runs for 52 minutes, what is the average length per film, in minutes, for the new group of films, in terms of t?

(A) $t + \dfrac{2}{3}$

(B) $t - \dfrac{2}{3}$

(C) $21t + 14$

(D) $t + \dfrac{3}{2}$

(E) $t - \dfrac{3}{2}$

PS08051
129. An open box in the shape of a cube measuring 50 centimeters on each side is constructed from plywood. If the plywood weighs 1.5 grams per square centimeter, which of the following is closest to the total weight, in kilograms, of the plywood used for the box? (1 kilogram = 1,000 grams)

(A) 2

(B) 4

(C) 8

(D) 13

(E) 19

PS03614
130. A garden center sells a certain grass seed in 5-pound bags at $13.85 per bag, 10-pound bags at $20.43 per bag, and 25-pound bags at $32.25 per bag. If a customer is to buy at least 65 pounds of the grass seed, but no more than 80 pounds, what is the least possible cost of the grass seed that the customer will buy?

(A) $94.03

(B) $96.75

(C) $98.78

(D) $102.07

(E) $105.36

PS12785
131. If $x = -|w|$, which of the following must be true?

(A) $x = -w$

(B) $x = w$

(C) $x^2 = w$

(D) $x^2 = w^2$

(E) $x^3 = w^3$

PS04160
132. A certain financial institution reported that its assets totaled $2,377,366.30 on a certain day. Of this amount, $31,724.54 was held in cash. Approximately what percent of the reported assets was held in cash on that day?

(A) 0.00013%

(B) 0.0013%

(C) 0.013%

(D) 0.13%

(E) 1.3%

$$\begin{array}{r} AB \\ + \ BA \\ \hline AAC \end{array}$$

PS09820
133. In the correctly worked addition problem shown, where the sum of the two-digit positive integers AB and BA is the three-digit integer AAC, and A, B, and C are different digits, what is the units digit of the integer AAC?

(A) 9

(B) 6

(C) 3

(D) 2

(E) 0

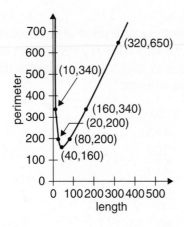

PS14060

134. Planning is in progress for a fenced, rectangular playground with an area of 1,600 square meters. The graph above shows the perimeter, in meters, as a function of the length of the playground. The length of the playground should be how many meters to minimize the perimeter and, therefore, the amount of fencing needed to enclose the playground?

   (A)   10
   (B)   40
   (C)   60
   (D)   160
   (E)   340

PS89670.02

135. The hard drive, monitor, and printer for a certain desktop computer system cost a total of $2,500. The cost of the printer and monitor together is equal to $\frac{2}{3}$ of the cost of the hard drive. If the cost of the printer is $100 more than the cost of the monitor, what is the cost of the printer?

   (A) $800
   (B) $600
   (C) $550
   (D) $500
   (E) $350

$$3r \leq 4s + 5$$
$$|s| \leq 5$$

PS06913

136. Given the inequalities above, which of the following CANNOT be the value of r ?

   (A)   −20
   (B)   −5
   (C)   0
   (D)   5
   (E)   20

PS11647

137. If m is an even integer, v is an odd integer, and m > v > 0, which of the following represents the number of even integers less than m and greater than v ?

   (A) $\dfrac{m-v}{2} - 1$

   (B) $\dfrac{m-v-1}{2}$

   (C) $\dfrac{m-v}{2}$

   (D) $m - v - 1$

   (E) $m - v$

PS02378

138. A positive integer is divisible by 9 if and only if the sum of its digits is divisible by 9. If n is a positive integer, for which of the following values of k is $25 \times 10^n + k \times 10^{2n}$ divisible by 9 ?

   (A)   9
   (B)   16
   (C)   23
   (D)   35
   (E)   47

PS17806

139. The perimeter of rectangle A is 200 meters. The length of rectangle B is 10 meters less than the length of rectangle A and the width of rectangle B is 10 meters more than the width of rectangle A. If rectangle B is a square, what is the width, in meters, of rectangle A ?

   (A)   10
   (B)   20
   (C)   40
   (D)   50
   (E)   60

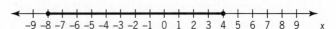

PS08598

140. On the number line, the shaded interval is the graph of which of the following inequalities?

   (A) $|x| \leq 4$
   (B) $|x| \leq 8$
   (C) $|x - 2| \leq 4$
   (D) $|x - 2| \leq 6$
   (E) $|x + 2| \leq 6$

PS12450

141. Last year members of a certain professional organization for teachers consisted of teachers from 49 different school districts, with an average (arithmetic mean) of 9.8 schools per district. Last year the average number of teachers at these schools who were members of the organization was 22. Which of the following is closest to the total number of members of the organization last year?

(A) 10^7

(B) 10^6

(C) 10^5

(D) 10^4

(E) 10^3

PS09294

142. Of all the students in a certain dormitory, $\frac{1}{2}$ are first-year students and the rest are second-year students. If $\frac{4}{5}$ of the first-year students have <u>not</u> declared a major and if the fraction of second-year students who have declared a major is 3 times the fraction of first-year students who have declared a major, what fraction of all the students in the dormitory are second-year students who have <u>not</u> declared a major?

(A) $\frac{1}{15}$

(B) $\frac{1}{5}$

(C) $\frac{4}{15}$

(D) $\frac{1}{3}$

(E) $\frac{2}{5}$

PS09050

143. If the average (arithmetic mean) of x, y, and z is $7x$ and $x \neq 0$, what is the ratio of x to the sum of y and z?

(A) 1:21

(B) 1:20

(C) 1:6

(D) 6:1

(E) 20:1

PS05413

144. Jonah drove the first half of a 100-mile trip in x hours and the second half in y hours. Which of the following is equal to Jonah's average speed, in miles per hour, for the entire trip?

(A) $\frac{50}{x+y}$

(B) $\frac{100}{x+y}$

(C) $\frac{25}{x}+\frac{25}{y}$

(D) $\frac{50}{x}+\frac{50}{y}$

(E) $\frac{100}{x}+\frac{100}{y}$

PS11454

145. In the xy-plane, the points (c,d), $(c,-d)$, and $(-c,-d)$ are three vertices of a certain square. If $c < 0$ and $d > 0$, which of the following points is in the same quadrant as the fourth vertex of the square?

(A) $(-5,-3)$

(B) $(-5,3)$

(C) $(5,-3)$

(D) $(3,-5)$

(E) $(3,5)$

PS05470

146. If the amount of federal estate tax due on an estate valued at $1.35 million is $437,000 plus 43 percent of the value of the estate in excess of $1.25 million, then the federal tax due is approximately what percent of the value of the estate?

A. 30%

B. 35%

C. 40%

D. 45%

E. 50%

$$7x + 6y \leq 38,000$$
$$4x + 5y \leq 28,000$$

PS30421.02

147. A manufacturer wants to produce x balls and y boxes. Resource constraints require that x and y satisfy the inequalities shown. What is the maximum number of balls and boxes combined that can be produced given the resource constraints?

(A)   5,000
(B)   6,000
(C)   7,000
(D)   8,000
(E)   10,000

PS05924

148. If $\dfrac{3}{10^4} = x\%$, then $x =$

(A)   0.3
(B)   0.03
(C)   0.003
(D)   0.0003
(E)   0.00003

PS01285

149. What is the remainder when 3^{24} is divided by 5 ?

(A)   0
(B)   1
(C)   2
(D)   3
(E)   4

PS16620.02

150. José has a collection of 100 coins, consisting of nickels, dimes, quarters, and half-dollars. If he has a total of 35 nickels and dimes, a total of 45 dimes and quarters, and a total of 50 nickels and quarters, how many half-dollars does he have?

(A)   15
(B)   20
(C)   25
(D)   30
(E)   35

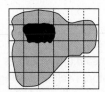

PS11692

151. In the figure shown, a square grid is superimposed on the map of a park, represented by the shaded region, in the middle of which is a pond, represented by the black region. If the area of the pond is 5,000 square yards, which of the following is closest to the area of the park, in square yards, including the area of the pond?

(A)   30,000
(B)   45,000
(C)   60,000
(D)   75,000
(E)   90,000

PS03623

152. If the volume of a ball is 32,490 cubic millimeters, what is the volume of the ball in cubic centimeters? (1 millimeter = 0.1 centimeter)

(A)   0.3249
(B)   3.249
(C)   32.49
(D)   324.9
(E)   3,249

PS07058

153. David used part of $100,000 to purchase a house. Of the remaining portion, he invested $\dfrac{1}{3}$ of it at 4 percent simple annual interest and $\dfrac{2}{3}$ of it at 6 percent simple annual interest. If after a year the income from the two investments totaled $320, what was the purchase price of the house?

(A) $96,000
(B) $94,000
(C) $88,000
(D) $75,000
(E) $40,000

PS09439

154. A certain manufacturer sells its product to stores in 113 different regions worldwide, with an average (arithmetic mean) of 181 stores per region. If last year these stores sold an average of 51,752 units of the manufacturer's product per store, which of the following is closest to the total number of units of the manufacturer's product sold worldwide last year?

(A) 10^6

(B) 10^7

(C) 10^8

(D) 10^9

(E) 10^{10}

PS17708

155. Andrew started saving at the beginning of the year and had saved $240 by the end of the year. He continued to save and by the end of 2 years had saved a total of $540. Which of the following is closest to the percent increase in the amount Andrew saved during the second year compared to the amount he saved during the first year?

(A) 11%

(B) 25%

(C) 44%

(D) 56%

(E) 125%

PS18180.02

156. If x is a positive integer, r is the remainder when x is divided by 4, and R is the remainder when x is divided by 9, what is the greatest possible value of $r^2 + R$?

(A) 25

(B) 21

(C) 17

(D) 13

(E) 11

PS34550.02

157. Each of the nine digits 0, 1, 1, 4, 5, 6, 8, 8, and 9 is used once to form 3 three-digit integers. What is the greatest possible sum of the 3 integers?

(A) 1,752

(B) 2,616

(C) 2,652

(D) 2,775

(E) 2,958

PS19941.02

158. Given that $1^2 + 2^2 + 3^2 + \ldots + 10^2 = 385$, what is the value of $3^2 + 6^2 + 9^2 + \ldots + 30^2$?

(A) 1,155

(B) 1,540

(C) 1,925

(D) 2,310

(E) 3,465

Questions 159 to 212 - Difficulty: Hard

PS19062

159. Two numbers differ by 2 and sum to S. Which of the following is the greater of the numbers in terms of S?

(A) $\dfrac{S}{2} - 1$

(B) $\dfrac{S}{2}$

(C) $\dfrac{S}{2} + \dfrac{1}{2}$

(D) $\dfrac{S}{2} + 1$

(E) $\dfrac{S}{2} + 2$

PS00904

160. The figure shown above consists of three identical circles that are tangent to each other. If the area of the shaded region is $64\sqrt{3} - 32\pi$, what is the radius of each circle?

(A) 4

(B) 8

(C) 16

(D) 24

(E) 32

PS24000.02

161. If m is an integer and $m = 10^{32} - 32$, what is the sum of the digits of m?

(A) 257

(B) 264

(C) 275

(D) 284

(E) 292

PS02053

162. In a numerical table with 10 rows and 10 columns, each entry is either a 9 or a 10. If the number of 9s in the nth row is $n - 1$ for each n from 1 to 10, what is the average (arithmetic mean) of all the numbers in the table?

(A)   9.45

(B)   9.50

(C)   9.55

(D)   9.65

(E)   9.70

PS76841.02

163. In 2004, the cost of 1 year-long print subscription to a certain newspaper was $4 per week. In 2005, the newspaper introduced a new rate plan for 1 year-long print subscription: $3 per week for the first 40 weeks of 2005 and $2 per week for the remaining weeks of 2005. How much less did 1 year-long print subscription to this newspaper cost in 2005 than in 2004 ?

(A) $64

(B) $78

(C) $112

(D) $144

(E) $304

PS08485

164. A positive integer n is a perfect number provided that the sum of all the positive factors of n, including 1 and n, is equal to $2n$. What is the sum of the reciprocals of all the positive factors of the perfect number 28 ?

(A) $\dfrac{1}{4}$

(B) $\dfrac{56}{27}$

(C)   2

(D)   3

(E)   4

PS11430

165. The infinite sequence $a_1, a_2, \ldots, a_n, \ldots$ is such that $a_1 = 2$, $a_2 = -3$, $a_3 = 5$, $a_4 = -1$, and $a_n = a_{n-4}$ for $n > 4$. What is the sum of the first 97 terms of the sequence?

(A)   72

(B)   74

(C)   75

(D)   78

(E)   80

PS09901

166. The sequence $a_1, a_2, \ldots a_n, \ldots$ is such that $a_n = 2a_{n-1} - x$ for all positive integers $n \geq 2$ and for a certain number x. If $a_5 = 99$ and $a_3 = 27$, what is the value of x ?

(A)   3

(B)   9

(C)   18

(D)   36

(E)   45

PS03779

167. A window is in the shape of a regular hexagon with each side of length 80 centimeters. If a diagonal through the center of the hexagon is w centimeters long, then $w =$

(A)   80

(B)   120

(C)   150

(D)   160

(E)   240

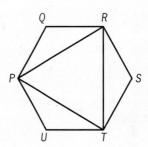

PS03695

168. In the figure shown, $PQRSTU$ is a regular polygon with sides of length x. What is the perimeter of triangle PRT in terms of x ?

(A) $\dfrac{x\sqrt{3}}{2}$

(B) $x\sqrt{3}$

(C) $\dfrac{3x\sqrt{3}}{2}$

(D) $3x\sqrt{3}$

(E) $4x\sqrt{3}$

PS11755
169. In a certain medical survey, 45 percent of the people surveyed had the type A antigen in their blood and 3 percent had both the type A antigen and the type B antigen. Which of the following is closest to the percent of those with the type A antigen who also had the type B antigen?

(A)   1.35%
(B)   6.67%
(C)   13.50%
(D)   15.00%
(E)   42.00%

PS05146
170. On a certain transatlantic crossing, 20 percent of a ship's passengers held round-trip tickets and also took their cars aboard the ship. If 60 percent of the passengers with round-trip tickets did not take their cars aboard the ship, what percent of the ship's passengers held round-trip tickets?

(A) $33\frac{1}{3}\%$
(B)   40%
(C)   50%
(D)   60%
(E) $66\frac{2}{3}\%$

PS03696
171. If x and k are integers and $(12^x)(4^{2x+1}) = (2^k)(3^2)$, what is the value of k?

(A)   5
(B)   7
(C)   10
(D)   12
(E)   14

PS11024
172. If S is the sum of the reciprocals of the 10 consecutive integers from 21 to 30, then S is between which of the following two fractions?

(A) $\frac{1}{3}$ and $\frac{1}{2}$

(B) $\frac{1}{4}$ and $\frac{1}{3}$

(C) $\frac{1}{5}$ and $\frac{1}{4}$

(D) $\frac{1}{6}$ and $\frac{1}{5}$

(E) $\frac{1}{7}$ and $\frac{1}{6}$

PS08729
173. For every even positive integer m, $f(m)$ represents the product of all even integers from 2 to m, inclusive. For example, $f(12) = 2 \times 4 \times 6 \times 8 \times 10 \times 12$. What is the greatest prime factor of $f(24)$?

(A)   23
(B)   19
(C)   17
(D)   13
(E)   11

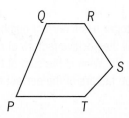

Note: Not drawn to scale.

PS08572
174. In pentagon $PQRST$, $PQ = 3$, $QR = 2$, $RS = 4$, and $ST = 5$. Which of the lengths 5, 10, and 15 could be the value of PT?

(A)   5 only
(B)   15 only
(C)   5 and 10 only
(D)   10 and 15 only
(E)   5, 10, and 15

3, *k*, 2, 8, *m*, 3

PS07771

175. The arithmetic mean of the list of numbers above is 4. If *k* and *m* are integers and *k* ≠ *m*, what is the median of the list?

(A) 2

(B) 2.5

(C) 3

(D) 3.5

(E) 4

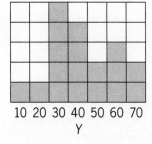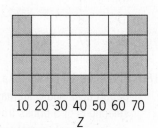

PS04987

176. If the variables, *X*, *Y*, and *Z* take on only the values 10, 20, 30, 40, 50, 60, or 70 with frequencies indicated by the shaded regions above, for which of the frequency distributions is the mean equal to the median?

(A) *X* only

(B) *Y* only

(C) *Z* only

(D) *X* and *Y*

(E) *X* and *Z*

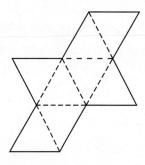

PS15538

177. When the figure above is cut along the solid lines, folded along the dashed lines, and taped along the solid lines, the result is a model of a geometric solid. This geometric solid consists of 2 pyramids, each with a square base that they share. What is the sum of the number of edges and the number of faces of this geometric solid?

(A) 10

(B) 18

(C) 20

(D) 24

(E) 25

$$2x + y = 12$$
$$|y| \le 12$$

PS03356

178. For how many ordered pairs (*x*,*y*) that are solutions of the system above are *x* and *y* both integers?

(A) 7

(B) 10

(C) 12

(D) 13

(E) 14

PS39160.02

179. The United States mint produces coins in 1-cent, 5-cent, 10-cent, 25-cent, and 50-cent denominations. If a jar contains exactly 100 cents worth of these coins, which of the following could be the total number of coins in the jar?

I.   91

II.   81

III. 76

(A) I only

(B) II only

(C) III only

(D) I and III only

(E) I, II, and III

139

PS08859

180. The points R, T, and U lie on a circle that has radius 4. If the length of arc RTU is $\dfrac{4\pi}{3}$, what is the length of line segment RU?

(A) $\dfrac{4}{3}$

(B) $\dfrac{8}{3}$

(C) 3

(D) 4

(E) 6

PS02955

181. A certain university will select 1 of 7 candidates eligible to fill a position in the mathematics department and 2 of 10 candidates eligible to fill 2 identical positions in the computer science department. If none of the candidates is eligible for a position in both departments, how many different sets of 3 candidates are there to fill the 3 positions?

(A) 42

(B) 70

(C) 140

(D) 165

(E) 315

PS06189

182. A survey of employers found that during 1993 employment costs rose 3.5 percent, where employment costs consist of salary costs and fringe-benefit costs. If salary costs rose 3 percent and fringe-benefit costs rose 5.5 percent during 1993, then fringe-benefit costs represented what percent of employment costs at the beginning of 1993?

(A) 16.5%

(B) 20%

(C) 35%

(D) 55%

(E) 65%

PS02528

183. The subsets of the set $\{w, x, y\}$ are $\{w\}$, $\{x\}$, $\{y\}$, $\{w, x\}$, $\{w, y\}$, $\{x, y\}$, $\{w, x, y\}$, and $\{\,\}$ (the empty subset). How many subsets of the set $\{w, x, y, z\}$ contain w?

(A) Four

(B) Five

(C) Seven

(D) Eight

(E) Sixteen

PS10309

184. There are 5 cars to be displayed in 5 parking spaces, with all the cars facing the same direction. Of the 5 cars, 3 are red, 1 is blue, and 1 is yellow. If the cars are identical except for color, how many different display arrangements of the 5 cars are possible?

(A) 20

(B) 25

(C) 40

(D) 60

(E) 125

PS17461

185. The number $\sqrt{63 - 36\sqrt{3}}$ can be expressed as $x + y\sqrt{3}$ for some integers x and y. What is the value of xy?

(A) −18

(B) −6

(C) 6

(D) 18

(E) 27

PS01334

186. There are 10 books on a shelf, of which 4 are paperbacks and 6 are hardbacks. How many possible selections of 5 books from the shelf contain at least one paperback and at least one hardback?

(A) 75

(B) 120

(C) 210

(D) 246

(E) 252

PS03774

187. If x is to be chosen at random from the set $\{1, 2, 3, 4\}$ and y is to be chosen at random from the set $\{5, 6, 7\}$, what is the probability that xy will be even?

(A) $\dfrac{1}{6}$

(B) $\dfrac{1}{3}$

(C) $\dfrac{1}{2}$

(D) $\dfrac{2}{3}$

(E) $\dfrac{5}{6}$

PS04254

188. The function f is defined for each positive three-digit integer n by $f(n) = 2^x \, 3^y \, 5^z$, where x, y, and z are the hundreds, tens, and units digits of n, respectively. If m and v are three-digit positive integers such that $f(m) = 9f(v)$, then $m - v =$

(A) 8
(B) 9
(C) 18
(C) 20
(E) 80

PS06312

189. If $10^{50} - 74$ is written as an integer in base 10 notation, what is the sum of the digits in that integer?

(A) 424
(B) 433
(C) 440
(D) 449
(E) 467

PS09056

190. A certain company that sells only cars and trucks reported that revenues from car sales in 1997 were down 11 percent from 1996 and revenues from truck sales in 1997 were up 7 percent from 1996. If total revenues from car sales and truck sales in 1997 were up 1 percent from 1996, what is the ratio of revenue from car sales in 1996 to revenue from truck sales in 1996 ?

(A) 1:2
(B) 4:5
(C) 1:1
(D) 3:2
(E) 5:3

PS14267

191. Becky rented a power tool from a rental shop. The rent for the tool was $12 for the first hour and $3 for each additional hour. If Becky paid a total of $27, excluding sales tax, to rent the tool, for how many hours did she rent it?

(A) 5
(B) 6
(C) 9
(D) 10
(E) 12

PS06959

192. If $4 < \dfrac{7 - x}{3}$, which of the following must be true?

I. $5 < x$
II. $|x + 3| > 2$
III. $-(x + 5)$ is positive.

(A) II only
(B) III only
(C) I and II only
(D) II and III only
(E) I, II, and III

PS08654

193. A certain right triangle has sides of length x, y, and z, where $x < y < z$. If the area of this triangular region is 1, which of the following indicates all of the possible values of y ?

(A) $y > \sqrt{2}$
(B) $\dfrac{\sqrt{3}}{2} < y < \sqrt{2}$
(C) $\dfrac{\sqrt{2}}{3} < y < \dfrac{\sqrt{3}}{2}$
(D) $\dfrac{\sqrt{3}}{4} < y < \dfrac{\sqrt{2}}{3}$
(E) $y < \dfrac{\sqrt{3}}{4}$

PS14397

194. On a certain day, a bakery produced a batch of rolls at a total production cost of $300. On that day, $\dfrac{4}{5}$ of the rolls in the batch were sold, each at a price that was 50 percent greater than the average (arithmetic mean) production cost per roll. The remaining rolls in the batch were sold the next day, each at a price that was 20 percent less than the price of the day before. What was the bakery's profit on this batch of rolls?

(A) $150
(B) $144
(C) $132
(D) $108
(E) $90

PS05972

195. A set of numbers has the property that for any number t in the set, $t + 2$ is in the set. If -1 is in the set, which of the following must also be in the set?

I. -3

II. 1

III. 5

(A)   I only

(B)   II only

(C)   I and II only

(D)   II and III only

(E)   I, II, and III

PS04780

196. A couple decides to have 4 children. If they succeed in having 4 children and each child is equally likely to be a boy or a girl, what is the probability that they will have exactly 2 girls and 2 boys?

(A) $\dfrac{3}{8}$

(B) $\dfrac{1}{4}$

(C) $\dfrac{3}{16}$

(D) $\dfrac{1}{8}$

(E) $\dfrac{1}{16}$

PS01564

197. The closing price of Stock X changed on each trading day last month. The percent change in the closing price of Stock X from the first trading day last month to each of the other trading days last month was less than 50 percent. If the closing price on the second trading day last month was $10.00, which of the following CANNOT be the closing price on the last trading day last month?

(A) $3.00

(B) $9.00

(C) $19.00

(D) $24.00

(E) $29.00

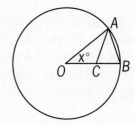

PS02389

198. In the figure above, point O is the center of the circle and $OC = AC = AB$. What is the value of x?

(A)   40

(B)   36

(C)   34

(D)   32

(E)   30

PS16967

199. An airline passenger is planning a trip that involves three connecting flights that leave from Airports A, B, and C, respectively. The first flight leaves Airport A every hour, beginning at 8:00 a.m., and arrives at Airport B $2\frac{1}{2}$ hours later. The second flight leaves Airport B every 20 minutes, beginning at 8:00 a.m., and arrives at Airport C $1\frac{1}{6}$ hours later. The third flight leaves Airport C every hour, beginning at 8:45 a.m. What is the least total amount of time the passenger must spend between flights if all flights keep to their schedules?

(A)   25 min

(B)   1 hr 5 min

(C)   1 hr 15 min

(D)   2 hr 20 min

(E)   3 hr 40 min

PS07426

200. If n is a positive integer and n^2 is divisible by 72, then the largest positive integer that must divide n is

(A)   6

(B)   12

(C)   24

(D)   36

(E)   48

PS16977

201. A certain grocery purchased x pounds of produce for p dollars per pound. If y pounds of the produce had to be discarded due to spoilage and the grocery sold the rest for s dollars per pound, which of the following represents the gross profit on the sale of the produce?

   (A) $(x - y)s - xp$

   (B) $(x - y)p - ys$

   (C) $(s - p)y - xp$

   (D) $xp - ys$

   (E) $(x - y)(s - p)$

PS16990

202. If x, y, and z are positive integers such that x is a factor of y, and x is a multiple of z, which of the following is NOT necessarily an integer?

   (A) $\dfrac{x+z}{z}$

   (B) $\dfrac{y+z}{x}$

   (C) $\dfrac{x+y}{z}$

   (D) $\dfrac{xy}{z}$

   (E) $\dfrac{yz}{x}$

PS08416

203. Running at their respective constant rates, Machine X takes 2 days longer to produce w widgets than Machine Y. At these rates, if the two machines together produce $\dfrac{5}{4}w$ widgets in 3 days, how many days would it take Machine X alone to produce $2w$ widgets?

   (A)   4

   (B)   6

   (C)   8

   (D)   10

   (E)   12

PS14051.02

204. What is the greatest positive integer n such that 5^n divides $10! - (2)(5!)^2$?

   (A)   2

   (B)   3

   (C)   4

   (D)   5

   (E)   6

PS12151.02

205. Yesterday, Candice and Sabrina trained for a bicycle race by riding around an oval track. They both began riding at the same time from the track's starting point. However, Candice rode at a faster pace than Sabrina, completing each lap around the track in 42 seconds, while Sabrina completed each lap around the track in 46 seconds. How many laps around the track had Candice completed the next time that Candice and Sabrina were together at the starting point?

   (A)   21

   (B)   23

   (C)   42

   (D)   46

   (E)   483

PS07117

206. A square wooden plaque has a square brass inlay in the center, leaving a wooden strip of uniform width around the brass square. If the ratio of the brass area to the wooden area is 25 to 39, which of the following could be the width, in inches, of the wooden strip?

   I.   1

   II.   3

   III.   4

   (A)   I only

   (B)   II only

   (C)   I and II only

   (D)   I and III only

   (E)   I, II, and III

PS66661.02

207. If $n = 9! - 6^4$, which of the following is the greatest integer k such that 3^k is a factor of n ?

   (A)   1

   (B)   3

   (C)   4

   (D)   6

   (E)   8

PS62451.02

208. The integer 120 has many factorizations. For example, $120 = (2)(60)$, $120 = (3)(4)(10)$, and $120 = (-1)(-3)(4)(10)$. In how many of the factorizations of 120 are the factors consecutive integers in ascending order?

(A) 2
(B) 3
(C) 4
(D) 5
(E) 6

PS65741.02

209. Jorge's bank statement showed a balance that was $0.54 greater than what his records showed. He discovered that he had written a check for $x.yz and had recorded it as $x.zy, where each of x, y, and z represents a digit from 0 though 9. Which of the following could be the value of z ?

(A) 2
(B) 3
(C) 4
(D) 5
(E) 6

PS79981.02

210. One side of a parking stall is defined by a straight stripe that consists of n painted sections of equal length with an unpainted section $\frac{1}{2}$ as long between each pair of consecutive painted sections. The total length of the stripe from the beginning of the first painted section to the end of the last painted section is 203 inches. If n is an integer and the length, in inches, of each unpainted section is an integer greater than 2, what is the value of n ?

(A) 5
(B) 9
(C) 10
(D) 14
(E) 29

PS16963

211. $\dfrac{2\frac{3}{5} - 1\frac{2}{3}}{\frac{2}{3} - \frac{3}{5}} =$

(A) 16
(B) 14
(C) 3
(D) 1
(E) −1

Machine	Consecutive Minutes Machine Is Off	Units of Power When On
A	17	15
B	14	18
C	11	12

PS67381.02

212. At a certain factory, each of Machines A, B, and C is periodically on for exactly 1 minute and periodically off for a fixed number of consecutive minutes. The table above shows that Machine A is on and uses 15 units of power every 18th minute, Machine B is on and uses 18 units of power every 15th minute, and Machine C is on and uses 12 units of power every 12th minute. The factory has a backup generator that operates only when the total power usage of the 3 machines exceeds 30 units of power. What is the time interval, in minutes, between consecutive times the backup generator begins to operate?

(A) 36
(B) 63
(C) 90
(D) 180
(E) 270

4.4 Answer Key

1.	A	33.	D	65.	B	97.	B	129.	E
2.	D	34.	E	66.	E	98.	B	130.	B
3.	A	35.	D	67.	B	99.	B	131.	D
4.	B	36.	C	68.	E	100.	B	132.	E
5.	D	37.	A	69.	D	101.	A	133.	E
6.	E	38.	C	70.	B	102.	C	134.	B
7.	C	39.	C	71.	C	103.	A	135.	C
8.	E	40.	E	72.	A	104.	B	136.	E
9.	A	41.	D	73.	E	105.	D	137.	B
10.	C	42.	D	74.	C	106.	D	138.	E
11.	C	43.	D	75.	C	107.	D	139.	C
12.	C	44.	A	76.	D	108.	D	140.	E
13.	C	45.	B	77.	B	109.	E	141.	D
14.	E	46.	C	78.	C	110.	D	142.	B
15.	E	47.	C	79.	D	111.	E	143.	B
16.	D	48.	D	80.	B	112.	D	144.	B
17.	B	49.	B	81.	A	113.	E	145.	E
18.	C	50.	C	82.	A	114.	E	146.	B
19.	D	51.	C	83.	E	115.	E	147.	B
20.	B	52.	E	84.	A	116.	C	148.	B
21.	D	53.	B	85.	B	117.	C	149.	B
22.	D	54.	B	86.	A	118.	A	150.	E
23.	B	55.	D	87.	E	119.	D	151.	B
24.	A	56.	D	88.	E	120.	C	152.	C
25.	B	57.	C	89.	D	121.	D	153.	B
26.	A	58.	B	90.	D	122.	A	154.	D
27.	C	59.	A	91.	C	123.	B	155.	B
28.	D	60.	C	92.	B	124.	D	156.	C
29.	B	61.	A	93.	B	125.	B	157.	C
30.	D	62.	C	94.	D	126.	C	158.	E
31.	E	63.	A	95.	D	127.	A	159.	D
32.	D	64.	D	96.	B	128.	B	160.	B

161.	D	172.	A	183.	D	194.	C	205.	B
162.	C	173.	E	184.	A	195.	D	206.	E
163.	A	174.	C	185.	A	196.	A	207.	D
164.	C	175.	C	186.	D	197.	A	208.	C
165.	B	176.	E	187.	D	198.	B	209.	E
166.	A	177.	C	188.	D	199.	B	210.	C
167.	D	178.	D	189.	C	200.	B	211.	B
168.	D	179.	D	190.	A	201.	A	212.	C
169.	B	180.	D	191.	B	202.	B		
170.	C	181.	E	192.	D	203.	E		
171.	E	182.	B	193.	A	204.	D		

4.5 Answer Explanations

The following discussion is intended to familiarize you with the most efficient and effective approaches to the kinds of problems common to Problem Solving questions. The particular questions in this chapter are generally representative of the kinds of problem solving questions you will encounter on the GMAT exam. Remember that it is the problem solving strategy that is important, not the specific details of a particular question.

Questions 1 to 81 - Difficulty: Easy

*PS03439

1. Working at a constant rate, a copy machine makes 20 copies of a one-page document per minute. If the machine works at this constant rate, how many hours does it take to make 4,800 copies of a one-page document?

    (A) 4
    (B) 5
    (C) 6
    (D) 7
    (E) 8

Arithmetic Rate

The copy machine produces 20 copies of the one-page document each minute. Because there are 60 minutes in an hour, the constant rate of 20 copies per minute is equal to $60 \times 20 = 1,200$ copies per hour. With the machine working at this rate, the amount of time that it takes to produce 4,800 copies of the document is

$$\frac{4800 \text{ copies}}{1200 \frac{\text{copies}}{\text{hour}}} = 4 \text{ hours.}$$

The correct answer is A.

PS11042

2. If $x + y = 2$ and $x^2 + y^2 = 2$, what is the value of xy?

    (A) −2
    (B) −1
    (C) 0
    (D) 1
    (E) 2

Algebra Second-Degree Equations

$x + y = 2$	given
$y = 2 - x$	subtract x from both sides
$x^2 + (2 - x)^2 = 2$	substitute $y = 2 - x$ into $x^2 + y^2 = 2$
$2x^2 - 4x + 4 = 2$	expand and combine like terms
$2x^2 - 4x + 2 = 0$	subtract 2 from both sides
$x^2 - 2x + 1 = 0$	divide both sides by 2
$(x - 1)(x - 1) = 0$	factor
$x = 1$	set each factor equal to 0
$y = 1$	use $x = 1$ and $y = 2 - x$
$xy = 1$	multiply 1 and 1

Alternatively, the value of xy can be found by first squaring both sides of the equation $x + y = 2$.

$x + y = 2$	given
$(x + y)^2 = 4$	square both sides
$x^2 + 2xy + y^2 = 4$	expand and combine like terms
$2 + 2xy = 4$	replace $x^2 + y^2$ with 2
$2xy = 2$	subtract 2 from both sides
$xy = 1$	divide both sides by 2

The correct answer is D.

PS02978

3. The sum S of the first n consecutive positive even integers is given by $S = n(n + 1)$. For what value of n is this sum equal to 110?

    (A) 10
    (B) 11
    (C) 12
    (D) 13
    (E) 14

---

*These numbers correlate with the online test bank question number. See the GMAT™ Official Guide Quantitative Review Question Index in the back of this book.

147

Algebra Factoring

Given that the sum of the first n even numbers is $n(n + 1)$, the sum is equal to 110 when $110 = n(n + 1)$. To find the value of n in this case, we need to find the two consecutive integers whose product is 110. These integers are 10 and 11; $10 \times 11 = 110$. The smaller of these numbers is n.

The correct answer is A.

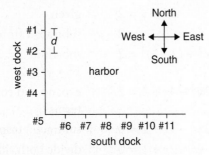

PS08375

4. A certain harbor has docking stations along its west and south docks, as shown in the figure; any two adjacent docking stations are separated by a uniform distance d. A certain boat left the west dock from docking station #2 and moved in a straight line diagonally until it reached the south dock. If the boat was at one time directly east of docking station #4 and directly north of docking station #7, at which docking station on the south dock did the boat arrive?

    (A) #7
    (B) #8
    (C) #9
    (D) #10
    (E) #11

Geometry Coordinate Geometry

The boat traveled in a straight line from docking station #2 on the west dock to one of the docking stations on the south dock, passing through a single point that is both due east of docking station #4 and due north of docking station #7. Call this point P. Having traveled to P, the boat was both $2d$ south of its starting point and $2d$ east of its starting point. Therefore, traveling in a straight line, the boat traveled one unit south for every one unit traveled east. And because at point P the boat was a distance d north of the south dock, the boat must have reached the south dock at a point which is a distance of d east of docking

station #7 (which is due south of point P). This point is the position of docking station #8. The boat therefore arrived at docking station #8.

The correct answer is B.

PS03887

5. $6(87.30 + 0.65) - 5(87.30) =$

    (A) 3.90
    (B) 39.00
    (C) 90.90
    (D) 91.20
    (E) 91.85

Arithmetic Factors, Multiples, and Divisibility

This question is most efficiently answered by distributing the 6 over 87.30 and 0.65, and then combining the terms that contain a factor of 87.30, as follows:

$6(87.30 + 0.65) - 5(87.30) = 6\ (87.30) + 6\ (0.65) - 5\ (87.30) = (6 - 5)\ 87.30 + 6(0.65) = 87.30 + 3.90 = 91.20$

The correct answer is D.

PS13800

6. Points A, B, C, and D, in that order, lie on a line. If $AB = 3$ cm, $AC = 4$ cm, and $BD = 6$ cm, what is CD, in centimeters?

    (A) 1
    (B) 2
    (C) 3
    (D) 4
    (E) 5

Geometry Lines and Segments

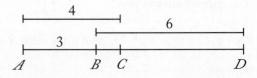

The figure shows points A, B, C, and D as well as the given measurements. Since $AC = AB + BC$, it follows that $4 = 3 + BC$, and so $BC = 1$. Then, since $BD = BC + CD$, it follows that $6 = 1 + CD$, and so $CD = 5$.

Alternately, $AD = AB + BD = 3 + 6 = 9$. Also, $AD = AC + CD$, so $9 = 4 + CD$ and $CD = 5$.

The correct answer is E.

PS05292

7. What is the value of $x^2yz - xyz^2$, if $x = -2$, $y = 1$, and $z = 3$?

    (A)   20
    (B)   24
    (C)   30
    (D)   32
    (E)   48

Algebra Operations on Integers

Given that $x = -2$, $y = 1$, and $z = 3$, it follows by substitution that

$$x^2yz - xyz^2 = (-2)^2(1)(3) - (-2)(1)(3^2)$$
$$= (4)(1)(3) - (-2)(1)(9)$$
$$= 12 - (-18)$$
$$= 12 + 18$$
$$= 30$$

The correct answer is C.

PS11468

8. A souvenir vendor purchased 1,000 shirts for a special event at a price of $5 each. The vendor sold 600 of the shirts on the day of the event for $12 each and 300 of the shirts in the week following the event for $4 each. The vendor was unable to sell the remaining shirts. What was the vendor's gross profit on the sale of these shirts?

    (A) $1,000
    (B) $2,200
    (C) $2,700
    (D) $3,000
    (E) $3,400

Arithmetic Applied Problems

The vendor's gross profit on the sale of the shirts is equal to the total revenue from the shirts that were sold minus the total cost for all of the shirts. The total cost for all of the shirts is equal to the number of shirts the vendor purchased multiplied by the price paid by the vendor for each shirt: $1,000 \times \$5 = \$5,000$. The total revenue from the shirts that were sold is equal to the total revenue from the 600 shirts sold for $12 each plus the total revenue from the 300 shirts that were sold

for $4 each: $600 \times \$12 + 300 \times \$4 = \$7,200 + \$1,200 = \$8,400$. The gross profit is therefore $\$8,400 - \$5,000 = \$3,400$.

The correct answer is E.

PS06937

9. If $x > y$ and $y > z$, which of the following represents the greatest number?

    (A) $x - z$
    (B) $x - y$
    (C) $y - x$
    (D) $z - y$
    (E) $z - x$

Algebra Inequalities

From $x > y$ and $y > z$, it follows that $x > z$. These inequalities imply the following about the differences that are given in the answer choices:

Answer choice	Difference	Algebraic sign	Reason
A	$x - z$	positive	$x > z$ implies $x - z > 0$
B	$x - y$	positive	$x > y$ implies $x - y > 0$
C	$y - x$	negative	$x - y > 0$ implies $y - x < 0$
D	$z - y$	negative	$y > z$ implies $0 > z - y$
E	$z - x$	negative	$x - z > 0$ implies $z - x < 0$

Since the expressions in A and B represent positive numbers and the expressions in C, D, and E represent negative numbers, the latter can be eliminated because every negative number is less than every positive number. To determine which of $x - z$ and $x - y$ is greater, consider the placement of points with coordinates x, y, and z on the number line.

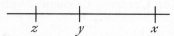

The distance between x and z (that is, $x - z$) is the sum of the distance between x and y (that is, $x - y$) and the distance between y and z (that is, $y - z$).

Therefore, $(x - z) > (x - y)$, which means that $x - z$ represents the greater of the numbers represented by $(x - z)$ and $(x - y)$. Thus, $x - z$ represents the greatest of the numbers represented by the answer choices.

Alternatively,

$y > z$	given
$-y < -z$	multiply both sides by -1
$x - y < x - z$	add x to both sides

Thus, $x - z$ represents the greater of the numbers represented by $(x - z)$ and $(x - y)$. Therefore, $x - z$ represents the greatest of the numbers represented by the answer choices.

The correct answer is A.

PS12926

10. To order certain plants from a catalog, it costs $3.00 per plant, plus a 5 percent sales tax, plus $6.95 for shipping and handling regardless of the number of plants ordered. If Company C ordered these plants from the catalog at the total cost of $69.95, how many plants did Company C order?

(A) 22
(B) 21
(C) 20
(D) 19
(E) 18

Algebra First-Degree Equations

Letting x represent the number of plants Company C bought from the catalog, then, in dollars, $3.00x$ is the cost of the plants, $(0.05)(3.00x)$ is the sales tax, and 6.95 is the shipping and handling fee. It follows that

$3.00x + (0.05)(3.00x) + 6.95 = 69.95$	plants + tax + shipping = total
$(3.00x)(1.05) + 6.95 = 69.95$	add like terms
$(3.00x)(1.05) = 63.00$	subtract 6.95 from both sides
$x = 20$	divide both sides by $(3.00)(1.05)$

Therefore, Company C bought 20 plants from the catalog.

The correct answer is C.

PS00812

11. A rug manufacturer produces rugs at a cost of $75 per rug. What is the manufacturer's gross profit from the sale of 150 rugs if $\frac{2}{3}$ of the rugs are sold for $150 per rug and the rest are sold for $200 per rug?

(A) $10,350
(B) $11,250
(C) $13,750
(D) $16,250
(E) $17,800

Arithmetic Applied Problems; Proportions

The gross profit from the sale of 150 rugs is equal to the revenue from the sale of the rugs minus the cost of producing them. For $\frac{2}{3}$ of the 150 rugs—100 of them—the gross profit per rug is $150 - $75 = 75. For the remaining 50 rugs, the gross profit per rug is $200 - $75 = 125. The gross profit from the sale of the 150 rugs is therefore $100 \times $75 + 50 \times $125 = $13,750$.

The correct answer is C.

PS07793

12. The value of Maureen's investment portfolio has decreased by 5.8 percent since her initial investment in the portfolio. If her initial investment was $16,800, what is the current value of the portfolio?

(A) $7,056.00
(B) $14,280.00
(C) $15,825.60
(D) $16,702.56
(E) $17,774.40

Arithmetic Percents

Maureen's initial investment was $16,800, and it has decreased by 5.8%. Its current value is therefore $(100\% - 5.8\%) = 94.2\%$ of $16,800, which is equal to $0.942 \times $16,800$. To make the multiplication simpler, this can be expressed as (942×16.8). Thus multiplying, we obtain the result of $15,825.60.

The correct answer is C.

PS03036

13. Company C produces toy trucks at a cost of $5.00 each for the first 100 trucks and $3.50 for each additional truck. If 500 toy trucks were produced by Company C and sold for $10.00 each, what was Company C's gross profit?

(A) $2,250
(B) $2,500
(C) $3,100
(D) $3,250
(E) $3,500

Arithmetic Applied Problems

The company's gross profit on the 500 toy trucks is the company's revenue from selling the trucks minus the company's cost of producing the trucks. The revenue is $(500)(\$10.00) = \$5,000$. The cost for the first 100 trucks is $(100)(\$5.00) = \$500$, and the cost for the other 400 trucks is $(400)(\$3.50) = \$1,400$ for a total cost of $\$500 + \$1,400 = \$1,900$. Thus, the company's gross profit is $\$5,000 - \$1,900 = \$3,100$.

The correct answer is C.

Division	Profit or Loss (in millions of dollars)				
	1991	1992	1993	1994	1995
A	1.1	(3.4)	1.9	2.0	0.6
B	(2.3)	5.5	(4.5)	3.9	(2.9)
C	10.0	(6.6)	5.3	1.1	(3.0)

PS02019

14. The annual profit or loss for the three divisions of Company T for the years 1991 through 1995 are summarized in the table shown, where losses are enclosed in parentheses. For which division and which three consecutive years shown was the division's profit or loss for the three-year period closest to $0 ?

(A) Division A for 1991–1993
(B) Division A for 1992–1994
(C) Division B for 1991–1993
(D) Division B for 1993–1995
(E) Division C for 1992–1994

Arithmetic Applied Problems

For completeness, the table shows all 9 of the profit or loss amounts, in millions of dollars, for each of the 3 divisions and the 3 three-year periods.

	1991–1993	1992–1994	1993–1995
A	−0.4	0.5	4.5
B	−1.3	4.9	−3.5
C	8.7	**−0.2**	3.4

The correct answer is E.

PS13583

15. Of the following, which is least?

(A) $\dfrac{0.03}{0.00071}$
(B) $\dfrac{0.03}{0.0071}$
(C) $\dfrac{0.03}{0.071}$
(D) $\dfrac{0.03}{0.71}$
(E) $\dfrac{0.03}{7.1}$

Arithmetic Operations on Rational Numbers

Since the numerator of all of the fractions in the answer choices is 0.03, the least of the fractions will be the fraction with the greatest denominator. The greatest denominator is 7.1, and so the least of the fractions is $\dfrac{0.03}{7.1}$.

The correct answer is E.

PS08011

16. If the average (arithmetic mean) of 5 numbers $j, j + 5, 2j - 1, 4j - 2$, and $5j - 1$ is 8, what is the value of j ?

(A) $\dfrac{1}{3}$
(B) $\dfrac{7}{13}$
(C) 1
(D) 3
(E) 8

Algebra First-Degree Equations

$$\frac{j + (j + 5) + (2j - 1) + (4j - 2) + (5j - 1)}{5} = 8 \quad \text{given}$$

$$j + (j + 5) + (2j - 1) + (4j - 2) + (5j - 1) = 40 \quad \begin{array}{l}\text{multiply}\\\text{both sides}\\\text{by 5}\end{array}$$

$$13j + 1 = 40 \quad \begin{array}{l}\text{combine}\\\text{like terms}\end{array}$$

$$13j = 39 \quad \begin{array}{l}\text{subtract 1}\\\text{from both}\\\text{sides}\end{array}$$

$$j = 3 \quad \begin{array}{l}\text{divide}\\\text{both sides}\\\text{by 13}\end{array}$$

The correct answer is D.

PS14037

17. Guadalupe owns 2 rectangular tracts of land. One is 300 m by 500 m and the other is 250 m by 630 m. The combined area of these 2 tracts is how many square meters?

(A) 3,360
(B) 307,500
(C) 621,500
(D) 704,000
(E) 2,816,000

Geometry Area

The area of a rectangle can be found by multiplying the length and width of the rectangle. Therefore, the combined area, in square meters, of the 2 rectangular tracts of land is $(300)(500) + (250)(630) = 150,000 + 157,500 = 307,500$.

The correct answer is B.

PS03918

18. There are five sales agents in a certain real estate office. One month Andy sold twice as many properties as Ellen, Bob sold 3 more than Ellen, Cary sold twice as many as Bob, and Dora sold as many as Bob and Ellen together. Who sold the most properties that month?

(A) Andy
(B) Bob
(C) Cary
(D) Dora
(E) Ellen

Algebra Order

Let x represent the number of properties that Ellen sold, where $x \geq 0$. Then, since Andy sold twice as many properties as Ellen, $2x$ represents the number of properties that Andy sold. Bob sold 3 more properties than Ellen, so $(x + 3)$ represents the number of properties that Bob sold. Cary sold twice as many properties as Bob, so $2(x + 3) = (2x + 6)$ represents the number of properties that Cary sold. Finally, Dora sold as many properties as Bob and Ellen combined, so $[(x + 3) + x] = (2x + 3)$ represents the number of properties that Dora sold. The following table summarizes these results.

Agent	Properties Sold
Andy	$2x$
Bob	$x + 3$
Cary	$2x + 6$
Dora	$2x + 3$
Ellen	x

Since $x \geq 0$, clearly $2x + 6$ exceeds x, $x + 3$, $2x$, and $2x + 3$. Therefore, Cary sold the most properties.

The correct answer is C.

PS10862

19. In a field day at a school, each child who competed in n events and scored a total of p points was given an overall score of $\frac{p}{n} + n$. Andrew competed in 1 event and scored 9 points. Jason competed in 3 events and scored 5, 6, and 7 points, respectively. What was the ratio of Andrew's overall score to Jason's overall score?

(A) $\dfrac{10}{23}$

(B) $\dfrac{7}{10}$

(C) $\dfrac{4}{5}$

(D) $\dfrac{10}{9}$

(E) $\dfrac{12}{7}$

Algebra Applied Problems; Substitution

Andrew participated in 1 event and scored

9 points, so his overall score was $\frac{9}{1} + 1 = 10$. Jason

participated in 3 events and scored $5 + 6 + 7 =$

18 points, so his overall score was $\frac{18}{3} + 3 = 9$. The

ratio of Andrew's overall score to Jason's overall

score was $\frac{10}{9}$.

The correct answer is D.

PS06719

20. A certain work plan for September requires that a
     work team, working every day, produce an average of
     200 items per day. For the first half of the month, the
     team produced an average of 150 items per day. How
     many items per day must the team average during the
     second half of the month if it is to attain the average
     daily production rate required by the work plan?

     (A) 225
     (B) 250
     (C) 275
     (D) 300
     (E) 350

Arithmetic Rate Problem

The work plan requires that the team produce
an average of 200 items per day in September.
Because the team has only produced an average of
150 items per day in the first half of September, it
has a shortfall of 200 − 150 = 50 items per day for
the first half of the month. The team must make
up for this shortfall in the second half of the
month, which has an equal number of days as the
first half of the month. The team must therefore
produce in the second half of the month an
average amount per day that is 50 items greater
than the required average of 200 items per day for
the entire month. This amount for the second half
of September is 250 items per day.

The correct answer is B.

PS01949

21. A company sells radios for $15.00 each. It costs the
     company $14.00 per radio to produce 1,000 radios
     and $13.50 per radio to produce 2,000 radios. How
     much greater will the company's gross profit be from
     the production and sale of 2,000 radios than from the
     production and sale of 1,000 radios?

     (A) $500
     (B) $1,000
     (C) $1,500
     (D) $2,000
     (E) $2,500

Arithmetic Applied Problems

If the company produces and sells 1,000 radios,
its gross profit from the sale of these radios is
equal to the total revenue from the sale of these
radios minus the total cost. The total cost is equal
to the number of radios produced multiplied by
the production cost per radio: $1,000 \times \$15.00$.
The total revenue is equal to the number of
radios sold multiplied by the selling price:
$1,000 \times \$14.00$. The gross profit in this case is
therefore $1,000 \times \$15.00 - 1,000 \times \$14.00 =$
$1,000 \times (\$15.00 - \$14.00) = 1,000 (\$1.00) =$
$\$1,000$. If 2,000 radios are produced and sold,
the total cost is equal to $2,000 \times \$13.50$ and the
total revenue is equal to $2,000 \times \$15.00$. The gross
profit in this case is therefore $2,000 \times \$15.00 -$
$2,000 \times \$13.50 = 2,000 \times (\$15.00 - \$13.50) =$
$2,000 \times (\$1.50) = \$3,000$. This profit of $3,000
is $2,000 greater than the gross profit of $1,000
from producing and selling 1,000 radios.

The correct answer is D.

PS06555

22. Which of the following represent positive numbers?

     I.   −3 − (−5)
     II.   (−3)(−5)
     III. −5 − (−3)

     (A) I only
     (B) II only
     (C) III only
     (D) I and II
     (E) II and III

Arithmetic Operations on Integers

Find the value of each expression to determine if it is positive.

  I. $-3 - (-5) = -3 + 5 = 2$, which is positive.

  II. $(-3)(-5) = 15$, which is positive.

  III. $-5 - (-3) = -5 + 3 = -2$, which is not positive.

The correct answer is D.

PS09983

23. Point *X* lies on side *BC* of rectangle *ABCD*, which has length 12 and width 8. What is the area of triangular region *AXD* ?

(A)   96
(B)   48
(C)   32
(D)   24
(E)   20

Geometry Area

Note that, in rectangle *ABCD*, the sides *BC* and *AD* do not share an endpoint and must therefore be on opposite sides of the rectangle. We thus see that the point *X*, which is both on triangle *AXD* and on side *BC* of the rectangle, lies on the side of the rectangle that is opposite the side *AD* of the rectangle. *AD* is also a side of the triangle. So if the rectangle is drawn with *AD* horizontal and on the bottom (see the diagram, which is not drawn to scale), the vertical height of the triangle from the base *AD* is equal to the length of the sides on the rectangle that are adjacent to *AD*. Given the formula for the area of a triangle, $\frac{1}{2} \times$ base $\times$ height, the area of the triangle *AXD* is thus $\frac{1}{2} \times AD \times AB$ (or equivalently $\frac{1}{2} \times AD \times CD$).

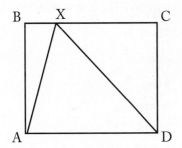

Now, *AD* may be either a length or a width of the rectangle—equal to 12 or equal to 8. If *AD* is equal to 12, then *AB* is a width and is equal to 8; the area of the triangle is thus $\frac{1}{2} \times 12 \times 8$. If *AD* is instead equal to 8, then *AB* is equal to 12, and the formula for the area of the triangle results in the expression $\frac{1}{2} \times 8 \times 12$. In both cases, the area of the triangle is equal to 48.

The correct answer is B.

PS07659

24. A grocer has 400 pounds of coffee in stock, 20 percent of which is decaffeinated. If the grocer buys another 100 pounds of coffee of which 60 percent is decaffeinated, what percent, by weight, of the grocer's stock of coffee is decaffeinated?

(A)   28%
(B)   30%
(C)   32%
(D)   34%
(E)   40%

Arithmetic Percents

The grocer has 400 pounds of coffee in stock, of which $(400)(20\%) = 80$ pounds is decaffeinated coffee. Therefore, if the grocer buys 100 pounds of coffee, of which $(100)(60\%) = 60$ pounds is decaffeinated coffee, then the percent of the grocer's stock of coffee that is decaffeinated would be $\frac{80 + 60}{400 + 100} = \frac{140}{500} = \frac{28}{100} = 28\%$.

The correct answer is A.

PS05129

25. The toll *T*, in dollars, for a truck using a certain bridge is given by the formula $T = 1.50 + 0.50(x - 2)$, where *x* is the number of axles on the truck. What is the toll for an 18-wheel truck that has 2 wheels on its front axle and 4 wheels on each of its other axles?

(A) $2.50
(B) $3.00
(C) $3.50
(D) $4.00
(E) $5.00

Algebra Operations on Rational Numbers

The 18-wheel truck has 2 wheels on its front axle and 4 wheels on each of its other axles, and so if A represents the number of axles on the truck in addition to the front axle, then $2 + 4A = 18$, from which it follows that $4A = 16$ and $A = 4$. Therefore, the total number of axles on the truck is $1 + A = 1 + 4 = 5$. Then, using $T = 1.50 + 0.50(x - 2)$, where x is the number of axles on the truck and $x = 5$, it follows that $T = 1.50 + 0.50(5 - 2) = 1.50 + 1.50 = 3.00$. Therefore, the toll for the truck is $3.00.

The correct answer is B.

PS13917

26. For what value of x between -4 and 4, inclusive, is the value of $x^2 - 10x + 16$ the greatest?

(A) -4

(B) -2

(C) 0

(D) 2

(E) 4

Algebra Second-Degree Equations

Given the expression $x^2 - 10x + 16$, a table of values can be created for the corresponding function $f(x) = x^2 - 10x + 16$ and the graph in the standard (x, y) coordinate plane can be sketched by plotting selected points:

x	$f(x)$
-4	72
-3	55
-2	40
-1	27
0	16
1	7
2	0
3	-5
4	-8
5	-9
6	-8
7	-5
8	0
9	7

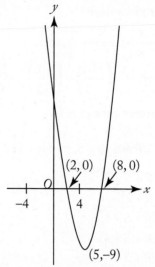

It is clear from both the table of values and the sketch of the graph that as the value of x increases from -4 to 4, the values of $x^2 - 10x + 16$ decrease. Therefore, the value of $x^2 - 10x + 16$ is greatest when $x = -4$.

Alternatively, the given expression, $x^2 - 10x + 16$, has the form $ax^2 + bx + c$, where $a = 1$, $b = -10$, and $c = 16$. The graph in the standard (x, y) coordinate plane of the corresponding function $f(x) = ax^2 + bx + c$ is a parabola with vertex at $x = -\dfrac{b}{2a}$, and so the vertex of the graph of $f(x) = x^2 - 10x + 16$ is at

$$x = -\left(\frac{-10}{2(1)}\right) = 5.$$

Because $a = 1$ and 1 is positive, this parabola opens upward and values of $x^2 - 10x + 16$ decrease as x increases from -4 to 4. Therefore, the greatest value of $x^2 - 10x + 16$ for all values of x between -4 and 4, inclusive, is at $x = -4$.

The correct answer is A.

PS15994

27. If $x = -\dfrac{5}{8}$ and $y = -\dfrac{1}{2}$, what is the value of the expression $-2x - y^2$?

(A) $-\dfrac{3}{2}$

(B) -1

(C) 1

(D) $\dfrac{3}{2}$

(E) $\dfrac{7}{4}$

Algebra Fractions

If $x = -\dfrac{5}{8}$ and $y = -\dfrac{1}{2}$, then

$$-2x - y^2 = -2\left(-\dfrac{5}{8}\right) - \left(-\dfrac{1}{2}\right)^2 = \dfrac{5}{4} - \dfrac{1}{4} = \dfrac{4}{4} = 1.$$

The correct answer is C.

PS13686

28. If $x - y = R$ and $xy = S$, then $(x - 2)(y + 2) =$

(A) $R + S - 4$

(B) $R + 2S - 4$

(C) $2R - S - 4$

(D) $2R + S - 4$

(E) $2R + S$

Algebra Simplifying Algebraic Expressions; Substitution

$$
\begin{aligned}
(x - 2)(y + 2) &= xy + 2x - 2y - 4 \quad \text{multiply binomials}\\
&= xy + 2(x - y) - 4 \quad \text{distributive principle}\\
&= S + 2R - 4 \quad\quad\quad\ \text{substitution}\\
&= 2R + S - 4 \quad\quad\quad \text{commutative principle}
\end{aligned}
$$

The correct answer is D.

PS01466

29. For positive integers a and b, the remainder when a is divided by b is equal to the remainder when b is divided by a. Which of the following could be a value of ab ?

I.   24

II. 30

III. 36

(A) II only

(B) III only

(C) I and II only

(D) II and III only

(E) I, II, and III

Arithmetic Properties of Integers

We are given that the remainder when a is divided by b is equal to the remainder when b is divided by a, and asked about possible values of ab. We thus need to find what our given condition implies about a and b.

We consider two cases: $a = b$ and $a \neq b$.

If $a = b$, then our given condition is trivially satisfied: the remainder when a is divided by a is equal to the remainder when a is divided by b. The condition thus allows that a be equal to b.

Now consider the case of $a \neq b$. Either $a < b$ or $b < a$. Supposing that $a < b$, the remainder when a is divided by b is simply a. (For example, if 7 is divided by 10, then the remainder is 7.) However, according to our given condition, this remainder, a, is also the remainder when b is divided by a, which is impossible. If b is divided by a, then the remainder must be less than a. (For example, for any number that is divided by 10, the remainder cannot be 10 or greater.) Similar reasoning applies if we suppose that $b < a$. This is also impossible.

We thus see that a must be equal to b, and consider the statements I, II, and III.

I.   Factored in terms of prime numbers, $24 = 3 \times 2 \times 2 \times 2$. Because "3" occurs only once in the factorization, we see that there is no integer a such that $a \times a = 24$. Based on the reasoning above, we see that 24 cannot be a value of ab.

II. Factored in terms of prime numbers, $30 = 5 \times 3 \times 2$. Because there is no integer a such that $a \times a = 30$, we see that 30 cannot be a value of ab.

III. Because $36 = 6 \times 6$, we see that 36 is a possible value of ab (with $a = b$).

The correct answer is B.

PS01867

30. List S consists of the positive integers that are multiples of 9 and are less than 100. What is the median of the integers in S ?

(A) 36

(B) 45

(C) 49

(D) 54

(E) 63

Arithmetic Series and Sequences

In the set of positive integers less than 100, the greatest multiple of 9 is 99 (9×11) and the least multiple of 9 is 9 (9×1). The sequence of positive multiples of 9 that are less than 100 is therefore the sequence of numbers $9 \times k$, where k ranges from 1 through 11. The median of the numbers k from 1 through 11 is 6. Therefore the median of the numbers $9 \times k$, where k ranges from 1 through 11, is $9 \times 6 = 54$.

The correct answer is D.

PS07380

31. A rope 20.6 meters long is cut into two pieces. If the length of one piece of rope is 2.8 meters shorter than the length of the other, what is the length, in meters, of the longer piece of rope?

(A)   7.5
(B)   8.9
(C)   9.9
(D)   10.3
(E)   11.7

Algebra First-Degree Equations

If x represents the length of the longer piece of rope, then $x - 2.8$ represents the length of the shorter piece, where both lengths are in meters. The total length of the two pieces of rope is 20.6 meters so,

$$
\begin{aligned}
x + (x - 2.8) &= 20.6 \quad \text{given} \\
2x - 2.8 &= 20.6 \quad \text{add like terms} \\
2x &= 23.4 \quad \text{add 2.8 to both sides} \\
x &= 11.7 \quad \text{divide both sides by 2}
\end{aligned}
$$

Thus, the length of the longer piece of rope is 11.7 meters.

The correct answer is E.

PS01120

32. If x and y are integers and x − y is odd, which of the following must be true?

I. xy is even.
II. $x^2 + y^2$ is odd.
III. $(x + y)^2$ is even.

(A)   I only
(B)   II only
(C)   III only
(D)   I and II only
(E)   I, II, and III

Arithmetic Properties of Numbers

We are given that x and y are integers and that $x - y$ is odd, and then asked, for various operations on x and y, whether the results of the operations are odd or even. It is therefore useful to determine, given that $x - y$ is odd, whether x and y are odd or even. If both x and y are even—that is, divisible by 2—then $x - y = 2m - 2n = 2(m - n)$ for integers m and n. We thus see if both x and y are even then $x - y$ cannot be odd. And because $x - y$ *is* odd, we see that x and y cannot both be even. Similarly, if both x and y are odd, then, for integers j and k, $x = 2j + 1$ and $y = 2k + 1$. Therefore, $x - y = (2j + 1) - (2k + 1)$. The ones cancel, and we are left with $x - y = 2j - 2k = 2(j - k)$. Because $2(j - k)$ would be even, x and y cannot both be odd if $x - y$ is odd. It follows from all of this that one of x or y must be even and the other odd.

Now consider the statements I through III.

I.   If one of x or y is even, then one of x or y is divisible by 2. It follows that xy is divisible by 2 and that xy is even.

II. Given that a number x or y is odd—not divisible by 2—we know that its product with itself is not divisible by 2 and is therefore odd. On the other hand, given that a number x or y is even, we know that its product with itself *is* divisible by 2 and is therefore even. The sum $x^2 + y^2$ is therefore the sum of an even number and an odd number. In such a case, the sum can be written as $(2m) + (2n + 1) = 2(m + n) + 1$, with m and n integers. It follows that $x^2 + y^2$ is not divisible by 2 and is therefore odd.

III. We know that one of x or y is even and the other is odd. We can therefore see from the discussion of statement II that $x + y$ is odd, and then also see, from the discussion of statement II, that the product of $x + y$ with itself, $(x + y)^2$, is odd.

The correct answer is D.

PS00335

33. On Monday, the opening price of a certain stock was $100 per share and its closing price was $110 per share. On Tuesday the closing price of the stock was 10 percent less than its closing price on Monday, and on Wednesday the closing price of the stock was 4 percent greater than its closing price on Tuesday. What was the approximate percent change in the price of the stock from its opening price on Monday to its closing price on Wednesday?

(A) A decrease of 6%
(B) A decrease of 4%
(C) A decrease of 1%
(D) An increase of 3%
(E) An increase of 4%

Arithmetic Percents

The closing share price on Tuesday was 10% less than the closing price on Monday, $110. 10% of $110 is equal to $0.1 \times \$110 = \$11$, so the closing price on Tuesday was $110 - \$11 = \$99$. The closing price on Wednesday was 4% greater than this: $99 + (0.04 \times \$99) = \$99 + \$3.96 = \$102.96$. This value, $102.96, is 2.96% greater than $100, the opening price on Monday. The percentage change from the opening share price on Monday is therefore an increase of approximately 3%, which is the closest of the available answers to an increase of 2.96%.

The correct answer is D.

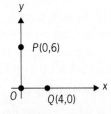

PS05109

34. In the rectangular coordinate system shown above, points O, P, and Q represent the sites of three proposed housing developments. If a fire station can be built at any point in the coordinate system, at which point would it be equidistant from all three developments?

(A) (3,1)
(B) (1,3)
(C) (3,2)
(D) (2,2)
(E) (2,3)

Geometry Coordinate Geometry

Any point equidistant from the points (0,0) and (4,0) must lie on the perpendicular bisector of the segment with endpoints (0,0) and (4,0), which is the line with equation $x = 2$. Any point equidistant from the points (0,0) and (0,6) must lie on the perpendicular bisector of the segment with endpoints (0,0) and (0,6), which is the line with equation $y = 3$. Therefore, the point that is equidistant from (0,0), (4,0), and (0,6) must lie on both of the lines $x = 2$ and $y = 3$, which is the point (2,3).

Alternatively, let (x,y) be the point equidistant from (0,0), (4,0), and (0,6). Since the distance between (x,y) and (0,0) is equal to the distance between (x,y) and (4,0), it follows from the distance formula that $\sqrt{x^2 + y^2} = \sqrt{(x-4)^2 + y^2}$. Squaring both sides gives $x^2 + y^2 = (x-4)^2 + y^2$. Subtracting y^2 from both sides of the last equation and then expanding the right side gives $x^2 = x^2 - 8x + 16$, or $0 = -8x + 16$, or $x = 2$. Also, since the distance between (x,y) and (0,0) is equal to the distance between (x,y) and (0,6), it follows from the distance formula that $\sqrt{x^2 + y^2} = \sqrt{x^2 + (y-6)^2}$. Squaring both sides of the last equation gives $x^2 + y^2 = x^2 + (y-6)^2$. Subtracting x^2 from both sides and then expanding the right side gives $y^2 = y^2 - 12y + 36$, or $0 = -12y + 36$, or $y = 3$.

The correct answer is E.

PS05008

35. What is the perimeter, in meters, of a rectangular garden 6 meters wide that has the same area as a rectangular playground 16 meters long and 12 meters wide?

(A) 48
(B) 56
(C) 60
(D) 76
(E) 192

Geometry Perimeter and Area

Let L represent the length, in meters, of the rectangular garden. It is given that the width of the garden is 6 meters and the area of the garden is the same as the area of a rectangular playground that is 16 meters long and 12 meters wide. It follows that $6L = (16)(12)$, and so $L = 32$. The perimeter of the garden is, then, $2(32 + 6) = 2(38) = 76$ meters.

The correct answer is D.

PS00918

36. $1 - 0.000001 =$

(A) $(1.01)(0.99)$

(B) $(1.11)(0.99)$

(C) $(1.001)(0.999)$

(D) $(1.111)(0.999)$

(E) $(1.0101)(0.0909)$

Arithmetic Place Value

The task in this question is to find among the available answers the expression that is equal to $1 - 0.000001 = 0.999999$. In the case of answer choice C, the first of the two factors, (1.001), is equal to $1 + 0.001$. One may therefore observe that $(1.001)(0.999) = (1 + 0.001)(0.999) = 0.999 + 0.000999 = 0.999999$. Answer choice C is therefore a correct answer.

For answer choice A, $(1.01)(0.99) = (1 + 0.01)(0.99) = 0.9999$. This answer choice is therefore incorrect. For answer choice B, $(1.11)(0.99) = (1 + 0.1 + 0.01)(0.99) = 0.99 + 0.099 + 0.0099 = 1.0989$. This answer choice is therefore incorrect. For answer choice D, $(1.111)(0.999) = 0.999 + 0.0999 + 0.00999 + 0.000999 = 1.109889$. This answer choice is therefore incorrect. For answer choice E, $(1.0101)(0.909) = 0.909 + 0.00909 + 0.0000909 = 0.9181809$. This answer choice is therefore incorrect.

The correct answer is C.

PS57330.02

37. In a certain history class of 17 juniors and seniors, each junior has written 2 book reports and each senior has written 3 book reports. If the 17 students have written a total of 44 book reports, how many juniors are in the class?

(A) 7

(B) 8

(C) 9

(D) 10

(E) 11

Algebra Simultaneous Equations

Letting j and s, respectively, represent the juniors and seniors in the class, it is given that $j + s = 17$ or $s = 17 - j$. Also, since it is given that each junior has written 2 book reports and each senior has written 3 book reports for a total of 44 book reports, it follows that $2j + 3s = 44$ or $2j + 3(17 - j) = 44$. Therefore, $j = 3(17) - 44 = 7$.

The correct answer is A.

PS04362

38. $|-4|(|-20|-|5|) =$

(A) -100

(B) -60

(C) 60

(D) 75

(E) 100

Arithmetic Absolute Value

$|-4|(|-20|-|5|) = 4(20 - 5) = 4 \times 15 = 60$

The correct answer is C.

PS12934

39. Of the total amount that Jill spent on a shopping trip, excluding taxes, she spent 50 percent on clothing, 20 percent on food, and 30 percent on other items. If Jill paid a 4 percent tax on the clothing, no tax on the food, and an 8 percent tax on all other items, then the total tax that she paid was what percent of the total amount that she spent, excluding taxes?

(A) 2.8%

(B) 3.6%

(C) 4.4%

(D) 5.2%

(E) 6.0%

Arithmetic Applied Problems

Let T represent the total amount Jill spent, excluding taxes. Jill paid a 4% tax on the clothing she bought, which accounted for 50% of the total amount she spent, and so the tax she paid on the clothing was $(0.04)(0.5T)$. Jill paid an 8% tax on the other items she bought, which accounted for 30% of the total amount she spent, and so the tax she paid on the other items was $(0.08)(0.3T)$. Therefore, the total amount of tax Jill paid was $(0.04)(0.5T) + (0.08)(0.3T) = 0.02T + 0.024T = 0.044T$. The tax as a percent of the total amount Jill spent, excluding taxes, was

$$\left(\frac{0.044T}{T} \times 100\right)\% = 4.4\%.$$

The correct answer is C.

PS15469

40. How many integers x satisfy both $2 < x \le 4$ and $0 \le x \le 3$?

(A) 5
(B) 4
(C) 3
(D) 2
(E) 1

Arithmetic Inequalities

The integers that satisfy $2 < x \le 4$ are 3 and 4. The integers that satisfy $0 \le x \le 3$ are 0, 1, 2, and 3. The only integer that satisfies both $2 < x \le 4$ and $0 \le x \le 3$ is 3, and so there is only one integer that satisfies both $2 < x \le 4$ and $0 \le x \le 3$.

The correct answer is E.

PS09322

41. At the opening of a trading day at a certain stock exchange, the price per share of stock K was $8. If the price per share of stock K was $9 at the closing of the day, what was the percent increase in the price per share of stock K for that day?

(A) 1.4%
(B) 5.9%
(C) 11.1%
(D) 12.5%
(E) 23.6%

Arithmetic Percents

An increase from $8 to $9 represents an increase of $\left(\frac{9-8}{8} \times 100\right)\% = \frac{100}{8}\% = 12.5\%$.

The correct answer is D.

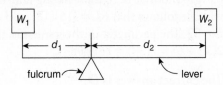

PS14237

42. As shown in the diagram above, a lever resting on a fulcrum has weights of w_1 pounds and w_2 pounds, located d_1 feet and d_2 feet from the fulcrum. The lever is balanced and $w_1 d_1 = w_2 d_2$. Suppose w_1 is 50 pounds and w_2 is 30 pounds. If d_1 is 4 feet less than d_2, what is d_2, in feet?

(A) 1.5
(B) 2.5
(C) 6
(D) 10
(E) 20

Algebra First-Degree Equations; Substitution

Given $w_1 d_1 = w_2 d_2$, $w_1 = 50$, $w_2 = 30$, and $d_1 = d_2 - 4$, it follows that $50(d_2 - 4) = 30d_2$, and so

$$50(d_2 - 4) = 30d_2 \quad \text{given}$$
$$50d_2 - 200 = 30d_2 \quad \text{distributive principle}$$
$$20d_2 = 200 \quad \text{add } 200 - 30d_2 \text{ to both sides}$$
$$d_2 = 10 \quad \text{divide both sides by 20}$$

The correct answer is D.

PS01650

43. If r and s are positive integers such that $(2^r)(4^s) = 16$, then $2r + s =$

(A) 2
(B) 3
(C) 4
(D) 5
(E) 6

Algebra Exponents

Using the rules of exponents,

$$(2^r)(4^s) = 16 \quad \text{given}$$
$$(2^r)(2^{2s}) = 2^4 \quad 4^s = (2^2)^s = 2^{2s}, 16 = 2^4$$
$$2^{r+2s} = 2^4 \quad \text{addition property of exponents}$$

Thus, $r + 2s = 4$. However, the problem asks for the value of $2r + s$. Since r and s are positive integers, $s < 2$; otherwise, r would not be positive. Therefore, $s = 1$, and it follows that $r + (2)(1) = 4$, or $r = 2$. The value of $2r + s$ is $(2)(2) + 1 = 5$.

Alternatively, since $(2^r)(4^s) = 16$ and both r and s are positive, it follows that $s < 2$; otherwise, $4^s \geq 16$ and r would not be positive. Therefore, $s = 1$ and $(2^r)(4) = 16$. It follows that $2^r = 4$ and $r = 2$. The value of $2r + s$ is $(2)(2) + 1 = 5$.

The correct answer is D.

PS06726
44. Three people each contributed x dollars toward the purchase of a car. They then bought the car for y dollars, an amount less than the total number of dollars contributed. If the excess amount is to be refunded to the three people in equal amounts, each person should receive a refund of how many dollars?

(A) $\dfrac{3x - y}{3}$

(B) $\dfrac{x - y}{3}$

(C) $\dfrac{x - 3y}{3}$

(D) $\dfrac{y - 3x}{3}$

(E) $3(x - y)$

Algebra Applied Problems

The total to be refunded is equal to the total contributed minus the amount paid, or $3x - y$. If $3x - y$ is divided into three equal amounts, then each amount will be $\dfrac{3x - y}{3}$.

The correct answer is A.

PS07080
45. Last week Jack worked 70 hours and earned $1,260. If he earned his regular hourly wage for the first 40 hours worked, $1\frac{1}{2}$ times his regular hourly wage for the next 20 hours worked, and 2 times his regular hourly wage for the remaining 10 hours worked, what was his regular hourly wage?

(A) $7.00
(B) $14.00
(C) $18.00
(D) $22.00
(E) $31.50

Algebra First-Degree Equations

If w represents Jack's regular hourly wage, then Jack's earnings for the week can be represented by the sum of the following amounts, in dollars: $40w$ (his earnings for the first 40 hours he worked), $(20)(1.5w)$ (his earnings for the next 20 hours he worked), and $(10)(2w)$ (his earnings for the last 10 hours he worked). Therefore,

$$40w + (20)(1.5w) + (10)(2w) = 1{,}260 \quad \text{given}$$
$$90w = 1{,}260 \quad \text{add like terms}$$
$$w = 14 \quad \text{divide both sides by 90}$$

Jack's regular hourly wage was $14.00.

The correct answer is B.

PS13426
46. If a and b are positive integers and $(2^a)^b = 2^3$, what is the value of $2^a\, 2^b$?

(A) 6
(B) 8
(C) 16
(D) 32
(E) 64

Algebra Exponents

It is given that $(2^a)^b = 2^3$, or $2^{ab} = 2^3$. Therefore, $ab = 3$. Since a and b are positive integers, it follows that either $a = 1$ and $b = 3$, or $a = 3$ and $b = 1$. In either case $a + b = 4$, and so $2^a 2^b = 2^{a+b} = 2^4 = 16$.

The correct answer is C.

PS01099
47. Five machines at a certain factory operate at the same constant rate. If four of these machines, operating simultaneously, take 30 hours to fill a certain production order, how many fewer hours does it take all five machines, operating simultaneously, to fill the same production order?

(A) 3
(B) 5
(C) 6
(D) 16
(E) 24

Arithmetic Applied Problems

If 4 machines, working simultaneously, each work for 30 hours to fill a production order, it takes $(4)(30)$ machine hours to fill the order. If 5 machines are working simultaneously, it will take $\frac{(4)(30)}{5} = 24$ hours. Thus, 5 machines working simultaneously will take $30 - 24 = 6$ fewer hours to fill the production order than 4 machines working simultaneously.

The correct answer is C.

PS01443

48. A certain toll station on a highway has 7 tollbooths, and each tollbooth collects $0.75 from each vehicle that passes it. From 6 o'clock yesterday morning to 12 o'clock midnight, vehicles passed each of the tollbooths at the average rate of 4 vehicles per minute. Approximately how much money did the toll station collect during that time period?

(A) $1,500
(B) $3,000
(C) $11,500
(D) $23,000
(E) $30,000

Arithmetic Rate Problem

On average, 4 vehicles pass each tollbooth every minute. There are 7 tollbooths at the station, and each passing vehicle pays $0.75. Therefore, the average rate, per minute, at which money is collected by the toll station is $ (7 \times 4 \times 0.75) = $ $ (7 \times 4 \times \frac{3}{4}) = $ $ (7 \times 3) = 21. From 6 a.m. through midnight there are 18 hours. And because 18 hours is equal to 18×60 minutes, from 6 a.m. through midnight there are 1,080 minutes. The total amount of money collected by the toll station during this period is therefore $1,080 \times $21 = $22,680$, which is approximately $23,000.

The correct answer is D.

PS13829

49. How many integers between 1 and 16, inclusive, have exactly 3 different positive integer factors?

(Note: 6 is NOT such an integer because 6 has 4 different positive integer factors: 1, 2, 3, and 6.)

(A) 1
(B) 2
(C) 3
(D) 4
(E) 6

Arithmetic Properties of Numbers

Using the process of elimination to eliminate integers that do NOT have exactly 3 different positive integer factors, the integer 1 can be eliminated since 1 has only 1 positive integer factor, namely 1 itself. Because each prime number has exactly 2 positive factors, each prime number between 1 and 16, inclusive, (namely, 2, 3, 5, 7, 11, and 13) can be eliminated. The integer 6 can also be eliminated since it was used as an example of an integer with exactly 4 positive integer factors. Check the positive integer factors of each of the remaining integers.

Integer	Positive integer factors	Number of factors
4	1, 2, 4	3
8	1, 2, 4, 8	4
9	1, 3, 9	3
10	1, 2, 5, 10	4
12	1, 2, 3, 4, 6, 12	6
14	1, 2, 7, 14	4
15	1, 3, 5, 15	4
16	1, 2, 4, 8, 16	5

Just the integers 4 and 9 have exactly 3 positive integer factors.

Alternatively, if the integer n, where $n > 1$, has exactly 3 positive integer factors, which include 1 and n, then n has exactly one other positive integer factor, say p. Since any factor of p would also be a factor of n, then p is prime, and so p is the only prime factor of n. It follows that $n = p^k$ for some integer $k > 1$. But if $k \geq 3$, then p^2 is a factor of n in addition to 1, p, and n, which contradicts the fact that n has exactly 3 positive integer factors. Therefore, $k = 2$ and $n = p^2$, which means that n is the square of a prime number. Of the integers between 1 and 16, inclusive, only 4 and 9 are the squares of prime numbers.

The correct answer is B.

PS14063

50. Stephanie has $2\frac{1}{4}$ cups of milk on hand and makes 2 batches of cookies, using $\frac{2}{3}$ cup of milk for each batch of cookies. Which of the following describes the amount of milk remaining after she makes the cookies?

(A) Less than $\frac{1}{2}$ cup

(B) Between $\frac{1}{2}$ cup and $\frac{3}{4}$ cup

(C) Between $\frac{3}{4}$ cup and 1 cup

(D) Between 1 cup and $1\frac{1}{2}$ cups

(E) More than $1\frac{1}{2}$ cups

Arithmetic Applied Problems

In cups, the amount of milk remaining is

$2\frac{1}{4} - 2\left(\frac{2}{3}\right) = \frac{9}{4} - \frac{4}{3} = \frac{27 - 16}{12} = \frac{11}{12}$, which is

greater than $\frac{3}{4} = \frac{9}{12}$ and less than 1.

The correct answer is C.

PS01656

51. The expression $n!$ is defined as the product of the integers from 1 through n. If p is the product of the integers from 100 through 299 and q is the product of the integers from 200 through 299, which of the following is equal to $\frac{p}{q}$?

(A) 99!

(B) 199!

(C) $\frac{199!}{99!}$

(D) $\frac{299!}{99!}$

(E) $\frac{299!}{199!}$

Arithmetic Series and Sequences

The number p is equal to $100 \times 101 \times 102 \times \ldots \times 299$ and the number q is equal to $200 \times 201 \times 202 \times \ldots \times 299$. The number $\frac{p}{q}$

is thus equal to $\dfrac{100 \times 101 \times 102 \times \ldots \times 299}{200 \times 201 \times 202 \times \ldots \times 299} =$

$\dfrac{100 \times 101 \times 102 \times \ldots \times 199 \times 200 \times 201 \times 202 \times \ldots \times 299}{200 \times 201 \times 202 \times \ldots \times 299}$.

Canceling $200 \times 201 \times 202 \times \ldots \times 299$ from the numerator and the denominator, we see that $\frac{p}{q} = 100 \times 101 \times 102 \times \ldots \times 199$. Note that the multiplication in this expression for $\frac{p}{q}$ begins with 100 (the smallest of the numbers being multiplied), whereas the multiplication in $n! = 1 \times 2 \times 3 \times \ldots \times n$ begins with 1. Starting with 199! as our numerator, we thus need to find a denominator that will cancel the undesired elements of the multiplication (in 199!). This number is $1 \times 2 \times 3 \times \ldots \times 99 = 99!$. That is, $\frac{p}{q} = 100 \times 101 \times 102 \times \ldots \times 199 =$

$\dfrac{1 \times 2 \times 3 \times \ldots \times 99 \times 100 \times 101 \times 102 \times \ldots \times 199}{1 \times 2 \times 3 \times \ldots \times 99} = \dfrac{199!}{99!}$.

The correct answer is C.

PS15753

52. A school club plans to package and sell dried fruit to raise money. The club purchased 12 containers of dried fruit, each containing $16\frac{3}{4}$ pounds. What is the maximum number of individual bags of dried fruit, each containing $\frac{1}{4}$ pounds, that can be sold from the dried fruit the club purchased?

(A) 50

(B) 64

(C) 67

(D) 768

(E) 804

Arithmetic Applied Problems; Operations with Fractions

The 12 containers, each containing $16\frac{3}{4}$ pounds

of dried fruit, contain a total of $(12)\left(16\frac{3}{4}\right) =$

$(12)\left(\dfrac{67}{4}\right) = (3)(67) = 201$ pounds of dried fruit, which will make $\dfrac{201}{\frac{1}{4}} = (201)(4) = 804$ individual bags that can be sold.

The correct answer is E.

Height	Price
Less than 5 ft	$14.95
5 ft to 6 ft	$17.95
Over 6 ft	$21.95

PS02498

53. A nursery sells fruit trees priced as shown in the chart above. In its inventory 54 trees are less than 5 feet in height. If the expected revenue from the sale of its entire stock is estimated at $2,450, approximately how much of this will come from the sale of trees that are at least 5 feet tall?

(A) $1,730
(B) $1,640
(C) $1,410
(D) $1,080
(E) $810

Arithmetic Applied Problems

If the nursery sells its entire stock of trees, it will sell the 54 trees that are less than 5 feet in height at the price per tree of $14.95 shown in the chart. The expected revenue from the sale of the trees that are less than 5 feet tall is therefore $54 \times \$14.95 = \$807.30$. The revenue from the sale of the trees that are at least 5 feet tall is thus equal to the total revenue from the sale of the entire stock of trees minus $807.30. The revenue from the sale of the entire stock of trees is estimated at $2,450. Based on this estimate, the revenue from the sale of the trees that are at least 5 feet tall will be $\$2,450 - \$807.30 = \$1,642.70$, which is approximately $1,640.

The correct answer is B.

PS04971

54. A certain bridge is 4,024 feet long. Approximately how many minutes does it take to cross this bridge at a constant speed of 20 miles per hour? (1 mile = 5,280 feet)

(A)   1
(B)   2
(C)   4
(D)   6
(E)   7

Arithmetic Applied Problems

First, convert 4,024 feet to miles since the speed is given in miles per hour:

$$4,024 \text{ ft} \times \frac{1 \text{ mi}}{5,280 \text{ ft}} = \frac{4,024}{5,280} \text{ mi.}$$

Now, divide by 20 mph: $\dfrac{4,024}{5,280} \text{ mi} \div \dfrac{20 \text{ mi}}{1 \text{ hr}}$

$$= \frac{4,024 \text{ mi}}{5,280} \times \frac{1 \text{ hr}}{20 \text{ mi}} = \frac{4,024 \text{ hr}}{(5,280)(20)}.$$

Last, convert $\dfrac{4,024 \text{ hr}}{(5,280)(20)}$ to minutes:

$$\frac{4,024 \text{ hr}}{(5,280)(20)} \times \frac{60 \text{ min}}{1 \text{ hr}} = \frac{(4,024)(60) \text{ min}}{(5,280)(20)} \approx$$

$\dfrac{4,000}{5,000} \times \dfrac{60}{20}$ min. Then, $\dfrac{4,000}{5,000} \times \dfrac{60}{20}$ min =

$= 0.8 \times 3 \text{ min} \approx 2 \text{ min}$. Thus, at a constant speed of 20 miles per hour, it takes approximately 2 minutes to cross the bridge.

The correct answer is B.

PS25440.02

55. A purse contains 57 coins, all of which are nickels, dimes, or quarters. If the purse contains x dimes and 8 more nickels than dimes, which of the following gives the number of quarters the purse contains in terms of x ?

(A)   2x – 49
(B)   2x + 49
(C)   2x – 65
(D)   49 – 2x
(E)   65 – 2x

Algebra First-Degree Equations

Letting Q be the number of quarters, there are $(x + 8)$ nickels, x dimes, and Q quarters for a total of 57 coins.

$$
\begin{aligned}
(x + 8) + x + Q &= 57 && \text{given} \\
2x + 8 + Q &= 57 && \text{combine like terms} \\
Q &= 49 - 2x && \text{subtract } 2x + 8 \text{ from} \\
&&& \text{both sides}
\end{aligned}
$$

The correct answer is D.

PS12657

56. The annual interest rate earned by an investment increased by 10 percent from last year to this year. If the annual interest rate earned by the investment this year was 11 percent, what was the annual interest rate last year?

(A)   1%
(B)   1.1%
(C)   9.1%
(D)   10%
(E)   10.8%

Arithmetic Percents

If L is the annual interest rate last year, then the annual interest rate this year is 10% greater than L, or $1.1L$. It is given that $1.1L = 11\%$. Therefore, $L = \dfrac{11\%}{1.1} = 10\%$. (Note that if the given information had been that the investment increased by *10 percentage points*, then the equation would have been $L + 10\% = 11\%$.)

The correct answer is D.

PS07394

57. A total of 5 liters of gasoline is to be poured into two empty containers with capacities of 2 liters and 6 liters, respectively, such that both containers will be filled to the same percent of their respective capacities. What amount of gasoline, in liters, must be poured into the 6-liter container?

(A) $4\dfrac{1}{2}$

(B)   4

(C) $3\dfrac{3}{4}$

(D)   3

(E) $1\dfrac{1}{4}$

Algebra Ratio and Proportion

If x represents the amount, in liters, of gasoline poured into the 6-liter container, then $5 - x$ represents the amount, in liters, of gasoline poured into the 2-liter container. After the gasoline is poured into the containers, the 6-liter container will be filled to $\left(\dfrac{x}{6} \times 100 \right)\%$ of its capacity and the 2-liter container will be filled to $\left(\dfrac{5 - x}{2} \times 100 \right)\%$ of its capacity. Because these two percents are equal,

$$
\begin{aligned}
\frac{x}{6} &= \frac{5 - x}{2} && \text{given} \\
2x &= 6(5 - x) && \text{multiply both sides by 12} \\
2x &= 30 - 6x && \text{use distributive property} \\
8x &= 30 && \text{add } 6x \text{ to both sides} \\
x &= 3\frac{3}{4} && \text{divide both sides by 8}
\end{aligned}
$$

Therefore, $3\dfrac{3}{4}$ liters of gasoline must be poured into the 6-liter container.

The correct answer is C.

PS13882

58. What is the larger of the 2 solutions of the equation $x^2 - 4x = 96$?

(A)   8
(B)   12
(C)   16
(D)   32
(E)   100

Algebra Second-Degree Equations

It is given that $x^2 - 4x = 96$, or $x^2 - 4x - 96 = 0$, or $(x - 12)(x + 8) = 0$. Therefore, $x = 12$ or $x = -8$, and the larger of these two numbers is 12.

Alternatively, from $x^2 - 4x = 96$ it follows that $x(x - 4) = 96$. By inspection, the left side is either the product of 12 and 8, where the value of x is 12, or the product of -8 and -12, where the value of x is -8, and the larger of these two values of x is 12.

The correct answer is B.

$$x = \frac{1}{6}gt^2$$

PS89821.02

59. In the formula shown, if g is a constant and $x = -6$ when $t = 2$, what is the value of x when $t = 4$?

(A) −24
(B) −20
(C) −15
(D) 20
(E) 24

Algebra Formulas

Since $x = -6$ when $t = 2$, it follows that

$-6 = \left(\frac{1}{6}\right)(g)(4)$ so $g = \frac{3}{2}(-6) = -9$. Then,

when $t = 4$, $x = \frac{1}{6}(-9)(16) = -24$.

The correct answer is A.

PS10921

60. $\dfrac{(39,897)(0.0096)}{198.76}$ is approximately

(A) 0.02
(B) 0.2
(C) 2
(D) 20
(E) 200

Arithmetic Estimation

$$\frac{(39,897)(0.0096)}{198.76} \approx \frac{(40,000)(0.01)}{200} = (200)(0.01) = 2$$

The correct answer is C.

PS13205

61. If a square region has area n, what is the length of the diagonal of the square in terms of n ?

(A) $\sqrt{2n}$
(B) $\sqrt{n}$
(C) $2\sqrt{n}$
(D) $2n$
(E) $2n^2$

Geometry Area; Pythagorean Theorem

If s represents the side length of the square, then $n = s^2$. By the Pythagorean theorem, the length of the diagonal of the square is $\sqrt{s^2 + s^2} = \sqrt{n + n} = \sqrt{2n}$.

The correct answer is A.

PS00817

62. The "prime sum" of an integer n greater than 1 is the sum of all the prime factors of n, including repetitions. For example, the prime sum of 12 is 7, since $12 = 2 \times 2 \times 3$ and $2 + 2 + 3 = 7$. For which of the following integers is the prime sum greater than 35 ?

(A) 440
(B) 512
(C) 620
(D) 700
(E) 750

Arithmetic Properties of Numbers

A Since $440 = 2 \times 2 \times 2 \times 5 \times 11$, the prime sum of 440 is $2 + 2 + 2 + 5 + 11 = 22$, which is not greater than 35.

B Since $512 = 2^9$, the prime sum of 512 is $9(2) = 18$, which is not greater than 35.

C Since $620 = 2 \times 2 \times 5 \times 31$, the prime sum of 620 is $2 + 2 + 5 + 31 = 40$, which is greater than 35.

Because there can be only one correct answer, D and E need not be checked. However, for completeness,

D Since $700 = 2 \times 2 \times 5 \times 5 \times 7$, the prime sum of 700 is $2 + 2 + 5 + 5 + 7 = 21$, which is not greater than 35.

E Since $750 = 2 \times 3 \times 5 \times 5 \times 5$, the prime sum of 750 is $2 + 3 + 5 + 5 + 5 = 20$, which is not greater than 35.

The correct answer is C.

PS02256

63. Each machine at a toy factory assembles a certain kind of toy at a constant rate of one toy every 3 minutes. If 40 percent of the machines at the factory are to be replaced by new machines that assemble this kind of toy at a constant rate of one toy every 2 minutes, what will be the percent increase in the number of toys assembled in one hour by all the machines at the factory, working at their constant rates?

(A)   20%
(B)   25%
(C)   30%
(D)   40%
(E)   50%

Arithmetic Applied Problems; Percents

Let n be the total number of machines working. Currently, it takes each machine 3 minutes to assemble 1 toy, so each machine assembles 20 toys in 1 hour and the total number of toys assembled in 1 hour by all the current machines is $20n$. It takes each new machine 2 minutes to assemble 1 toy, so each new machine assembles 30 toys in 1 hour. If 60% of the machines assemble 20 toys each hour and 40% assemble 30 toys each hour, then the total number of toys produced by the machines each hour is $(0.60n)(20) + (0.40n)(30) = 24n$. The percent increase in hourly production is $\dfrac{24n - 20n}{20n} = \dfrac{1}{5}$ or 20%.

The correct answer is A.

PS10339

64. When a subscription to a new magazine was purchased for m months, the publisher offered a discount of 75 percent off the regular monthly price of the magazine. If the total value of the discount was equivalent to buying the magazine at its regular monthly price for 27 months, what was the value of m?

(A)   18
(B)   24
(C)   30
(D)   36
(E)   48

Algebra Percents

Let P represent the regular monthly price of the magazine. The discounted monthly price is then $0.75P$. Paying this price for m months is equivalent to paying the regular price for 27 months. Therefore, $0.75mP = 27P$, and so $0.75m = 27$. It follows that $m = \dfrac{27}{0.75} = 36$.

The correct answer is D.

PS10422

65. At a garage sale, all of the prices of the items sold were different. If the price of a radio sold at the garage sale was both the 15th highest price and the 20th lowest price among the prices of the items sold, how many items were sold at the garage sale?

(A)   33
(B)   34
(C)   35
(D)   36
(E)   37

Arithmetic Operations with Integers

If the price of the radio was the 15th highest price, there were 14 items that sold for prices higher than the price of the radio. If the price of the radio was the 20th lowest price, there were 19 items that sold for prices lower than the price of the radio. Therefore, the total number of items sold is $14 + 1 + 19 = 34$.

The correct answer is B.

PS11738

66. Half of a large pizza is cut into 4 equal-sized pieces, and the other half is cut into 6 equal-sized pieces. If a person were to eat 1 of the larger pieces and 2 of the smaller pieces, what fraction of the pizza would remain uneaten?

(A) $\dfrac{5}{12}$

(B) $\dfrac{13}{24}$

(C) $\dfrac{7}{12}$

(D) $\dfrac{2}{3}$

(E) $\dfrac{17}{24}$

Arithmetic Operations with Fractions

Each of the 4 equal-sized pieces represents $\frac{1}{8}$ of the whole pizza since each slice is $\frac{1}{4}$ of $\frac{1}{2}$ of the pizza. Each of the 6 equal-sized pieces represents $\frac{1}{12}$ of the whole pizza since each slice is $\frac{1}{6}$ of $\frac{1}{2}$ of the pizza. The fraction of the pizza remaining after a person eats one of the larger pieces and 2 of the smaller pieces is $1 - \left[\frac{1}{8} + 2\left(\frac{1}{12}\right)\right] = 1 - \left(\frac{1}{8} + \frac{1}{6}\right) = 1 - \frac{6+8}{48} = 1 - \frac{7}{24} = \frac{17}{24}$.

The correct answer is E.

PS14293

67. If $a = 1 + \frac{1}{4} + \frac{1}{16} + \frac{1}{64}$ and $b = 1 + \frac{1}{4}a$, then what is the value of $a - b$?

(A) $-\frac{85}{256}$

(B) $-\frac{1}{256}$

(C) $-\frac{1}{4}$

(D) $\frac{125}{256}$

(E) $\frac{169}{256}$

Arithmetic Operations with Fractions

Given that $a = 1 + \frac{1}{4} + \frac{1}{16} + \frac{1}{64}$, it follows that $\frac{1}{4}a = \frac{1}{4} + \frac{1}{16} + \frac{1}{64} + \frac{1}{256}$ and so $b = 1 + \frac{1}{4} + \frac{1}{16} + \frac{1}{64} + \frac{1}{256}$. Then $a - b = \left(1 + \frac{1}{4} + \frac{1}{16} + \frac{1}{64}\right) - \left(1 + \frac{1}{4} + \frac{1}{16} + \frac{1}{64} + \frac{1}{256}\right) = -\frac{1}{256}$.

The correct answer is B.

PS10174

68. In a certain learning experiment, each participant had three trials and was assigned, for each trial, a score of either −2, −1, 0, 1, or 2. The participant's final score consisted of the sum of the first trial score, 2 times the second trial score, and 3 times the third trial score. If Anne received scores of 1 and −1 for her first two trials, not necessarily in that order, which of the following could NOT be her final score?

(A) −4

(B) −2

(C) 1

(D) 5

(E) 6

Arithmetic Applied Problems

If x represents Anne's score on the third trial, then Anne's final score is either $1 + 2(-1) + 3x = 3x - 1$ or $-1 + 2(1) + 3x = 3x + 1$, where x can have the value −2, −1, 0, 1, or 2. The following table shows Anne's final score for each possible value of x.

x	$3x - 1$	$3x + 1$
−2	−7	−5
−1	−4	−2
0	−1	1
1	2	4
2	5	7

Among the answer choices, the only one not found in the table is 6.

The correct answer is E.

PS00111

69. For all positive integers m and v, the expression $m \ominus v$ represents the remainder when m is divided by v. What is the value of $((98 \ominus 33) \ominus 17) - (98 \ominus (33 \ominus 17))$?

(A) −10

(B) −2

(C) 8

(D) 13

(E) 17

Arithmetic Operations with Integers

First, for $((98 \ominus 33) \ominus 17)$, determine $98 \ominus 33$, which equals 32, since 32 is the remainder when 98 is divided by 33 ($98 = 2(33) + 32$). Then, determine $32 \ominus 17$, which equals 15, since 15 is the remainder when 32 is divided by 17 (32 = 1(17) + 15). Thus, ((98 Θ 33) Θ 17) = 15.

Next, for (98 Θ (33 Θ 17)), determine 33 Θ 17, which equals 16, since 16 is the remainder when 33 is divided by 17 (33 = 1(17) + 16). Then, determine 98 Θ 16, which equals 2, since 2 is the remainder when 98 is divided by 16 (98 = 6(16) + 2). Thus, (98 Θ (33 Θ 17)) = 2.

Finally, ((98 Θ 33) Θ 17 - (98 Θ (33 Θ 17)) = 15 - 2 = 13.

The correct answer is D.

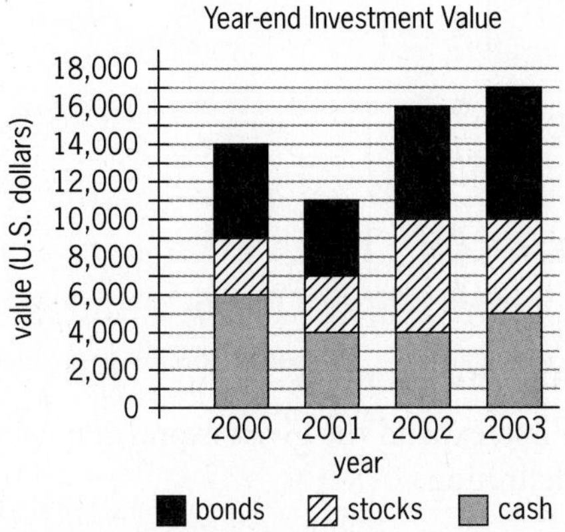

PS13841

70. The chart above shows year-end values for Darnella's investments. For just the stocks, what was the increase in value from year-end 2000 to year-end 2003 ?

(A) $1,000
(B) $2,000
(C) $3,000
(D) $4,000
(E) $5,000

Arithmetic Interpretation of Graphs

From the graph, the year-end 2000 value for stocks is 9,000 – 6,000 = 3,000 and the year-end 2003 value for stocks is 10,000 – 5,000 = 5,000. Therefore, for just the stocks, the increase in value from year-end 2000 to year-end 2003 is 5,000 – 3,000 = 2,000.

The correct answer is B.

PS05775

71. If the sum of the reciprocals of two consecutive odd integers is $\frac{12}{35}$, then the greater of the two integers is

(A) 3
(B) 5
(C) 7
(D) 9
(E) 11

Arithmetic Operations with Fractions

The sum of the reciprocals of 2 integers, a and b, is $\frac{1}{a}+\frac{1}{b}=\frac{a+b}{ab}$. Therefore, since $\frac{12}{35}$ is the sum of the reciprocals of 2 consecutive odd integers, the integers must be such that their sum is a multiple of 12 and their product is the same multiple of 35 so that the fraction reduces to $\frac{12}{35}$. Considering the simplest case where $a + b = 12$ and $ab = 35$, it is easy to see that the integers are 5 and 7 since 5 and 7 are the only factors of 35 that are consecutive odd integers. The larger of these is 7.

Algebraically, if a is the greater of the two integers, then $b = a - 2$ and

$$\frac{a+(a-2)}{a(a-2)}=\frac{12}{35}$$

$$\frac{2a-2}{a(a-2)}=\frac{12}{35}$$

$$35(2a-2)=12a(a-2)$$
$$70a-70=12a^2-24a$$
$$0=12a^2-94a+70$$
$$0=2(6a-5)(a-7)$$

Thus, $6a - 5 = 0$, so $a=\frac{5}{6}$, or $a - 7 = 0$, so $a = 7$. Since a must be an integer, it follows that $a = 7$.

The correct answer is C.

PS05916

72. What is the sum of the odd integers from 35 to 85, inclusive?

(A) 1,560
(B) 1,500
(C) 1,240
(D) 1,120
(E) 1,100

Arithmetic Operations on Integers

The odd integers from 35 through 85 form an arithmetic sequence with first term 35 and each subsequent term 2 more than the preceding term. Thus the sum $35 + 37 + 39 + \ldots + 85$ can be found as follows:

1st term	35	= 35		
2nd term	37	= 35	+	1(2)
3rd term	39	= 35	+	2(2)
4th term	41	= 35	+	3(2)
...	...	......	...	...
26th term	85	= 35	+	25(2)

$$\text{Sum} = 35(26) + (1 + 2 + 3 + \ldots + 25)(2)$$

$$= 35(26) + \frac{(25)(26)}{2}(2)$$

see note below

$$= 910 + 650$$

$$= 1{,}560$$

Note that if $s = 1 + 2 + 3 + \ldots + 25$, then $2s = (1 + 2 + 3 + \ldots + 25) + (25 + 24 + 23 + \ldots + 1)$, and so $2s = (1 + 25) + (2 + 24) + (3 + 23) + \ldots + (25 + 1) = (25)(26)$. Therefore, $s = \frac{(25)(26)}{2}$.

Alternatively, to determine the number of odd integers from 35 to 85, inclusive, consider that 3 of them (35, 37, and 39) have tens digit 3. Half of the integers with tens digit 4 are odd, so 5 of the odd integers between 35 and 85, inclusive, have tens digit 4. Similarly, 5 of the odd integers between 35 and 85, inclusive, have tens digit 5; 5 have tens digit 6; and 5 have tens digit 7. Finally, 3 have tens digit 8 (81, 83, and 85), and so the number of odd integers between 35 and 85, inclusive, is $3 + 5 + 5 + 5 + 5 + 3 = 26$. Now, let $S = 35 + 37 + 39 + \ldots + 85$. Then, $S = 85 + 83 + 81 + \ldots + 35$, and it follows that $2S = (35 + 85) + (37 + 83) + (39 + 81) + \ldots + (85 + 35) = (120)(26)$. Thus, $S = 35 + 37 + 39 + \ldots + 85 = \frac{(120)(26)}{2} = 1{,}560$.

The correct answer is A.

PS21080.02

73. For all numbers a, b, c, and d, $\begin{vmatrix} a & b \\ c & d \end{vmatrix}$ is defined by the equation $\begin{vmatrix} a & b \\ c & d \end{vmatrix} = ad - cb$. Which of the following is equal to $\begin{vmatrix} s & t \\ 1 & 3 \end{vmatrix} - \begin{vmatrix} -t & 2 \\ s & 4 \end{vmatrix} + \begin{vmatrix} 2 & 2 \\ t & s \end{vmatrix}$?

(A) $\begin{vmatrix} s & t \\ 1 & 5 \end{vmatrix}$

(B) $\begin{vmatrix} s & t \\ 7 & 1 \end{vmatrix}$

(C) $\begin{vmatrix} s & t \\ 5 & 7 \end{vmatrix}$

(D) $\begin{vmatrix} s & -t \\ 1 & 5 \end{vmatrix}$

(E) $\begin{vmatrix} s & -t \\ 1 & 7 \end{vmatrix}$

Algebra Formulas

First, expand the given expression using the given definition.

$$\begin{vmatrix} s & t \\ 1 & 3 \end{vmatrix} - \begin{vmatrix} -t & 2 \\ s & 4 \end{vmatrix} + \begin{vmatrix} 2 & 2 \\ t & s \end{vmatrix}$$

$$= (3s - t) - (-4t - 2s) + (2s - 2t) = 3s - t + 4t + 2s + 2s - 2t = 7s + t$$

Next, compare the result, $7s + t$, with the expanded versions of the answer choices.

A $\begin{vmatrix} s & t \\ 1 & 5 \end{vmatrix} = 5s - t$ (not correct)

B $\begin{vmatrix} s & t \\ 7 & 1 \end{vmatrix} = s - 7t$ (not correct)

C $\begin{vmatrix} s & t \\ 5 & 7 \end{vmatrix} = 7s - 5t$ (not correct)

D $\begin{vmatrix} s & -t \\ 1 & 5 \end{vmatrix} = 5s + t$ (not correct)

E $\begin{vmatrix} s & -t \\ 1 & 7 \end{vmatrix} = 7s + t$ (correct)

The correct answer is E.

PS00777

74. In a certain sequence, each term after the first term is one-half the previous term. If the tenth term of the sequence is between 0.0001 and 0.001, then the twelfth term of the sequence is between

(A) 0.0025 and 0.025
(B) 0.00025 and 0.0025
(C) 0.000025 and 0.00025
(D) 0.0000025 and 0.000025
(E) 0.00000025 and 0.0000025

Arithmetic Sequences

Let a_n represent the nth term of the sequence. It is given that each term after the first term is $\frac{1}{2}$ the previous term and that $0.0001 < a_{10} < 0.001$.

Then for a_{11}, $\frac{0.0001}{2} < a_{11} < \frac{0.001}{2}$, or $0.00005 < a_{11} < 0.0005$. For a_{12}, $\frac{0.00005}{2} < a_{12} < \frac{0.0005}{2}$, or $0.000025 < a_{12} < 0.00025$. Thus, the twelfth term of the sequence is between 0.000025 and 0.00025.

The correct answer is C.

PS04765

75. A certain drive-in movie theater has a total of 17 rows of parking spaces. There are 20 parking spaces in the first row and 21 parking spaces in the second row. In each subsequent row there are 2 more parking spaces than in the previous row. What is the total number of parking spaces in the movie theater?

(A) 412
(B) 544
(C) 596
(D) 632
(E) 692

Arithmetic Operations on Integers

Row	Number of parking spaces
1st row	20
2nd row	21
3rd row	21 + 1(2)
4th row	21 + 2(2)
…	… … …
17th row	21 + 15(2)

Then, letting S represent the total number of parking spaces in the theater,

$$S = 20 + (16)(21) + (1 + 2 + 3 + \dots + 15)(2)$$
$$= 20 + 336 + \frac{(15)(16)}{2}(2) \text{ see note below}$$
$$= 356 + 240$$
$$= 596$$

Note that if $s = 1 + 2 + 3 + \dots + 15$, then $2s = (1 + 2 + 3 + \dots + 15) + (15 + 14 + 13 + \dots + 1)$, and so $2s = (1 + 15) + (2 + 14) + (3 + 13) + \dots + (15 + 1) = (15)(16)$. Therefore, $s = \frac{(15)(16)}{2}$.

The correct answer is C.

PS10810

76. Ada and Paul received their scores on three tests. On the first test, Ada's score was 10 points higher than Paul's score. On the second test, Ada's score was 4 points higher than Paul's score. If Paul's average (arithmetic mean) score on the three tests was 3 points higher than Ada's average score on the three tests, then Paul's score on the third test was how many points higher than Ada's score?

(A) 9
(B) 14
(C) 17
(D) 23
(E) 25

Algebra Statistics

Let a_1, a_2, and a_3 be Ada's scores on the first, second, and third tests, respectively, and let p_1, p_2, and p_3 be Paul's scores on the first, second, and third tests, respectively. Then, Ada's average score is $\dfrac{a_1 + a_2 + a_3}{3}$ and Paul's average score is $\dfrac{p_1 + p_2 + p_3}{3}$. But, Paul's average score is 3 points higher than Ada's average score, so $\dfrac{p_1 + p_2 + p_3}{3} = \dfrac{a_1 + a_2 + a_3}{3} + 3$. Also, it is given that $a_1 = p_1 + 10$ and $a_2 = p_2 + 4$, so by substitution, $\dfrac{p_1 + p_2 + p_3}{3} = \dfrac{(p_1 + 10) + (p_2 + 4) + a_3}{3} + 3$. Then, $p_1 + p_2 + p_3 = (p_1 + 10) + (p_2 + 4) + a_3 + 9$ and so $p_3 = a_3 + 23$. On the third test, Paul's score was 23 points higher than Ada's score.

The correct answer is D.

PS06180

77. The price of a certain stock increased by 0.25 of 1 percent on a certain day. By what fraction did the price of the stock increase that day?

(A) $\dfrac{1}{2,500}$

(B) $\dfrac{1}{400}$

(C) $\dfrac{1}{40}$

(D) $\dfrac{1}{25}$

(E) $\dfrac{1}{4}$

Arithmetic Percents

It is given that the price of a certain stock increased by 0.25 of 1 percent on a certain day. This is equivalent to an increase of $\dfrac{1}{4}$ of $\dfrac{1}{100}$, which is $\left(\dfrac{1}{4}\right)\left(\dfrac{1}{100}\right)$, and $\left(\dfrac{1}{4}\right)\left(\dfrac{1}{100}\right) = \dfrac{1}{400}$.

The correct answer is B.

PS03831

78. For each trip, a taxicab company charges $4.25 for the first mile and $2.65 for each additional mile or fraction thereof. If the total charge for a certain trip was $62.55, how many miles at most was the trip?

(A) 21

(B) 22

(C) 23

(D) 24

(E) 25

Arithmetic Applied Problems

Subtracting the charge for the first mile leaves a charge of $62.55 − $4.25 = $58.30 for the miles after the first mile. Divide this amount by $2.65 to find the number of miles to which $58.30 corresponds: $\dfrac{58.30}{2.65} = 22$ miles. Therefore, the total number of miles is at most 1 (the first mile) added to 22 (the number of miles after the first mile), which equals 23.

The correct answer is C.

PS12857

79. When 24 is divided by the positive integer n, the remainder is 4. Which of the following statements about n must be true?

   I. n is even.

   II. n is a multiple of 5.

   III. n is a factor of 20.

(A) III only

(B) I and II only

(C) I and III only

(D) II and III only

(E) I, II, and III

Arithmetic Properties of Numbers

Since the remainder is 4 when 24 is divided by the positive integer n and the remainder must be less than the divisor, it follows that $24 = qn + 4$ for some positive integer q and $4 < n$, or $qn = 20$ and $n > 4$. It follows that $n = 5$, or $n = 10$, or $n = 20$ since these are the only factors of 20 that exceed 4.

   I. n is not necessarily even. For example, n could be 5.

II. n is necessarily a multiple of 5 since the value of n is either 5, 10, or 20.

III. n is a factor of 20 since $20 = qn$ for some positive integer q.

The correct answer is D.

PS80871.02

80.   Terry needs to purchase some pipe for a plumbing job that requires pipes with lengths of 1 ft 4 in, 2 ft 8 in, 3 ft 4 in, 3 ft 8 in, 4 ft 8 in, 5 ft 8 in, and 9 ft 4 in. The store from which Terry will purchase the pipe sells pipe only in 10-ft lengths. If each 10-ft length can be cut into shorter pieces, what is the minimum number of 10-ft pipe lengths that Terry needs to purchase for the plumbing job?

(Note: 1 ft = 12 in)

(A)   3
(B)   4
(C)   5
(D)   6
(E)   7

Arithmetic Operations with Integers; Measurement Conversion

The 7 lengths of pipe Terry needs total 30 feet plus 8 inches, which means Terry will need to buy at least 4 pipes, each 10 feet long. Four pipes will suffice if Terry cuts pieces of the following lengths:

1st pipe: 9 feet 4 inches (with 8 inches left)

2nd pipe: 5 feet 8 inches and 3 feet 8 inches (with 8 inches left)

3rd pipe: 4 feet 8 inches, 3 feet 4 inches, and 1 foot 4 inches (with 8 inches left)

4th pipe: 2 feet 8 inches (with 7 feet 4 inches left)

The correct answer is B.

PS12759

81.   What is the thousandths digit in the decimal equivalent of $\dfrac{53}{5,000}$?

(A)   0
(B)   1
(C)   3
(D)   5
(E)   6

Arithmetic Place Value

$\dfrac{53}{5,000} = \dfrac{106}{10,000} = 0.0106$ and the thousandths digit is 0.

The correct answer is A.

Questions 82 to 158 - Difficulty: **Medium**

PS67502.01

82.   If $\dfrac{1}{2}$ the result obtained when 2 is subtracted from $5x$ is equal to the sum of 10 and $3x$, what is the value of x ?

(A)   −22
(B)   −4
(C)   4
(D)   18
(E)   22

Algebra First-Degree Equations

The result obtained when 2 is subtracted from $5x$ is $5x - 2$, and the sum of 10 and $3x$ is $10 + 3x$. Therefore, it is given that $\dfrac{1}{2}$ of $5x - 2$ is equal to $10 + 3x$, or $\dfrac{1}{2}(5x - 2) = 10 + 3x$.

$$\dfrac{1}{2}(5x - 2) = 10 + 3x \quad \text{given}$$

$$5x - 2 = 20 + 6x \quad \text{multiply both sides by 2}$$

$$-22 = x \quad \begin{array}{l} \text{subtract both } 5x \text{ and } 20 \\ \text{from both sides} \end{array}$$

The correct answer is A.

PS48502.01

83.   In a rectangular coordinate system, straight line k passes through points (0, 0) and (3, 2). Which of the following are coordinates of a point on k ?

(A)   (9, 4)
(B)   (4, 9)
(C)   (−4, 6)
(D)   (−6, −9)
(E)   (−6, −4)

Geometry Simple Coordinate Geometry

Line k has slope $m = \dfrac{2 - 0}{3 - 0} = \dfrac{2}{3}$ and y-intercept $b = 0$. Therefore, an equation of line k is $y = mx + b = \dfrac{2}{3}x + 0$, or $y = \dfrac{2}{3}x$. It follows that a point is on k if and only if $\dfrac{2}{3}$ times the x-coordinate of the point is equal to the y-coordinate of the point. The table below shows that, among the answer choices, only the point $(-6, -4)$ is on k.

x-coordinate	$\frac{2}{3}$ times x-coordinate
9	6
4	$\frac{8}{3}$
-4	$-\frac{8}{3}$
-6	-4

The correct answer is E.

PS78502.01

84. If Car A took n hours to travel 2 miles and Car B took m hours to travel 3 miles, which of the following expresses the time it would take Car C, traveling at the average (arithmetic mean) of those rates, to travel 5 miles?

(A) $\dfrac{10nm}{3n+2m}$

(B) $\dfrac{3n+2m}{10(n+m)}$

(C) $\dfrac{2n+3m}{5nm}$

(D) $\dfrac{10(n+m)}{2n+3m}$

(E) $\dfrac{5(n+m)}{2n+3m}$

Algebra Applied Problems

This is a rate problem that can be solved by several applications of the formula

$$\text{rate} \times \text{time} = \text{distance}.$$

Let r_A and r_B be the rates, respectively and in miles per hour, of Car A and Car B. Then omitting units for simplicity, for Car A this formula becomes $r_A \times n = 2$, or $r_A = \dfrac{2}{n}$, and for Car B this formula becomes $r_B \times m = 3$, or $r_B = \dfrac{3}{m}$. Thus, the average of the two rates is

$$\frac{1}{2}(r_A + r_B) = \frac{1}{2}\left(\frac{2}{n} + \frac{3}{m}\right) = \frac{1}{2}\left(\frac{2m+3n}{mn}\right) = \frac{3n+2m}{2mn}.$$

Therefore, if t is the desired time, in hours, that Car C traveled, then the above formula for Car C becomes $\dfrac{3n+2m}{2mn} \times t = 5$, or

$$t = 5 \times \frac{2mn}{3n+2m} = \frac{10mn}{3n+2m}.$$

The correct answer is A.

PS87502.01

85. If x, y, and k are positive and x is less than y, then $\dfrac{x+k}{y+k}$ is

(A) 1

(B) greater than $\dfrac{x}{y}$

(C) equal to $\dfrac{x}{y}$

(D) less than $\dfrac{x}{y}$

(E) less than $\dfrac{x}{y}$ or greater than $\dfrac{x}{y}$, depending on the value of k

Algebra Ratios

$x < y$		given
$kx < ky$		multiply by positive k
$xy + kx < xy + ky$		add xy
$x(y+k) < y(x+k)$		factor
$x < \dfrac{y(x+k)}{y+k}$		divide by positive $y+k$
$\dfrac{x}{y} < \dfrac{x+k}{y+k}$		divide by positive y

Thus, $\dfrac{x+k}{y+k} > \dfrac{x}{y}$.

The correct answer is B.

PS09502.01

86. Consider the following set of inequalities: $p > q$, $s > r$, $q > t$, $s > p$, and $r > q$. Between which two quantities is no relationship established?

(A) p and r

(B) s and t

(C) s and q

(D) p and t

(E) r and t

Algebra Order

Using $r > q$ and $q > t$ gives $r > t$, so a relationship is established between r and t. The correct answer is NOT E.

Using $p > q$ and $q > t$ gives $p > t$, so a relationship is established between p and t. The correct answer is NOT D.

Using $s > r$ and $r > q$ gives $s > q$, so a relationship is established between s and q. The correct answer is NOT C.

Using $s > r$, $r > q$, and $q > t$ gives $s > t$, so a relationship is established between s and t. The correct answer is NOT B.

Alternately, the diagram below shows the given relationships and does not establish a relationship between p and r.

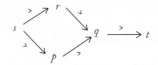

The correct answer is A.

PS68502.01

87. Carl averaged $2m$ miles per hour on a trip that took him h hours. If Ruth made the same trip in $\frac{2}{3}h$ hours, what was her average speed in miles per hour?

(A) $\frac{1}{3}mh$

(B) $\frac{2}{3}mh$

(C) m

(D) $\frac{3}{2}m$

(E) $3m$

Algebra Applied Problems

Using

$$\text{distance} = \text{rate} \times \text{time},$$

the distance Carl traveled on the trip was $2mh$ miles. Using rate $= \dfrac{\text{distance}}{\text{time}}$, Ruth's rate was $\dfrac{2mh}{\frac{2}{3}h} = \dfrac{3}{2}(2m) = 3m$.

The correct answer is E.

PS29502.01

88. Of three persons, two take relish, two take pepper, and two take salt. The one who takes no salt takes no pepper, and the one who takes no pepper takes no relish. Which of the following statements must be true?

I.   The person who takes no salt also takes no relish.

II. Any of the three persons who takes pepper also takes relish and salt.

III. The person who takes no relish is not one of those who takes salt.

(A) I only

(B) II only

(C) III only

(D) I and II only

(E) I, II, and III

Arithmetic Sets (Venn Diagrams)

Although this problem can be solved by the use of a Venn diagram, it is probably simpler to use ordinary reasoning. The single person who takes no salt takes no pepper, and the single person who takes no pepper takes no relish, so exactly one person does not take any of the three. Thus, each of the other two people take all three. The table below shows these results where Person 1 does not take any of the three and Persons 2 and 3 each take all three.

Person	Relish	Pepper	Salt
1	no	no	no
2	yes	yes	yes
3	yes	yes	yes

The only person who takes no salt is Person 1, who also takes no relish, so I must be true.

The only people who take pepper are Persons 2 and 3, and each of them also takes relish and salt, so II must be true.

The only person who takes no relish is Person 1, who is not a person who takes salt, so III must be true.

The correct answer is E.

PS88502.01

89. If a rectangle of area 24 can be partitioned into exactly 3 nonoverlapping squares of equal area, what is the length of the longest side of the rectangle?

(A) $2\sqrt{2}$
(B) 6
(C) 8
(D) $6\sqrt{2}$
(E) $12\sqrt{2}$

Geometry Rectangles

Because the squares all have the same area, the sides of the squares all have the same length. Let s be the common side length of the squares. Then the area of one of the squares is s^2 and the total area of the 3 nonoverlapping squares is $3s^2$. From the given information, it follows that $3s^2 = 24$, or $s^2 = 8$, or $s = \sqrt{8} = 2\sqrt{2}$. The diagram below shows how these squares must be arranged in the rectangle.

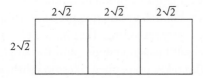

From the diagram, it follows that the length of the longest side of the rectangle is $2\sqrt{2} + 2\sqrt{2} + 2\sqrt{2} = 6\sqrt{2}$.

The correct answer is D.

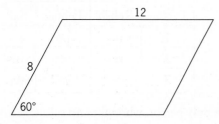

PS50602.01

90. In the figure above, the area of the parallelogram is

(A) 40
(B) $24\sqrt{3}$
(C) 72
(D) $48\sqrt{3}$
(E) 96

Geometry Quadrilaterals

The area of a parallelogram is the product of its base and its height. Letting the length

of the horizontal sides in the given figure be the parallelogram's base, then the area of the parallelogram is the product of 12 and the value of AC in the figure below. To determine the value of AC, observe that $\triangle ABC$ is a 30°-60°-90° triangle with hypotenuse of length 8. Therefore, the side opposite the 30° angle has length $BC = \frac{1}{2}(8) = 4$ and the side opposite the 60° angle has length $AC = \sqrt{3}(BC) = 4\sqrt{3}$. Hence, the area of the parallelogram is $(12)(4\sqrt{3}) = 48\sqrt{3}$.

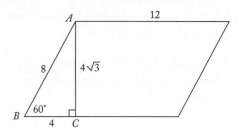

The correct answer is D.

PS91602.01

91. If the smaller of 2 consecutive odd integers is a multiple of 5, which of the following could NOT be the sum of these 2 integers?

(A) −8
(B) 12
(C) 22
(D) 52
(E) 252

Algebra Operations with Integers

Since the smaller of the 2 consecutive odd integers is a multiple of 5, let it be represented by $5n$ for some integer n. Then the other odd integer can be represented by $5n + 2$. The sum of these two integers is $10n + 2$. The sum is −8 when $n = -1$ and $5n = (5)(-1)$ is odd. The sum is 12 when $n = 1$ and $5n = (5)(1)$ is odd. The sum is 22 when $n = 2$, but $5n = (5)(2)$ is not odd. There is no need to check the D and E because it has been determined that 22 cannot be the sum of the 2 consecutive odd integers. For completeness, the sum is 52 when $n = 5$ and $5n = (5)(5)$ is odd. The sum is 252 when $n = 25$ and $5n = (5)(25)$ is odd.

The correct answer is C.

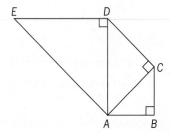

PS73602.01

92. In the figure above, if triangles *ABC*, *ACD*, and *ADE* are isosceles right triangles and the area of △*ABC* is 6, then the area of △*ADE* is

(A) 18

(B) 24

(C) 36

(D) $12\sqrt{2}$

(E) $24\sqrt{2}$

Geometry Triangles; Pythagorean Theorem

Because △*ABC* is an isosceles right triangle with legs $\overline{AB}$ and $\overline{BC}$, it follows that $AB = BC$ and the area of △*ABC* is $\frac{1}{2}(AB)(BC) = \frac{1}{2}(AB)^2$. It is given that the area of △*ABC* is 6, and thus $\frac{1}{2}(AB)^2 = 6$, or $(AB)^2 = 12$, or $AB = \sqrt{12}$. Applying the Pythagorean theorem to △*ABC* gives $(AC)^2 = (AB)^2 + (BC)^2$, and hence $(AC)^2 = \left(\sqrt{12}\right)^2 + \left(\sqrt{12}\right)^2 = 12 + 12 = 24$, or $AC = \sqrt{24}$. Because △*ACD* is an isosceles right triangle with legs $\overline{AC}$ and $\overline{CD}$, and $AC = \sqrt{24}$, it follows that $AC = CD = \sqrt{24}$. Applying the Pythagorean theorem to △*ACD* gives $(AD)^2 = (AC)^2 + (CD)^2$, and hence $(AD)^2 = \left(\sqrt{24}\right)^2 + \left(\sqrt{24}\right)^2 = 24 + 24 = 48$, or $AD = \sqrt{48}$. Because △*ADE* is an isosceles right triangle with legs $\overline{AD}$ and $\overline{DE}$, and $AD = \sqrt{48}$, it follows that $AD = DE = \sqrt{48}$, and hence the area of △*ADE* is $\frac{1}{2}(AD)(DE) = \frac{1}{2}\left(\sqrt{48}\right)\left(\sqrt{48}\right) = \frac{1}{2}(48) = 24$.

The correct answer is B.

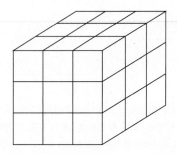

PS93602.01

93. Each of 27 white 1-centimeter cubes will have exactly one face painted red. If these 27 cubes are joined together to form one large cube, as shown above, what is the greatest possible fraction of the surface area that could be red?

(A) $\frac{11}{27}$

(B) $\frac{13}{27}$

(C) $\frac{1}{2}$

(D) $\frac{5}{9}$

(E) $\frac{19}{27}$

Geometry Rectangular Solids and Cylinders

All but one of the 1-centimeter cubes, namely the 1-centimeter cube in the center, has at least one face lying on the surface of the large cube. The greatest possible fraction of the surface of the large cube will be red when each of these $27 - 1 = 26$ non-center 1-centimeter cubes is oriented so that its red face lies on the surface of the large cube. Since the surface of the large cube has 6 faces, each consisting of 9 faces from the 1-centimeter cubes, the surface of the large cube consists of a total of $(6)(9) = 54$ faces from the 1-centimeter cubes. Therefore, the greatest possible fraction of the surface area that could be red is $\frac{26}{54} = \frac{13}{27}$.

The correct answer is B.

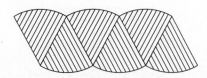

PS44602.01

94. The figure above is constructed by separating a circular region into 6 equal parts and rearranging the parts as shown. If the diameter of the circle is d, what is the perimeter of the figure above?

(A) πd

(B) $2\pi d$

(C) $\pi d + 2$

(D) $\pi d + d$

(E) $2\pi d + d$

Geometry Circles

The perimeter consists of 6 arcs and 2 segments. The total length of the 6 arcs is the circumference of the circle, which is πd. Each segment is a radius of the circle with length $\dfrac{d}{2}$. Therefore the perimeter of the figure is $\pi d + 2\left(\dfrac{d}{2}\right) = \pi d + d$.

The correct answer is D.

PS54602.01

95. On a scale drawing of a triangular piece of land, the sides of the triangle have lengths 5, 12, and 13 centimeters. If 1 centimeter on the drawing represents 3 meters, what is the area, in square meters, of the piece of land?

(A) 90

(B) 180

(C) 240

(D) 270

(E) 540

Geometry Triangles; Area; Measurement Conversion

Since $5^2 + 12^2 = 13^2$, the piece of land is in the shape of a right triangle. The lengths of the legs of the piece of land, in meters, are $(3)(5) = 15$ and $(3)(12) = 36$ since 1 centimeter on the drawing represents 3 meters on the piece of land. Therefore, the area, in square meters, of the piece of land is $\dfrac{1}{2}(15)(36) = 270$ square meters.

The correct answer is D.

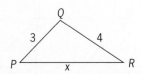

Note: Figure not drawn to scale.

PS05602.01

96. Which of the following gives all possible values of x in the figure above?

(A) $1 < x < 4$

(B) $1 < x < 7$

(C) $3 < x < 5$

(D) $4 < x < 7$

(E) $5 < x < 12$

Geometry Triangles

Because the sum of the lengths of two sides of a triangle must be greater than the length of the third side, $3 + 4 = 7 > x$ and $3 + x > 4$ or $x > 1$. Combining $7 > x$ and $x > 1$ gives $7 > x > 1$ or $1 < x < 7$.

The correct answer is B.

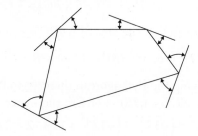

PS15602.01

97. In the figure above, lines are drawn at the vertices of the quadrilateral as shown. What is the sum of the degree measures of the marked angles?

(A) 450

(B) 360

(C) 270

(D) 240

(E) 180

Geometry Angles

The sum of the marked angles is the sum of 4 straight angles minus the sum of the interior angles of the quadrilateral or $(4)(180) - 360 = 360$.

The correct answer is B.

PS25602.01

98. The dimensions of a ream of paper are $8\frac{1}{2}$ inches by 11 inches by $2\frac{1}{2}$ inches. The inside dimensions of a carton that will hold exactly 12 reams of paper could be

(A) $8\frac{1}{2}$ in by 11 in by 12 in

(B) 17 in by 11 in by 15 in

(C) 17 in by 22 in by 3 in

(D) 51 in by 66 in by 15 in

(E) 102 in by 132 in by 30 in

Geometry Volume

In cubic inches, the total volume of 12 reams of paper is $12(8.5 \times 11 \times 2.5) = 2(8.5) \times 11 \times 6(2.5) = 17 \times 11 \times 15$, which is exactly the total volume represented by B.

The correct answer is B.

PS35602.01

99. In the racetrack shown above, regions I and III are semicircular with radius r. If region II is rectangular and its length is twice its width, what is the perimeter of the track in terms of r?

(A) $2r(\pi + 2)$

(B) $2r(\pi + 4)$

(C) $2r(\pi + 8)$

(D) $4r(\pi + 2)$

(E) $4r(\pi + 4)$

Geometry Perimeter

The figure shows that the (vertical) width of the racetrack is equal to the diameter of the semicircles, which is $2r$, and thus the (horizontal) length of the racetrack is $2(2r) = 4r$. Therefore, the perimeter of the racetrack, which consists of two semicircular arcs and two lengths of the rectangle, is $2(\pi r) + 2(4r) = 2r(\pi + 4)$.

The correct answer is B.

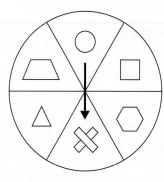

PS85602.01

100. The figure above, which is divided into 6 sectors of equal area, contains an arrow representing a spinner. If the spinner is rotated 3,840 degrees in a clockwise direction from the position shown, which of the following indicates the sector to which the arrow on the spinner will point?

(A) △

(B) □

(C) ○

(D) ⬠ (trapezoid)

(E) ⬡

Geometry Angle Measure in Degrees

The spinner rotates $\frac{3,840}{360} = \frac{32}{3} = 10\frac{2}{3}$ revolutions, which can also be seen by observing that 3,840 degrees − 3,600 degrees = 240 degrees $= \frac{2}{3}$ of a revolution. After making 10 revolutions, the spinner is back to the starting point and still needs to rotate $\frac{2}{3}$ of the way around the circle. Since rotating $\frac{2}{3}$ of the way around the circle is equivalent to rotating through 4 of the 6 sectors of the circle, the spinner will point to the sector with the square.

The correct answer is B.

PS95602.01

101. When a rectangular vat that is 3 feet deep is filled to $\frac{2}{3}$ of its capacity, it contains 60 gallons of water. If $7\frac{1}{2}$ gallons of water occupies 1 cubic foot of space, what is the area, in square feet, of the base of the vat?

(A)   4
(B)   8
(C)   12
(D)   150
(E)   225

Geometry Rectangular Solids and Cylinders

When filled to $\frac{2}{3}$ capacity, the vat contains 60 gallons of water (i.e., $\frac{2}{3}$(capacity) = 60), and so when it is filled to capacity it contains $\frac{3}{2}(60) = 90$ gallons of water, which occupies $\frac{90}{7.5} = 12$ cubic feet. If A represents the area of the base of the vat, in square feet, then the volume of the vat is $3A = 12$ cubic feet, and hence $A = 4$.

The correct answer is A.

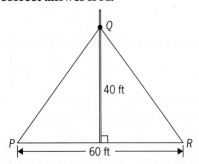

PS06602.01

102. The figure above represents an antenna tower with two guy wires that extend from point Q, 40 feet above the ground, to points P and R as shown. If the two wires have equal length, approximately what is the total length, in feet, of the two wires?

(A)   60
(B)   80
(C)   100
(D)   120
(E)   180

Geometry Triangles; Pythagorean Theorem

Because $PQ = QR$, it follows that $\triangle PQR$ is isosceles and the perpendicular from Q to $\overline{PR}$ bisects $\overline{PR}$. Therefore, each of the right triangles in the figure has legs that are 30 ft and 40 ft. By the Pythagorean theorem, $PQ = \sqrt{30^2 + 40^2} = 50$ and the total length of the two guy wires is 2(50 ft) = 100 ft.

The correct answer is C.

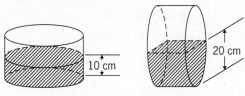

PS16602.01

103. The figures above show a sealed container that is a right circular cylinder filled with liquid to $\frac{1}{2}$ its capacity. If the container is placed on its base, the depth of the liquid in the container is 10 centimeters and if the container is placed on its side, the depth of the liquid is 20 centimeters. How many cubic centimeters of liquid are in the container?

(A) $4,000\pi$
(B) $2,000\pi$
(C) $1,000\pi$
(D) 400π
(E) 200π

Geometry Volume

The figure on the right, which shows the cylinder filled to $\frac{1}{2}$ its capacity, indicates that the radius of the cylinder is 20 cm. The figure on the left indicates that the height of the liquid is 10 cm. Using $V = \pi r^2 h$, where r is the radius and h is the height of the liquid in the cylinder, the volume of liquid in the cylindrical container is $\pi(20)^2(10) = 4,000\pi$ cubic centimeters.

The correct answer is A.

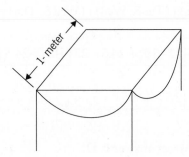

PS26602.01

104. The figure above shows a drop-leaf table. With all four leaves down the tabletop is a square, and with all four leaves up the tabletop is a circle. What is the radius, in meters, of the tabletop when all four leaves are up?

(A) $\frac{1}{2}$

(B) $\frac{\sqrt{2}}{2}$

(C) 1

(D) $\sqrt{2}$

(E) 2

Geometry Triangle

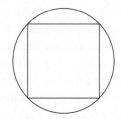

The figure above shows the circular tabletop viewed from above. The diameter of the circle is the diagonal of the square, which is 1 meter on a side. By the Pythagorean theorem, the diagonal is $\sqrt{1^2+1^2} = \sqrt{2}$ meters and the radius is $\frac{\sqrt{2}}{2}$ meters.

The correct answer is B.

PS36602.01

105. If the diameter of a circular skating rink is 60 meters, the area of the rink is approximately how many square meters?

(A) 90

(B) 180

(C) 900

(D) 2,800

(E) 10,800

Geometry Circles

If the diameter of the circular skating rink is 60 meters, then the radius is 30 meters and the area is $\pi(30)^2 = 900\pi$ square meters. Assuming the value of π to be slightly greater than 3, the rink is approximately 2,800 square meters.

The correct answer is D.

PS46602.01

106. What is the greatest number of blocks 8 centimeters by 6 centimeters by 9 centimeters that will fit into a storage space that is 60 centimeters by 72 centimeters by 96 centimeters?

(A) 60

(B) 840

(C) 896

(D) 960

(E) 1,080

Geometry Volume

The volume of the storage space is $60 \times 72 \times 96$ and each block is $6 \times 8 \times 9$, so the number of blocks that will fit is $\frac{60 \times 72 \times 96}{6 \times 8 \times 9} = \frac{60}{6} \times \frac{72}{9} \times \frac{96}{8} = 10 \times 8 \times 12 = 960$.

The correct answer is D.

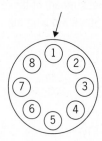

PS56602.01

107. Eight light bulbs numbered 1 through 8 are arranged in a circle as shown above. The bulbs are wired so that every third bulb, counting in a clockwise direction, flashes until all bulbs have flashed once. If the bulb numbered 1 flashes first, which numbered bulb will flash last?

(A) 2

(B) 3

(C) 4

(D) 6

(E) 7

Arithmetic Properties of Integers

The easiest way to do this problem might be by just counting every third bulb going clockwise around the circle starting at Bulb 1, which flashes, skipping 2 bulbs and getting to Bulb 4, which flashes, skipping 2 bulbs and getting to Bulb 7, which flashes, skipping 2 bulbs and getting to Bulb 2, which flashes, skipping 2 bulbs and getting to Bulb 5, which flashes, skipping 2 bulbs and getting to Bulb 8, which flashes, skipping 2 bulbs and getting to Bulb 3, which flashes, and finally skipping 2 bulbs and getting to Bulb 6, which flashes. Now, all 8 bulbs have flashed once and the last one to flash was Bulb 6.

The correct answer is D.

Closing Prices of Stock X
During a Certain Week
(in dollars)

Monday	Tuesday	Wednesday	Thursday	Friday
21	19	22	$24\frac{1}{2}$	23

PS28580.02

108. A certain financial analyst defines the "volatility" of a stock during a given week to be the result of the following procedure: find the absolute value of the difference in the stock's closing price for each pair of consecutive days in the week and then find the average (arithmetic mean) of these 4 values. What is the volatility of Stock X during the week shown in the table?

(A) 0.50
(B) 1.80
(C) 2.00
(D) 2.25
(E) 2.50

Arithmetic Statistics

The volatility of Stock X during the week is the average of the 4 values associated with the 4 pairs of consecutive days during the week.

$$\frac{(\text{Mon} \& \text{Tue}) + (\text{Tue} \& \text{Wed}) + (\text{Wed} \& \text{Thu}) + (\text{Thu} \& \text{Fri})}{4}$$

$$= \frac{|19 - 21| + |22 - 19| + |24.5 - 22| + |23 - 24.5|}{4}$$

$$= \frac{|-2| + |3| + |2.5| + |-1.5|}{4} = \frac{2 + 3 + 2.5 + 1.5}{4} = \frac{9}{4} = 2.25$$

The correct answer is D.

PS29580.02

109. If $y = \dfrac{|3x - 5|}{-x^2 - 3}$, for what value of x will the value of y be greatest?

(A) -5
(B) $-\dfrac{3}{5}$
(C) 0
(D) $\dfrac{3}{5}$
(E) $\dfrac{5}{3}$

Algebra Functions; Absolute Value

Since the absolute value of any real number is greater than or equal to zero, it follows that $|3x - 5| \geq 0$. Also, for any real number x we have $x^2 \geq 0$, and hence $-x^2 \leq 0$. Subtracting 3 from both sides of the last inequality gives $-x^2 - 3 \leq -3$. Therefore, the numerator of the expression for y is greater than or equal to zero and the denominator of the expression for y is negative. It follows that the value of y cannot be greater than 0. However, the value of y is equal to 0 when $|3x - 5| = 0$, or $3x - 5 = 0$, or $x = \dfrac{5}{3}$. Therefore, the value of x for which the value of y is greatest (i.e., when $y = 0$) is $x = \dfrac{5}{3}$.

The correct answer is E.

PS22680.02

110. What values of x have a corresponding value of y that satisfies both $xy > 0$ and $xy = x + y$?

(A) $x \leq -1$
(B) $-1 < x \leq 0$
(C) $0 < x \leq 1$
(D) $x > 1$
(E) All real numbers

Algebra Equations; Inequalities

First, use $xy = x + y$ to solve for y in terms of x.

$$
\begin{aligned}
xy &= x + y & \text{given} \\
xy - y &= x & \text{subtract } y \text{ from both sides} \\
y(x - 1) &= x & \text{factor} \\
y &= \frac{x}{x-1} & \text{divide both sides by } x - 1
\end{aligned}
$$

Note that the division by $x - 1$ requires $x \neq 1$, and thus $x = 1$ needs to be considered separately. However, if $x = 1$, then $xy = x + y$ becomes $y = 1 + y$, which is not true for any value of y.

Using $y = \frac{x}{x-1}$, it follows that the inequality $xy > 0$ is equivalent to $\frac{x^2}{x-1} > 0$. Since $x^2 \geq 0$ for each value of x, the quotient $\frac{x^2}{x-1}$ can only be positive when $x \neq 0$ and $x - 1$ is positive, or when $x > 1$.

Alternatively, the correct answer can be found by eliminating the incorrect answers, which can be accomplished by considering the endpoints of the intervals given in the answer choices.

Case 1: If $x = -1$, then $xy = x + y$ becomes $-y = -1 + y$, or $y = \frac{1}{2}$. However, in this case $xy = (-1)\left(\frac{1}{2}\right)$ is negative, and thus $xy > 0$ is not true. Therefore, the answer cannot be A or E.

Case 2: If $x = 0$, then $xy = 0$, and thus $xy > 0$ is not true. Therefore, the answer cannot be B or E.

Case 3: If $x = 1$, then $xy = x + y$ becomes $y = 1 + y$, which is not true for any value of y. Therefore, the answer cannot be C or E.

Since the answer cannot be A, B, C, or E, it follows that the answer is D.

The correct answer is D.

PS17680.02

111. Employee X's annual salary is $12,000 more than half of Employee Y's annual salary. Employee Z's annual salary is $15,000 more than half of Employee X's annual salary. If Employee X's annual salary is $27,500, which of the following lists these three people in order of increasing annual salary?

(A) Y, Z, X

(B) Y, X, Z

(C) Z, X, Y

(D) X, Y, Z

(E) X, Z, Y

Algebra First-Degree Equations

Letting x, y, and z represent the annual salary, in dollars, of Employee X, Employee Y, and Employee Z, respectively, the following information is given:

(1) $x = 12{,}000 + \dfrac{y}{2}$

(2) $z = 15{,}000 + \dfrac{x}{2}$

(3) $x = 27{,}500$

From (1) and (3), it follows that $27{,}500 = 12{,}000 + \dfrac{y}{2}$ or $y = 2(27{,}500 - 12{,}000) = 31{,}000$.
From (2) and (3), it follows that $z = 15{,}000 + \dfrac{27{,}500}{2} = 28{,}750$. Therefore, $x < z < y$.

The correct answer is E.

PS27680.02

112.
$$
C = \begin{cases} 0.10s, \text{ if } s \leq 60{,}000 \\ 0.10s + 0.04(s - 60{,}000), \text{ if } s > 60{,}000 \end{cases}
$$

The formula above gives the contribution C, in dollars, to a certain profit-sharing plan for a participant with a salary of s dollars. How many more dollars is the contribution for a participant with a salary of $70,000 than for a participant with a salary of $50,000 ?

(A) $800

(B) $1,400

(C) $2,000

(D) $2,400

(E) $2,800

GMAT™ Official Guide Quantitative Review 2022

Algebra Applied Problems; Formulas

For a participant with a salary of $70,000,
$C = 0.1(\$70,000) + 0.04(\$70,000 - \$60,000)$
$= \$7,000 + \$400 = \$7,400$. For a participant with
a salary of $50,000, $C = 0.1(\$50,000) = \$5,000$.
The difference is $7,400 - \$5,000 = \$2,400$.

The correct answer is D.

PS39680.02

113. Next month, Ron and Cathy will each begin working
part-time at $\frac{3}{5}$ of their respective current salaries.

If the sum of their reduced salaries will be equal to
Cathy's current salary, then Ron's current salary is what
fraction of Cathy's current salary?

(A) $\frac{1}{3}$

(B) $\frac{2}{5}$

(C) $\frac{1}{2}$

(D) $\frac{3}{5}$

(E) $\frac{2}{3}$

Algebra First-Degree Equations

Letting R and C, respectively, represent Ron's
and Cathy's current salaries, it is given that
$\frac{3}{5}R + \frac{3}{5}C = C$. It follows that $\frac{3}{5}R = \frac{2}{5}C$ and
$R = \frac{5}{3}\left(\frac{2}{5}C\right) = \frac{2}{3}C$.

The correct answer is E.

PS84780.02

114. David and Ron are ordering food for a business lunch.
David thinks that there should be twice as many
sandwiches as there are pastries, but Ron thinks the
number of pastries should be 12 more than one-fourth
of the number of sandwiches. How many sandwiches
should be ordered so that David and Ron can agree on
the number of pastries to order?

(A) 12
(B) 16
(C) 20
(D) 24
(E) 48

Algebra Simultaneous Equations

Let S be the number of sandwiches that should
be ordered and let P be the number of pastries
that should be ordered. Then David desires $S = 2P$
and Ron desires $P = 12 + \frac{1}{4}S$.

$S = 2P$ given

$S = 2(12 + \frac{1}{4}S)$ $P = 12 + \frac{1}{4}S$

$S = 24 + \frac{1}{2}S$ distributive law

$\frac{1}{2}S = 24$ subtract $\frac{1}{2}S$ from both sides

$S = 48$ multiply both sides by 2

The correct answer is E.

PS34880.02

115. The cost of purchasing each box of candy from a
certain mail order catalog is v dollars per pound of
candy, plus a shipping charge of h dollars. How many
dollars does it cost to purchase 2 boxes of candy, one
containing s pounds of candy and the other containing
t pounds of candy, from this catalog?

(A) $h + stv$
(B) $2h + stv$
(C) $2hstv$
(D) $2h + s + t + v$
(E) $2h + v(s + t)$

Algebra Formulas

The cost, in dollars, to purchase the 2 boxes of
candy is the sum of 2 shipping charges and the
cost of $s + t$ pounds of candy.

cost $=$ (2 shipping charges) $+ (v)(s + t)$
cost $=$ $2(h) + (v)(s + t)$
cost $=$ $2h + v(s + t)$

The correct answer is E.

PS16980.02

116. If $x \neq -\dfrac{1}{2}$, then $\dfrac{6x^3 + 3x^2 - 8x - 4}{2x + 1} =$

(A) $3x^2 + \dfrac{3}{2}x - 8$

(B) $3x^2 + \dfrac{3}{2}x - 4$

(C) $3x^2 - 4$

(D) $3x - 4$

(E) $3x + 4$

Algebra Factoring

$$\dfrac{6x^3 + 3x^2 - 8x - 4}{2x + 1} = \dfrac{(6x^3 + 3x^2) - (8x + 4)}{2x + 1} \qquad \text{group}$$

$$= \dfrac{3x^2(2x + 1) - 4(2x + 1)}{2x + 1} \qquad \text{factor}$$

$$= \dfrac{(3x^2 - 4)(2x + 1)}{2x + 1} \qquad \text{factor}$$

$$= 3x^2 - 4 \qquad \begin{array}{l}\text{cancel since}\\ x \neq \dfrac{1}{2}\end{array}$$

Alternatively, sometimes it is easier or quicker to test one-variable expressions for equality by substituting a convenient value for the variable and eliminating answer choices for which the value of the expression in that answer choice does not equal the value of the given expression. For example, choose $x = 0$, since calculations for $x = 0$ are minimal. Then, as shown in the table below, $\dfrac{6x^3 + 3x^2 - 8x - 4}{2x + 1} = \dfrac{-4}{1} = -4$, but $3x^2 + \dfrac{3}{2}x - 8 = -8$ and $3x + 4 = 4$, neither of which equals -4, so answer choices A and E can be eliminated. Another convenient value to choose for x is 1. There is no need to evaluate answer choices A and E at 1 since they have already been eliminated. As shown, when $x = 1$, $\dfrac{6x^3 + 3x^2 - 8x - 4}{2x + 1} = -1$, but $3x^2 + \dfrac{3}{2}x - 4 = \dfrac{1}{2} \neq -1$, so answer choice B can be eliminated. A third convenient value for x is -1. There is no need to evaluate answer choices A, B, and E at -1 since they have already been eliminated. As shown, when $x = -1$, $\dfrac{6x^3 + 3x^2 - 8x - 4}{2x + 1} = -1$, but $3x - 4 = -7 \neq -1$, so answer choice D can be

eliminated. Note that, if $x = -1$ had been chosen initially, A, B, D, and E would have been eliminated immediately since $3x^2 + \dfrac{3}{2}x - 8 = -6\dfrac{1}{2} \neq -1$, $3x^2 + \dfrac{3}{2}x - 4 = -2\dfrac{1}{2} \neq -1$, $3x - 4 = -7 \neq -1$, and $3x + 4 = 1 \neq -1$.

		$x = 0$	$x = 1$	$x = -1$
	$\dfrac{6x^3 + 3x^2 - 8x - 4}{2x + 1}$	-4	-1	-1
A	$3x^2 + \dfrac{3}{2}x - 8$	-8		
B	$3x^2 + \dfrac{3}{2}x - 4$	-4	$\dfrac{1}{2}$	
C	$3x^2 - 4$	-4	-1	-1
D	$3x - 4$	-4	-1	-7
E	$3x + 4$	4		

The correct answer is C.

PS29980.02

117. If $x^2 + bx + 5 = (x + c)^2$ for all numbers x, where b and c are positive constants, what is the value of b?

(A) $\sqrt{5}$

(B) $\sqrt{10}$

(C) $2\sqrt{5}$

(D) $2\sqrt{10}$

(E) 10

Algebra Second-Degree Equations

Given that $x^2 + bx + 5 = (x + c)^2$, since $(x + c)^2 = x^2 + 2cx + c^2$, it follows that $5 = c^2$ and $b = 2c$. The possible values of c are $-\sqrt{5}$ and $\sqrt{5}$, but since c is positive, $c = \sqrt{5}$ and $b = 2c = 2\sqrt{5}$.

The correct answer is C.

PS08090.02

118. Last year Shannon listened to a certain public radio station 10 hours per week and contributed $35 to the station. Of the following, which is closest to Shannon's contribution per minute of listening time last year?

(A) $0.001

(B) $0.010

(C) $0.025

(D) $0.058

(E) $0.067

Arithmetic Measurement Conversion

Since there are 52 weeks in 1 year and 60 minutes in 1 hour, 10 hours per week is equivalent to (10)(52)(60) = 31,200 minutes per year. Shannon's $35 contribution is then $\frac{35}{31,200}$ dollars per minute, which is closest to $0.001 per minute.

The correct answer is A.

PS97190.02
119. Each of the 20 employees at Company J is to receive an end-of-year bonus this year. Agnes will receive a larger bonus than any other employee, but only $500 more than Cheryl will receive. None of the employees will receive a smaller bonus than Cheryl. If the amount of money to be distributed in bonuses at Company J this year totals $60,000, what is the largest bonus Agnes can receive?

(A) $3,250
(B) $3,325
(C) $3,400
(D) $3,475
(E) $3,500

Algebra Applied Problems

Since the total amount of the bonuses is fixed, the largest possible bonus that Agnes can receive will occur when the total amount received by the 19 employees other than Agnes is the smallest possible. Let A be the bonus, in dollars, that Agnes receives. Then, in dollars, Cheryl will receive $(A-500)$, and each of the remaining 18 employees will receive between $(A-500)$ and A. Therefore, the total amount received by the 19 employees other than Agnes is smallest when each of these 19 employees receives $(A-500)$ dollars.

$19(A-500)+A$	=	60,000	total of 20 bonuses is $60,000
$19A-9,500+A$	=	60,000	distributive law
$20A-9,500$	=	60,000	combine like terms
$20A$	=	69,500	add 9,500 to both sides
A	=	3,475	divide both sides by 20

The correct answer is D.

PS90731.02
120. Beth, Naomi, and Juan raised a total of $55 for charity. Naomi raised $5 less than Juan, and Juan raised twice as much as Beth. How much did Beth raise?

(A) $9
(B) $10
(C) $12
(D) $13
(E) $15

Algebra Simultaneous Equations

Let B, N, and J be the amounts raised, respectively and in dollars, by Beth, Naomi, and Juan.

$B+N+J$	=	55	given
N	=	$J-5$	given
J	=	$2B$	given
J	=	$55-B-N$	subtract $B+N$ from both sides of first equation
J	=	$55-B-(J-5)$	$N=J-5$
$2B$	=	$55-B-(2B-5)$	$J=2B$
B	=	12	solve for B

The correct answer is C.

PS16731.02
121. The set of solutions for the equation $(x^2-25)^2 = x^2-10x+25$ contains how many real numbers?

(A) 0
(B) 1
(C) 2
(D) 3
(E) 4

Algebra Second-Degree Equations

$(x^2-25)^2$	$= x^2-10x+25$	given
$(x+5)^2(x-5)^2$	$= (x-5)^2$	factor
$(x+5)^2(x-5)^2-(x-5)^2$	$= 0$	subtract $(x-5)^2$
$(x-5)^2[(x+5)^2-1]$	$= 0$	factor
$(x-5)^2[(x+5)-1]$		
$[(x+5)+1]$	$= 0$	factor
$(x-5)^2(x+4)(x+6)$	$= 0$	subtraction, addition

Thus the solution set of $(x^2 - 25)^2 = x^2 - 10x + 25$ contains 3 real numbers: 5, −4, and −6.

The correct answer is D.

PS67941.02

122. An aerosol can is designed so that its bursting pressure, B, in pounds per square inch, is 120% of the pressure, F, in pounds per square inch, to which it is initially filled. Which of the following formulas expresses the relationship between B and F?

(A) $B = 1.2F$

(B) $B = 120F$

(C) $B = 1 + 0.2F$

(D) $B = \dfrac{F}{1.2}$

(E) $B = \dfrac{1.2}{F}$

Algebra Formulas; Percents

We are given that B is 120% of F, so $B = (120\%)F$, or $B = 1.2F$. Note that both B and F are given in pounds per square inch, so there are no unit conversions involved.

The correct answer is A.

PS00986

123. The average (arithmetic mean) of the positive integers x, y, and z is 3. If $x < y < z$, what is the greatest possible value of z?

(A) 5

(B) 6

(C) 7

(D) 8

(E) 9

Algebra Inequalities

It is given that $\dfrac{x + y + z}{3} = 3$, or $x + y + z = 9$, or $z = 9 + (-x - y)$. It follows that the greatest possible value of z occurs when $-x - y = -(x + y)$ has the greatest possible value, which occurs when $x + y$ has the least possible value. Because x and y are different positive integers, the least possible value of $x + y$ occurs when $x = 1$ and $y = 2$. Therefore, the greatest possible value of z is $9 - 1 - 2 = 6$.

The correct answer is B.

PS14087

124. The product of 3,305 and the 1-digit integer x is a 5-digit integer. The units (ones) digit of the product is 5 and the hundreds digit is y. If A is the set of all possible values of x and B is the set of all possible values of y, then which of the following gives the members of A and B?

	A	B
(A)	{1, 3, 5, 7, 9}	{0, 1, 2, 3, 4, 5, 6, 7, 8, 9}
(B)	{1, 3, 5, 7, 9}	{1, 3, 5, 7, 9}
(C)	{3, 5, 7, 9}	{1, 5, 7, 9}
(D)	{5, 7, 9}	{1, 5, 7}
(E)	{5, 7, 9}	{1, 5, 9}

Arithmetic Properties of Numbers

Since the products of 3,305 and 1, 3,305 and 2, and 3,305 and 3 are the 4-digit integers 3,305, 6,610, and 9,915, respectively, it follows that x must be among the 1-digit integers 4, 5, 6, 7, 8, and 9. Also, since the units digit of the product of 3,305 and x is 5, it follows that x cannot be 4 (product has units digit 0), 6 (product has units digit 0), or 8 (product has units digit 0). Therefore, $A = \{5, 7, 9\}$. The possibilities for y will be the hundreds digits of the products $(3,305)(5) = 16,525$, $(3,305)(7) = 23,135$, and $(3,305)(9) = 29,745$. Thus, y can be 5, 1, or 7, and so $B = \{1, 5, 7\}$.

The correct answer is D.

PS07001

125. If x and y are integers such that $2 < x \le 8$ and $2 < y \le 9$, what is the maximum value of $\dfrac{1}{x} - \dfrac{x}{y}$?

(A) $-3\dfrac{1}{8}$

(B) 0

(C) $\dfrac{1}{4}$

(D) $\dfrac{5}{18}$

(E) 2

Algebra Inequalities

Because x and y are both positive, the maximum value of $\dfrac{1}{x} - \dfrac{x}{y}$ will occur when the value of $\dfrac{1}{x}$ is maximum and the value of $\dfrac{x}{y}$ is minimum. The value of $\dfrac{1}{x}$ is maximum when the value of

x is minimum or when $x = 3$. The value of $\frac{x}{y}$ is minimum when the value of x is minimum (or when $x = 3$) and the value of y is maximum (or when $y = 9$). Thus, the maximum value of $\frac{1}{x} - \frac{x}{y}$ is $\frac{1}{3} - \frac{3}{9} = 0$.

The correct answer is B.

PS01875

126. Items that are purchased together at a certain discount store are priced at $3 for the first item purchased and $1 for each additional item purchased. What is the maximum number of items that could be purchased together for a total price that is less than $30 ?

(A)   25

(B)   26

(C)   27

(D)   28

(E)   29

Arithmetic Applied Problems

After the first item is purchased, $29.99 − $3.00 = $26.99 remains to purchase the additional items. Since the price for each of the additional items is $1.00, a maximum of 26 additional items could be purchased. Therefore, a maximum of $1 + 26 = 27$ items could be purchased for less than $30.00.

The correct answer is C.

PS00774

127. What is the least integer z for which (0.000125) $(0.0025)(0.00000125) \times 10^z$ is an integer?

(A)   18

(B)   10

(C)   0

(D)   −10

(E)   −18

Arithmetic Decimals

Considering each of the three decimal numbers in parentheses separately, we know that 0.000125×10^6 is the integer 125, 0.0025×10^4 is the integer 25, and 0.00000125×10^8 is the integer 125. We thus know that $(0.000125) \times 10^6 \times (0.0025) \times 10^4 \times (0.00000125) \times 10^8 = (0.000125)(0.0025)(0.00000125) \times 10^6 \times 10^4 \times 10^8 = (0.000125)(0.0025)(0.00000125) \times$

$10^{6+4+8} = (0.000125)(0.0025)(0.00000125) \times 10^{18}$ is the integer $125 \times 25 \times 125$. We therefore know that if $z = 18$, then $(0.000125)(0.0025)$ $(0.00000125) \times 10^z$ is an integer.

Now, if the product $125 \times 25 \times 125$ were divisible by 10, then for at least one integer z less than 18, $(0.000125)(0.0025)(0.00000125) \times 10^z$ would be an integer. However, each of the three numbers being multiplied in the product $125 \times 25 \times 125$ is odd (not divisible by 2). We thus know that $125 \times 25 \times 125$ is not divisible by 2 and is therefore odd. Because only even numbers are divisible by 10, we know that $125 \times 25 \times 125$ is not divisible by 10. We thus know that 18 is the *least* integer z such that $(0.000125)(0.0025)$ $(0.00000125) \times 10^z$ is an integer.

Note that it is not necessary to perform the multiplication $125 \times 25 \times 125$.

The correct answer is A.

PS08407

128. The average (arithmetic mean) length per film for a group of 21 films is t minutes. If a film that runs for 66 minutes is removed from the group and replaced by one that runs for 52 minutes, what is the average length per film, in minutes, for the new group of films, in terms of t ?

(A) $t + \frac{2}{3}$

(B) $t - \frac{2}{3}$

(C) $21t + 14$

(D) $t + \frac{3}{2}$

(E) $t - \frac{3}{2}$

Arithmetic Statistics

Let S denote the sum of the lengths, in minutes, of the 21 films in the original group. Since the average length is t minutes, it follows that $\frac{S}{21} = t$.

If a 66-minute film is replaced by a 52-minute film, then the sum of the lengths of the 21 films in the resulting group is $S - 66 + 52 = S - 14$. Therefore, the average length of the resulting 21 films is $\frac{S - 14}{21} = \frac{S}{21} - \frac{14}{21} = t - \frac{2}{3}$.

The correct answer is B.

PS08051

129. An open box in the shape of a cube measuring 50 centimeters on each side is constructed from plywood. If the plywood weighs 1.5 grams per square centimeter, which of the following is closest to the total weight, in kilograms, of the plywood used for the box? (1 kilogram = 1,000 grams)

(A)   2
(B)   4
(C)   8
(D)   13
(E)   19

Geometry Surface Area

The total weight of the box is the sum of the weights of the 4 lateral sides of the box and the bottom of the box. Since the sides of the box all have the same area and the same density throughout, the total weight of the box is 5 times the weight of a side of the box. In grams, the weight of a side of the box is $(A \text{ cm}^2)\left(1.5 \dfrac{\text{g}}{\text{cm}^2}\right)$, where A is the area of a side of the box in square centimeters. Since $A = (50 \text{ cm})(50 \text{ cm}) = 2{,}500 \text{ cm}^2$, the weight of a side of the box is $(2{,}500)(1.5) = 3{,}750$ grams = 3.75 kilograms. Therefore, the total weight of the box is $5(3.75) = 18.75$ kilograms.

The correct answer is E.

PS03614

130. A garden center sells a certain grass seed in 5-pound bags at $13.85 per bag, 10-pound bags at $20.43 per bag, and 25-pound bags at $32.25 per bag. If a customer is to buy at least 65 pounds of the grass seed, but no more than 80 pounds, what is the least possible cost of the grass seed that the customer will buy?

(A) $94.03
(B) $96.75
(C) $98.78
(D) $102.07
(E) $105.36

Arithmetic Applied Problems

Let x represent the amount of grass seed, in pounds, the customer is to buy. It follows that $65 \le x \le 80$. Since the grass seed is available in only 5-pound, 10-pound, and 25-pound bags, then the customer must buy either 65, 70, 75, or 80 pounds of grass seed. Because the seed is more expensive per pound for smaller bags, the customer should minimize the number of the smaller bags and maximize the number of 25-pound bags to incur the least possible cost for the grass seed. The possible purchases are given in the table below.

x	Number of 25-pound bags	Number of 10-pound bags	Number of 5-pound bags	Total cost
65	2	1	1	$98.78
70	2	2	0	$105.36
75	3	0	0	$96.75
80	3	0	1	$110.60

The least possible cost is then $3(\$32.25) = \$96.75$.

The correct answer is B.

PS12785

131. If $x = -|w|$, which of the following must be true?

(A) $x = -w$
(B) $x = w$
(C) $x^2 = w$
(D) $x^2 = w^2$
(E) $x^3 = w^3$

Algebra Absolute Value

Squaring both sides of $x = -|w|$ gives $x^2 = (-|w|)^2$, or $x^2 = |w|^2 = w^2$.

Alternatively, if (x, w) is equal to either of the pairs $(-1,1)$ or $(-1,-1)$, then $x = -|w|$ is true. However, each of the answer choices except $x^2 = w^2$ is false for at least one of these two pairs.

The correct answer is D.

PS04160
132. A certain financial institution reported that its assets totaled $2,377,366.30 on a certain day. Of this amount, $31,724.54 was held in cash. Approximately what percent of the reported assets was held in cash on that day?

(A)   0.00013%

(B)   0.0013%

(C)   0.013%

(D)   0.13%

(E)   1.3%

Arithmetic Percents; Estimation

The requested percent can be estimated by converting the values into scientific notation.

$$\frac{31,724.54}{2,377,366.30}$$ value as fraction

$$=\frac{3.172454\times10^{4}}{2.37736630\times10^{6}}$$ convert to scientific notation

$$=\frac{3.172454}{2.37736630}\times\frac{10^{4}}{10^{6}}$$ arithmetic property of fractions

$$=\frac{3.172454}{2.37736630}\times10^{-2}$$ subtract exponents

$$\approx\frac{3}{2}\times10^{-2}$$ approximate

$$=1.5\times10^{-2}$$ convert to decimal fraction

$$=0.015$$ multiply

$$=1.5\%$$ convert to percent

A more detailed computation would show that 1.3% is a better approximation. However, in order to select the best value from the values given as answer choices, the above computation is sufficient.

The correct answer is E.

$$
\begin{array}{r}
AB \\
+\ BA \\
\hline
AAC
\end{array}
$$

PS09820
133. In the correctly worked addition problem shown, where the sum of the two-digit positive integers AB and BA is the three-digit integer AAC, and A, B, and C are different digits, what is the units digit of the integer AAC?

(A)   9

(B)   6

(C)   3

(D)   2

(E)   0

Arithmetic Place Value

Determine the value of C.

It is given that $(10A+B)+(10B+A)=100A+10A+C$ or $11A+11B=110A+C$. Thus, $11B-99A=C$, or $11(B-9A)=C$. Therefore, C is divisible by 11, and 0 is the only digit that is divisible by 11.

The correct answer is E.

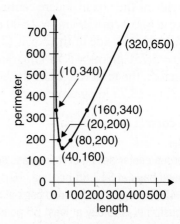

PS14060
134. Planning is in progress for a fenced, rectangular playground with an area of 1,600 square meters. The graph above shows the perimeter, in meters, as a function of the length of the playground. The length of the playground should be how many meters to minimize the perimeter and, therefore, the amount of fencing needed to enclose the playground?

(A)   10

(B)   40

(C)   60

(D)   160

(E)   340

Geometry Simple Coordinate Geometry

Since values of the perimeter are represented on the vertical axis, the point on the graph that corresponds to the minimum perimeter is the point on the graph that has the least y-coordinate, which is (40,160). This point corresponds to a length of 40 meters, which is what the question asked, and a perimeter of 160 meters.

The correct answer is B.

PS89670.02

135. The hard drive, monitor, and printer for a certain desktop computer system cost a total of $2,500. The cost of the printer and monitor together is equal to $\frac{2}{3}$ of the cost of the hard drive. If the cost of the printer is $100 more than the cost of the monitor, what is the cost of the printer?

(A) $800
(B) $600
(C) $550
(D) $500
(E) $350

Algebra Simultaneous Equations

Letting d, m, and p, respectively, represent the cost of the hard drive, monitor, and printer, the following equations are given:

(1) $d + m + p = 2,500$

(2) $p + m = \frac{2}{3}d$

(3) $p = m + 100$

Using (2) and substituting $\frac{2}{3}d$ for $m + p$ in (1) gives $\frac{5}{3}d = 2,500$, from which $d = 1,500$. Then from (1), $p + m = 1,000$, but $m = p - 100$ from (2), so $2p - 100 = 1,000$, $2p = 1,100$, and $p = 550$.

The correct answer is C.

$$3r \leq 4s + 5$$
$$|s| \leq 5$$

PS06913

136. Given the inequalities above, which of the following CANNOT be the value of r?

(A) −20
(B) −5
(C) 0
(D) 5
(E) 20

Algebra Inequalities

Since $|s| \leq 5$, it follows that $-5 \leq s \leq 5$. Therefore, $-20 \leq 4s \leq 20$, and hence $-15 \leq 4s + 5 \leq 25$. Since $3r \leq 4s + 5$ (given) and $4s + 5 \leq 25$ (end of previous sentence), it follows that $3r \leq 25$. Among the answer choices, $3r \leq 25$ is false only for $r = 20$.

The correct answer is E.

PS11647

137. If m is an even integer, v is an odd integer, and $m > v > 0$, which of the following represents the number of even integers less than m and greater than v?

(A) $\dfrac{m-v}{2} - 1$

(B) $\dfrac{m-v-1}{2}$

(C) $\dfrac{m-v}{2}$

(D) $m - v - 1$

(E) $m - v$

Arithmetic Properties of Numbers

Since there is only one correct answer, one method of solving the problem is to choose values for m and v and determine which of the expressions gives the correct number for these values. For example, if $m = 6$ and $v = 1$, then there are 2 even integers less than 6 and greater than 1, namely the even integers 2 and 4. As the table below shows, $\dfrac{m-v-1}{2}$ is the only expression given that equals 2.

$$\frac{m-v}{2}-1=1.5$$

$$\frac{m-v-1}{2}=2$$

$$\frac{m-v}{2}=2.5$$

$$m-v-1=4$$

$$m-v=5$$

To solve this problem it is not necessary to show that $\dfrac{m-v-1}{2}$ always gives the correct number of even integers. However, one way this can be done is by the following method, first shown for a specific example and then shown in general. For the specific example, suppose $v=15$ and $m=144$. Then a list—call it the first list—of the even integers greater than v and less than m is 16, 18, 20, …, 140, 142. Now subtract 14 (chosen so that the second list will begin with 2) from each of the integers in the first list to form a second list, which has the same number of integers as the first list: 2, 4, 6, …, 128. Finally, divide each of the integers in the second list (all of which are even) by 2 to form a third list, which also has the same number of integers as the first list: 1, 2, 3, …, 64. Since the number of integers in the third list is 64, it follows that the number of integers in the first list is 64. For the general situation, the first list is the following list of even integers: $v+1$, $v+3$, $v+5$, …, $m-4$, $m-2$. Now subtract the even integer $v-1$ from (i.e., add $-v+1$ to) each of the integers in the first list to obtain the second list: 2, 4, 6, …, $m-v-3$, $m-v-1$. (Note, for example, that $m-4-(v-1)=m-v-3$.) Finally, divide each of the integers (all of which are even) in the second list by 2 to obtain the third list: 1, 2, 3, …, $\dfrac{m-v-3}{2}$, $\dfrac{m-v-1}{2}$.

Since the number of integers in the third list is $\dfrac{m-v-1}{2}$, it follows that the number of integers in the first list is $\dfrac{m-v-1}{2}$.

The correct answer is B.

PS02378
138. A positive integer is divisible by 9 if and only if the sum of its digits is divisible by 9. If n is a positive integer, for which of the following values of k is $25 \times 10^n + k \times 10^{2n}$ divisible by 9 ?

(A) 9
(B) 16
(C) 23
(D) 35
(E) 47

Arithmetic Properties of Numbers

Since n can be any positive integer, let $n=2$. Then $25 \times 10^n = 2{,}500$, so its digits consist of the digits 2 and 5 followed by two digits of 0. Also, $k \times 10^{2n} = k \times 10{,}000$, so its digits consist of the digits of k followed by four digits of 0. Therefore, the digits of $(25 \times 10^n)+(k \times 10^{2n})$ consist of the digits of k followed by the digits 2 and 5, followed by two digits of 0. The table below shows this for $n=2$ and $k=35$:

$$25 \times 10^n = \quad 2{,}500$$
$$35 \times 10^{2n} = 350{,}000$$
$$(25 \times 10^n)+(35 \times 10^{2n}) = 352{,}500$$

Thus, when $n=2$, the sum of the digits of $(25 \times 10^n)+(k \times 10^{2n})$ will be $2+5=7$ plus the sum of the digits of k. Of the answer choices, this sum of digits is divisible by 9 only for $k=47$, which gives $2+5+4+7=18$. It can also be verified that, for each positive integer n, the only such answer choice is $k=47$, although this additional verification is not necessary to obtain the correct answer.

The correct answer is E.

PS17806
139. The perimeter of rectangle A is 200 meters. The length of rectangle B is 10 meters less than the length of rectangle A and the width of rectangle B is 10 meters more than the width of rectangle A. If rectangle B is a square, what is the width, in meters, of rectangle A ?

(A) 10
(B) 20
(C) 40
(D) 50
(E) 60

Geometry Rectangles; Perimeter

Let L meters and W meters be the length and width, respectively, of rectangle A. Then $(L - 10)$ meters and $(W + 10)$ meters are the length and width, respectively, of rectangle B. Since the perimeter of rectangle A is 200 meters, it follows that $2L + 2W = 200$, or $L + W = 100$. Since rectangle B is a square, it follows that $L - 10 = W + 10$, or $L - W = 20$. Adding the equations $L + W = 100$ and $L - W = 20$ gives $2L = 120$, or $L = 60$. From $L - W = 20$ and $L = 60$, it follows that $W = 40$, and so the width of rectangle A is 40 meters.

The correct answer is C.

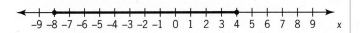

PS08598

140. On the number line, the shaded interval is the graph of which of the following inequalities?

(A) $|x| \leq 4$

(B) $|x| \leq 8$

(C) $|x - 2| \leq 4$

(D) $|x - 2| \leq 6$

(E) $|x + 2| \leq 6$

Algebra Inequalities; Absolute Value

The midpoint of the interval from –8 to 4, inclusive, is $\dfrac{-8 + 4}{2} = -2$ and the length of the interval from –8 to 4, inclusive, is $4 - (-8) = 12$, so the interval consists of all numbers within a distance of $\dfrac{12}{2} = 6$ from –2. Using an inequality involving absolute values, this can be described by $|x - (-2)| \leq 6$, or $|x + 2| \leq 6$.

Alternatively, the inequality $-8 \leq x \leq 4$ can be written as the conjunction $-8 \leq x$ and $x \leq 4$. Rewrite this conjunction so that the lower value, –8, and the upper value, 4, are shifted to values that have the same magnitude. This can be done by adding 2 to each side of each inequality, which gives $-6 \leq x + 2$ and $x + 2 \leq 6$. Thus, $x + 2$ lies between –6 and 6, inclusive, and it follows that $|x + 2| \leq 6$.

The correct answer is E.

PS12450

141. Last year members of a certain professional organization for teachers consisted of teachers from 49 different school districts, with an average (arithmetic mean) of 9.8 schools per district. Last year the average number of teachers at these schools who were members of the organization was 22. Which of the following is closest to the total number of members of the organization last year?

(A) 10^7

(B) 10^6

(C) 10^5

(D) 10^4

(E) 10^3

Arithmetic Statistics

There are 49 school districts and an average of 9.8 schools per district, so the number of schools is $(49)(9.8) \approx (50)(10) = 500$. There are approximately 500 schools and an average of 22 teachers at each school, so the number of teachers is approximately $(500)(22) \approx (500)(20) = 10,000 = 10^4$.

The correct answer is D.

PS09294

142. Of all the students in a certain dormitory, $\dfrac{1}{2}$ are first-year students and the rest are second-year students. If $\dfrac{4}{5}$ of the first-year students have <u>not</u> declared a major and if the fraction of second-year students who have declared a major is 3 times the fraction of first-year students who have declared a major, what fraction of all the students in the dormitory are second-year students who have <u>not</u> declared a major?

(A) $\dfrac{1}{15}$

(B) $\dfrac{1}{5}$

(C) $\dfrac{4}{15}$

(D) $\dfrac{1}{3}$

(E) $\dfrac{2}{5}$

Arithmetic Applied Problems

Consider the table below in which T represents the total number of students in the dormitory. Since $\frac{1}{2}$ of the students are first-year students and the rest are second-year students, it follows that $\frac{1}{2}$ of the students are second-year students, and so the totals for the first-year and second-year columns are both $0.5T$. Since $\frac{4}{5}$ of the first-year students have not declared a major, it follows that the middle entry in the first-year column is $\frac{4}{5}(0.5T) = 0.4T$ and the first entry in the first-year column is $0.5T - 0.4T = 0.1T$. Since the fraction of second-year students who have declared a major is 3 times the fraction of first-year students who have declared a major, it follows that the first entry in the second-year column is $3(0.1T) = 0.3T$ and the second entry in the second-year column is $0.5T - 0.3T = 0.2T$. Thus, the fraction of students that are second-year students who have not declared a major is $\frac{0.2T}{T} = 0.2 = \frac{1}{5}$.

	First-year	Second-year	Total
Declared major	$0.1T$	$0.3T$	$0.4T$
Not declared major	$0.4T$	$0.2T$	$0.6T$
Total	$0.5T$	$0.5T$	T

The correct answer is B.

PS09050

143. If the average (arithmetic mean) of x, y, and z is $7x$ and $x \neq 0$, what is the ratio of x to the sum of y and z?

(A)   1:21
(B)   1:20
(C)   1:6
(D)   6:1
(E)   20:1

Algebra Ratio and Proportion

Given that the average of x, y, and z is $7x$, it follows that $\frac{x+y+z}{3} = 7x$, or $x + y + z = 21x$, or $y + z = 20x$. Dividing both sides of the last

equation by $20(y + z)$ gives $\frac{1}{20} = \frac{x}{y+z}$, so the ratio of x to the sum of y and z is 1:20.

The correct answer is B.

PS05413

144. Jonah drove the first half of a 100-mile trip in x hours and the second half in y hours. Which of the following is equal to Jonah's average speed, in miles per hour, for the entire trip?

(A) $\dfrac{50}{x+y}$

(B) $\dfrac{100}{x+y}$

(C) $\dfrac{25}{x} + \dfrac{25}{y}$

(D) $\dfrac{50}{x} + \dfrac{50}{y}$

(E) $\dfrac{100}{x} + \dfrac{100}{y}$

Algebra Applied Problems

Using average speed $= \dfrac{\text{total distance}}{\text{total time}}$, it follows that Jonah's average speed for his entire 100-mile trip is $\dfrac{100}{x+y}$.

The correct answer is B.

PS11454

145. In the xy-plane, the points (c,d), $(c,-d)$, and $(-c,d)$ are three vertices of a certain square. If $c < 0$ and $d > 0$, which of the following points is in the same quadrant as the fourth vertex of the square?

(A) $(-5,-3)$
(B) $(-5,3)$
(C) $(5,-3)$
(D) $(3,-5)$
(E) $(3,5)$

Geometry Coordinate Geometry

Because the points (c,d) and $(c,-d)$ lie on the same vertical line (the line with equation $x = c$), one side of the square has length $2d$ and is vertical. Therefore, the side of the square opposite this side has length $2d$, is vertical, and contains the vertex $(-c,-d)$. From this it follows that the remaining vertex is $(-c,d)$, because $(-c,d)$ lies on the same vertical line as $(-c,-d)$ (the line with equation $x = -c$) and these two vertices are a distance $2d$ apart. Because $c < 0$ and $d > 0$, the point $(-c,d)$ has positive x-coordinate and positive y-coordinate. Thus, the point $(-c,d)$ is in Quadrant I. Of the answer choices, only $(3,5)$ is in Quadrant I.

The correct answer is E.

PS05470

146. If the amount of federal estate tax due on an estate valued at $1.35 million is $437,000 plus 43 percent of the value of the estate in excess of $1.25 million, then the federal tax due is approximately what percent of the value of the estate?

(A) 30%
(B) 35%
(C) 40%
(D) 45%
(E) 50%

Arithmetic Percents; Estimation

The amount of tax divided by the value of the estate is

$$\frac{[0.437 + (0.43)(1.35 - 1.25)] \text{ million}}{1.35 \text{ million}} \quad \text{value as fraction}$$

$$= \frac{0.437 + (0.43)(0.1)}{1.35} \quad \text{arithmetic}$$

$$= \frac{0.48}{1.35} = \frac{48}{135} \quad \text{arithmetic}$$

By long division, $\dfrac{48}{135}$ is approximately 35.6, so the closest answer choice is 35%.

Alternatively, $\dfrac{48}{135}$ can be estimated by

$\dfrac{48}{136} = \dfrac{6}{17} \approx \dfrac{6}{18} = \dfrac{1}{3} \approx 33\%$, so the closest answer choice is 35%. Note that $\dfrac{48}{135}$ is greater than $\dfrac{48}{136}$, and $\dfrac{6}{17}$ is greater than $\dfrac{6}{18}$, so the correct value is greater than 33%, which rules out 30% being the closest.

The correct answer is B.

$$7x + 6y \le 38,000$$
$$4x + 5y \le 28,000$$

PS30421.02

147. A manufacturer wants to produce x balls and y boxes. Resource constraints require that x and y satisfy the inequalities shown. What is the maximum number of balls and boxes combined that can be produced given the resource constraints?

(A) 5,000
(B) 6,000
(C) 7,000
(D) 8,000
(E) 10,000

Algebra Inequalities

We are to determine the maximum value of $x + y$ given the inequalities above. Note that if $A \le B$ and $C \le D$, then we can "add inequalities" to obtain $A + C \le B + D$, since (roughly speaking) the sum of two smaller numbers is less than the sum of two larger numbers. Adding the inequalities shown above gives $(7x + 6y) + (4x + 5y) \le 38,000 + 28,000$, or $11x + 11y \le 66,000$. Dividing both sides of this last inequality by 11 gives $x + y \le 6,000$. Therefore, the values of $x + y$ are at most 6,000, and hence the maximum value of $x + y$ is *at most* 6,000.

The fact that the maximum value of $x + y$ is *equal* to 6,000 follows from the fact that the system of simultaneous equations $7x + 6y = 38,000$ and $4x + 5y = 28,000$ has a solution, which in turn follows from the fact that these two equations correspond to a pair of nonparallel lines in the standard (x,y) coordinate plane. In particular, the pair $x = 2,000$ and $y = 4,000$ satisfy both the two inequalities and the equation $x + y = 6,000$.

The correct answer is B.

PS05924

148. If $\dfrac{3}{10^4} = x\%$, then $x =$

(A) 0.3
(B) 0.03
(C) 0.003
(D) 0.0003
(E) 0.00003

Arithmetic Percents

Given that $\dfrac{3}{10^4} = x\,\%$, and writing $x\,\%$ as $\dfrac{x}{100}$, it follows that $\dfrac{3}{10^4} = \dfrac{x}{100}$. Multiplying both sides by 100 gives $x = \dfrac{300}{10^4} = \dfrac{300}{10,000} = \dfrac{3}{100} = 0.03$.

The correct answer is B.

PS01285

149. What is the remainder when 3^{24} is divided by 5 ?

(A)   0
(B)   1
(C)   2
(D)   3
(E)   4

Arithmetic Properties of Numbers

A pattern in the units digits of the numbers $3, 3^2 = 9, 3^3 = 27, 3^4 = 81, 3^5 = 243$, etc., can be found by observing that the units digit of a product of two integers is the same as the units digit of the product of the units digit of the two integers. For example, the units digit of $3^5 = 3 \times 3^4 = 3 \times 81$ is 3 since the units digit of 3×1 is 3, and the units digit of $3^6 = 3 \times 3^5 = 3 \times 243$ is 9 since the units digit of 3×3 is 9. From this it follows that the units digit of the powers of 3 follow the pattern 3, 9, 7, 1, 3, 9, 7, 1, etc., with a units digit of 1 for $3^4, 3^8, 3^{12}, \ldots$, $3^{24}, \ldots$. Therefore, the units digit of 3^{24} is 1. Thus, 3^{24} is 1 more than a multiple of 10, and hence 3^{24} is 1 more than a multiple of 5, and so the remainder when 3^{24} is divided by 5 is 1.

The correct answer is B.

PS16620.02

150. José has a collection of 100 coins, consisting of nickels, dimes, quarters, and half-dollars. If he has a total of 35 nickels and dimes, a total of 45 dimes and quarters, and a total of 50 nickels and quarters, how many half-dollars does he have?

(A)   15
(B)   20
(C)   25
(D)   30
(E)   35

Algebra Simultaneous Equations

Letting n, d, q, and h, respectively, represent the numbers of nickels, dimes, quarters, and half-dollars José has, determine the value of h.

The following are given:

(1) $n + d + q + h = 100$
(2) $n + d = 35$
(3) $d + q = 45$
(4) $n + q = 50$

Adding (2), (3), and (4) gives $2n + 2d + 2q = 130$ or $n + d + q = 65$. Subtracting this equation from (1) gives $h = 100 - 65 = 35$.

The correct answer is E.

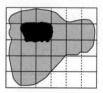

PS11692

151. In the figure shown, a square grid is superimposed on the map of a park, represented by the shaded region, in the middle of which is a pond, represented by the black region. If the area of the pond is 5,000 square yards, which of the following is closest to the area of the park, in square yards, including the area of the pond?

(A)   30,000
(B)   45,000
(C)   60,000
(D)   75,000
(E)   90,000

Geometry Estimation; Area

Let s be the side length, in yards, represented by each of the squares that form the square grid. By inspection, the map of the pond fills approximately 2 squares, so the area of the pond is approximately $2s^2$ yd². Since it is given that the area of the pond is 5,000 yd², it follows that $2s^2 = 5,000$, or $s^2 = 2,500$, or $s = 50$. The entire rectangular figure has a horizontal length of 6 squares, which represents $6(50 \text{ yd}) = 300 \text{ yd}$, and a vertical length of 5 squares, which represents $5(50 \text{ yd}) = 250 \text{ yd}$, so the area of the entire rectangular figure represents $(300 \text{ yd})(250 \text{ yd}) = 75,000 \text{ yd}^2$.

In the rectangular figure, less area is not shaded than is shaded, so to estimate the area represented by the shaded portion it will be easier to estimate the area represented by the portion that is not shaded and subtract this estimate from 75,000 yd^2, the area represented by the entire rectangular figure. By inspection, the area not shaded in the upper right corner represents approximately 2 squares, the area not shaded in the lower right corner represents approximately 6 squares, and the area not shaded on the left side represents approximately 2 squares. Thus, the area not shaded represents approximately $(2 + 6 + 2)$ squares, or approximately 10 squares, or approximately $10(2,500$ yd$^2) = 25,000$ yd^2. Therefore, the area of the park is approximately 75,000 yd^2 − 25,000 yd^2 = 50,000 yd^2, and of the values available, 45,000 is the closest.

The correct answer is B.

PS03623

152. If the volume of a ball is 32,490 cubic millimeters, what is the volume of the ball in cubic centimeters? (1 millimeter = 0.1 centimeter)

(A) 0.3249
(B) 3.249
(C) 32.49
(D) 324.9
(E) 3,249

Arithmetic Measurement Conversion

Since 1 mm = 0.1 cm, it follows that 1 mm^3 = $(0.1)^3$ cm^3 = 0.001 cm^3. Therefore, 32,490 mm^3 = $(32,490)(0.001)$ cm^3 = 32.49 cm^3.

The correct answer is C.

PS07058

153. David used part of $100,000 to purchase a house. Of the remaining portion, he invested $\frac{1}{3}$ of it at 4 percent simple annual interest and $\frac{2}{3}$ of it at 6 percent simple annual interest. If after a year the income from the two investments totaled $320, what was the purchase price of the house?

(A) $96,000
(B) $94,000
(C) $88,000
(D) $75,000
(E) $40,000

Algebra Applied Problems; Percents

Let x be the amount, in dollars, that David used to purchase the house. Then David invested $(100,000 - x)$ dollars, $\frac{1}{3}$ at 4% simple annual interest and $\frac{2}{3}$ at 6% simple annual interest. After one year the total interest, in dollars, on this investment was $\frac{1}{3}(100,000 - x)(0.04) + \frac{2}{3}(100,000 - x)(0.06) = 320$. Solve this equation to find the value of x.

$$\frac{1}{3}(100,000 - x)(0.04) +$$

$\frac{2}{3}(100,000 - x)(0.06) = 320$	given
$(100,000 - x)(0.04) +$ $2(100,000 - x)(0.06) = 960$	multiply both sides by 3
$4,000 - 0.04x +$ $12,000 - 0.12x = 960$	distributive property
$16,000 - 0.16x = 960$	combine like terms
$16,000 - 960 = 0.16x$	add $0.16x - 960$ to both sides
$100,000 - 6,000 = x$	divide both sides by 0.16
$94,000 = x$	

Therefore, the purchase price of the house was $94,000.

The correct answer is B.

PS09439

154. A certain manufacturer sells its product to stores in 113 different regions worldwide, with an average (arithmetic mean) of 181 stores per region. If last year these stores sold an average of 51,752 units of the manufacturer's product per store, which of the following is closest to the total number of units of the manufacturer's product sold worldwide last year?

(A) 10^6
(B) 10^7
(C) 10^8
(D) 10^9
(E) 10^{10}

Arithmetic Estimation

$(113)(181)(51,752) \approx (100)(200)(50,000)$

$$= 10^2 \times (2 \times 10^2) \times (5 \times 10^4)$$
$$= (2 \times 5) \times 10^{2+2+4}$$
$$= 10^1 \times 10^8 = 10^9$$

The correct answer is D.

PS17708

155. Andrew started saving at the beginning of the year and had saved $240 by the end of the year. He continued to save and by the end of 2 years had saved a total of $540. Which of the following is closest to the percent increase in the amount Andrew saved during the second year compared to the amount he saved during the first year?

(A) 11%
(B) 25%
(C) 44%
(D) 56%
(E) 125%

Arithmetic Percents

Andrew saved $240 in the first year and $540 − $240 = $300 in the second year. The percent increase in the amount Andrew saved in the second year compared to the amount he saved in the first year is $\left(\dfrac{300 - 240}{240} \times 100 \right)\% = $ $\left(\dfrac{60}{240} \times 100 \right)\% = \left(\dfrac{1}{4} \times 100 \right)\% = 25\%$.

The correct answer is B.

PS18180.02

156. If x is a positive integer, r is the remainder when x is divided by 4, and R is the remainder when x is divided by 9, what is the greatest possible value of $r^2 + R$?

(A) 25
(B) 21
(C) 17
(D) 13
(E) 11

Arithmetic Properties of Integers

If r is the remainder when the positive integer x is divided by 4, then $0 \le r < 4$, so the maximum value of r is 3. If R is the remainder when the

positive integer x is divided by 9, then $0 \le R < 9$, so the maximum value of R is 8. Thus, the maximum value of $r^2 + R$ is $3^2 + 8 = 17$.

The correct answer is C.

PS34550.02

157. Each of the nine digits 0, 1, 1, 4, 5, 6, 8, 8, and 9 is used once to form 3 three-digit integers. What is the greatest possible sum of the 3 integers?

(A) 1,752
(B) 2,616
(C) 2,652
(D) 2,775
(E) 2,958

Arithmetic Place Value

To create 3 three-digit numbers using each of the digits 0, 1, 1, 4, 5, 6, 8, 8, and 9 and having the maximum possible sum, the greatest three digits must be in hundreds place, the next greatest three in tens place, and the three smallest digits in units place. The sum will then be $(9 + 8 + 8)(100) + (4 + 5 + 6)(10) + (0 + 1 + 1) = 25(100) + 15(10) + 2 = 2,500 + 150 + 2 = 2,652$.

The correct answer is C.

PS19941.02

158. Given that $1^2 + 2^2 + 3^2 + \ldots + 10^2 = 385$, what is the value of $3^2 + 6^2 + 9^2 + \ldots + 30^2$?

(A) 1,155
(B) 1,540
(C) 1,925
(D) 2,310
(E) 3,465

Arithmetic Series and Sequences

We can use the fact that each term of the second series is $3^2 = 9$ times greater than the corresponding term of the first series to find the sum of the second series.

$3^2 + 6^2 + 9^2 + \ldots + 30^2$
$= (3 \cdot 1)^2 + (3 \cdot 2)^2 + (3 \cdot 3)^2 + \ldots + (3 \cdot 10)^2$
$= (3^2 \cdot 1^2) + (3^2 \cdot 2^2) + (3^2 \cdot 3^2) + \ldots + (3^2 \cdot 10^2)$
$= 3^2(1^2 + 2^2 + 3^2 + \ldots + 10^2) = 9(385) = 3,465$

The correct answer is E.

PS19062

159. Two numbers differ by 2 and sum to S. Which of the following is the greater of the numbers in terms of S?

(A) $\dfrac{S}{2} - 1$

(B) $\dfrac{S}{2}$

(C) $\dfrac{S}{2} + \dfrac{1}{2}$

(D) $\dfrac{S}{2} + 1$

(E) $\dfrac{S}{2} + 2$

Algebra First-Degree Equations

Let x represent the greater of the two numbers that differ by 2. Then, $x - 2$ represents the lesser of the two numbers. The two numbers sum to S, so $x + (x - 2) = S$. It follows that $2x - 2 = S$, or $2x = S + 2$, or $x = \dfrac{S}{2} + 1$.

The correct answer is D.

PS00904

160. The figure shown above consists of three identical circles that are tangent to each other. If the area of the shaded region is $64\sqrt{3} - 32\pi$, what is the radius of each circle?

(A) 4

(B) 8

(C) 16

(D) 24

(E) 32

Geometry Circles; Triangles; Area

Let r represent the radius of each circle. Then the triangle shown dashed in the figure is equilateral with sides $2r$ units long. The interior of the triangle is comprised of the shaded region and three circular sectors. The area of the shaded region can be found as the area of the triangle minus the sum of the areas of the three sectors. Since the triangle is equilateral, its side lengths are in the proportions as shown in the diagram

below. The area of the interior of the triangle is $\dfrac{1}{2}(2r)\left(r\sqrt{3}\right) = r^2\sqrt{3}$.

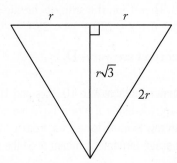

Each of the three sectors has a central angle of $60°$ because the central angle is an angle of the equilateral triangle. Therefore, the area of each sector is $\dfrac{60}{360} = \dfrac{1}{6}$ of the area of the circle. The sum of the areas of the three sectors is then $3\left(\dfrac{1}{6}\pi r^2\right) = \dfrac{1}{2}\pi r^2$. Thus, the area of the shaded region is $r^2\sqrt{3} - \dfrac{1}{2}\pi r^2 = r^2\left(\sqrt{3} - \dfrac{1}{2}\pi\right)$. But, this area is given as $64\sqrt{3} - 32\pi = 64\left(\sqrt{3} - \dfrac{1}{2}\pi\right)$. Thus $r^2 = 64$, and $r = 8$.

The correct answer is B.

PS24000.02

161. If m is an integer and $m = 10^{32} - 32$, what is the sum of the digits of m?

(A) 257

(B) 264

(C) 275

(D) 284

(E) 292

Arithmetic Arithmetic Operations

When written in standard base 10 notation, 10^{32} is the digit 1 followed by 32 digits of 0. Now consider the following subtractions and the digit pattern they suggest, a pattern which is easily seen to continue.

$$
\begin{aligned}
100 - 32 &= 68 \\
1{,}000 - 32 &= 968 \\
10{,}000 - 32 &= 9{,}968 \\
100{,}000 - 32 &= 99{,}968 \\
1{,}000{,}000 - 32 &= 999{,}968
\end{aligned}
$$

Using this digit pattern, $m = 10^{32} - 32$ in standard base 10 notation consists of $32 - 2 = 30$ occurrences of the digit 9 followed by the digits 6 and 8. Therefore, the sum of the digits of m is $30(9) + 6 + 8 = 270 + 14 = 284$.

The correct answer is D.

PS02053

162. In a numerical table with 10 rows and 10 columns, each entry is either a 9 or a 10. If the number of 9s in the nth row is $n - 1$ for each n from 1 to 10, what is the average (arithmetic mean) of all the numbers in the table?

(A) 9.45
(B) 9.50
(C) 9.55
(D) 9.65
(E) 9.70

Arithmetic Operations with Integers

There are $(10)(10) = 100$ entries in the table. In rows $1, 2, 3, \ldots, 10$, the number of 9s is $0, 1, 2, \ldots, 9$, respectively, giving a total of $0 + 1 + 2 + \ldots + 9 = 45$ entries with a 9. This leaves a total of $100 - 45 = 55$ entries with a 10. Therefore, the sum of the 100 entries is $45(9) + 55(10) = 405 + 550 = 955$, and the average of the 100 entries is $\frac{955}{100} = 9.55$

The correct answer is C.

PS76841.02

163. In 2004, the cost of 1 year-long print subscription to a certain newspaper was $4 per week. In 2005, the newspaper introduced a new rate plan for 1 year-long print subscription: $3 per week for the first 40 weeks of 2005 and $2 per week for the remaining weeks of 2005. How much less did 1 year-long print subscription to this newspaper cost in 2005 than in 2004 ?

(A) $64
(B) $78
(C) $112
(D) $144
(E) $304

Arithmetic Applied Problems

The cost, in dollars, of 1 year-long print subscription in 2004 was $52(4) = 208$ and the cost, in dollars, of 1 year-long print subscription in 2005 was $40(3) + 12(2) = 120 + 24 = 144$. Therefore, the cost in 2005 was less than the cost in 2004 by $208 - 144 = 64$ dollars.

The correct answer is A.

PS08485

164. A positive integer n is a perfect number provided that the sum of all the positive factors of n, including 1 and n, is equal to $2n$. What is the sum of the reciprocals of all the positive factors of the perfect number 28 ?

(A) $\dfrac{1}{4}$

(B) $\dfrac{56}{27}$

(C) 2

(D) 3

(E) 4

Arithmetic Properties of Numbers

The factors of 28 are $1, 2, 4, 7, 14,$ and 28. Therefore, the sum of the reciprocals of the factors of 28 is $\dfrac{1}{1} + \dfrac{1}{2} + \dfrac{1}{4} + \dfrac{1}{7} + \dfrac{1}{14} + \dfrac{1}{28} =$

$\dfrac{28}{28} + \dfrac{14}{28} + \dfrac{7}{28} + \dfrac{4}{28} + \dfrac{2}{28} + \dfrac{1}{28} =$

$\dfrac{28 + 14 + 7 + 4 + 2 + 1}{28} = \dfrac{56}{28} = 2.$

The correct answer is C.

PS11430

165. The infinite sequence $a_1, a_2, \ldots, a_n, \ldots$ is such that $a_1 = 2$, $a_2 = -3$, $a_3 = 5$, $a_4 = -1$, and $a_n = a_{n-4}$ for $n > 4$. What is the sum of the first 97 terms of the sequence?

(A) 72
(B) 74
(C) 75
(D) 78
(E) 80

Arithmetic Sequences and Series

Because $a_n = a_{n-4}$ for $n > 4$, it follows that the terms of the sequence repeat in groups of 4 terms:

Values for n	Values for a_n
1, 2, 3, 4	2, −3, 5, −1
5, 6, 7, 8	2, −3, 5, −1
9, 10, 11, 12	2, −3, 5, −1
13, 14, 15, 16	2, −3, 5, −1

Thus, since $97 = 24(4) + 1$, the sum of the first 97 terms can be grouped into 24 groups of 4 terms each, with one remaining term, which allows the sum to be easily found:

$$(a_1 + a_2 + a_3 + a_4) + (a_5 + a_6 + a_7 + a_8) + \ldots + (a_{93} + a_{94} + a_{95} + a_{96}) + a_{97}$$

$$= (2 - 3 + 5 - 1) + (2 - 3 + 5 - 1) + \ldots + (2 - 3 + 5 - 1) + 2$$

$$= 24(2 - 3 + 5 - 1) + 2 = 24(3) + 2 = 74$$

The correct answer is B.

PS09901

166. The sequence $a_1, a_2, \ldots, a_n, \ldots$ is such that $a_n = 2a_{n-1} - x$ for all positive integers $n \geq 2$ and for a certain number x. If $a_5 = 99$ and $a_3 = 27$, what is the value of x?

(A)   3
(B)   9
(C)   18
(D)   36
(E)   45

Algebra Sequences and Series

An expression for a_5 that involves x can be obtained using $a_3 = 27$ and applying the equation $a_n = 2a_{n-1} - x$ twice, once for $n = 4$ and once for $n = 5$.

$a_4 = 2a_3 - x$	using $a_n = 2a_{n-1} - x$ for $n = 4$
$= 2(27) - x$	using $a_3 = 27$
$a_5 = 2a_4 - x$	using $a_n = 2a_{n-1} - x$ for $n = 5$
$= 2[2(27) - x] - x$	using $a_4 = 2(27) - x$
$= 4(27) - 3x$	combine like terms

Therefore, using $a_5 = 99$, we have

$99 = 4(27) - 3x$	given
$3x = 4(27) - 99$	adding $(3x - 99)$ to both sides
$x = 4(9) - 33$	dividing both sides by 3
$x = 3$	arithmetic

The correct answer is A.

PS03779

167. A window is in the shape of a regular hexagon with each side of length 80 centimeters. If a diagonal through the center of the hexagon is w centimeters long, then $w =$

(A)   80
(B)   120
(C)   150
(D)   160
(E)   240

Geometry Polygons

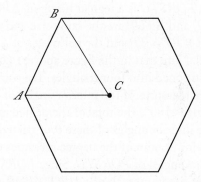

Let A and B be the endpoints of one of the sides of the hexagon and let C be the center of the hexagon. Then the degree measure of $\angle ACB$ is $\frac{360}{6} = 60$ and the sum of the degree measures of $\angle ABC$ and $\angle BAC$ is $180 - 60 = 120$. Also, since $AC = BC$, the degree measures of $\angle ABC$ and $\angle BAC$ are equal. Therefore, the degree measure of each of $\angle ABC$ and $\angle BAC$ is 60. Thus, $\triangle ABC$ is an equilateral triangle with side length $AB = 80$. It follows that the length of a diagonal through the center of the hexagon is $2(AC) = 2(80) = 160$.

The correct answer is D.

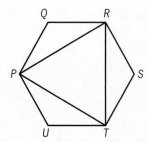

PS03695

168. In the figure shown, *PQRSTU* is a regular polygon with sides of length *x*. What is the perimeter of triangle *PRT* in terms of *x* ?

(A) $\dfrac{x\sqrt{3}}{2}$

(B) $x\sqrt{3}$

(C) $\dfrac{3x\sqrt{3}}{2}$

(D) $3x\sqrt{3}$

(E) $4x\sqrt{3}$

Geometry Polygons

Since *PQRSTU* is a regular hexagon, $\triangle PQR$, $\triangle RST$, and $\triangle TUP$ are the same size and shape, so $PR = RT = TP$ and the perimeter of $\triangle PRT$ is $3(PR)$. Note that in the figure above, *PQRSTU* is partitioned into four triangles. The sum of the degree measures of the interior angles of each triangle is 180°. The total of the degree measures of the interior angles of these four triangles is equal to the sum of the degree measures of the six interior angles of *PQRSTU*. Since *PQRSTU* is a regular hexagon, each of $\angle UPQ$, $\angle PQR$, $\angle QRS$, $\angle RST$, $\angle STU$, and $\angle TUP$ has the same measure, which is $\dfrac{(4)(180°)}{6} = 120°$.

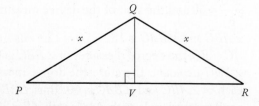

In the figure above, $\triangle PQR$ is isosceles with $PQ = QR = x$. The measure of $\angle PQR$ is 120°, and the measure of $\angle P =$ the measure of $\angle R = \dfrac{180° - 120°}{2} = 30°$. $\overline{QV}$ is perpendicular to $\overline{PR}$ and $PV = VR$. Since $\triangle PVQ$ is a

30°–60°–90° triangle, its side lengths are in the ratio $1:\sqrt{3}:2$, and so $PV = \dfrac{x\sqrt{3}}{2}$ and $PR = x\sqrt{3}$. Therefore, the perimeter of $\triangle PRT$ is

$$3(x\sqrt{3}) = 3x\sqrt{3}.$$

The correct answer is D.

PS11755

169. In a certain medical survey, 45 percent of the people surveyed had the type A antigen in their blood and 3 percent had both the type A antigen and the type B antigen. Which of the following is closest to the percent of those with the type A antigen who also had the type B antigen?

(A) 1.35%

(B) 6.67%

(C) 13.50%

(D) 15.00%

(E) 42.00%

Arithmetic Applied Problems; Percents

Let *n* be the total number of people surveyed. Then, the proportion of the people who had type A who also had type B is $\dfrac{(3\%)n}{(45\%)n} = \dfrac{3}{45} = \dfrac{1}{15}$, which as a percent is approximately 6.67%. Note that by using $\dfrac{1}{15} = \dfrac{1}{3} \times \dfrac{1}{5}$, which equals $\dfrac{1}{3}$ of 20%, we can avoid dividing by a 2-digit integer.

The correct answer is B.

PS05146

170. On a certain transatlantic crossing, 20 percent of a ship's passengers held round-trip tickets and also took their cars aboard the ship. If 60 percent of the passengers with round-trip tickets did <u>not</u> take their cars aboard the ship, what percent of the ship's passengers held round-trip tickets?

(A) $33\dfrac{1}{3}\%$

(B) 40%

(C) 50%

(D) 60%

(E) $66\dfrac{2}{3}\%$

Problem Solving **Answer Explanations**

Arithmetic Percents

Since the number of passengers on the ship is immaterial, let the number of passengers on the ship be 100 for convenience. Let x be the number of passengers that held round-trip tickets. Then, since 20 percent of the passengers held a round-trip ticket and took their cars aboard the ship, $0.20(100) = 20$ passengers held round-trip tickets and took their cars aboard the ship. The remaining passengers with round-trip tickets did not take their cars aboard, and they represent $0.6x$ (that is, 60 percent of the passengers with round-trip tickets). Thus $0.6x + 20 = x$, from which it follows that $20 = 0.4x$, and so $x = 50$. The percent of passengers with round-trip tickets is, then,

$$\frac{50}{100} = 50\%.$$

The correct answer is C.

PS03696

171. If x and k are integers and $(12^x)(4^{2x+1}) = (2^k)(3^2)$, what is the value of k?

(A) 5
(B) 7
(C) 10
(D) 12
(E) 14

Arithmetic Exponents

Rewrite the expression on the left so that it is a product of powers of 2 and 3.

$$(12^x)(4^{2x+1}) = [(3 \cdot 2^2)^x][(2^2)^{2x+1}]$$
$$= (3^x)[(2^2)^x][2^{2(2x+1)}]$$
$$= (3^x)(2^{2x})(2^{4x+2})$$
$$= (3^x)(2^{6x+2})$$

Then, since $(12^x)(4^{2x+1}) = (2^k)(3^2)$, it follows that $(3^x)(2^{6x+2}) = (2^k)(3^2) = (3^2)(2^k)$, so $x = 2$ and $k = 6x + 2$. Substituting 2 for x gives $k = 6(2) + 2 = 14$.

The correct answer is E.

PS11024

172. If S is the sum of the reciprocals of the 10 consecutive integers from 21 to 30, then S is between which of the following two fractions?

(A) $\frac{1}{3}$ and $\frac{1}{2}$

(B) $\frac{1}{4}$ and $\frac{1}{3}$

(C) $\frac{1}{5}$ and $\frac{1}{4}$

(D) $\frac{1}{6}$ and $\frac{1}{5}$

(E) $\frac{1}{7}$ and $\frac{1}{6}$

Arithmetic Estimation

The value of $\frac{1}{21} + \frac{1}{22} + \frac{1}{23} + \ldots + \frac{1}{30}$ is LESS than $\frac{1}{20} + \frac{1}{20} + \frac{1}{20} + \ldots + \frac{1}{20}$ (10 numbers added), which equals $10\left(\frac{1}{20}\right) = \frac{1}{2}$, and GREATER than $\frac{1}{30} + \frac{1}{30} + \frac{1}{30} + \ldots + \frac{1}{30}$ (10 numbers added), which equals $10\left(\frac{1}{30}\right) = \frac{1}{3}$. Therefore, the value of $\frac{1}{21} + \frac{1}{22} + \frac{1}{23} + \ldots + \frac{1}{30}$ is between $\frac{1}{3}$ and $\frac{1}{2}$.

The correct answer is A.

PS08729

173. For every even positive integer m, $f(m)$ represents the product of all even integers from 2 to m, inclusive. For example, $f(12) = 2 \times 4 \times 6 \times 8 \times 10 \times 12$. What is the greatest prime factor of $f(24)$?

(A) 23
(B) 19
(C) 17
(D) 13
(E) 11

Arithmetic Properties of Numbers

Rewriting $f(24) = 2 \times 4 \times 6 \times 8 \times 10 \times 12 \times 14 \times \ldots \times 20 \times 22 \times 24$ as $2 \times 4 \times 2(3) \times 8 \times 2(5) \times 12 \times 2(7) \times \ldots \times 20 \times 2(11) \times 24$ shows that all of the prime numbers from 2 through 11 are factors of $f(24)$. The next prime number is 13, but 13 is not a factor of $f(24)$ because none of the even integers from 2 through 24 has 13 as a factor. Therefore, the largest prime factor of $f(24)$ is 11.

The correct answer is E.

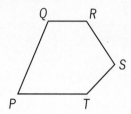

Note: Not drawn to scale.

PS08572

174. In pentagon $PQRST$, $PQ = 3$, $QR = 2$, $RS = 4$, and $ST = 5$. Which of the lengths 5, 10, and 15 could be the value of PT?

(A)   5 only

(B)   15 only

(C)   5 and 10 only

(D)   10 and 15 only

(E)   5, 10, and 15

Geometry Polygons; Triangles

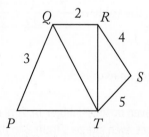

Note: Not drawn to scale.

In the figure above, diagonals $\overline{TQ}$ and $\overline{TR}$ have been drawn in to show $\triangle TRS$ and $\triangle TRQ$. Because the length of any side of a triangle must be less than the sum of the lengths of the other two sides, $RT < 5 + 4 = 9$ in $\triangle TRS$, and $QT < RT + 2$ in $\triangle TRQ$. Since $RT < 9$, then $RT + 2 < 9 + 2 = 11$, which then implies $QT < 11$. Now, $PT < QT + 3$ in $\triangle TQP$, and since $QT < 11$, $QT + 3 < 11 + 3 = 14$. It follows that $PT < 14$. Therefore, 15 cannot be the length of $\overline{PT}$ since $15 \not< 14$.

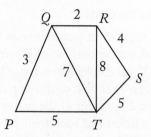

Note: Not drawn to scale.

To show that 5 can be the length of $\overline{PT}$, consider the figure above. For $\triangle TQP$, the length of any side is less than the sum of the lengths of the other two sides as shown below.

$$QT = 7 < 8 = 5 + 3 = PT + PQ$$
$$PQ = 3 < 12 = 5 + 7 = PT + TQ$$
$$PT = 5 < 10 = 3 + 7 = PQ + TQ$$

For $\triangle RQT$, the length of any side is less than the sum of the lengths of the other two sides as shown below.

$$RT = 8 < 9 = 7 + 2 = QT + QR$$
$$RQ = 2 < 15 = 7 + 8 = QT + RT$$
$$QT = 7 < 10 = 2 + 8 = QR + RT$$

For $\triangle RST$, the length of any side is less than the sum of the lengths of the other two sides as shown below.

$$RS = 4 < 13 = 8 + 5 = TR + TS$$
$$RT = 8 < 9 = 5 + 4 = ST + SR$$
$$ST = 5 < 12 = 8 + 4 = TR + RS$$

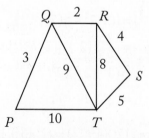

Note: Not drawn to scale.

To show that 10 can be the length of $\overline{PT}$, consider the figure above. For $\triangle TQP$, the length of any side is less than the sum of the lengths of the other two sides as shown below.

$$QT = 9 < 13 = 10 + 3 = PT + PQ$$
$$PQ = 3 < 19 = 10 + 9 = PT + TQ$$
$$PT = 10 < 12 = 3 + 9 = PQ + TQ$$

For $\triangle RQT$, the length of any side is less than the sum of the lengths of the other two sides as shown below.

$$RT = 8 < 11 = 9 + 2 = QT + QR$$
$$RQ = 2 < 17 = 9 + 8 = QT + RT$$
$$QT = 9 < 10 = 2 + 8 = QT + RT$$

For $\triangle RST$, the length of any side is less than the sum of the lengths of the other two sides as shown below.

$$RS = 4 < 13 = 8 + 5 = TR + TS$$
$$RT = 8 < 9 = 5 + 4 = ST + SR$$
$$ST = 5 < 12 = 8 + 4 = TR + RS$$

Therefore, 5 and 10 can be the length of $\overline{PT}$, and 15 cannot be the length of $\overline{PT}$.

The correct answer is C.

$$3, k, 2, 8, m, 3$$

PS07771

175. The arithmetic mean of the list of numbers above is 4. If k and m are integers and $k \ne m$ what is the median of the list?

(A) 2
(B) 2.5
(C) 3
(D) 3.5
(E) 4

Arithmetic Statistics

Since the arithmetic mean $= \dfrac{\text{sum of values}}{\text{number of values}}$, then $\dfrac{3+k+2+8+m+3}{6} = 4$, and so $\dfrac{16+k+m}{6} = 4$, $16 + k + m = 24$, $k + m = 8$. Since $k \ne m$, then either $k < 4$ and $m > 4$ or $k > 4$ and $m < 4$. Because k and m are integers, either $k \le 3$ and $m \ge 5$ or $k \ge 5$ and $m \le 3$.

Case (i): If $k \le 2$, then $m \ge 6$ and the six integers in ascending order are $k, 2, 3, 3, m, 8$ or $k, 2, 3, 3, 8, m$. The two middle integers are both 3 so the median is $\dfrac{3+3}{2} = 3$.

Case (ii): If $k = 3$, then $m = 5$ and the six integers in ascending order are $2, k, 3, 3, m, 8$. The two middle integers are both 3 so the median is $\dfrac{3+3}{2} = 3$.

Case (iii): If $k = 5$, then $m = 3$ and the six integers in ascending order are $2, m, 3, 3, k, 8$. The two middle integers are both 3 so the median is $\dfrac{3+3}{2} = 3$.

Case (iv): If $k \ge 6$, then $m \le 2$ and the six integers in ascending order are $m, 2, 3, 3, k, 8$ or $m, 2, 3, 3, 8, k$. The two middle integers are both 3 so the median is $\dfrac{3+3}{2} = 3$.

The correct answer is C.

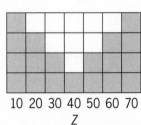

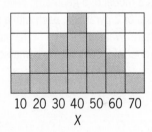
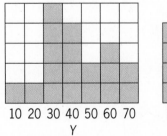

PS04987

176. If the variables X, Y, and Z take on only the values 10, 20, 30, 40, 50, 60, or 70 with frequencies indicated by the shaded regions above, for which of the frequency distributions is the mean equal to the median?

(A) X only
(B) Y only
(C) Z only
(D) X and Y
(E) X and Z

Arithmetic Statistics

The frequency distributions for both X and Z are symmetric about 40, and thus both X and Z have mean = median = 40. Therefore, any answer choice that does not include both X and Z can be eliminated. This leaves only answer choice E.

The correct answer is E.

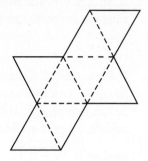

PS15538

177. When the figure above is cut along the solid lines, folded along the dashed lines, and taped along the solid lines, the result is a model of a geometric solid. This geometric solid consists of 2 pyramids, each with a square base that they share. What is the sum of the number of edges and the number of faces of this geometric solid?

(A)   10
(B)   18
(C)   20
(D)   24
(E)   25

Geometry Solids

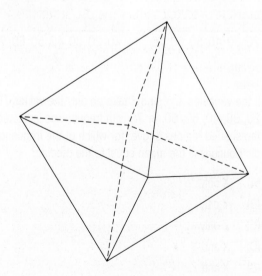

A geometric solid consisting of 2 pyramids, each with a square base that they share, is shown in the figure above. From the figure it can be seen that the solid has 12 edges and 8 faces. Therefore, the sum of the number of edges and the number of faces of the solid is 12 + 8 = 20.

Alternatively, the solid has 7 + 5 = 12 edges because each edge in the solid is generated from either a dashed segment (there are 7 dashed segments) or from a pair of solid segments taped together (there are $\frac{10}{2} = 5$ such pairs of solid segments), and the solid has 8 faces because there are 8 small triangles in the given figure. Therefore, the sum of the number of edges and the number of faces of the solid is 12 + 8 = 20.

The correct answer is C.

$$2x + y = 12$$
$$|y| \leq 12$$

PS03356

178. For how many ordered pairs (x,y) that are solutions of the system above are x and y both integers?

(A)   7
(B)   10
(C)   12
(D)   13
(E)   14

Algebra Absolute Value

From $|y| \leq 12$, if y must be an integer, then y must be in the set

$S = \{\pm 12, \pm 11, \pm 10, \ldots, \pm 3, \pm 2, \pm 1, 0\}$.

Since $2x + y = 12$, then $x = \frac{12 - y}{2}$. If x must be an integer, then $12 - y$ must be divisible by 2; that is, $12 - y$ must be even. Since 12 is even, $12 - y$ is even if and only if y is even. This eliminates all odd integers from S, leaving only the even integers $\pm 12, \pm 10, \pm 8, \pm 6, \pm 4, \pm 2$, and 0. Thus, there are 13 possible integer y-values, each with a corresponding integer x-value and, therefore, there are 13 ordered pairs (x,y), where x and y are both integers, that solve the system.

The correct answer is D.

PS39160.02

179. The United States mint produces coins in 1-cent, 5-cent, 10-cent, 25-cent, and 50-cent denominations. If a jar contains exactly 100 cents worth of these coins, which of the following could be the total number of coins in the jar?

    I.   91
    II.   81
    III. 76

    (A)   I only
    (B)   II only
    (C)   III only
    (D)   I and III only
    (E)   I, II, and III

Arithmetic Operations with Integers

Letting p, n, d, q, and h, respectively, represent the numbers of pennies (1-cent coins), nickels (5-cent coins), dimes (10-cent coins), quarters (25-cent coins), and half-dollars (50-cent coins) with a total worth of 100 cents, it follows that $p + 5n + 10d + 25q + 50h = 100$. Then $p = 100 - (5n + 10d + 25q + 50h) = 5(20 - n - 2d - 5q - 10h)$, so p must be a multiple of 5.

    I.   If the jar contained 90 pennies and 1 dime, the total number of coins would be $90 + 1 = 91$ and the coins would be worth $90 + 10 = 100$ cents.

    II.   For the jar to contain 81 coins with a total worth of 100 cents, there could be 80 pennies, but then the one coin remaining would have to amount to 20 cents to make the coins' total worth 100 cents. This is not possible since none of the coins is a 20-cent coin. If there were 75 pennies, then the remaining 6 coins would have to amount to 25 cents. This is not possible because 6 coins of the next smallest denomination would be worth 30 cents. If there were 70 pennies, then the remaining 11 coins would have to amount to 30 cents. This is not possible because 11 coins of the next smallest denomination would be worth 55 cents. Continuing in this manner shows that it is not possible for the jar to contain 81 coins with a total worth of 100 cents.

    III. If the jar contained 70 pennies and 6 nickels, the total number of coins would be $70 + 6 = 76$ and the coins would be worth $70 + 30 = 100$ cents.

The correct answer is D.

PS08859

180. The points R, T, and U lie on a circle that has radius 4. If the length of arc RTU is $\frac{4\pi}{3}$ what is the length of line segment RU?

    (A) $\dfrac{4}{3}$
    (B) $\dfrac{8}{3}$
    (C)   3
    (D)   4
    (E)   6

Geometry Circles; Triangles; Circumference

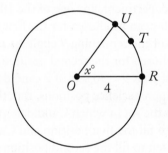

In the figure above, O is the center of the circle that contains R, T, and U and x is the degree measure of $\angle ROU$. Since the circumference of the circle is $2\pi(4) = 8\pi$ and there are 360° in the circle, the ratio of the length of arc RTU to the circumference of the circle is the same as the ratio of x to 360. Therefore, $\dfrac{\frac{4\pi}{3}}{8\pi} = \dfrac{x}{360}$. Then $x = \dfrac{\frac{4\pi}{3}(360)}{8\pi} = \dfrac{480\pi}{8\pi} = 60$. This means that $\triangle ROU$ is an isosceles triangle with side lengths $OR = OU = 4$ and vertex angle measuring 60°. The base angles of $\triangle ROU$ must have equal measures and the sum of their measures must be $180° - 60° = 120°$. Therefore, each base angle measures 60°, $\triangle ROU$ is equilateral, and $RU = 4$.

The correct answer is D.

PS02955

181. A certain university will select 1 of 7 candidates eligible to fill a position in the mathematics department and 2 of 10 candidates eligible to fill 2 identical positions in the computer science department. If none of the candidates is eligible for a position in both departments, how many different sets of 3 candidates are there to fill the 3 positions?

(A)   42
(B)   70
(C)   140
(D)   165
(E)   315

Arithmetic Elementary Combinatorics

To fill the position in the math department, 1 candidate will be selected from a group of 7 eligible candidates, and so there are 7 sets of 1 candidate each to fill the position in the math department. To fill the positions in the computer science department, any one of the 10 eligible candidates can be chosen for the first position and any of the remaining 9 eligible candidates can be chosen for the second position, making a total of $10 \times 9 = 90$ sets of 2 candidates to fill the computer science positions. But, this number includes the set in which Candidate A was chosen to fill the first position and Candidate B was chosen to fill the second position as well as the set in which Candidate B was chosen for the first position and Candidate A was chosen for the second position. These sets are not different essentially since the positions are identical and in both sets Candidates A and B are chosen to fill the 2 positions. Therefore, there are $\frac{90}{2} = 45$ sets of 2 candidates to fill the computer science positions. Then, using the multiplication principle, there are $7 \times 45 = 315$ different sets of 3 candidates to fill the 3 positions.

The correct answer is E.

PS06189

182. A survey of employers found that during 1993 employment costs rose 3.5 percent, where employment costs consist of salary costs and fringe-benefit costs. If salary costs rose 3 percent and fringe-benefit costs rose 5.5 percent during 1993, then fringe-benefit costs represented what percent of employment costs at the beginning of 1993 ?

(A)   16.5%
(B)   20%
(C)   35%
(D)   55%
(E)   65%

Algebra; Arithmetic First-Degree Equations; Percents

Let E represent employment costs, S represent salary costs, and F represent fringe-benefit costs. Then $E = S + F$. An increase of 3 percent in salary costs and a 5.5 percent increase in fringe-benefit costs resulted in a 3.5 percent increase in employment costs. Therefore $1.03S + 1.055F = 1.035E$. But, $E = S + F$, so $1.03S + 1.055F = 1.035(S + F) = 1.035S + 1.035F$.

Combining like terms gives $(1.055 - 1.035)F = (1.035 - 1.03)S$ or $0.02F = 0.005S$. Then, $S = \frac{0.02}{0.005}F = 4F$. Thus, since $E = S + F$, it follows that $E = 4F + F = 5F$. Then, F as a percent of E is $\frac{F}{E} = \frac{F}{5F} = \frac{1}{5} = 20\%$.

The correct answer is B.

PS02528

183. The subsets of the set {w, x, y} are {w}, {x}, {y}, {w, x}, {w, y}, {x, y}, {w, x, y}, and { } (the empty subset). How many subsets of the set {w, x, y, z} contain w ?

(A)   Four
(B)   Five
(C)   Seven
(D)   Eight
(E)   Sixteen

Arithmetic Sets

As shown in the table, the subsets of $\{w, x, y, z\}$ can be organized into two columns, those subsets of $\{w, x, y, z\}$ that do not contain w (left column) and the corresponding subsets of $\{w, x, y, z\}$ that contain w (right column), and each of these collections has the same number of sets. Therefore, there are 8 subsets of $\{w, x, y, z\}$ that contain w.

subsets not containing w	subsets containing w
{ }	$\{w\}$
$\{x\}$	$\{w, x\}$
$\{y\}$	$\{w, y\}$
$\{z\}$	$\{w, z\}$
$\{x, y\}$	$\{w, x, y\}$
$\{x, z\}$	$\{w, x, z\}$
$\{y, z\}$	$\{w, y, z\}$
$\{x, y, z\}$	$\{w, x, y, z\}$

The correct answer is D.

PS10309

184. There are 5 cars to be displayed in 5 parking spaces, with all the cars facing the same direction. Of the 5 cars, 3 are red, 1 is blue, and 1 is yellow. If the cars are identical except for color, how many different display arrangements of the 5 cars are possible?

(A)   20
(B)   25
(C)   40
(D)   60
(E)   125

Arithmetic Elementary Combinatorics

There are 5 parking spaces from which 3 must be chosen to display the 3 identical red cars. Thus, there are $\binom{5}{3} = \dfrac{5!}{3!2!} = 10$ different arrangements of the 3 identical red cars in the parking spaces. There are 2 spaces remaining for displaying the single blue car and 1 space left for displaying the single yellow car. Therefore, there are $(10)(2)(1) = 20$ arrangements possible for displaying the 5 cars in the 5 parking spaces.

The correct answer is A.

PS17461

185. The number $\sqrt{63 - 36\sqrt{3}}$ can be expressed as $x + y\sqrt{3}$ for some integers x and y. What is the value of xy?

(A)   −18
(B)   −6
(C)   6
(D)   18
(E)   27

Algebra Operations on Radical Expressions

Squaring both sides of $\sqrt{63 - 36\sqrt{3}} = x + y\sqrt{3}$ gives $63 - 36\sqrt{3} = x^2 + 2xy\sqrt{3} + 3y^2 = (x^2 + 3y^2) + (2xy)\sqrt{3}$, which implies that $-36 = 2xy$, or $xy = -18$. Indeed, if $-36 \neq 2xy$, or equivalently, if $36 + 2xy \neq 0$, then we could write $\sqrt{3}$ as a quotient of the two integers $63 - x^2 - 3y^2$ and $36 + 2xy$, which is not possible because $\sqrt{3}$ is an irrational number. To be more explicit, $63 - 36\sqrt{3} = x^2 + 2xy\sqrt{3} + 3y^2$ implies $63 - x^2 - 3y^2 = (36 + 2xy)\sqrt{3}$, and if $36 + 2xy \neq 0$, then we could divide both sides of the equation $63 - x^2 - 3y^2 = (36 + 2xy)\sqrt{3}$ by $36 + 2xy$ to get $\dfrac{63 - x^2 - 3y^2}{36 + 2xy} = \sqrt{3}$.

The correct answer is A.

PS01334

186. There are 10 books on a shelf, of which 4 are paperbacks and 6 are hardbacks. How many possible selections of 5 books from the shelf contain at least one paperback and at least one hardback?

(A)   75
(B)   120
(C)   210
(D)   246
(E)   252

Arithmetic Elementary Combinatorics

The number of selections of 5 books containing at least one paperback and at least one hardback is equal to $T - N$, where T is the total number of selections of 5 books and N is the number of selections that do not contain both a paperback and a hardback. The value of T is

$$\binom{10}{5} = \frac{10!}{5!(10-5)!} = \frac{(6)(7)(8)(9)(10)}{(1)(2)(3)(4)(5)}$$

$$= (7)(2)(9)(2) = 252.$$

To find the value of N, first note that no selection of 5 books can contain all paperbacks, since there are only 4 paperback books. Thus, the value of N is equal to the number of selections of 5 books that contain all hardbacks, which is equal to 6 since there are 6 ways that a single hardback can be left out when choosing the 5 hardback books. It follows that the number of selections of 5 books containing at least one paperback and at least one hardback is $T - N = 252 - 6 = 246$.

The correct answer is D.

PS03774

187. If x is to be chosen at random from the set {1, 2, 3, 4} and y is to be chosen at random from the set {5, 6, 7}, what is the probability that xy will be even?

(A) $\dfrac{1}{6}$

(B) $\dfrac{1}{3}$

(C) $\dfrac{1}{2}$

(D) $\dfrac{2}{3}$

(E) $\dfrac{5}{6}$

Arithmetic; Algebra Probability; Concepts of Sets

By the principle of multiplication, since there are 4 elements in the first set and 3 elements in the second set, there are $(4)(3) = 12$ possible products of xy, where x is chosen from the first set and y is chosen from the second set. These products will be even EXCEPT when both x and y are odd. Since there are 2 odd numbers in the first set and 2 odd numbers in the second set, there are $(2)(2) = 4$ products of x and y that are odd. This means that the remaining $12 - 4 = 8$ products are even.

Thus, the probability that xy is even is $\dfrac{8}{12} = \dfrac{2}{3}$.

The correct answer is D.

PS04254

188. The function f is defined for each positive three-digit integer n by $f(n) = 2^x\, 3^y\, 5^z$, where x, y, and z are the hundreds, tens, and units digits of n, respectively. If m and v are three-digit positive integers such that $f(m) = 9f(v)$, then $m - v =$

(A) 8

(B) 9

(C) 18

(D) 20

(E) 80

Algebra Place Value

Let the hundreds, tens, and units digits of m be A, B, and C, respectively; and let the hundreds, tens, and units digits of v be a, b, and c, respectively. From $f(m) = 9f(v)$ it follows that $2^A 3^B 5^C = 9(2^a 3^b 5^c) = 3^2(2^a 3^b 5^c) = 2^a 3^{b+2} 5^c$. Therefore, $A = a$, $B = b + 2$, and $C = c$. Now calculate $m - v$.

$$
\begin{aligned}
m - v &= (100A + 10B + C) && \text{place value} \\
      &\quad - (100a + 10b + c) && \text{property} \\
      &= (100a + 10(b + 2) + c) && \text{obtained above} \\
      &\quad - (100a + 10b + c) \\
      &= 10(b + 2) - 10b && \text{combine like terms} \\
      &= 10b + 20 - 10b && \text{distributive property} \\
      &= 20 && \text{combine like terms}
\end{aligned}
$$

The correct answer is D.

PS06312

189. If $10^{50} - 74$ is written as an integer in base 10 notation, what is the sum of the digits in that integer?

(A) 424

(B) 433

(C) 440

(D) 449

(E) 467

Arithmetic Properties of Numbers

$10^2 - 74$	=	$100 - 74$	=	26
$10^3 - 74$	=	$1,000 - 74$	=	926
$10^4 - 74$	=	$10,000 - 74$	=	9,926
$10^5 - 74$	=	$100,000 - 74$	=	99,926
$10^6 - 74$	=	$1,000,000 - 74$	=	999,926

From the table above it is clear that $10^{50} - 74$ in base 10 notation will be 48 digits of 9 followed by the digits 2 and 6. Therefore, the sum of the digits of $10^{50} - 74$ is equal to $48(9) + 2 + 6 = 440$.

The correct answer is C.

PS09056

190. A certain company that sells only cars and trucks reported that revenues from car sales in 1997 were down 11 percent from 1996 and revenues from truck sales in 1997 were up 7 percent from 1996. If total revenues from car sales and truck sales in 1997 were up 1 percent from 1996, what is the ratio of revenue from car sales in 1996 to revenue from truck sales in 1996 ?

(A)   1:2
(B)   4:5
(C)   1:1
(D)   3:2
(E)   5:3

Algebra; Arithmetic First-Degree Equations; Percents

Let C_{96} and C_{97} represent revenues from car sales in 1996 and 1997, respectively, and let T_{96} and T_{97} represent revenues from truck sales in 1996 and 1997, respectively. A decrease of 11 percent in revenue from car sales from 1996 to 1997 can be represented as $(1 - 0.11)C_{96} = C_{97}$, and a 7 percent increase in revenue from truck sales from 1996 to 1997 can be represented as $(1 + 0.07)T_{96} = T_{97}$. An overall increase of 1 percent in revenue from car and truck sales from 1996 to 1997 can be represented as $C_{97} + T_{97} = (1 + 0.01)(C_{96} + T_{96})$. Then, by substitution of expressions for C_{97} and T_{97} that were derived above, $(1 - 0.11)C_{96} + (1 + 0.07)T_{96} = (1 + 0.01)(C_{96} + T_{96})$ and so $0.89C_{96} + 1.07T_{96} = 1.01(C_{96} + T_{96})$ or $0.89C_{96} + 1.07T_{96} = 1.01C_{96} + 1.01T_{96}$. Then, combining like terms gives $(1.07 - 1.01)T_{96} = (1.01 - 0.89)C_{96}$ or

$0.06T_{96} = 0.12C_{96}$. Thus $\frac{C_{96}}{T_{96}} = \frac{0.06}{0.12} = \frac{1}{2}$. The ratio of revenue from car sales in 1996 to revenue from truck sales in 1996 is 1:2.

The correct answer is A.

PS14267

191. Becky rented a power tool from a rental shop. The rent for the tool was $12 for the first hour and $3 for each additional hour. If Becky paid a total of $27, excluding sales tax, to rent the tool, for how many hours did she rent it?

(A)   5
(B)   6
(C)   9
(D)   10
(E)   12

Arithmetic Applied Problems

Becky paid a total of $27 to rent the power tool. She paid $12 to rent the tool for the first hour and $27 − $12 = $15 to rent the tool for the additional hours at the rate of $3 per additional hour. It follows that she rented the tool for $\frac{15}{3} = 5$ additional hours and a total of $1 + 5 = 6$ hours.

The correct answer is B.

PS06959

192. If $4 < \dfrac{7 - x}{3}$, which of the following must be true?

I. $5 < x$

II. $|x + 3| > 2$

III. $-(x + 5)$ is positive.

(A)   II only
(B)   III only
(C)   I and II only
(D)   II and III only
(E)   I, II, and III

Algebra Inequalities

Given that $4 < \dfrac{7-x}{3}$, it follows that $12 < 7 - x$. Then, $5 < -x$ or, equivalently, $x < -5$.

I. If $4 < \dfrac{7-x}{3}$, then $x < -5$. If $5 < x$ were true then, by combining $5 < x$ and $x < -5$, it would follow that $5 < -5$, which cannot be true. Therefore, it is not the case that, if $4 < \dfrac{7-x}{3}$, then Statement I must be true. In fact, Statement I is never true.

II. If $4 < \dfrac{7-x}{3}$, then $x < -5$, and it follows that $x + 3 < -2$. Since $-2 < 0$, then $x + 3 < 0$ and $|x+3| = -(x+3)$. If $x + 3 < -2$, then $-(x+3) > 2$ and by substitution, $|x + 3| > 2$. Therefore, Statement II must be true for every value of x such that $x < -5$. Therefore, Statement II must be true if $4 < \dfrac{7-x}{3}$.

III. If $4 < \dfrac{7-x}{3}$, then $x < -5$ and $x + 5 < 0$. But if $x + 5 < 0$, then it follows that $-(x+5) > 0$ and so $-(x+5)$ is positive. Therefore Statement III must be true if $4 < \dfrac{7-x}{3}$.

The correct answer is D.

PS08654

193. A certain right triangle has sides of length x, y, and z, where $x < y < z$. If the area of this triangular region is 1, which of the following indicates all of the possible values of y?

(A) $y > \sqrt{2}$

(B) $\dfrac{\sqrt{3}}{2} < y < \sqrt{2}$

(C) $\dfrac{\sqrt{2}}{3} < y < \dfrac{\sqrt{3}}{2}$

(D) $\dfrac{\sqrt{3}}{4} < y < \dfrac{\sqrt{2}}{3}$

(E) $y < \dfrac{\sqrt{3}}{4}$

Geometry; Algebra Triangles; Area; Inequalities

Since x, y, and z are the side lengths of a right triangle and $x < y < z$, it follows that x and y are the lengths of the legs of the triangle and so the area of the triangle is $\dfrac{1}{2}xy$. But, it is given that the area is 1 and so $\dfrac{1}{2}xy = 1$. Then, $xy = 2$ and $y = \dfrac{2}{x}$. Under the assumption that x, y, and z are all positive since they are the side lengths of a triangle, $x < y$ implies $\dfrac{1}{x} > \dfrac{1}{y}$ and then $\dfrac{2}{x} > \dfrac{2}{y}$. But, $y = \dfrac{2}{x}$, so by substitution, $y > \dfrac{2}{y}$, which implies that $y^2 > 2$ since y is positive. Thus, $y > \sqrt{2}$.

Alternatively, if $x < \sqrt{2}$ and $y < \sqrt{2}$ then $xy < 2$. If $x > \sqrt{2}$ and $y > \sqrt{2}$, then $xy > 2$. But, $xy = 2$ so one of x or y must be less than $\sqrt{2}$ and the other must be greater than $\sqrt{2}$. Since $x < y$, it follows that $x < \sqrt{2} < y$ and $y > \sqrt{2}$.

The correct answer is A.

PS14397

194. On a certain day, a bakery produced a batch of rolls at a total production cost of $300. On that day, $\dfrac{4}{5}$ of the rolls in the batch were sold, each at a price that was 50 percent greater than the average (arithmetic mean) production cost per roll. The remaining rolls in the batch were sold the next day, each at a price that was 20 percent less than the price of the day before. What was the bakery's profit on this batch of rolls?

(A) $150

(B) $144

(C) $132

(D) $108

(E) $90

Arithmetic Applied Problems

Let n be the number of rolls in the batch and p be the average production price, in dollars, per roll. Then the total cost of the batch is $np = 300$ dollars, and the total revenue from selling the rolls in the batch is $\left(\frac{4}{5}n\right)(1.5p) + \left(\frac{1}{5}n\right)(0.8)(1.5p) =$

$\left(\frac{4}{5}n\right)\left(\frac{3}{2}p\right) + \left(\frac{1}{5}n\right)\left(\frac{4}{5}\right)\left(\frac{3}{2}p\right) = \left(\frac{6}{5} + \frac{6}{25}\right)np$

$= \left(\frac{36}{25}\right)np$. Therefore, the profit from selling the

rolls in the batch is $\left(\frac{36}{25}\right)np - np = \left(\frac{11}{25}\right)np =$

$\left(\frac{11}{25}\right)(300)$ dollars $= 132$ dollars.

The correct answer is C.

PS05972

195. A set of numbers has the property that for any number t in the set, $t + 2$ is in the set. If -1 is in the set, which of the following must also be in the set?

   I. -3

   II. 1

   III. 5

(A) I only
(B) II only
(C) I and II only
(D) II and III only
(E) I, II, and III

Arithmetic Properties of Numbers

It is given that -1 is in the set and, if t is in the set, then $t + 2$ is in the set.

  I. Since $\{-1, 1, 3, 5, 7, 9, 11, \ldots\}$ contains -1 and satisfies the property that if t is in the set, then $t + 2$ is in the set, it is not true that -3 must be in the set.

  II. Since -1 is in the set, $-1 + 2 = 1$ is in the set. Therefore, it must be true that 1 is in the set.

  III. Since -1 is in the set, $-1 + 2 = 1$ is in the set. Since 1 is in the set, $1 + 2 = 3$ is in the set. Since 3 is in the set, $3 + 2 = 5$ is in the set. Therefore, it must be true that 5 is in the set.

The correct answer is D.

PS04780

196. A couple decides to have 4 children. If they succeed in having 4 children and each child is equally likely to be a boy or a girl, what is the probability that they will have exactly 2 girls and 2 boys?

(A) $\dfrac{3}{8}$

(B) $\dfrac{1}{4}$

(C) $\dfrac{3}{16}$

(D) $\dfrac{1}{8}$

(E) $\dfrac{1}{16}$

Arithmetic Probability

Representing the birth order of the 4 children as a sequence of 4 letters, each of which is B for boy and G for girl, there are 2 possibilities (B or G) for the first letter, 2 for the second letter, 2 for the third letter, and 2 for the fourth letter, making a total of $2^4 = 16$ sequences. The table below categorizes some of these 16 sequences.

# of boys	# of girls	Sequences	# of sequences
0	4	GGGG	1
1	3	BGGG, GBGG, GGBG, GGGB	4
3	1	GBBB, BGBB, BBGB, BBBG	4
4	0	BBBB	1

The table accounts for $1 + 4 + 4 + 1 = 10$ sequences. The other 6 sequences will have 2Bs and 2Gs. Therefore the probability that the couple will have exactly 2 boys and 2 girls is $\dfrac{6}{16} = \dfrac{3}{8}$.

For the mathematically inclined, if it is assumed that a couple has a fixed number of children, that the probability of having a girl each time is p, and that the sex of each child is independent of the sex of the other children, then the number of girls, x, born to a couple with n children is a random variable having the binomial probability distribution. The probability of having exactly x girls born to a couple with n children is given by the formula $\binom{n}{x} p^x (1-p)^{n-x}$. For the problem at hand, it is given that each child is equally likely to be a boy or a girl, and so $p = \frac{1}{2}$. Thus, the probability of having exactly 2 girls born to a couple with 4 children is

$$\binom{4}{2} \left(\frac{1}{2}\right)^2 \left(\frac{1}{2}\right)^2 = \frac{4!}{2!2!} \left(\frac{1}{2}\right)^2 \left(\frac{1}{2}\right)^2 =$$

$$(6)\left(\frac{1}{4}\right)\left(\frac{1}{4}\right) = \frac{6}{16} = \frac{3}{8}.$$

The correct answer is A.

PS01564

197. The closing price of Stock X changed on each trading day last month. The percent change in the closing price of Stock X from the first trading day last month to each of the other trading days last month was less than 50 percent. If the closing price on the second trading day last month was $10.00, which of the following CANNOT be the closing price on the last trading day last month?

(A) $3.00
(B) $9.00
(C) $19.00
(D) $24.00
(E) $29.00

Arithmetic Applied Problems; Percents

Let P be the first-day closing price, in dollars, of the stock. It is given that the second-day closing price was $(1 + n\%)P = 10$, so $P = \dfrac{10}{1 + n\%}$, for some value of n such that $-50 < n < 50$. Therefore, P is between $\dfrac{10}{1 + 0.50} \approx 6.67$ and $\dfrac{10}{1 - 0.50} = 20$. Hence, if Q is the closing price, in dollars, of the stock on the last day, then Q is between $(0.50)(6.67) \approx 3.34$ (50% decrease from the lowest possible first-day closing price) and $(1.50)(20) = 30$ (50% increase from the greatest possible first-day closing price). The only answer choice that gives a number of dollars not between 3.34 and 30 is the first answer choice.

The correct answer is A.

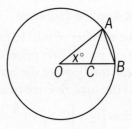

PS02389

198. In the figure above, point O is the center of the circle and $OC = AC = AB$. What is the value of x?

(A)   40
(B)   36
(C)   34
(D)   32
(E)   30

Geometry Angles

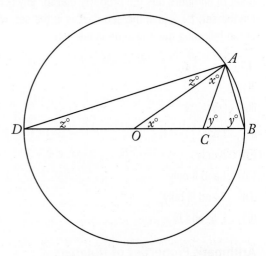

Consider the figure above, where $\overline{DB}$ is a diameter of the circle with center O and $\overline{AD}$ is a chord. Since $OC = AC$, $\triangle OCA$ is isosceles and so the base angles, $\angle AOC$ and $\angle OAC$, have the same degree measure. The measure of $\angle AOC$ is given as $x°$, so the measure of $\angle OAC$ is $x°$. Since $AC = AB$, $\triangle CAB$ is isosceles and so the base angles, $\angle ACB$ and $\angle ABC$, have the same degree measure. The measure of each is marked as $y°$. Likewise, since $\overline{OD}$ and $\overline{OA}$ are radii of the circle, $OD = OA$, and $\triangle DOA$ is isosceles with base angles, $\angle ADO$ and $\angle DAO$, each measuring $z°$. Each of the following statements is true:

(i) The measure of $\angle CAB$ is $180 - 2y$ since the sum of the measures of the angles of $\triangle CAB$ is 180.

(ii) $\angle DAB$ is a right angle (because $\overline{DB}$ is a diameter of the circle) and so $z + x + (180 - 2y) = 90$, or, equivalently, $2y - x - z = 90$.

(iii) $z + 90 + y = 180$ since the sum of the measures of the angles of right triangle $\triangle DAB$ is 180, or, equivalently, $z = 90 - y$.

(iv) $x = 2z$ because the measure of exterior angle $\angle AOC$ to $\triangle AOD$ is the sum of the measures of the two opposite interior angles, $\angle ODA$ and $\angle OAD$.

(v) $y = 2x$ because the measure of exterior angle $\angle ACB$ to $\triangle OCA$ is the sum of the measures of the two opposite interior angles, $\angle COA$ and $\angle CAO$.

Multiplying the final equation in (iii) by 2 gives $2z = 180 - 2y$. But, $x = 2z$ in (iv), so $x = 180 - 2y$. Finally, the sum of the measures of the angles of $\triangle CAB$ is 180 and so $y + y + x = 180$. Then from (v), $2x + 2x + x = 180$, $5x = 180$, and $x = 36$.

The correct answer is B.

PS16967
199. An airline passenger is planning a trip that involves three connecting flights that leave from Airports A, B, and C, respectively. The first flight leaves Airport A every hour, beginning at 8:00 a.m., and arrives at Airport B $2\frac{1}{2}$ hours later. The second flight leaves Airport B every 20 minutes, beginning at 8:00 a.m., and arrives at Airport C $1\frac{1}{6}$ hours later. The third flight leaves Airport C every hour, beginning at 8:45 a.m. What is the least total amount of time the passenger must spend between flights if all flights keep to their schedules?

(A) 25 min
(B) 1 hr 5 min
(C) 1 hr 15 min
(D) 2 hr 20 min
(E) 3 hr 40 min

Arithmetic Operations on Rational Numbers

Since the flight schedules at each of Airports A, B, and C are the same hour after hour, assume that the passenger leaves Airport A at 8:00 and arrives at Airport B at 10:30. Since flights from Airport B leave at 20-minute intervals beginning on the hour, the passenger must wait 10 minutes at Airport B for the flight that leaves at 10:40 and arrives at Airport C $1\frac{1}{6}$ hours or 1 hour 10 minutes later. Thus, the passenger arrives at Airport C at 11:50. Having arrived too late for the 11:45 flight from Airport C, the passenger must wait 55 minutes for the 12:45 flight. Thus, the least total amount of time the passenger must spend waiting between flights is $10 + 55 = 65$ minutes, or 1 hour 5 minutes.

The correct answer is B.

PS07426
200. If n is a positive integer and n^2 is divisible by 72, then the largest positive integer that must divide n is

(A) 6
(B) 12
(C) 24
(D) 36
(E) 48

Arithmetic Properties of Numbers

Since n^2 is divisible by 72, $n^2 = 72k$ for some positive integer k. Since $n^2 = 72k$, then $72k$ must be a perfect square. Since $72k = (2^3)(3^2)k$, then $k = 2m^2$ for some positive integer m in order for $72k$ to be a perfect square. Then, $n^2 = 72k = (2^3)(3^2)(2m^2) = (2^4)(3^2)m^2 = [(2^2)(3)(m)]^2$, and $n = (2^2)(3)(m)$. The positive integers that MUST divide n are 1, 2, 3, 4, 6, and 12. Therefore, the largest positive integer that must divide n is 12.

The correct answer is B.

PS16977
201. A certain grocery purchased x pounds of produce for p dollars per pound. If y pounds of the produce had to be discarded due to spoilage and the grocery sold the rest for s dollars per pound, which of the following represents the gross profit on the sale of the produce?

(A) $(x - y)s - xp$

(B) $(x - y)p - ys$

(C) $(s - p)y - xp$

(D) $xp - ys$

(E) $(x - y)(s - p)$

Algebra Simplifying Algebraic Expressions;
        Applied Problems

Since the grocery bought x pounds of produce for p dollars per pound, the total cost of the produce was xp dollars. Since y pounds of the produce was discarded, the grocery sold $x - y$ pounds of produce at the price of s dollars per pound, yielding a total revenue of $(x - y)s$ dollars. Then, the grocery's gross profit on the sale of the produce is its total revenue minus its total cost or $(x - y)s - xp$ dollars.

The correct answer is A.

PS16990
202. If x, y, and z are positive integers such that x is a factor of y, and x is a multiple of z, which of the following is NOT necessarily an integer?

(A) $\dfrac{x + z}{z}$

(B) $\dfrac{y + z}{x}$

(C) $\dfrac{x + y}{z}$

(D) $\dfrac{xy}{z}$

(E) $\dfrac{yz}{x}$

Arithmetic Properties of Numbers

Since the positive integer x is a factor of y, then $y = kx$ for some positive integer k. Since x is a multiple of the positive integer z, then $x = mz$ for some positive integer m.

Substitute these expressions for x and/or y into each answer choice to find the one expression that is NOT necessarily an integer.

A $\dfrac{x + z}{z} = \dfrac{mz + z}{z} = \dfrac{(m+1)z}{z} = m + 1$, which MUST be an integer

B $\dfrac{y + z}{x} = \dfrac{y}{x} + \dfrac{z}{x} = \dfrac{kx}{x} + \dfrac{z}{mz} = k + \dfrac{1}{m}$, which NEED NOT be an integer

Because only one of the five expressions need not be an integer, the expressions given in C, D, and E need not be tested. However, for completeness,

C $\dfrac{x + y}{z} = \dfrac{mz + kx}{z} = \dfrac{mz + k(mz)}{z} = \dfrac{mz(1 + k)}{z}$
    $= m(1 + k)$, which MUST be an integer

D $\dfrac{xy}{z} = \dfrac{(mz)y}{z} = my$, which MUST be an integer

E $\dfrac{yz}{x} = \dfrac{(kx)(z)}{x} = kz$, which MUST be an integer

The correct answer is B.

PS08416
203. Running at their respective constant rates, Machine X takes 2 days longer to produce w widgets than Machine Y. At these rates, if the two machines together produce $\dfrac{5}{4}w$ widgets in 3 days, how many days would it take Machine X alone to produce $2w$ widgets?

(A)   4

(B)   6

(C)   8

(D)   10

(E)   12

Algebra Applied Problems

If x, where $x > 2$, represents the number of days Machine X takes to produce w widgets, then Machine Y takes $x - 2$ days to produce w widgets. It follows that Machines X and Y can produce $\dfrac{w}{x}$ and $\dfrac{w}{x-2}$ widgets, respectively, in 1 day and together they can produce $\dfrac{w}{x} + \dfrac{w}{x-2}$ widgets in 1 day. Since it is given that, together, they can produce $\dfrac{5}{4}w$ widgets in 3 days, it follows that, together, they can produce $\dfrac{1}{3}\left(\dfrac{5}{4}w\right) = \dfrac{5}{12}w$ widgets in 1 day. Thus,

$$\frac{w}{x} + \frac{w}{x-2} = \frac{5}{12}w$$

$$\left(\frac{1}{x} + \frac{1}{x-2}\right)w = \frac{5}{12}w$$

$$\left(\frac{1}{x} + \frac{1}{x-2}\right) = \frac{5}{12}$$

$$12x(x-2)\left(\frac{1}{x} + \frac{1}{x-2}\right) = 12x(x-2)\left(\frac{5}{12}\right)$$

$$12[(x-2) + x] = 5x(x-2)$$

$$12(2x-2) = 5x(x-2)$$

$$24x - 24 = 5x^2 - 10x$$

$$0 = 5x^2 - 34x + 24$$

$$0 = (5x-4)(x-6)$$

$$x = \frac{4}{5} \text{ or } 6$$

Therefore, since $x > 2$, it follows that $x = 6$. Machine X takes 6 days to produce w widgets and $2(6) = 12$ days to produce $2w$ widgets.

The correct answer is E.

PS14051.02

204. What is the greatest positive integer n such that 5^n divides $10! - (2)(5!)^2$?

(A) 2

(B) 3

(C) 4

(D) 5

(E) 6

Arithmetic Properties of Numbers; Exponents

The greatest positive integer n such that 5^n divides a given integer is the number of factors of 5 in the prime factorization of the given integer. By repeated identification of common factors, the indicated difference can be factored sufficiently to determine the number of factors of 5 in its prime factorization. In the computations that follow, we have used the equalities $10! = (5!)(6)(7)(8)(9)(10)$ and $5! = (2)(3)(4)(5)$.

$10! - (2)(5!)^2$

$= (5! \cdot 6 \cdot 7 \cdot 8 \cdot 9 \cdot 10) - (2 \cdot 5! \cdot 5!)$

$= (5!)(6 \cdot 7 \cdot 8 \cdot 9 \cdot 10 - 2 \cdot 5!)$

$= (5!)(6 \cdot 7 \cdot 8 \cdot 9 \cdot 10 - 2 \cdot 2 \cdot 3 \cdot 4 \cdot 5)$

$= (5!)(2^4)(3 \cdot 7 \cdot 9 \cdot 10 - 3 \cdot 5)$

$= (5!)(2^4)(3)(7 \cdot 9 \cdot 10 - 5)$

$= (5!)(2^4)(3)(5)(7 \cdot 9 \cdot 2 - 1)$

$= (5!)(2^4)(3)(5)(63 \cdot 2 - 1)$

$= (5!)(2^4)(3)(5)(126 - 1)$

$= (5!)(2^4)(3)(5)(125)$

Since there is exactly 1 factor of 5 in $5! = (2)(3)(4)(5)$, no factors of 5 in either 2^4 or 3, exactly 1 factor of 5 in 5, and exactly 3 factors of 5 in $125 = 5^3$, it follows that there are $1 + 1 + 3 = 5$ factors of 5 in $10! - (2)(5!)^2 = (5!)(2^4)(3)(5)(125)$.

The correct answer is D.

PS12151.02

205. Yesterday, Candice and Sabrina trained for a bicycle race by riding around an oval track. They both began riding at the same time from the track's starting point. However, Candice rode at a faster pace than Sabrina, completing each lap around the track in 42 seconds, while Sabrina completed each lap around the track in 46 seconds. How many laps around the track had

Candice completed the next time that Candice and Sabrina were together at the starting point?

(A)   21

(B)   23

(C)   42

(D)   46

(E)   483

Arithmetic Applied Problems; Properties of Integers

Let C and S be the number of laps around the track, respectively, whenever Candice and Sabrina were together again at the starting point. Since Candice completes each lap in 42 seconds, Candice had been riding for a total of $42C$ seconds, and since Sabrina completes each lap in 46 seconds, Sabrina had been riding for a total of $46S$ seconds. Because they had been riding for the same total amount of time, we have $42C = 46S$, or $21C = 23S$, where C and S are positive integers.

Because 23 is a prime number that divides the product of 21 and C (note that 23 divides $23S$ and $23S = 21C$), it follows that 23 divides 21 (not true) or 23 divides C, and hence 23 divides C. Also, because 3 is a prime number that divides the product of 23 and S (note that 3 divides $21C$ and $21C = 23S$), it follows that 3 divides 23 (not true) or 3 divides S, and hence 3 divides S. Finally, because 7 is a prime number that divides the product of 23 and S (note that 7 divides $21C$ and $21C = 23S$), it follows that 7 divides 23 (not true) or 7 divides S, and hence 7 divides S

It follows that C is a multiple of 23 and S is a multiple of both 3 and 7. The least positive integer values for C and S with this property are $C = 23$ and $S = 3 \times 7 = 21$. Therefore, the next time after beginning that Candice and Sabrina were together at the starting point, Candice had completed 23 laps and Sabrina had completed 21 laps.

The correct answer is B.

PS07117

206. A square wooden plaque has a square brass inlay in the center, leaving a wooden strip of uniform width around the brass square. If the ratio of the brass area to the wooden area is 25 to 39, which of the following could be the width, in inches, of the wooden strip?

I.   1

II.   3

III.   4

(A)   I only

(B)   II only

(C)   I and II only

(D)   I and III only

(E)   I, II, and III

Geometry Area

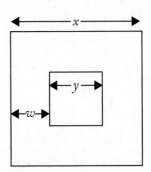

Note: Not drawn to scale.

Let x represent the side length of the entire plaque, let y represent the side length of the brass inlay, and w represent the uniform width of the wooden strip around the brass inlay, as shown in the figure above. Since the ratio of the area of the brass inlay to the area of the wooden strip is 25 to 39, the ratio of the area of the brass inlay to the area of the entire plaque is $\dfrac{y^2}{x^2} = \dfrac{25}{25+39} = \dfrac{25}{64}$.

Then, $\dfrac{y}{x} = \sqrt{\dfrac{25}{64}} = \dfrac{5}{8}$ and $y = \dfrac{5}{8}x$. Also, $x = y + 2w$ and $w = \dfrac{x-y}{2}$. Substituting $\dfrac{5}{8}x$ for y into this expression for w gives $w = \dfrac{x - \frac{5}{8}x}{2} = \dfrac{\frac{3}{8}x}{2} = \dfrac{3}{16}x$. Thus,

I. If the plaque were $\frac{16}{3}$ inches on a side, then the width of the wooden strip would be 1 inch, and so 1 inch is a possible width for the wooden strip.

II. If the plaque were 16 inches on a side, then the width of the wooden strip would be 3 inches, and so 3 inches is a possible width for the wooden strip.

III. If the plaque were $\frac{64}{3}$ inches on a side, then the width of the wooden strip would be 4 inches, and so 4 inches is a possible width for the wooden strip.

The correct answer is E.

PS66661.02

207. If $n = 9! - 6^4$, which of the following is the greatest integer k such that 3^k is a factor of n?

(A) 1
(B) 3
(C) 4
(D) 6
(E) 8

Arithmetic Properties of Integers

The following charts isolate and count the occurrences of 2 and of 3 in the factorizations of $9! = (9)(8)(7)(6)(5)(4)(3)(2)$ and $6^4 = (6)(6)(6)(6)$.

9!	=	(9)	(8)	(7)	(6)	(5)	(4)	(3)	(2)
Occurrences of 2		0	3	0	1	0	2	0	1
Occurrences of 3		2	0	0	1	0	0	1	0

6^4	=	(6)	(6)	(6)	(6)
Occurrences of 2		1	1	1	1
Occurrences of 3		1	1	1	1

So, $9! - 6^4 = (2^7 \cdot 3^4 \cdot 5 \cdot 7) - (2^4 \cdot 3^4) = (2^4 \cdot 3^4)(2^3 \cdot 5 \cdot 7 - 1) = (2^4 \cdot 3^4)(279) = (2^4 \cdot 3^4)(3^2 \cdot 31) = 2^4 \cdot 3^6 \cdot 31$, where 31 is prime. Therefore $k = 6$.

Alternatively, express $n = 9! - 6^4$ as $(9)(8)(7)(6)(5)(4)(3)(2)(1) - 6^4 = [(9)(8)](7)(6)(5)(4)[(3)(2)](1) - 6^4$. Then factor $(9)(8)$ as $(36)(2) = (6^2)(2)$

and multiply $(3)(2)$ to get 6. Factoring 6^4 from $n = (6^2)(2)(7)(6)(5)(4)(6)(1) - 6^4$ gives $n = 6^4[(2)(7)(5)(4)(1) - 1] = 6^4(279)$. It follows that 6^4 has 4 factors of 3 and 279 has 2 additional factors of 3 since $279 = (3^2)(31)$, so the greatest integer k such that 3^k is a factor of n is $4 + 2 = 6$.

The correct answer is D.

PS62451.02

208. The integer 120 has many factorizations. For example, $120 = (2)(60)$, $120 = (3)(4)(10)$, and $120 = (-1)(-3)(4)(10)$. In how many of the factorizations of 120 are the factors consecutive integers in ascending order?

(A) 2
(B) 3
(C) 4
(D) 5
(E) 6

Arithmetic Properties of Integers

All of the positive factors of 120 listed in ascending order are 1, 2, 3, 4, 5, 6, 8, 10, 12, 15, 20, 24, 30, 40, 60, and 120. The negative factors of 120 listed in ascending order are −120, −60, −40, −30, −24, −20, −15, −12, −10, −8, −6, −5, −4, −3, −2, and −1. Examining these lists for groups of consecutive factors whose product is 120 gives $(1)(2)(3)(4)(5)$, $(2)(3)(4)(5)$, $(4)(5)(6)$, and $(-5)(-4)(-3)(-2)$.

The correct answer is C.

PS65741.02

209. Jorge's bank statement showed a balance that was \$0.54 greater than what his records showed. He discovered that he had written a check for \$$x.yz$ and had recorded it as \$$x.zy$, where each of x, y, and z represents a digit from 0 though 9. Which of the following could be the value of z?

(A) 2
(B) 3
(C) 4
(D) 5
(E) 6

Arithmetic Place Value

Since the amount Jorge recorded for the check (\$$x.zy$) was \$0.54 more than the actual amount of the check (\$$x.yz$), it follows that

$x.zy - x.yz = \$0.54$. This is equivalent to $x + \frac{z}{10} + \frac{y}{100} - (x + \frac{y}{10} + \frac{z}{100}) = \frac{54}{100}$. Then $\frac{10z + y}{100} - \frac{10y + z}{100} = \frac{54}{100}$ or, equivalently, $10z + y - (10y + z) = 54$. It follows that $9z - 9y = 54$ or $z - y = 6$. Since y and z are digits, the possible values of y and z, respectively, are 0 and 6, 1 and 7, 2 and 8, and 3 and 9. Of the possible values of z, only 6 is given as one of the answer choices.

The correct answer is E.

PS79981.02

210. One side of a parking stall is defined by a straight stripe that consists of n painted sections of equal length with an unpainted section $\frac{1}{2}$ as long between each pair of consecutive painted sections. The total length of the stripe from the beginning of the first painted section to the end of the last painted section is 203 inches. If n is an integer and the length, in inches, of each unpainted section is an integer greater than 2, what is the value of n?

(A)   5
(B)   9
(C)   10
(D)   14
(E)   29

Algebra Applied Problems

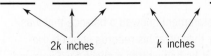

2k inches   k inches

The figure above is a schematic diagram of the parking stall's painted sections, where each painted section has length $2k$ inches and each unpainted section has length k inches. Since there is a total of n painted sections and a total of $(n-1)$ unpainted sections, it follows that $n(2k) + (n-1)k = 203$, or $(3n-1)k = 203$. Also, since n and k are positive integers with $n \geq 2$, and $203 = (7)(29)$ is the only factorization of 203 with integer factors greater than or equal to 2, we have two cases.

Case 1: $3n - 1 = 7$ and $k = 29$. In this case we have $n = \frac{8}{3}$.

Case 2: $3n - 1 = 29$ and $k = 7$. In this case we have $n = 10$.

Because $\frac{8}{3}$ is not an integer, we discard Case 1, and hence $n = 10$.

The correct answer is C.

PS16963

211. $\dfrac{2\frac{3}{5} - 1\frac{2}{3}}{\frac{2}{3} - \frac{3}{5}} =$

(A)   16
(B)   14
(C)   3
(D)   1
(E)   −1

Arithmetic Operations on Rational Numbers

Work the problem:

$$\frac{2\frac{3}{5} - 1\frac{2}{3}}{\frac{2}{3} - \frac{3}{5}} =$$

$$\frac{\frac{13}{5} - \frac{5}{3}}{\frac{2}{3} - \frac{3}{5}} = \frac{\frac{39 - 25}{15}}{\frac{10 - 9}{15}} = \frac{\frac{14}{15}}{\frac{1}{15}} = \frac{14}{15} \times \frac{15}{1} = 14$$

The correct answer is B.

Machine	Consecutive Minutes Machine Is Off	Units of Power When On
A	17	15
B	14	18
C	11	12

PS67381.02

212. At a certain factory, each of Machines A, B, and C is periodically on for exactly 1 minute and periodically off for a fixed number of consecutive minutes. The table above shows that Machine A is on and uses 15 units of power every 18th minute, Machine B is on and uses 18 units of power every 15th minute, and Machine C is on and uses 12 units of power every 12th minute. The factory has a backup generator that operates only when the total power usage of the 3 machines

exceeds 30 units of power. What is the time interval, in minutes, between consecutive times the backup generator begins to operate?

(A) 36
(B) 63
(C) 90
(D) 180
(E) 270

Arithmetic Applied Problems

The given table shows that the backup generator will not operate when only one of the machines is operating, since none of the machines uses more than 30 units of power. The table below shows the power usage when more than one machine is operating at the same time.

Machines	Units of power when on	Backup generator
A & B	$15 + 18 = 33$	On
B & C	$18 + 12 = 30$	Off
C & A	$12 + 15 = 27$	Off
A & B & C	$15 + 18 + 12 = 45$	On

Thus, the backup generator will be on whenever Machines A and B are both on, this being true regardless of whether Machine C is on. We are given that Machine A is on for 1 minute every 18 minutes and Machine B is on for 1 minute every 15 minutes. Therefore, if Machines A and B are both on for a certain minute, then the following are the minutes when these machines are again on.

Minutes when Machine A is on: 1st, 19th, 37th, 55th, 73rd, **91st**, 109th, …

Minutes when Machine B is on: 1st, 16th, 31st, 46th, 61st, 76th, **91st**, 106th, …

Therefore, the next time Machines A and B are both on is the 91st minute, which is 90 minutes after the first minute.

Alternatively, Machine A is on every 18 = $(2)(3^2)$ minutes and Machine B is on every $15 = (3)(5)$ minutes, so the machines are both on every $(2)(3^2)(5) = 90$ minutes (least common multiple of 18 and 15).

The correct answer is C.

5.0 Data Sufficiency

5.0 Data Sufficiency

Data Sufficiency questions appear in the Quantitative Reasoning section of the GMAT exam. Multiple-choice Data Sufficiency questions are intermingled with Problem Solving questions throughout the section. You will have 62 minutes to complete the Quantitative Reasoning section of the GMAT exam, or about 2 minutes to answer each question. These questions require knowledge of the following topics:

- Arithmetic
- Elementary algebra
- Commonly known concepts of geometry.

Data Sufficiency questions are designed to measure your ability to analyze a quantitative problem, recognize which given information is relevant, and determine at what point there is sufficient information to solve a problem. In these questions, you are to classify each problem according to the five fixed answer choices, rather than find a solution to the problem.

Each Data Sufficiency question consists of a question, often accompanied by some initial information, and two statements, labeled (1) and (2), which contain additional information. You must decide whether the information in each statement is sufficient to answer the question or—if neither statement provides enough information—whether the information in the two statements together is sufficient. It is also possible that the statements, in combination do not give enough information to answer the question.

Begin by reading the initial information and the question carefully. Next, consider the first statement. Does the information provided by the first statement enable you to answer the question? Go on to the second statement. Try to ignore the information given in the first statement when you consider whether the second statement provides information that, by itself, allows you to answer the question. Now you should be able to say, for each statement, whether it is sufficient to determine the answer.

Next, consider the two statements in tandem. Do they, together, enable you to answer the question?

Look again at your answer choices. Select the one that most accurately reflects whether the statements provide the information required to answer the question.

5.1 Test-Taking Strategies

1. **Do not waste valuable time solving a problem.**

   You only need to determine whether sufficient information is given to solve it.

2. **Consider each statement separately.**

   First, decide whether each statement alone gives sufficient information to solve the problem. Be sure to disregard the information given in statement (1) when you evaluate the information given in statement (2). If either, or both, of the statements give(s) sufficient information to solve the problem, select the answer corresponding to the description of which statement(s) give(s) sufficient information to solve the problem.

3. **Judge the statements in tandem if neither statement is sufficient by itself.**

   It is possible that the two statements together do not provide sufficient information. Once you decide, select the answer corresponding to the description of whether the statements together give sufficient information to solve the problem.

4. **Answer the question asked.**

   For example, if the question asks, "What is the value of y ?" for an answer statement to be sufficient, you must be able to find one and only one value for y. Being able to determine minimum or maximum values for an answer (e.g., $y = x + 2$) is not sufficient, because such answers constitute a range of values rather than the specific value of y.

5. **Be very careful not to make unwarranted assumptions based on the images represented.**

   Figures are not necessarily drawn to scale; they are generalized figures showing little more than intersecting line segments and the relationships of points, angles, and regions. For example, if a figure described as a rectangle looks like a square, do not conclude that it is actually a square just by looking at the figure.

If statement 1 is sufficient, then the answer must be **A or D.**

If statement 2 is not sufficient, then the answer must be **A.**

If statement 2 is sufficient, then the answer must be **D.**

If statement 1 is not sufficient, then the answer must be **B, C, or E.**

If statement 2 is sufficient, then the answer must be **B.**

If statement 2 is not sufficient, then the answer must be **C or E.**

If both statements together are sufficient, then the answer must be **C.**

If both statements together are still not sufficient, then the answer must be **E.**

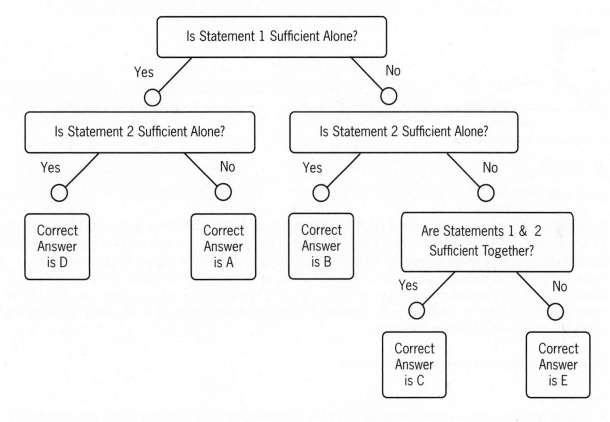

5.2 Section Instructions

Go to www.mba.com/tutorial to view instructions for the section and get a feel for what the test center screens will look like on the actual GMAT exam.

To register for the GMAT™ exam go to www.mba.com

5.3 Practice Questions

Each Data Sufficiency problem consists of a question and two statements, labeled (1) and (2), which contain certain data. Using these data and your knowledge of mathematics and everyday facts (such as the number of days in July or the meaning of the word *counterclockwise*), decide whether the data given are sufficient for answering the question and then indicate one of the following answer choices:

A   Statement (1) ALONE is sufficient, but statement (2) alone is not sufficient.

B   Statement (2) ALONE is sufficient, but statement (1) alone is not sufficient.

C   BOTH statements TOGETHER are sufficient, but NEITHER statement ALONE is sufficient.

D   EACH statement ALONE is sufficient.

E   Statements (1) and (2) TOGETHER are not sufficient.

Note: In Data Sufficiency problems that ask for the value of a quantity, the data given in the statements are sufficient only when it is possible to determine exactly one numerical value for the quantity.

Example:

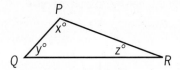

In $\triangle PQR$, what is the value of x ?

(1) $PQ = PR$

(2) $y = 40$

Explanation: According to statement (1) $PQ = PR$; therefore, $\triangle PQR$ is isosceles and $y = z$. Since $x + y + z = 180$, it follows that $x + 2y = 180$. Since statement (1) does not give a value for y, you cannot answer the question using statement (1) alone. According to statement (2), $y = 40$; therefore, $x + z = 140$. Since statement (2) does not give a value for z, you cannot answer the question using statement (2) alone. Using both statements together, since $x + 2y = 180$ and the value of y is given, you can find the value of x. Therefore, BOTH statements (1) and (2) TOGETHER are sufficient to answer the questions, but NEITHER statement ALONE is sufficient.

Numbers: All numbers used are real numbers.

Figures:
- Figures conform to the information given in the question, but will not necessarily conform to the additional information given in statements (1) and (2).
- Lines shown as straight are straight, and lines that appear jagged are also straight.
- The positions of points, angles, regions, etc., exist in the order shown, and angle measures are greater than zero.
- All figures lie in a plane unless otherwise indicated.

Questions 213 to 265 - Difficulty: Easy

*DS05149

213. Does $2x + 8 = 12$?

    (1) $2x + 10 = 14$
    (2) $3x + 8 = 14$

DS96720.02

214. Each car at a certain dealership is either blue or white. What is the average (arithmetic mean) sticker price of all the cars at the dealership?

    (1)   Of all the cars at the dealership, $\frac{1}{3}$ are blue and have an average sticker price of $21,000.

    (2)   Of all the cars at the dealership, $\frac{2}{3}$ are white and have an average sticker price of $24,000.

DS01503

215. If M is a set of consecutive even integers, is 0 in set M ?

    (1)   −6 is in set M.
    (2)   −2 is in set M.

DS35330.02

216. A box contains only white balls and black balls. What is the probability that a ball selected at random from the box is white?

    (1)   There are 100 balls in the box.
    (2)   There are 40 black balls in the box.

DS15510

217. Rita's monthly salary is $\frac{2}{3}$ Juanita's monthly salary. What is their combined monthly salary?

    (1)   Rita's monthly salary is $4,000.
    (2)   Either Rita's monthly salary or Juanita's monthly salary is $6,000.

DS37130.02

218. Each of the 120 students in a certain dormitory is either a junior or a senior. How many of the juniors have credit cards?

    (1) $\frac{2}{3}$ of the 120 juniors and seniors have credit cards.

    (2)   The number of seniors who have credit cards is 20 more than the number of juniors who have credit cards.

DS13384

219. What is the value of the integer x ?

    (1) x rounded to the nearest hundred is 7,200.
    (2)   The hundreds digit of x is 2.

DS04644

220. Is $2x > 2y$?

    (1) $x > y$
    (2) $3x > 3y$

DS38720.02

221. If the average (arithmetic mean) cost per sweater for 3 pullover sweaters and 1 cardigan sweater was $65, what was the cost of the cardigan sweater?

    (1)   The average cost per sweater for the 3 pullover sweaters was $55.

    (2)   The most expensive of the 3 pullover sweaters cost $30 more than the least expensive.

DS04636

222. If p and q are positive, is $\frac{p}{q}$ less than 1 ?

    (1) p is less than 4.
    (2) q is less than 4.

DS02779

223. In each quarter of 1998, Company M earned more money than in the previous quarter. What was the range of Company M's quarterly earnings in 1998?

    (1)   In the 2nd and 3rd quarters of 1998, Company M earned $4.0 million and $4.6 million, respectively.

    (2)   In the 1st and 4th quarters of 1998, Company M earned $3.8 million and $4.9 million, respectively.

DS69610.02

224. The range of the heights of a group of high school juniors and seniors is 20 centimeters. What is the average (arithmetic mean) of the height of the tallest senior in the group and the height of the shortest junior in the group?

    (1)   The average of the heights of the juniors in the group is 165 centimeters.

    (2)   The average of the heights of the seniors in the group is 179 centimeters.

*These numbers correlate with the online test bank question number. See the GMAT™ Official Guide Quantitative Review Question Index in the back of this book.

227

DS04510
225. In a certain factory, hours worked by each employee in excess of 40 hours per week are overtime hours and are paid for at $1\frac{1}{2}$ times the employee's regular hourly pay rate. If an employee worked a total of 42 hours last week, how much was the employee's gross pay for the hours worked last week?

   (1) The employee's gross pay for overtime hours worked last week was $30.

   (2) The employee's gross pay for all hours worked last week was $30 more than for the previous week.

DS01104
226. Is the integer p even?

   (1) The integer $p^2 + 1$ is odd.

   (2) The integer $p + 2$ is even.

DS05172
227. If $x > 0$, what is the value of x^5?

   (1) $\sqrt{x} = 32$

   (2) $x^2 = 2^{20}$

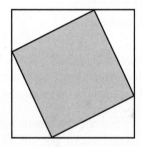

DS17640
228. In the quilting pattern shown above, a small square has its vertices on the sides of a larger square. What is the side length, in centimeters, of the larger square?

   (1) The side length of the smaller square is 10 cm.

   (2) Each vertex of the small square cuts 1 side of the larger square into 2 segments with lengths in the ratio of 1:2.

DS02589
229. Did Insurance Company K have more than $300 million in total net profits last year?

   (1) Last year Company K paid out $0.95 in claims for every dollar of premiums collected.

   (2) Last year Company K earned a total of $150 million in profits from the investment of accumulated surplus premiums from previous years.

DS15349
230. How many hours would it take Pump A and Pump B working together, each at its own constant rate, to empty a tank that was initially full?

   (1) Working alone at its constant rate, Pump A would empty the full tank in 4 hours 20 minutes.

   (2) Working alone, Pump B would empty the full tank at its constant rate of 72 liters per minute.

DS04573
231. What is the value of the integer N?

   (1) $101 < N < 103$

   (2) $202 < 2N < 206$

DS12033
232. Is zw positive?

   (1) $z + w^3 = 20$

   (2) z is positive.

DS03006
233. On the scale drawing of a certain house plan, if 1 centimeter represents x meters, what is the value of x?

   (1) A rectangular room that has a floor area of 12 square meters is represented by a region of area 48 square centimeters.

   (2) The 15-meter length of the house is represented by a segment 30 centimeters long.

DS23820.02
234. Maria left home $\frac{1}{4}$ hour after her husband and drove over the same route as he had in order to overtake him. From the time she left, how many hours did it take Maria to overtake her husband?

   (1) Maria drove 60 miles before overtaking her husband.

   (2) While overtaking her husband, Maria drove at an average rate of 60 miles per hour, which was 12 miles per hour faster than her husband's average rate.

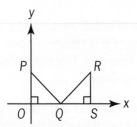

DS03939

235. In the rectangular coordinate system above, if $\triangle OPQ$ and $\triangle QRS$ have equal area, what are the coordinates of point R?

(1)   The coordinates of point P are (0,12).

(2) $OP = OQ$ and $QS = RS$.

DS07258

236. In a school that had a total of 600 students enrolled in the junior and senior classes, the students contributed to a certain fund. If all of the juniors but only half of the seniors contributed, was the total amount contributed more than $740?

(1)   Each junior contributed $1 and each senior who contributed gave $3.

(2)   There were more juniors than seniors enrolled in the school.

DS06650

237. How much did credit-card fraud cost United States banks in year X to the nearest $10 million?

(1)   In year X, counterfeit cards and telephone and mail-order fraud accounted for 39 percent of the total amount that card fraud cost the banks.

(2)   In year X, stolen cards accounted for $158.4 million, or 16 percent, of the total amount that credit-card fraud cost the banks.

DS17319

238. Is the positive integer n odd?

(1) $n^2 + (n + 1)^2 + (n + 2)^2$ is even.

(2) $n^2 - (n + 1)^2 - (n + 2)^2$ is even.

DS01130

239. In the xy-plane, circle C has center (1,0) and radius 2. If line k is parallel to the y-axis, is line k tangent to circle C?

(1)   Line k passes through the point (–1,0).

(2)   Line k passes through the point (–1,–1).

DS14170

240. Company X's profits this year increased by 25% over last year's profits. Was the dollar amount of Company X's profits this year greater than the dollar amount of Company Y's?

(1)   Last year, the ratio of Company Y's profits to Company X's profits was 5:2.

(2)   Company Y experienced a 40% drop in profits from last year to this year.

DS87910.02

241. A certain company consists of three divisions, A, B, and C. Of the employees in the three divisions, the employees in Division C have the greatest average (arithmetic mean) annual salary. Is the average annual salary of the employees in the three divisions combined less than $55,000?

(1)   The average annual salary of the employees in Divisions A and B combined is $45,000.

(2)   The average annual salary of the employees in Division C is $55,000.

DS09385

242. For all x, the expression x^* is defined to be $ax + a$, where a is a constant. What is the value of 2^*?

(1) $3^* = 2$

(2) $5^* = 3$

DS09260

243. Is $k + m < 0$?

(1) $k < 0$

(2) $km > 0$

DS08352

244. The symbol Δ represents which one of the following operations: addition, subtraction, or multiplication?

(1) $a \Delta (b \Delta c) \neq a \Delta (c \Delta b)$ for some numbers a, b, and c.

(2) $a \Delta (b \Delta c) \neq (a \Delta b) \Delta c$ for some numbers a, b, and c.

DS05989

245. What is the value of $2^x + 2^{-x}$?

(1) $x > 0$

(2) $4^x + 4^{-x} = 23$

DS13457

246. What is the ratio of c to d?

(1)   The ratio of $3c$ to $3d$ is 3 to 4.

(2)   The ratio of $c + 3$ to $d + 3$ is 4 to 5.

DS15099

247. A candle company determines that, for a certain specialty candle, the supply function is $p = m_1x + b_1$ and the demand function is $p = m_2x + b_2$, where p is the price of each candle, x is the number of candles supplied or demanded, and m_1, m_2, b_1, and b_2 are constants. At what value of x do the graphs of the supply function and demand function intersect?

    (1) $m_1 = -m_2 = 0.005$

    (2) $b_2 - b_1 = 6$

DS40410.02

248. A certain ski shop sold 125 pairs of skis and 100 pairs of ski boots for a total of $75,000. What was the average (arithmetic mean) selling price of a pair of the ski boots?

    (1) The average selling price of a pair of skis was $300.

    (2) The selling price of a pair of ski boots varied from $150 to $900.

DS93510.02

249. Is the standard deviation of the numbers in list R less than the standard deviation of the numbers in list S?

    (1) The range of the numbers in R is less than the range of the numbers in S.

    (2) Each number in R occurs once and each number in S is repeated.

DS96502.01

250. Is the length of rectangular field F greater than the length of rectangular field G?

    (1) The area of F is greater than the area of G.

    (2) The width of F is less than the width of G.

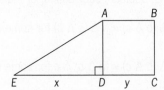

DS17502.01

251. In the figure above, is the area of triangular region ADE equal to the area of rectangular region $ABCD$?

    (1) $x = 10$ and $y = 5$.

    (2) $x = 2y$

DS97502.01

252. Last year Publisher X published 1,100 books, consisting of first editions, revised editions, and reprints. How many first editions did Publisher X publish last year?

    (1) The number of first editions published was 50 more than twice the number of reprints published.

    (2) The number of revised editions published was half the number of reprints published.

DS89502.01

253. How old is Jane?

    (1) Ten years ago she was one-third as old as she is now.

    (2) In 15 years, she will be twice as old as she is now.

DS99502.01

254. What was the population of City X in 2002?

    (1) X's population in 2002 increased by 2 percent, or 20,000 people, over 2001.

    (2) In 2001, X's population was 1,000,000.

DS79502.01

255. What is the perimeter of triangle ABC?

    (1) $AB = 16$ inches

    (2) $\triangle ABC$ is equilateral.

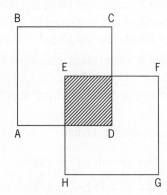

DS60602.01

256. In the figure above, is the shaded region a square region?

    (1) $ABCD$ and $EFGH$ are squares.

    (2) $BC = EF$

DS02602.01

257. *P* is a particle on the circle shown above. What is the length of the path traveled by *P* in one complete revolution around the circle?

  (1) The diameter of the circle is 1.5 meters.

  (2) The particle *P* moves in a clockwise direction at 0.5 meter per second.

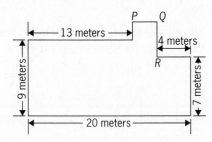

DS62602.01

258. The figure above shows the floor plan and inside dimensions of the ground level of a building. If all lines that intersect meet at right angles, what is the total floor area of this level of the building?

  (1) *QR* = 4 meters

  (2) *PQ* is less than *QR*.

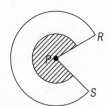

DS82602.01

259. The figure above shows the top of a circular cake with a slice removed. The shaded region on top of the cake is the remaining part of a circular decoration that was centered on the cake. What is the area of the shaded region?

  (1) *P* was the center of the top of the cake before the slice was removed and the angle of the slice, ∠*RPS*, is 60°.

  (2) *PR* = *PS* = 11 centimeters

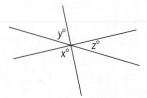

DS03602.01

260. If three straight lines intersect at a point as shown in the figure above, what is the value of *x* ?

  (1) *x* = *y* = *z*

  (2) *z* = 60

DS23602.01

261. What is the distance between City A and City C ?

  (1) The distance between City A and City B is 75 kilometers.

  (2) The distance between City B and City C is 135 kilometers.

DS33602.01

262. A person walked completely around the edge of a park beginning at the midpoint of one edge and making the minimum number of turns, each with the minimum number of degrees necessary, as shown in the figure above. What is the sum of the degrees of all the turns that the person made?

  (1) One of the turns is 80 degrees.

  (2) The number of sides of the park is 4, all of the sides are straight, and each interior angle is less than 180 degrees.

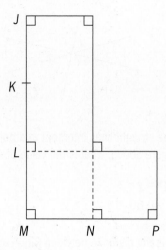

DS55602.01

263. What is the area, in square meters, of the building plot shown in the figure above?

(1) $KM = MP = 30$ meters

(2) $JK = KL = LM = MN = NP = 15$ meters

DS90820.02

264. Yesterday Bookstore B sold twice as many softcover books as hardcover books. Was Bookstore B's revenue from the sale of softcover books yesterday greater than its revenue from the sale of hardcover books yesterday?

(1)   The average (arithmetic mean) price of the hardcover books sold at the store yesterday was $10 more than the average price of the softcover books sold at the store yesterday.

(2)   The average price of the softcover and hardcover books sold at the store yesterday was greater than $14.

DS11820.02

265. What is the median of the nine consecutive even integers in a certain list?

(1)   The median of the integers in the list is greater than 0.

(2)   Of the integers in the list, the sum of the least of the negative integers and the least of the positive integers is –4.

DS18502.01

266. The heart-shaped decoration shown in the figure above consists of a square and two semicircles. What is the radius of each semicircle?

(1)   The diagonal of the square is $10\sqrt{2}$ centimeters long.

(2)   The area of the square region minus the sum of the areas of the semicircular regions is $100 - 25\pi$ square centimeters.

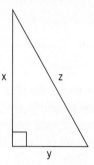

DS20602.01

267. If A is the area of a triangle with sides of lengths x, y, and z as shown above, what is the value of A?

(1) $z = 13$

(2) $A = \dfrac{5y}{2}$

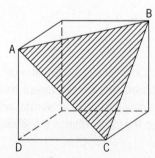

DS80602.01

268. The figure above shows a piece of cheese with a corner cut off to expose plane surface ABC. What is the area of surface ABC?

(1) $AD = 10$ centimeters

(2)   The shape of the cheese was a cube before the corner was cut off.

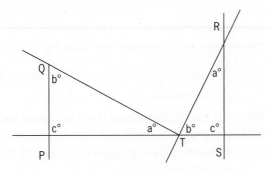

DS31602.01

269. The figure above shows a portion of a road map on which the measures of certain angles are indicated. If all lines shown are straight and intersect as shown, is road *PQ* parallel to road *RS* ?

   (1) $b = 2a$

   (2) $c = 3a$

DS14602.01

270. It costs $2,250 to fill right circular cylindrical Tank R with a certain industrial chemical. If the cost to fill any tank with this chemical is directly proportional to the volume of the chemical needed to fill the tank, how much does it cost to fill right circular cylindrical Tank S with the chemical?

   (1)   The diameter of the interior of Tank R is twice the diameter of the interior of Tank S.

   (2)   The interiors of Tanks R and S have the same height.

	Yes	No	Don't Know
Program X	400	200	400
Program Y	300	350	350

DS17700.02

271. The table shows the number of people who responded "yes" or "no" or "don't know" when asked whether their city council should implement environmental programs X and Y. If a total of 1,000 people responded to the question about both programs, what was the number of people who did not respond "yes" to implementing either of the two programs?

   (1)   The number of people who responded "yes" to implementing only Program X was 300.

   (2)   The number of people who responded "no" to implementing Program X and "no" to implementing Program Y was 100.

DS39510.02

272. An estimate of an actual data value has an error of p percent if $p = \dfrac{100|e - a|}{a}$, where e is the estimated value and a is the actual value. Emma's estimate for her total income last year had an error of less than 20 percent. Emma's estimate of her income from tutoring last year also had an error of less than 20 percent. Was Emma's actual income from tutoring last year at most 45 percent of her actual total income last year?

   (1)   Emma's estimated income last year from tutoring was 30 percent of her estimated total income last year.

   (2)   Emma's estimated total income last year was $40,000.

DS97030.02

273. Was Store K's profit last month at least 10 percent greater than its profit the previous month?

   (1)   Store K's expenses last month were 5 percent greater than its expenses the previous month.

   (2)   Store K's revenues last month were 10 percent greater than its revenues the previous month.

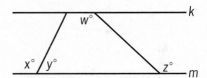

DS12862

274. In the figure shown, lines *k* and *m* are parallel to each other. Is $x = z$?

   (1) $x = w$

   (2) $y = 180 - w$

DS13097

275. If *k* and ℓ are lines in the *xy*-plane, is the slope of *k* less than the slope of ℓ ?

   (1)   The *x*-intercept of line *k* is positive, and the *x*-intercept of line ℓ is negative.

   (2)   Lines *k* and ℓ intersect on the positive *y*-axis.

DS73340.02

276. Is *n* less than 1?

   (1)   *n* is less than 0.01 percent of 10,000.

   (2)   *n* is less than 0.1 percent of 1,200.

DS18630.02
277. Gross profit is equal to selling price minus cost. A car dealer's gross profit on the sale of a certain car was what percent of the cost of the car?

   (1)   The selling price of the car was $\frac{11}{10}$ of the cost of the car.

   (2)   The cost of the car was $14,500.

DS09642
278. When the wind speed is 9 miles per hour, the wind-chill factor w is given by

$$w = -17.366 + 1.19t,$$

where t is the temperature in degrees Fahrenheit. If at noon yesterday the wind speed was 9 miles per hour, was the wind-chill factor greater than 0 ?

   (1)   The temperature at noon yesterday was greater than 10 degrees Fahrenheit.

   (2)   The temperature at noon yesterday was less than 20 degrees Fahrenheit.

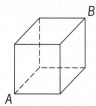

DS08852
279. What is the volume of the cube above?

   (1)   The surface area of the cube is 600 square inches.

   (2)   The length of diagonal AB is $10\sqrt{3}$ inches.

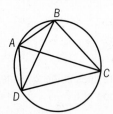

DS03989
280. In the figure shown, quadrilateral ABCD is inscribed in a circle of radius 5. What is the perimeter of quadrilateral ABCD ?

   (1)   The length of AB is 6 and the length of CD is 8.

   (2)   AC is a diameter of the circle.

DS05766
281. How many members of a certain legislature voted against the measure to raise their salaries?

   (1) $\frac{1}{4}$ of the members of the legislature did not vote on the measure.

   (2)   If 5 additional members of the legislature had voted against the measure, then the fraction of members of the legislature voting against the measure would have been $\frac{1}{3}$.

DS05986
282. If $y \neq 0$, is $|x| = 1$?

   (1) $x = \dfrac{y}{|y|}$

   (2) $|x| = -x$

DS08306
283. If x is a positive integer, what is the value of x ?

   (1) $x^2 = \sqrt{x}$

   (2) $\dfrac{n}{x} = n$ and $n \neq 0$.

DS07568
284. Is the median of the five numbers a, b, c, d, and e equal to d ?

   (1) $a < c < e$

   (2) $b < d < c$

DS10383
285. During a certain bicycle ride, was Sherry's average speed faster than 24 kilometers per hour? (1 kilometer = 1,000 meters)

   (1)   Sherry's average speed during the bicycle ride was faster than 7 meters per second.

   (2)   Sherry's average speed during the bicycle ride was slower than 8 meters per second.

DS13907
286. Working together, Rafael and Salvador can tabulate a certain set of data in 2 hours. In how many hours can Rafael tabulate the data working alone?

   (1)   Working alone, Rafael can tabulate the data in 3 hours less time than Salvador, working alone, can tabulate the data.

   (2)   Working alone, Rafael can tabulate the data in $\frac{1}{2}$ the time that Salvador, working alone, can tabulate the data.

DS04039
287. If x and y are integers, what is the value of x ?

(1) $xy = 1$

(2) $x \neq -1$

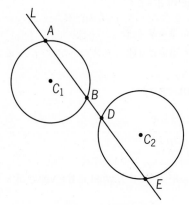

Note: Figure not drawn to scale.

DS18386
288. The figure above shows Line L, Circle 1 with center at C_1, and Circle 2 with center at C_2. Line L intersects Circle 1 at points A and B, Line L intersects Circle 2 at points D and E, and points C_1 and C_2 are equidistant from line L. Is the area of $\triangle ABC_1$ less than the area of $\triangle DEC_2$?

(1) The radius of Circle 1 is less than the radius of Circle 2.

(2) The length of chord $\overline{AB}$ is less than the length of chord $\overline{DE}$.

DS15938
289. Yesterday between 9:00 a.m. and 6:00 p.m. at Airport X, all flights to Atlanta departed at equally spaced times and all flights to New York City departed at equally spaced times. A flight to Atlanta and a flight to New York City both departed from Airport X at 1:00 p.m. yesterday. Between 1:00 p.m. and 3:00 p.m. yesterday, did another pair of flights to these 2 cities depart from Airport X at the same time?

(1) Yesterday at Airport X, a flight to Atlanta and a flight to New York City both departed at 10:00 a.m.

(2) Yesterday at Airport X, flights to New York City departed every 15 minutes between 9:00 a.m. and 6:00 p.m.

DS07206
290. Of the total number of copies of Magazine X sold last week, 40 percent were sold at full price. What was the total number of copies of the magazine sold last week?

(1) Last week, full price for a copy of Magazine X was $1.50 and the total revenue from full-price sales was $112,500.

(2) The total number of copies of Magazine X sold last week at full price was $75,000.

DS11614
291. If p, s, and t are positive, is $|ps - pt| > p(s - t)$?

(1) $p < s$

(2) $s < t$

DS04468
292. Is $x > y$?

(1) $x + y > x - y$

(2) $3x > 2y$

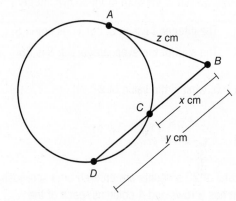

DS17588
293. In the figure above, $\overline{AB}$, which has length z cm, is tangent to the circle at point A, and $\overline{BD}$, which has length y cm, intersects the circle at point C. If $BC = x$ cm and $z = \sqrt{xy}$, what is the value of x ?

(1) $CD = x$ cm

(2) $z = 5\sqrt{2}$

DS15863
294. Is the integer n a prime number?

(1) $24 \leq n \leq 28$

(2) n is not divisible by 2 or 3.

DS03615
295. What is the average (arithmetic mean) annual salary of the 6 employees of a toy company?

(1) If the 6 annual salaries were ordered from least to greatest, each annual salary would be $6,300 greater than the preceding annual salary.

(2) The range of the 6 annual salaries is $31,500.

DS17503
296. In a certain order, the pretax price of each regular pencil was $0.03, the pretax price of each deluxe pencil was $0.05, and there were 50% more deluxe pencils than regular pencils. All taxes on the order are a fixed percent of the pretax prices. The sum of the total pretax price of the order and the tax on the order was $44.10. What was the amount, in dollars, of the tax on the order?

(1) The tax on the order was 5% of the total pretax price of the order.

(2) The order contained exactly 400 regular pencils.

DS06785
297. If m is an integer greater than 1, is m an even integer?

(1) 32 is a factor of m.

(2) m is a factor of 32.

DS05657
298. If the set S consists of five consecutive positive integers, what is the sum of these five integers?

(1) The integer 11 is in S, but 10 is not in S.

(2) The sum of the even integers in S is 26.

DS17543
299. If $x > 0$, what is the value of x?

(1) $x^3 - x = 0$

(2) $\sqrt[3]{x} - x = 0$

DS08307
300. A total of 20 amounts are entered on a spreadsheet that has 5 rows and 4 columns; each of the 20 positions in the spreadsheet contains one amount. The average (arithmetic mean) of the amounts in row i is R_i ($1 \le i \le 5$). The average of the amounts in column j is C_j ($1 \le j \le 4$). What is the average of all 20 amounts on the spreadsheet?

(1) $R_1 + R_2 + R_3 + R_4 + R_5 = 550$

(2) $C_1 + C_2 + C_3 + C_4 = 440$

DS13132
301. Was the range of the amounts of money that Company Y budgeted for its projects last year equal to the range of the amounts of money that it budgeted for its projects this year?

(1) Both last year and this year, Company Y budgeted money for 12 projects and the least amount of money that it budgeted for a project was $400.

(2) Both last year and this year, the average (arithmetic mean) amount of money that Company Y budgeted per project was $2,000.

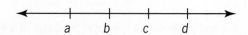

DS01633
302. If a, b, c, and d are numbers on the number line shown and if the tick marks are equally spaced, what is the value of $a + c$?

(1) $a + b = -8$

(2) $a + d = 0$

DS06067
303. Is $xm < ym$?

(1) $x > y$

(2) $m < 0$

DS02899
304. If $y = x^2 - 6x + 9$, what is the value of x?

(1) $y = 0$

(2) $x + y = 3$

DS06810
305. What is the probability that Lee will make exactly 5 errors on a certain typing test?

(1) The probability that Lee will make 5 or more errors on the test is 0.27.

(2) The probability that Lee will make 5 or fewer errors on the test is 0.85.

DS19208
306. If p is a positive integer, is $2^p + 1$ a prime number?

(1) p is a prime number.

(2) p is an even number.

Questions 307 to 373 - Difficulty: Hard

DS60130
307. What percent of the students at University X are enrolled in a science course but are not enrolled in a biology course?

(1) 28 percent of the students at University X are enrolled in a biology course.

(2) 70 percent of the students at University X who are enrolled in a science course are enrolled in a biology course.

DS02741
308. In the xy-plane, point (r,s) lies on a circle with center at the origin. What is the value of $r^2 + s^2$?

(1) The circle has radius 2.

(2) The point $\left(\sqrt{2}, -\sqrt{2}\right)$ lies on the circle.

DS06368

309. If r, s, and t are nonzero integers, is $r^5 s^3 t^4$ negative?

    (1) rt is negative.
    (2) s is negative.

DS13706

310. Each Type A machine fills 400 cans per minute, each Type B machine fills 600 cans per minute, and each Type C machine installs 2,400 lids per minute. A lid is installed on each can that is filled and on no can that is not filled. For a particular minute, what is the total number of machines working?

    (1) A total of 4,800 cans are filled that minute.
    (2) For that minute, there are 2 Type B machines working for every Type C machine working.

DS08660

311. If a and b are constants, what is the value of a?

    (1) $a < b$
    (2) $(t - a)(t - b) = t^2 + t - 12$, for all values of t.

DS04474

312. If x is a positive integer, is $\sqrt{x}$ an integer?

    (1) $\sqrt{4x}$ is an integer.
    (2) $\sqrt{3x}$ is not an integer.

DS16456

313. If p, q, x, y, and z are different positive integers, which of the five integers is the median?

    (1) $p + x < q$
    (2) $y < z$

DS16277

314. If $w + z = 28$, what is the value of wz?

    (1) w and z are positive integers.
    (2) w and z are consecutive odd integers.

DS02474

315. If $abc \neq 0$, is $\dfrac{\frac{a}{b}}{c} = \dfrac{a}{\frac{b}{c}}$?

    (1) $a = 1$
    (2) $c = 1$

DS14471

316. The arithmetic mean of a collection of 5 positive integers, not necessarily distinct, is 9. One additional positive integer is included in the collection and the arithmetic mean of the 6 integers is computed. Is the arithmetic mean of the 6 integers at least 10?

    (1) The additional integer is at least 14.
    (2) The additional integer is a multiple of 5.

DS11003

317. A certain list consists of 400 different numbers. Is the average (arithmetic mean) of the numbers in the list greater than the median of the numbers in the list?

    (1) Of the numbers in the list, 280 are less than the average.
    (2) Of the numbers in the list, 30 percent are greater than or equal to the average.

DS03678

318. In a two-month survey of shoppers, each shopper bought one of two brands of detergent, X or Y, in the first month and again bought one of these brands in the second month. In the survey, 90 percent of the shoppers who bought Brand X in the first month bought Brand X again in the second month, while 60 percent of the shoppers who bought Brand Y in the first month bought Brand Y again in the second month. What percent of the shoppers bought Brand Y in the second month?

    (1) In the first month, 50 percent of the shoppers bought Brand X.
    (2) The total number of shoppers surveyed was 5,000.

DS15902

319. If m and n are positive integers, is $m + n$ divisible by 4?

    (1) m and n are each divisible by 2.
    (2) Neither m nor n is divisible by 4.

DS02940

320. What is the area of rectangular region R?

    (1) Each diagonal of R has length 5.
    (2) The perimeter of R is 14.

DS17137

321. How many integers n are there such that $r < n < s$?

    (1) $s - r = 5$
    (2) r and s are not integers.

DS17147

322. If the total price of n equally priced shares of a certain stock was \$12,000, what was the price per share of the stock?

    (1) If the price per share of the stock had been \$1 more, the total price of the n shares would have been \$300 more.
    (2) If the price per share of the stock had been \$2 less, the total price of the n shares would have been 5 percent less.

DS02865
323. If n is positive, is $\sqrt{n} > 100$?

    (1) $\sqrt{n-1} > 99$

    (2) $\sqrt{n+1} > 101$

DS17150
324. Is $xy > 5$?

    (1) $1 \le x \le 3$ and $2 \le y \le 4$.

    (2) $x + y = 5$

DS17151
325. In Year X, 8.7 percent of the men in the labor force were unemployed in June compared with 8.4 percent in May. If the number of men in the labor force was the same for both months, how many men were unemployed in June of that year?

    (1)   In May of Year X, the number of unemployed men in the labor force was 3.36 million.

    (2)   In Year X, 120,000 more men in the labor force were unemployed in June than in May.

DS17112
326. If $x \ne 0$, what is the value of $\left(\dfrac{x^p}{x^q} \right)^4$?

    (1) $p = q$

    (2) $x = 3$

DS17153
327. On Monday morning a certain machine ran continuously at a uniform rate to fill a production order. At what time did it completely fill the order that morning?

    (1)   The machine began filling the order at 9:30 a.m.

    (2)   The machine had filled $\dfrac{1}{2}$ of the order by 10:30 a.m. and $\dfrac{5}{6}$ of the order by 11:10 a.m.

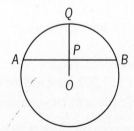

DS17107
328. What is the radius of the circle above with center O ?

    (1)   The ratio of OP to PQ is 1 to 2.

    (2) P is the midpoint of chord AB.

DS15618
329. If a and b are positive integers, what is the value of the product ab ?

    (1)   The least common multiple of a and b is 48.

    (2)   The greatest common factor of a and b is 4.

DS17095
330. What is the number of 360-degree rotations that a bicycle wheel made while rolling 100 meters in a straight line without slipping?

    (1)   The diameter of the bicycle wheel, including the tire, was 0.5 meter.

    (2)   The wheel made twenty 360-degree rotations per minute.

DS17168
331. In the equation $x^2 + bx + 12 = 0$, x is a variable and b is a constant. What is the value of b ?

    (1) $x - 3$ is a factor of $x^2 + bx + 12$.

    (2)   4 is a root of the equation $x^2 + bx + 12 = 0$.

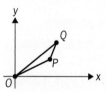

DS07715
332. In the figure above, line segment OP has slope $\dfrac{1}{2}$ and line segment PQ has slope 2. What is the slope of line segment OQ ?

    (1)   Line segment OP has length $2\sqrt{5}$.

    (2)   The coordinates of point Q are (5,4).

DS17164
333. In $\triangle XYZ$, what is the length of YZ ?

    (1)   The length of XY is 3.

    (2)   The length of XZ is 5.

DS07217
334. If the average (arithmetic mean) of n consecutive odd integers is 10, what is the least of the integers?

    (1)   The range of the n integers is 14.

    (2)   The greatest of the n integers is 17.

DS16044
335. If x, y, and z are positive numbers, is $x > y > z$?

    (1) $xz > yz$

    (2) $yx > yz$

DS06644

336. K is a set of numbers such that

   (i)   if x is in K, then $-x$ is in K, and

   (ii) if each of x and y is in K, then xy is in K.

   Is 12 in K ?

   (1)   2 is in K.

   (2)   3 is in K.

DS05637

337. If $x^2 + y^2 = 29$, what is the value of $(x - y)^2$?

   (1) $xy = 10$

   (2) $x = 5$

DS16470

338. After winning 50 percent of the first 20 games it played, Team A won all of the remaining games it played. What was the total number of games that Team A won?

   (1)   Team A played 25 games altogether.

   (2)   Team A won 60 percent of all the games it played.

DS17181

339. Is x between 0 and 1 ?

   (1) x^2 is less than x.

   (2) x^3 is positive.

DS04083

340. If m and n are nonzero integers, is m^n an integer?

   (1) n^m is positive.

   (2) n^m is an integer.

DS16034

341. What is the value of xy ?

   (1) $x + y = 10$

   (2) $x - y = 6$

DS13189

342. If n is the least of three different integers greater than 1, what is the value of n ?

   (1)   The product of the three integers is 90.

   (2)   One of the integers is twice one of the other two integers.

DS16461

343. Is x^2 greater than x ?

   (1) x^2 is greater than 1.

   (2) x is greater than -1.

DS03503

344. Michael arranged all his books in a bookcase with 10 books on each shelf and no books left over. After Michael acquired 10 additional books, he arranged all his books in a new bookcase with 12 books on each shelf and no books left over. How many books did Michael have before he acquired the 10 additional books?

   (1)   Before Michael acquired the 10 additional books, he had fewer than 96 books.

   (2)   Before Michael acquired the 10 additional books, he had more than 24 books.

DS16469

345. If $xy > 0$, does $(x - 1)(y - 1) = 1$?

   (1) $x + y = xy$

   (2) $x = y$

DS06842

346. Last year in a group of 30 businesses, 21 reported a net profit and 15 had investments in foreign markets. How many of the businesses did not report a net profit nor invest in foreign markets last year?

   (1)   Last year 12 of the 30 businesses reported a net profit and had investments in foreign markets.

   (2)   Last year 24 of the 30 businesses reported a net profit or invested in foreign markets, or both.

DS17110

347. Is the perimeter of square S greater than the perimeter of equilateral triangle T ?

   (1)   The ratio of the length of a side of S to the length of a side of T is 4:5.

   (2)   The sum of the lengths of a side of S and a side of T is 18.

DS17136

348. If $x + y + z > 0$, is $z > 1$?

   (1) $z > x + y + 1$

   (2) $x + y + 1 < 0$

DS07832

349. For all z, $\lceil z \rceil$ denotes the least integer greater than or equal to z. Is $\lceil x \rceil = 0$?

   (1) $-1 < x < -0.1$

   (2) $\lceil x + 0.5 \rceil = 1$

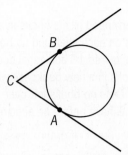

DS16464

350. The circular base of an above-ground swimming pool lies in a level yard and just touches two straight sides of a fence at points A and B, as shown in the figure above. Point C is on the ground where the two sides of the fence meet. How far from the center of the pool's base is point A?

    (1)   The base has area 250 square feet.
    (2)   The center of the base is 20 feet from point C.

DS16050

351. If $xy = -6$, what is the value of $xy(x + y)$?

    (1) $x - y = 5$
    (2) $xy^2 = 18$

DS05519

352. $[y]$ denotes the greatest integer less than or equal to y. Is $d < 1$?

    (1) $d = y - [y]$
    (2) $[d] = 0$

DS14052

353. If N is a positive odd integer, is N prime?

    (1) $N = 2^k + 1$ for some positive integer k.
    (2) $N + 2$ and $N + 4$ are both prime.

DS01140

354. If m is a positive integer, then m^3 has how many digits?

    (1) m has 3 digits.
    (2) m^2 has 5 digits.

DS03308

355. What is the value of $x^2 - y^2$?

    (1) $(x - y)^2 = 9$
    (2) $x + y = 6$

DS01267

356. For each landscaping job that takes more than 4 hours, a certain contractor charges a total of r dollars for the first 4 hours plus $0.2r$ dollars for each additional hour or fraction of an hour, where $r > 100$. Did a particular landscaping job take more than 10 hours?

    (1)   The contractor charged a total of \$288 for the job.
    (2)   The contractor charged a total of $2.4r$ dollars for the job.

DS17600

357. If $x^2 = 2^x$, what is the value of x?

    (1) $2x = \left(\dfrac{x}{2}\right)^3$
    (2) $x = 2^{x-2}$

DS01169

358. The sequence $s_1, s_2, s_3, \ldots, s_n, \ldots$ is such that $s_n = \dfrac{1}{n} - \dfrac{1}{n+1}$ for all integers $n \geq 1$. If k is a positive integer, is the sum of the first k terms of the sequence greater than $\dfrac{9}{10}$?

    (1) $k > 10$
    (2) $k < 19$

DS05518

359. In the sequence S of numbers, each term after the first two terms is the sum of the two immediately preceding terms. What is the 5th term of S?

    (1)   The 6th term of S minus the 4th term equals 5.
    (2)   The 6th term of S plus the 7th term equals 21.

DS01121

360. If 75 percent of the guests at a certain banquet ordered dessert, what percent of the guests ordered coffee?

    (1)   60 percent of the guests who ordered dessert also ordered coffee.
    (2)   90 percent of the guests who ordered coffee also ordered dessert.

DS05302

361. A tank containing water started to leak. Did the tank contain more than 30 gallons of water when it started to leak? (Note: 1 gallon = 128 ounces)

    (1)   The water leaked from the tank at a constant rate of 6.4 ounces per minute.
    (2)   The tank became empty less than 12 hours after it started to leak.

DS12752
362. In the *xy*-plane, lines *k* and *ℓ* intersect at the point (1,1). Is the *y*-intercept of *k* greater than the *y*-intercept of *ℓ* ?

    (1)   The slope of *k* is less than the slope of *ℓ*.
    (2)   The slope of *ℓ* is positive.

DS14588
363. A triangle has side lengths of *a*, *b*, and *c* centimeters. Does each angle in the triangle measure less than 90 degrees?

    (1)   The 3 semicircles whose diameters are the sides of the triangle have areas that are equal to 3 cm², 4 cm², and 6 cm², respectively.
    (2) $c < a + b < c + 2$

DS00890
364. Each of the 45 books on a shelf is written either in English or in Spanish, and each of the books is either a hardcover book or a paperback. If a book is to be selected at random from the books on the shelf, is the probability less than $\frac{1}{2}$ that the book selected will be a paperback written in Spanish?

    (1)   Of the books on the shelf, 30 are paperbacks.
    (2)   Of the books on the shelf, 15 are written in Spanish.

DS06683
365. A small school has three foreign language classes, one in French, one in Spanish, and one in German. How many of the 34 students enrolled in the Spanish class are also enrolled in the French class?

    (1)   There are 27 students enrolled in the French class, and 49 students enrolled in either the French class, the Spanish class, or both of these classes.
    (2)   One-half of the students enrolled in the Spanish class are enrolled in more than one foreign language class.

DS04910
366. If *S* is a set of four numbers *w*, *x*, *y*, and *z*, is the range of the numbers in *S* greater than 2 ?

    (1) $w - z > 2$
    (2)   *z* is the least number in *S*.

DS12187
367. Last year $\frac{3}{5}$ of the members of a certain club were males. This year the members of the club include all the members from last year plus some new members. Is the fraction of the members of the club who are males greater this year than last year?

    (1)   More than half of the new members are male.
    (2)   The number of members of the club this year is $\frac{6}{5}$ the number of members last year.

DS13640
368. If *a*, *b*, and *c* are consecutive integers and $0 < a < b < c$, is the product *abc* a multiple of 8 ?

    (1)   The product *ac* is even.
    (2)   The product *bc* is a multiple of 4.

DS13837
369. *M* and *N* are integers such that $6 < M < N$. What is the value of *N* ?

    (1)   The greatest common divisor of *M* and *N* is 6.
    (2)   The least common multiple of *M* and *N* is 36.

DS98530.02
370. Machines K, M, and N, each working alone at its constant rate, produce 1 widget in *x*, *y*, and 2 minutes, respectively. If Machines K, M, and N work simultaneously at their respective constant rates, does it take them less than 1 hour to produce a total of 50 widgets?

    (1) $x < 1.5$
    (2) $y < 1.2$

DS07575
371. Stations X and Y are connected by two separate, straight, parallel rail lines that are 250 miles long. Train P and train Q simultaneously left Station X and Station Y, respectively, and each train traveled to the other's point of departure. The two trains passed each other after traveling for 2 hours. When the two trains passed, which train was nearer to its destination?

    (1)   At the time when the two trains passed, train P had averaged a speed of 70 miles per hour.
    (2)   Train Q averaged a speed of 55 miles per hour for the entire trip.

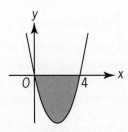

DS01613

372. In the xy-plane shown, the shaded region consists of all points that lie above the graph of $y = x^2 - 4x$ and below the x-axis. Does the point (a,b) (not shown) lie in the shaded region if $b < 0$?

 (1) $0 < a < 4$
 (2) $a^2 - 4a < b$

DS01685

373. If a and b are positive integers, is $\sqrt[3]{ab}$ an integer?

 (1) $\sqrt{a}$ is an integer.
 (2) $b = \sqrt{a}$

5.4 Answer Key

213.	D	249.	E	285.	A	321.	C	357.	D
214.	C	250.	C	286.	D	322.	D	358.	A
215.	E	251.	D	287.	C	323.	B	359.	A
216.	C	252.	C	288.	D	324.	E	360.	C
217.	A	253.	D	289.	E	325.	D	361.	E
218.	C	254.	A	290.	D	326.	A	362.	A
219.	E	255.	C	291.	B	327.	B	363.	A
220.	D	256.	E	292.	E	328.	E	364.	B
221.	A	257.	A	293.	C	329.	C	365.	A
222.	E	258.	A	294.	A	330.	A	366.	A
223.	B	259.	E	295.	E	331.	D	367.	E
224.	E	260.	A	296.	D	332.	B	368.	A
225.	A	261.	E	297.	D	333.	E	369.	C
226.	D	262.	B	298.	D	334.	D	370.	D
227.	D	263.	B	299.	D	335.	E	371.	A
228.	C	264.	C	300.	D	336.	C	372.	B
229.	E	265.	B	301.	E	337.	A	373.	B
230.	E	266.	D	302.	C	338.	D		
231.	D	267.	C	303.	C	339.	A		
232.	E	268.	C	304.	A	340.	E		
233.	D	269.	C	305.	C	341.	C		
234.	B	270.	C	306.	C	342.	C		
235.	C	271.	A	307.	C	343.	A		
236.	E	272.	A	308.	D	344.	A		
237.	B	273.	C	309.	E	345.	A		
238.	D	274.	D	310.	C	346.	D		
239.	D	275.	C	311.	C	347.	A		
240.	C	276.	A	312.	A	348.	B		
241.	B	277.	A	313.	E	349.	A		
242.	D	278.	E	314.	B	350.	A		
243.	C	279.	D	315.	B	351.	B		
244.	D	280.	C	316.	C	352.	D		
245.	B	281.	E	317.	D	353.	E		
246.	A	282.	A	318.	A	354.	E		
247.	C	283.	D	319.	C	355.	E		
248.	A	284.	E	320.	C	356.	B		

5.5 Answer Explanations

The following discussion of Data Sufficiency is intended to familiarize you with the most efficient and effective approaches to the kinds of problems common to Data Sufficiency. The particular questions in this chapter are generally representative of the kinds of Data Sufficiency questions you will encounter on the GMAT exam. Remember that it is the problem solving strategy that is important, not the specific details of a particular question.

Questions 213 to 265 - Difficulty: **Easy**

*DS05149

213. Does $2x + 8 = 12$?

  (1) $2x + 10 = 14$
  (2) $3x + 8 = 14$

Algebra First-Degree Equations

We need to determine, for each of statements 1 and 2, whether the statement is sufficient for determining whether $2x + 8 = 12$. Solving for x, we see that the equation $2x + 8 = 12$ is equivalent to $2x = 12 - 8 = 4$ and is thus equivalent to $x = 2$. We thus need to find whether the statements are sufficient for determining whether $x = 2$.

  (1) Given that $2x + 10 = 14$, it follows that $2x = 14 - 10 = 4$, and that $x = 2$; SUFFICIENT.

  (2) Similarly, given that $3x + 8 = 14$, it follows that $3x = 14 - 8 = 6$, and that $x = 2$; SUFFICIENT.

Alternatively, for both statements 1 and 2, it is only necessary to determine that it is possible to solve each of 1 and 2 to produce a unique value for x. Care must be taken with such an approach (there are cases such as, for example, $3y = 5 + 3y$, that cannot be solved for a unique value of the variable). However, the approach can save time.

**The correct answer is D;
each statement alone is sufficient.**

DS96720.02

214. Each car at a certain dealership is either blue or white. What is the average (arithmetic mean) sticker price of all the cars at the dealership?

  (1) Of all the cars at the dealership, $\frac{1}{3}$ are blue and have an average sticker price of $21,000.

  (2) Of all the cars at the dealership, $\frac{2}{3}$ are white and have an average sticker price of $24,000.

Algebra Statistics

Let Σ_b and Σ_w be the sum of the sticker prices, respectively and in dollars, of the blue cars and the white cars at the dealership, and let n be the number of cars at the dealership. Determine the value of $\dfrac{\Sigma_b + \Sigma_w}{n}$.

  (1) Given that there are $\frac{1}{3}n$ blue cars having an average sticker price of $21,000, it follows that $\Sigma_b = \left(\frac{1}{3}n\right)21,000 = 7,000n$. Therefore,
$$\frac{\Sigma_b + \Sigma_w}{n} = \frac{7,000n + \Sigma_w}{n} = 7,000 + \frac{\Sigma_w}{n},$$
which can have more than one possible value by suitably varying Σ_w and n; NOT sufficient.

  (2) Given that there are $\frac{2}{3}n$ white cars having an average sticker price of $24,000, it follows that $\Sigma_w = \left(\frac{2}{3}n\right)24,000 = 16,000n$. Therefore, $\dfrac{\Sigma_b + \Sigma_w}{n} = \dfrac{\Sigma_b + 16,000n}{n} = \dfrac{\Sigma_b}{n} + 16,000$, which can have more than one possible value by suitably varying Σ_b and n; NOT sufficient.

Taking (1) and (2) together, $\dfrac{\Sigma_b + \Sigma_w}{n} = \dfrac{7,000n + 16,000n}{n} = \dfrac{23,000n}{n} = 23,000$.

**The correct answer is C;
both statements together are sufficient.**

---

*These numbers correlate with the online test bank question number. See the GMAT™ Official Guide Quantitative Review Question Index in the back of this book.

244

DS01503
215. If *M* is a set of consecutive even integers, is 0 in set *M*?

   (1)   –6 is in set *M*.
   (2)   –2 is in set *M*.

Arithmetic Series and Sequences

For a set *M* of consecutive even integers, can we determine whether *M* contains the number 0?

   (1)   Given that –6 is in the set *M*, *M* could be a set of strictly negative integers or a set that contains both negative integers and zero (and perhaps positive integers). For example, it could be the set {–8, –6, –4} or the set {–8, –6, –4, –2, 0, 2}; NOT sufficient.

   (2)   Similarly, given that –2 is in *M*, *M* could be a set of strictly negative integers or a set that contains both negative integers and zero (and perhaps positive integers). For example, it could be the set {–4, –2} or the set {–8, –6, –4, –2, 0, 2}; NOT sufficient.

Furthermore we can see that statements 1 and 2 together are not sufficient. For example, {–8, –6, –4, –2, 0, 2} contains –6, –2, and 0, while {–8, –6, –4, –2} contains –6 and –2 but not 0.

The correct answer is E; both statements together are not sufficient.

DS35330.02
216. A box contains only white balls and black balls. What is the probability that a ball selected at random from the box is white?

   (1)   There are 100 balls in the box.
   (2)   There are 40 black balls in the box.

Arithmetic Probability

Determine the probability of selecting a white ball from a box that contains only white and black balls.

   (1)   Given that there are 100 balls in the box, it is impossible to determine the probability of selecting a white ball because there is no information on the white/black split of the 100 balls in the box; NOT sufficient.

   (2)   Given that there are 40 black balls in the box, it is impossible to determine the probability of selecting a white ball because

there is no indication of either the total number of balls in the box or the number of white balls; NOT sufficient.

Taking (1) and (2) together, there are 100 balls in the box, 40 of which are black. It follows that the number of white balls is $100 - 40 = 60$ and the probability of selecting a white ball is $\frac{60}{100} = \frac{3}{5}$.

The correct answer is C; both statements together are sufficient.

DS15510
217. Rita's monthly salary is $\frac{2}{3}$ Juanita's monthly salary. What is their combined monthly salary?

   (1)   Rita's monthly salary is $4,000.
   (2)   Either Rita's monthly salary or Juanita's monthly salary is $6,000.

Arithmetic Applied Problems

Let *R* and *J* be Rita's and Juanita's monthly salaries, respectively, in dollars. It is given that $R = \frac{2}{3} J$. Determine the value of their combined salary, which can be expressed as $R + J = \frac{2}{3} J + J = \frac{5}{3} J$.

   (1)   Given that $R = 4{,}000$, it follows that $4{,}000 = \frac{2}{3} J$, or $J = \frac{3}{2}(4{,}000) = 6{,}000$. Therefore, $\frac{5}{3} J = \frac{5}{3}(6{,}000) = 10{,}000$; SUFFICIENT.

   (2)   Given that $R = 6{,}000$ or $J = 6{,}000$, then $J = \frac{3}{2}(6{,}000) = 9{,}000$ or $J = 6{,}000$. Thus, $\frac{5}{3} J = \frac{5}{3}(9{,}000) = 15{,}000$ or $\frac{5}{3} J = \frac{5}{3}(6{,}000) = 10{,}000$, and so it is not possible to determine the value of $\frac{5}{3} J$; NOT sufficient.

The correct answer is A; statement 1 alone is sufficient.

DS37130.02
218. Each of the 120 students in a certain dormitory is either a junior or a senior. How many of the juniors have credit cards?

   (1) $\frac{2}{3}$ of the 120 juniors and seniors have credit cards.

(2) The number of seniors who have credit cards is 20 more than the number of juniors who have credit cards.

Algebra First-Degree Equations

Determine the number of juniors who have credit cards among the 120 students in a certain junior/senior dormitory.

(1) Given that $\frac{2}{3}$ of the 120 students have credit cards, it follows that 80 students have credit cards. There is no information regarding the number of juniors in this group of 80; NOT sufficient.

(2) Given that the number of seniors with credit cards is 20 more than the number of juniors with credit cards, it is impossible to determine how many juniors have credit cards because no information is given about the junior/senior split nor about the have/do not have credit cards split of the 120 students; NOT sufficient.

Taking (1) and (2) together, 80 students have credit cards from (1) and the number of seniors with credit cards is 20 more than the number of juniors with credit cards from (2). Thus, $J + S = 80$ or $J + (J + 20) = 80$, which can be solved for a unique value of J.

The correct answer is C;
both statements together are sufficient.

DS13384

219. What is the value of the integer x?

(1) x rounded to the nearest hundred is 7,200.
(2) The hundreds digit of x is 2.

Arithmetic Rounding

(1) Given that x rounded to the nearest hundred is 7,200, the value of x cannot be determined. For example, x could be 7,200 or x could be 7,201; NOT sufficient.

(2) Given that the hundreds digit of x is 2, the value of x cannot be determined. For example, x could be 7,200 or x could be 7,201; NOT sufficient.

Taking (1) and (2) together is of no more help than either (1) or (2) taken separately because the same examples were used in both (1) and (2).

The correct answer is E;
both statements together are still not sufficient.

DS04644

220. Is $2x > 2y$?

(1) $x > y$
(2) $3x > 3y$

Algebra Inequalities

(1) It is given that $x > y$. Thus, multiplying both sides by the positive number 2, it follows that $2x > 2y$; SUFFICIENT.

(2) It is given that $3x > 3y$. Thus, multiplying both sides by the positive number $\frac{2}{3}$, it follows that $2x > 2y$; SUFFICIENT.

The correct answer is D;
each statement alone is sufficient.

DS38720.02

221. If the average (arithmetic mean) cost per sweater for 3 pullover sweaters and 1 cardigan sweater was $65, what was the cost of the cardigan sweater?

(1) The average cost per sweater for the 3 pullover sweaters was $55.
(2) The most expensive of the 3 pullover sweaters cost $30 more than the least expensive.

Algebra Statistics

Letting P represent the average cost, in dollars, of 1 pullover sweater and C, the cost, in dollars, of the cardigan, it is given that $\frac{3P + C}{4} = 65$ or $3P + C = 260$. Determine the value of C.

(1) It is given that $P = 55$. Therefore, $3P = 3(55) = 165$ and $C = 260 - 165 = 95$; SUFFICIENT.

(2) Given that the most expensive pullover sweater cost $30 more than the least expensive, it is impossible to determine the value of C. For example, if the price of the most expensive pullover sweater was $60, the price of the least expensive was $30, and the price of the other

pullover sweater was $40, then the value of $C = 260 - 60 - 30 - 40 = 130$. But if the price of the most expensive pullover sweater was $60, the price of the least expensive was $30, and the price of the other pullover sweater was $50, then the value of $C = 260 - 60 - 30 - 50 = 120$; NOT sufficient.

The correct answer is A; statement 1 alone is sufficient.

DS04636
222. If p and q are positive, is $\dfrac{p}{q}$ less than 1 ?

(1)　p is less than 4.
(2)　q is less than 4.

Arithmetic Properties of Numbers

(1)　Given that p is less than 4, then it is not possible to determine whether $\dfrac{p}{q}$ is less than 1. For example, if $p = 1$ and $q = 2$, then $\dfrac{p}{q} = \dfrac{1}{2}$ and $\dfrac{1}{2}$ is less than 1. However, if $p = 2$ and $q = 1$, then $\dfrac{p}{q} = 2$ and 2 is not less than 1; NOT sufficient.

(2)　Given that q is less than 4, then it is not possible to determine whether $\dfrac{p}{q}$ is less than 1. For example, if $p = 1$ and $q = 2$, then $\dfrac{p}{q} = \dfrac{1}{2}$ and $\dfrac{1}{2}$ is less than 1. However, if $p = 2$ and $q = 1$, then $\dfrac{p}{q} = 2$ and 2 is not less than 1; NOT sufficient.

Taking (1) and (2) together is of no more help than either (1) or (2) taken separately because the same examples were used in both (1) and (2).

The correct answer is E; both statements together are still not sufficient.

DS02779
223. In each quarter of 1998, Company M earned more money than in the previous quarter. What was the range of Company M's quarterly earnings in 1998?

(1)　In the 2nd and 3rd quarters of 1998, Company M earned $4.0 million and $4.6 million, respectively.

(2)　In the 1st and 4th quarters of 1998, Company M earned $3.8 million and $4.9 million, respectively.

Arithmetic Statistics

We know that for each of the quarters in 1998, Company M earned more money than in the previous quarter. Is it possible to determine the range of the company's quarterly earnings in 1998?

(1)　Although we are told the value of the earnings for the 2nd and 3rd quarters, Company M's 4th quarter earnings could, consistent with statement 1, be any amount that is greater than the 3rd quarter earnings. Likewise, the company's 1st quarter earnings could be any positive amount that is less than the company's 2nd quarter earnings. The difference between these two values would be the range, and we see that it cannot be determined; NOT sufficient.

(2)　We are given the earnings for the 1st and 4th quarters, and we already know that, from quarter to quarter, the earnings in 1998 have always increased. We can thus infer that Company M's earnings for the 2nd and 3rd quarters are less than the 4th quarter earnings but greater than the 1st quarter earnings. The difference between the greatest quarterly earnings and the least quarter earnings for 1998 is thus the difference between the 4th quarter earnings and the 1st quarter earnings—the values $4.9 million and $3.8 million, respectively, that we have been given; SUFFICIENT.

The correct answer is B; statement 2 alone is sufficient.

DS69610.02
224. The range of the heights of a group of high school juniors and seniors is 20 centimeters. What is the average (arithmetic mean) of the height of the tallest senior in the group and the height of the shortest junior in the group?

(1)　The average of the heights of the juniors in the group is 165 centimeters.

(2)　The average of the heights of the seniors in the group is 179 centimeters.

Arithmetic Statistics

Determine the average of the height of the tallest senior and the height of the shortest junior.

(1) Given that the average of the heights of the juniors is 165 cm, it is not possible to determine the average of the height of the tallest senior and the height of the shortest junior. For example, the heights of the juniors could all be 165 cm and there could be three seniors with heights 176 cm, 176 cm, and 185 cm. In this case the range of all the heights is 185 − 165 = 20 cm, the average of the heights of the juniors is 165 cm, and the average of the height of the tallest senior and the height of the shortest junior is $\frac{185 + 165}{2} = 175$. On the other hand, the heights of the seniors could all be 179 cm and there could be three juniors with heights 159 cm, 168 cm, and 168 cm. In this case the range of all the heights is 179 − 159 = 20 cm, the average of the heights of the juniors is 165 cm, and the average of the height of the tallest senior and the height of the shortest junior is $\frac{179 + 159}{2} = 169$; NOT sufficient.

(2) Given that the average of the heights of the seniors is 179 cm, it is not possible to determine the average of the height of the tallest senior and the height of the shortest junior because, for each of the examples used in (1) above, the average of the heights of the seniors is 179 cm; NOT sufficient.

Taking (1) and (2) together, it is not possible to determine the average of the height of the tallest senior and the height of the shortest junior because each of the examples used in (1) above satisfies both (1) and (2).

The correct answer is E; both statements together are still not sufficient.

DS04510

225. In a certain factory, hours worked by each employee in excess of 40 hours per week are overtime hours and are paid for at $1\frac{1}{2}$ times the employee's regular hourly pay rate. If an employee worked a total of 42 hours last week, how much was the employee's gross pay for the hours worked last week?

(1) The employee's gross pay for overtime hours worked last week was $30.

(2) The employee's gross pay for all hours worked last week was $30 more than for the previous week.

Arithmetic Applied Problems

If an employee's regular hourly rate was $R and the employee worked 42 hours last week, then the employee's gross pay for hours worked last week was $40R + 2(1.5R)$. Determine the value of $40R + 2(1.5R) = 43R$, or equivalently, the value of R.

(1) Given that the employee's gross pay for overtime hours worked last week was $30, it follows that $2(1.5R) = 30$ and $R = 10$; SUFFICIENT.

(2) Given that the employee's gross pay for all hours worked last week was $30 more than for the previous week, the value of R cannot be determined because nothing specific is known about the value of the employee's pay for all hours worked the previous week; NOT sufficient.

The correct answer is A; statement 1 alone is sufficient.

DS01104

226. Is the integer p even?

(1) The integer $p^2 + 1$ is odd.

(2) The integer $p + 2$ is even.

Arithmetic Properties of Integers

(1) For any odd number m, $m - 1$ must be even. Therefore, given that $p^2 + 1$ is odd, p^2 must be even. Now, if in this case p were odd, p would not be divisible by 2 and so would not have 2 as one of its prime factors. p^2 would also not have 2 as one of its prime factors, and so, if p were odd, p^2 would be odd. Therefore, given that $p^2 + 1$ is odd (and p^2 is even), p must not be odd. That is, p must be even; SUFFICIENT.

(2) Given that $p + 2$ is even, it follows that $p + 2$ is divisible by 2. That is, $p + 2 = 2k$, where k is an integer. Thus, $p = 2k - 2 = 2(k - 1)$, where $k - 1$ is an integer. The integer p is thus divisible by 2 and is therefore even; SUFFICIENT.

The correct answer is D; each statement alone is sufficient.

DS05172

227. If $x > 0$, what is the value of x^5 ?

(1) $\sqrt{x} = 32$

(2) $x^2 = 2^{20}$

Algebra Exponents

(1) Given that $\sqrt{x} = 32$, it follows that $x = 32^2$ and $x^5 = (32^2)^5$; SUFFICIENT.

(2) Given that $x^2 = 2^{20}$, since x is positive, it follows that $x = \sqrt{2^{20}} = 2^{10}$ and $x^5 = (2^{10})^5$; SUFFICIENT.

The correct answer is D;
each statement alone is sufficient.

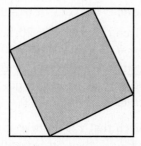

DS17640

228. In the quilting pattern shown above, a small square has its vertices on the sides of a larger square. What is the side length, in centimeters, of the larger square?

(1) The side length of the smaller square is 10 cm.

(2) Each vertex of the small square cuts 1 side of the larger square into 2 segments with lengths in the ratio of 1:2.

Geometry Triangles; Pythagorean Theorem

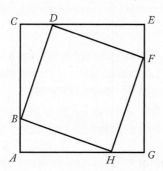

Determine the side length of the larger square or, in the figure above, determine $AG = AH + HG$. Note that $\triangle BAH$, $\triangle DCB$, $\triangle FED$, and $\triangle HGF$ are the same size and shape and that $AB = CD = EF = GH$ and $BC = DE = FG = HA$.

(1) This indicates that $HF = 10$, but it is possible that $HG = 6$ and $GF = 8$ $\left(\sqrt{6^2 + 8^2} = 10\right)$, from which it follows that the side length of the larger square is $6 + 8 = 14$, and it is possible that $HG = 1$ and $GF = \sqrt{99}$ $\left(\sqrt{1^2 + \left(\sqrt{99}\right)^2} = 10\right)$, from which it follows that the side length of the larger square is $1 + \sqrt{99}$; NOT sufficient.

(2) This indicates that if $HG = x$, then $AH = 2x$. If $x = 2$, then the side length of the larger square is $2 + 2(2) = 6$, but if $x = 5$, then the side length of the larger square is $5 + 2(5) = 15$; NOT sufficient.

Taking (1) and (2) together, $10 = \sqrt{x^2 + (2x)^2}$, which can be solved for x. Then taking 3 times the value of x gives the side length of the larger square.

The correct answer is C;
both statements together are sufficient.

DS02589

229. Did Insurance Company K have more than $300 million in total net profits last year?

(1) Last year Company K paid out $0.95 in claims for every dollar of premiums collected.

(2) Last year Company K earned a total of $150 million in profits from the investment of accumulated surplus premiums from previous years.

Arithmetic Applied Problems

Letting R and E, respectively, represent the company's total revenue and total expenses last year, determine if $R - E > \$300$ million.

(1) This indicates that, for $\$x$ in premiums collected, the company paid $\$0.95x$ in claims, but gives no information about other sources of revenue or other types of expenses; NOT sufficient.

(2) This indicates that the company's profits from the investment of accumulated surplus premiums was $150 million last year, but gives no information about other sources of revenue or other types of expenses; NOT sufficient.

Taking (1) and (2) together gives information on profit resulting from collecting premiums and paying claims as well as profit resulting from investments from accumulated surplus premiums, but gives no indication whether there were other sources of revenue or other types of expenses.

**The correct answer is E;
both statements together are still not sufficient.**

DS15349

230. How many hours would it take Pump A and Pump B working together, each at its own constant rate, to empty a tank that was initially full?

(1) Working alone at its constant rate, Pump A would empty the full tank in 4 hours 20 minutes.

(2) Working alone, Pump B would empty the full tank at its constant rate of 72 liters per minute.

Arithmetic Applied Problems

Determine how long it would take Pumps A and B working together, each at its own constant rate, to empty a full tank.

(1) This indicates how long it would take Pump A to empty the tank, but gives no information about Pump B's constant rate; NOT sufficient.

(2) This indicates the rate at which Pump B can empty the tank, but without information about the capacity of the tank or Pump A's rate, it is not possible to determine how long both pumps working together would take to empty the tank; NOT sufficient.

Taking (1) and (2) together gives the amount of time it would take Pump A to empty the tank and the rate at which Pump B can empty the tank, but without knowing the capacity of the tank, it is not possible to determine how long the pumps working together would take to empty the tank.

**The correct answer is E;
both statements together are still not sufficient.**

DS04573

231. What is the value of the integer N?

(1) $101 < N < 103$

(2) $202 < 2N < 206$

Arithmetic Inequalities

(1) Given that N is an integer and $101 < N < 103$, it follows that $N = 102$; SUFFICIENT.

(2) Given that N is an integer and $202 < 2N < 206$, it follows that $101 < N < 103$ and $N = 102$; SUFFICIENT.

**The correct answer is D;
each statement alone is sufficient.**

DS12033

232. Is zw positive?

(1) $z + w^3 = 20$

(2) z is positive.

Arithmetic Properties of Numbers

(1) Given that $z + w^3 = 20$, if $z = 1$ and $w = \sqrt[3]{19}$ then $z + w^3 = 20$ and zw is positive. However, if $z = 20$ and $w = 0$, then $z + w^3 = 20$ and zw is not positive; NOT sufficient.

(2) Given that z is positive, if $z = 1$ and $w = \sqrt[3]{19}$, then zw is positive. However, if $z = 20$ and $w = 0$, then zw is not positive; NOT sufficient.

Taking (1) and (2) together is of no more help than either (1) or (2) taken separately because the same examples were used in both (1) and (2).

**The correct answer is E;
both statements together are still not sufficient.**

DS03006

233. On the scale drawing of a certain house plan, if 1 centimeter represents x meters, what is the value of x?

(1) A rectangular room that has a floor area of 12 square meters is represented by a region of area 48 square centimeters.

(2) The 15-meter length of the house is represented by a segment 30 centimeters long.

Arithmetic Ratio and Proportion

It is given that on the scale drawing, 1 centimeter represents x meters. Determine the value of x. Note that 1 cm^2 represents x^2 m^2.

(1) This indicates that an area of 12 m² is represented by an area of 48 cm². Then, dividing both 12 and 48 by 48, it follows that an area of $\frac{12}{48} = \frac{1}{4}$ m² is represented by an area of $\frac{48}{48} = 1$ cm² and so $x^2 = \frac{1}{4}$ or $x = \frac{1}{2}$; SUFFICIENT.

(2) This indicates that a length of 15 m is represented by a length of 30 cm. Then, dividing both 15 and 30 by 30, it follows that a length of $\frac{15}{30} = \frac{1}{2}$ m is represented by a length of $\frac{30}{30} = 1$ cm and so $x = \frac{1}{2}$; SUFFICIENT.

The correct answer is D; each statement alone is sufficient.

DS23820.02

234. Maria left home $\frac{1}{4}$ hour after her husband and drove over the same route as he had in order to overtake him. From the time she left, how many hours did it take Maria to overtake her husband?

(1) Maria drove 60 miles before overtaking her husband.

(2) While overtaking her husband, Maria drove at an average rate of 60 miles per hour, which was 12 miles per hour faster than her husband's average rate.

Arithmetic Rate Problem

(1) Given that Maria drove 60 miles before overtaking her husband, it is not possible to determine how many hours she spent in driving this distance. For example, she could have been driving this distance at a rate of 30 miles per hour, and thus spent 2 hours in driving this distance. However, she could also have been driving this distance at a rate of 60 miles per hour, and thus spent 1 hour in driving this distance; NOT sufficient.

(2) Given that Maria drove at an average of 60 miles per hour and her husband drove at an average of $60 - 12 = 48$ miles per hour, and letting t be the number of hours it took for Maria to overtake her husband, it follows that $60t = 48(t + \frac{1}{4})$ since the distance Maria drove, $60t$ miles, is the same as the distance her husband drove, $48(t + \frac{1}{4})$ miles. Therefore, $60t = 48t + 12$, or $t = 1$, and hence it took 1 hour for Maria to overtake her husband; SUFFICIENT.

The correct answer is B; statement 2 alone is sufficient.

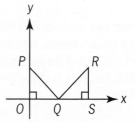

DS03939

235. In the rectangular coordinate system above, if $\triangle OPQ$ and $\triangle QRS$ have equal area, what are the coordinates of point R?

(1) The coordinates of point P are $(0,12)$.

(2) $OP = OQ$ and $QS = RS$.

Geometry Coordinate Geometry; Triangles

Since the area of $\triangle OPQ$ is equal to the area of $\triangle QRS$, it follows that $\frac{1}{2}(OQ)(OP) = \frac{1}{2}(QS)(SR)$, or $(OQ)(OP) = (QS)(SR)$. Also, if both OS and SR are known, then the coordinates of point R will be known.

(1) Given that the y-coordinate of P is 12, it is not possible to determine the coordinates of point R. For example, if $OQ = QS = SR = 12$, then the equation $(OQ)(OP) = (QS)(SR)$ becomes $(12)(12) = (12)(12)$, which is true, and the x-coordinate of R is $OQ + QS = 24$ and the y-coordinate of R is $SR = 12$. However, if $OQ = 12$, $QS = 24$, and $SR = 6$, then the equation $(OQ)(OP) = (QS)(SR)$ becomes $(12)(12) = (24)(6)$, which is true, and the x-coordinate of R is $OQ + QS = 36$ and the y-coordinate of R is $SR = 6$; NOT sufficient.

(2) Given that $OP = OQ$ and $QS = RS$, it is not possible to determine the coordinates of point R, since everything given would still be true if all the lengths were doubled, but doing this would change the coordinates of point R; NOT sufficient.

Taking (1) and (2) together, it follows that $OP = OQ = 12$. Therefore, $(OQ)(OP) = (QS)(SR)$ becomes $(12)(12) = (QS)(SR)$, or $144 = (QS)(SR)$. Using $QS = RS$ in the last equation gives $144 = (QS)^2$, or $12 = QS$. Thus, $OQ = QS = SR = 12$ and point R has coordinates $(24,12)$.

**The correct answer is C;
both statements together are sufficient.**

DS07258

236. In a school that had a total of 600 students enrolled in the junior and senior classes, the students contributed to a certain fund. If all of the juniors but only half of the seniors contributed, was the total amount contributed more than $740 ?

(1) Each junior contributed $1 and each senior who contributed gave $3.

(2) There were more juniors than seniors enrolled in the school.

Arithmetic Applied Problems

The task in this question is to determine whether the respective statements are sufficient for answering the question of whether the total amount contributed was more than $740. In making this determination, it is important to remember that we are to use only the information that has been given. For example, it may seem plausible to assume that the number of seniors at the school is roughly equal to the number of juniors. However, because no such information has been provided, we cannot assume that this assumption holds. With this in mind, consider statements 1 and 2.

(1) If it were the case that half of the 600 students were seniors, then, given that half of the 300 seniors would have contributed $3, there would have been $150 \times \$3 = \$450$ in contributions from the seniors and $300 \times \$1 = \$300$ in contributions from the juniors, for a total of $750—more than the figure of $740 with which the question is concerned. However, as noted, we cannot make such an assumption. To test the conditions that we have actually been given, we can consider extreme cases, which are often relatively simple. For example, given the information provided, it is possible that only two of the students are seniors and the other 598 students are juniors. If this were the case,

then the contributions from the juniors would be $598 ($1 per student) and the contributions from the seniors would be $3 ($3 for the one senior who contributes, given that only half of the 2 seniors contribute). The total contributions would then be $598 + $3 = $601; NOT sufficient.

(2) Merely with this statement—and not statement 1—we have no information as to how much the students contributed. We therefore cannot determine the total amount contributed; NOT sufficient.

We still need to consider whether statements 1 and 2 are sufficient *together* for determining whether a minimum of $740 has been contributed. However, note that the reasoning in connection with statement 1 applies here as well. We considered there the possibility that the 600 students included only two seniors, with the other 598 students being juniors. Because this scenario also satisfies statement 2, we see that statements 1 and 2 taken together are not sufficient.

**The correct answer is E;
both statements together are still not sufficient.**

DS06650

237. How much did credit-card fraud cost United States banks in year X to the nearest $10 million?

(1) In year X, counterfeit cards and telephone and mail-order fraud accounted for 39 percent of the total amount that card fraud cost the banks.

(2) In year X, stolen cards accounted for $158.4 million, or 16 percent, of the total amount that credit-card fraud cost the banks.

Arithmetic Percents

(1) It is given that certain parts of the total fraud cost have a total that is 39% of the total fraud cost, but since no actual dollar amounts are specified, it is not possible to estimate the total fraud cost to the nearest $10 million; NOT sufficient.

(2) Given that $158.4 million represents 16% of the total fraud cost, it follows that the total fraud cost equals $158.4 million divided by 0.16; SUFFICIENT.

**The correct answer is B;
statement 2 alone is sufficient.**

DS17319
238. Is the positive integer *n* odd?

(1) $n^2 + (n + 1)^2 + (n + 2)^2$ is even.
(2) $n^2 - (n + 1)^2 - (n + 2)^2$ is even.

Arithmetic Properties of Numbers

The positive integer *n* is either odd or even. Determine if it is odd.

(1) This indicates that the sum of the squares of three consecutive integers, n^2, $(n + 1)^2$, and $(n + 2)^2$, is even. If *n* is even, then *n* + 1 is odd and *n* + 2 is even. It follows that n^2 is even, $(n + 1)^2$ is odd, and $(n + 2)^2$ is even and, therefore, that $n^2 + (n + 1)^2 + (n + 2)^2$ is odd. But, this contradicts the given information, and so, *n* must be odd; SUFFICIENT.

(2) This indicates that $n^2 - (n + 1)^2 - (n + 2)^2$ is even. Adding the even number represented by $2(n + 1)^2 + 2(n + 2)^2$ to the even number represented by $n^2 - (n + 1)^2 - (n + 2)^2$ gives the even number represented by $n^2 + (n + 1)^2 + (n + 2)^2$. This is Statement (1); SUFFICIENT.

The correct answer is D; each statement alone is sufficient.

DS01130
239. In the *xy*-plane, circle *C* has center (1,0) and radius 2. If line *k* is parallel to the *y*-axis, is line *k* tangent to circle *C* ?

(1) Line *k* passes through the point (–1,0).
(2) Line *k* passes through the point (–1,–1).

Geometry Coordinate Geometry

Can we determine whether line *k*, which is parallel to the *y*-axis, is tangent to the circle *C* ?

(1) Given that line *k* passes through the point (–1,0), we can represent the scenario in the following diagram, which is not drawn to scale.

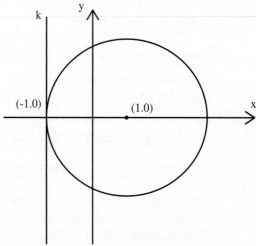

The points (1,0) and (–1,0) are two units apart on the *x* axis. We therefore know that circle *C*, with center (1,0) and radius 2, passes through the point (–1,0) and that, given that *k* passes through the point (–1,0), the circle intersects line *k* at this point. Furthermore, the radial line from the center (1,0) of the circle to point (–1,0) on the circle rests on the *x*-axis and is therefore perpendicular to the *y*-axis. Line *k*, being parallel to the *y*-axis, must also be perpendicular to this radial line. Therefore, because line *k* both intersects the circle at a point at which a radial line intersects the circle and is perpendicular to this radial line, we see that that line *k* must be tangent to circle *C*; SUFFICIENT.

(2) The sufficiency of statement 2 follows from the sufficiency of statement 1. For, if *k* is perpendicular to the *y*-axis and passes through point (–1,–1), then *k* must also pass through point (–1,0); *k* is simply the line *x* = –1. The reasoning for statement 1 now applies; SUFFICIENT.

The correct answer is D; Each statement alone is sufficient.

DS14170
240. Company X's profits this year increased by 25% over last year's profits. Was the dollar amount of Company X's profits this year greater than the dollar amount of Company Y's?

(1) Last year, the ratio of Company Y's profits to Company X's profits was 5:2.

(2) Company Y experienced a 40% drop in profits from last year to this year.

Algebra Applied Problems

Let P_X and P_X', respectively, be the profits of Company X last year and this year, and let P_Y and P_Y', respectively, be the profits of Company Y last year and this year. Then $P_X' = 1.25P_X$. Is $P_X' > P_Y'$?

(1) Given that $\dfrac{P_Y}{P_X} = \dfrac{5}{2}$, it is not possible to determine whether $P_X' > P_Y'$ because nothing is known about the value of P_Y' other than P_Y' is positive; NOT sufficient.

(2) Given that $P_Y' = 0.6P_Y$, it is not possible to determine whether $P_X' > P_Y'$ because nothing is known that relates the profits of Company X for either year to the profits of Company Y for either year; NOT sufficient.

Taking (1) and (2) together, it is given that $P_X' = 1.25P_X$ and from (1) it follows that $\dfrac{P_Y}{P_X} = \dfrac{5}{2}$, or $P_X = \dfrac{2}{5}P_Y$, and thus $P_X' = (1.25)\left(\dfrac{2}{5}P_Y\right)$. From (2) it follows that $P_Y' = 0.6P_Y$, or $P_Y = \dfrac{1}{0.6}P_Y'$, and thus $P_X' = (1.25)\left(\dfrac{2}{5}\right)\left(\dfrac{1}{0.6}P_Y'\right)$. Since the last equation expresses P_X' as a specific number times P_Y', it follows that it can be determined whether or not $P_X' > P_Y'$. Note that $(1.25)\left(\dfrac{2}{5}\right)\left(\dfrac{1}{0.6}\right) = \left(\dfrac{5}{4}\right)\left(\dfrac{2}{5}\right)\left(\dfrac{5}{3}\right) = \dfrac{5}{6}$, and so the answer to the question "Is $P_X' > P_Y'$" is no.

The correct answer is C; both statements together are sufficient.

DS87910.02

241. A certain company consists of three divisions, A, B, and C. Of the employees in the three divisions, the employees in Division C have the greatest average (arithmetic mean) annual salary. Is the average annual salary of the employees in the three divisions combined less than $55,000 ?

(1) The average annual salary of the employees in Divisions A and B combined is $45,000.

(2) The average annual salary of the employees in Division C is $55,000.

Algebra Statistics

(1) Given that the average annual salary of the employees in Divisions A and B combined is $45,000, each of the divisions could have exactly two employees such that the annual salaries in Division A are $45,000 and $45,000, the annual salaries in Division B are $45,000 and $45,000, and the annual salaries in Division C are $50,000 and $50,000, in which case Division C has the greatest average annual salary and the average annual salary in Divisions A, B, and C combined is less than $55,000. On the other hand, each of the divisions could have exactly two employees such that the annual salaries in Division A are $45,000 and $45,000, the annual salaries in Division B are $45,000 and $45,000, and the annual salaries in Division C are $1 million and $1 million, in which case Division C has the greatest average annual salary and the average annual salary in Divisions A, B, and C combined is greater than $55,000; NOT sufficient.

(2) Given that the average annual salary in Division C is $55,000, we have $\dfrac{\Sigma_C}{N_C} = 55{,}000$, where Σ_C is the sum of the annual salaries, in dollars, of the employees in Division C and N_C is the number of employees in Division C. Moreover, letting Σ_A and Σ_B be the sums of the annual salaries, respectively and in dollars, of the employees in Divisions A and B, and letting N_A and N_B be the numbers of employees, respectively, in Divisions A and B, then we have $\dfrac{\Sigma_A}{N_A} < 55{,}000$ and $\dfrac{\Sigma_B}{N_B} < 55{,}000$, since the employees in Division C have the greatest average annual salary. Note that these two inequalities and this equation can be rewritten as $\Sigma_A < 55{,}000N_A$, $\Sigma_B < 55{,}000N_B$, and $\Sigma_C = 55{,}000N_C$. Therefore, the average annual salary of the employees in the three divisions combined is $\dfrac{\Sigma_A + \Sigma_B + \Sigma_C}{N_A + N_B + N_C} = \dfrac{\Sigma_A + \Sigma_B + 55{,}000N_C}{N_A + N_B + N_C}$, which is less than $\dfrac{55{,}000N_A + 55{,}000N_B + 55{,}000N_C}{N_A + N_B + N_C} =$

$$\frac{55{,}000\left(N_A + N_B + N_C\right)}{N_A + N_B + N_C} = 55{,}000;$$

SUFFICIENT.

**The correct answer is B;
statement 2 alone is sufficient.**

DS09385

242. For all x, the expression x* is defined to be $ax + a$, where a is a constant. What is the value of 2* ?

   (1) $3^* = 2$
   (2) $5^* = 3$

Algebra Linear Equations

Determine the value of $2^* = (a)(2) + a = 3a$, or equivalently, determine the value of a.

   (1)   Given that $3^* = 2$, it follows that $(a)(3) + a = 2$, or $4a = 2$, or $a = \frac{1}{2}$; SUFFICIENT.

   (2)   Given that $5^* = 3$, it follows that $(a)(5) + a = 3$, or $6a = 3$, or $a = \frac{1}{2}$; SUFFICIENT.

**The correct answer is D;
each statement alone is sufficient.**

DS09260

243. Is $k + m < 0$?

   (1) $k < 0$
   (2) $km > 0$

Arithmetic Properties of Numbers

   (1)   Given that k is negative, it is not possible to determine whether $k + m$ is negative. For example, if $k = -2$ and $m = 1$, then $k + m$ is negative. However, if $k = -2$ and $m = 3$, then $k + m$ is not negative; NOT sufficient.

   (2)   Given that km is positive, it is not possible to determine whether $k + m$ is negative. For example, if $k = -2$ and $m = -1$, then km is positive and $k + m$ is negative. However, if $k = 2$ and $m = 1$, then km is positive and $k + m$ is not negative; NOT sufficient.

Taking (1) and (2) together, k is negative and km is positive, it follows that m is negative. Therefore, both k and m are negative, and hence $k + m$ is negative.

**The correct answer is C;
both statements together are sufficient.**

DS08352

244. The symbol Δ represents which one of the following operations: addition, subtraction, or multiplication?

   (1) $a \Delta (b \Delta c) \neq a \Delta (c \Delta b)$ for some numbers a, b, and c.
   (2) $a \Delta (b \Delta c) \neq (a \Delta b) \Delta c$ for some numbers a, b, and c.

Arithmetic Arithmetic Operations

Can we determine which of the operations—addition, subtraction, or multiplication—is the operation Δ?

   (1)   Given the condition that Δ has the property that, for some numbers a, b, and c, $a \Delta (b \Delta c) \neq a \Delta (c \Delta b)$, we can infer that, for some numbers b and c, $b \Delta c \neq c \Delta b$. Both addition and multiplication have the commutative property, whereby, for any numbers x and y, $x + y = y + x$ and $x \times y = y \times x$. For example, $7 + 2 = 9 = 2 + 7$, and $7 \times 2 = 14 = 2 \times 7$. We thus see that, for *all* numbers x, y, and z, both of the statements $x + (y + z) = x + (z + y)$ and $x \times (y \times z) = x \times (z \times y)$ are true. The operation Δ therefore cannot be addition or multiplication.

   Subtraction, on the other hand, lacks the commutative property; for example, $7 - 2 = 5$ and $2 - 7 = -5$. The operation Δ could therefore be subtraction. Subtraction is therefore the one operation among addition, subtraction, and multiplication that satisfies statement 1; SUFFICIENT.

   (2)   The reasoning in this case is similar to the reasoning for statement 1, but concerning the associative property rather than the commutative property. Both addition and multiplication have this property. For any numbers x, y, and z, the statements $x + (y + z) = (x + y) + z$ and $x \times (y \times z) = (x \times y) \times z$ are always true. For example, in the case of multiplication, $2 \times (3 \times 5) = 2 \times 15 = 30 = 6 \times 5 = (2 \times 3) \times 5$. However, in contrast to addition and multiplication, the operation of subtraction does not have the associative property. For example, for the numbers 2, 3, and 5, $2 - (3 - 5) = 2 - (-2) = 4$, whereas $(2 - 3) - 4 = -1 - 4 = -5$. Subtraction is therefore the one operation among addition,

subtraction, and multiplication that satisfies statement 2; SUFFICIENT.

**The correct answer is D;
each statement alone is sufficient.**

DS05989

245. What is the value of $2^x + 2^{-x}$?

(1) $x > 0$
(2) $4^x + 4^{-x} = 23$

Algebra Equations

Can we determine the value of $2^x + 2^{-x}$?

(1) The condition $x > 0$ by itself is not sufficient for determining the value of $2^x + 2^{-x}$. For example, if $x = 1$, then $2^x + 2^{-x} = 2^1 + 2^{-1} = 2\frac{1}{2}$. And if $x = 2$, then $2^x + 2^{-x} = 2^2 + 2^{-2} = 4\frac{1}{4}$; NOT sufficient.

(2) Given $4^x + 4^{-x} = 23$, it may be tempting to reason that this is an equation with only one unknown, and that it is therefore possible to determine the value of x and then the value of $2^x + 2^{-x}$. However, this reasoning can often produce erroneous results. For example the equation $(y - 1)(y - 3) = 0$ has only one unknown but is consistent with two values for y (1 and 3). To be sure that the statement $4^x + 4^{-x} = 23$ is sufficient for determining the value of $2^x + 2^{-x}$, consider first the square of $2^x + 2^{-x}$.

$$(2^x + 2^{-x})^2 = (2^x)^2 + (2^{-x})^2 + 2(2^x)(2^{-x})$$
$$= 2^{2x} + 2^{-2x} + 2(2^{x-x})$$
$$= (2^2)^x + (2^{-2})^x + 2$$
$$= 4^x + 4^{-x} + 2.$$

So $4^x + 4^{-x} = (2^x + 2^{-x})^2 - 2$. The condition that $4^x + 4^{-x} = 23$ thus becomes

$(2^x + 2^{-x})^2 - 2 = 23$, or $(2^x + 2^{-x})^2 = 25$. And because we know that $2^x + 2^{-x} > 0$ (because both $2^x > 0$ and $2^{-x} > 0$), we see that statement 1 implies $(2^x + 2^{-x}) = \sqrt{25} = 5$; SUFFICIENT.

**The correct answer is B;
statement 2 alone is sufficient.**

DS13457

246. What is the ratio of c to d?

(1) The ratio of $3c$ to $3d$ is 3 to 4.
(2) The ratio of $c + 3$ to $d + 3$ is 4 to 5.

Arithmetic Ratio and Proportion

Determine the value of $\frac{c}{d}$.

(1) Given that $\frac{3c}{3d} = \frac{3}{4}$, it follows that $\frac{3c}{3d} = \frac{c}{d} = \frac{3}{4}$; SUFFICIENT.

(2) Given that $\frac{c+3}{d+3} = \frac{4}{5}$, then it is not possible to determine the value of $\frac{c}{d}$. For example, if $c = 1$ and $d = 2$, then $\frac{c+3}{d+3} = \frac{4}{5}$ and $\frac{c}{d} = \frac{1}{2}$. However, if $c = 5$ and $d = 7$, then $\frac{c+3}{d+3} = \frac{8}{10} = \frac{4}{5}$ and $\frac{c}{d} = \frac{5}{7}$; NOT sufficient.

**The correct answer is A;
statement 1 alone is sufficient.**

DS15099

247. A candle company determines that, for a certain specialty candle, the supply function is $p = m_1 x + b_1$ and the demand function is $p = m_2 x + b_2$, where p is the price of each candle, x is the number of candles supplied or demanded, and m_1, m_2, b_1, and b_2 are constants. At what value of x do the graphs of the supply function and demand function intersect?

(1) $m_1 = -m_2 = 0.005$
(2) $b_2 - b_1 = 6$

Algebra First-Degree Equations

The graphs will intersect at the value of x such that $m_1 x + b_1 = m_2 x + b_2$ or $(m_1 - m_2)x = b_2 - b_1$.

(1) This indicates that $m_1 = -m_2 = 0.005$. It follows that $m_1 - m_2 = 0.01$, and so $0.01x = b_2 - b_1$ or $x = 100(b_2 - b_1)$, which can vary as the values of b_2 and b_1 vary; NOT sufficient.

(2) This indicates that $b_2 - b_1 = 6$. It follows that $(m_1 - m_2)x = 6$. This implies that $m_1 \neq m_2$, and so $x = \frac{b_2 - b_1}{m_1 - m_2} = \frac{6}{m_1 - m_2}$, which can vary as the values of m_1 and m_2 vary; NOT sufficient.

Taking (1) and (2) together, $m_1 - m_2 = 0.01$ and $b_2 - b_1 = 6$ and so the value of x is $\dfrac{6}{0.01} = 600$.

The correct answer is C;
both statements together are sufficient.

DS40410.02

248. A certain ski shop sold 125 pairs of skis and 100 pairs of ski boots for a total of $75,000. What was the average (arithmetic mean) selling price of a pair of the ski boots?

(1)   The average selling price of a pair of skis was $300.

(2)   The selling price of a pair of ski boots varied from $150 to $900.

Arithmetic Statistics

Let Σ_{skis} be the sum of the selling prices, in dollars, of all 125 pairs of skis and let Σ_{boots} be the sum of the selling prices, in dollars, of all 100 pairs of ski boots. We are given that $\Sigma_{\text{skis}} + \Sigma_{\text{boots}} = 75{,}000$. Determine the value of $\dfrac{\Sigma_{\text{boots}}}{100}$, or equivalently, determine the value of Σ_{boots}.

(1)   Given that $\dfrac{\Sigma_{\text{skis}}}{125} = 300$, or $\Sigma_{\text{skis}} = 300(125) = 37{,}500$, it follows from $\Sigma_{\text{skis}} + \Sigma_{\text{boots}} = 75{,}000$ that $\Sigma_{\text{boots}} = 75{,}000 - \Sigma_{\text{skis}} = 75{,}000 - 37{,}500 = 37{,}500$; SUFFICIENT.

(2)   Given that the selling price of a pair of ski boots varied from $150 to $900, it is possible that there were 40 pairs of ski boots each with a selling price of $150, 60 pairs of ski boots each with a selling price of $900, and 125 pairs of skis each with a selling price of $120 for a total selling price of 40($150) + 60($900) + 125($120) = $75,000, and thus it is possible that $\Sigma_{\text{boots}} = 40(150) + 60(900) = 6{,}000 + 54{,}000 = 60{,}000$. However, it is also possible that there were 60 pairs of ski boots each with a selling price of $150, 40 pairs of ski boots each with a selling price of $900, and 125 pairs of skis each with a selling price of $240 for a total selling price of 60($150) + 40($900) + 125($240) = $75,000, and thus it is also possible that $\Sigma_{\text{boots}} = 60(150) + 40(900) = 9{,}000 + 36{,}000 = 45{,}000$; NOT sufficient.

The correct answer is A;
statement 1 alone is sufficient.

DS93510.02

249. Is the standard deviation of the numbers in list R less than the standard deviation of the numbers in list S?

(1)   The range of the numbers in R is less than the range of the numbers in S.

(2)   Each number in R occurs once and each number in S is repeated.

Arithmetic Statistics

Let σ_R be the standard deviation of the numbers in R and let σ_S be the standard deviation of the numbers in S. Determine whether $\sigma_R < \sigma_S$ is true.

(1)   Given that the range of the numbers in R is less than the range of the numbers in S, Example 1 below shows that $\sigma_R < \sigma_S$ can be true and Example 2 below shows that $\sigma_R < \sigma_S$ can be false.

Example 1: Let the numbers in R be 0 and 2 and let the numbers in S be 0, 0, 4, and 4. Then the range of the numbers in R is $2 - 0 = 2$ and the range of the numbers in S is $4 - 0 = 4$, so the range of the numbers in R is less than the range of the numbers in S. Since the average of the numbers in R is $\dfrac{0+2}{2} = 1$, it follows that $\sigma_R = \sqrt{\dfrac{(0-1)^2 + (2-1)^2}{2}} = \sqrt{\dfrac{2(1^2)}{2}} = 1$. Also, since the average of the numbers in S is $\dfrac{0+0+4+4}{4} = 2$, it follows that $\sigma_S = \sqrt{\dfrac{(0-2)^2 + (0-2)^2 + (4-2)^2 + (4-2)^2}{4}} = \sqrt{\dfrac{4(2^2)}{4}} = 2$. Therefore, $\sigma_R = 1$ and $\sigma_S = 2$, so $\sigma_R < \sigma_S$ is true.

Example 2: Let the numbers in R be 0 and 2 and let the numbers in S be 0, 0, and a large number of repetitions of 4. Then the range of the numbers in R is $2 - 0 = 2$ and the range of the numbers in S is $4 - 0 = 4$, so the range of the numbers in R is less than the range of the numbers in S. Since the numbers in R are the same as in Example 1, we have $\sigma_R = 1$. Also, since the standard deviation of the numbers in a list is small when a large percentage of the numbers are clustered near their average, it is possible that $\sigma_S < 1$ when there are sufficiently many repetitions of 4 among the numbers in S. For example, if the numbers in S consist of 2 occurrences of 0 and 98 occurrences of 4, then the average of the numbers in S is $\dfrac{2(0) + 98(4)}{100} = 3.92$. Therefore,

$$\sigma_S = \sqrt{\dfrac{(0-3.92)^2 + (0-3.92)^2 + (4-3.92)^2 + \cdots + (4-3.92)^2}{100}}$$

$$= \sqrt{\dfrac{2(0-3.92)^2 + 98(4-3.92)^2}{100}} <$$

$$\sqrt{\dfrac{2(4)^2 + 100(0.08)^2}{100}} = \sqrt{\dfrac{32 + 0.64}{100}} < 1.$$

Therefore, $\sigma_R = 1$ and $\sigma_S < 1$, so $\sigma_R < \sigma_S$ is false; NOT sufficient.

(2)   Given that each number in R occurs once and each number in S is repeated, the same examples used in (1) above show that it is not possible to determine whether $\sigma_R < \sigma_S$ is true; NOT sufficient.

Taking (1) and (2) together, it is not possible to determine whether $\sigma_R < \sigma_S$ is true because each of the examples used in (1) above satisfies both (1) and (2).

**The correct answer is E;
both statements together are still not sufficient.**

DS96502.01
250. Is the length of rectangular field F greater than the length of rectangular field G ?

(1)   The area of F is greater than the area of G.

(2)   The width of F is less than the width of G.

Geometry Rectangles

(1)   Given that the area of F is greater than the area of G, it is not possible to determine whether the length of F is greater than the length of G. For example, suppose F has length 2 and width 1, and G has length 1 and width 1. Then the area of F is $(2)(1) = 2$, the area of G is $(1)(1) = 1$, the area of F is greater than the area of G, and the length of F is greater than the length of G. However, suppose F has length 1 and width 2, and G has length 1 and width 1. Then the area of F is $(1)(2) = 2$, the area of G is $(1)(1) = 1$,

the area of F is greater than the area of G, and the length of F is not greater than the length of G; NOT sufficient.

(2)   Given that the width of F is less than the width of G, it is not possible to determine whether the length of F is greater than the length of G, since unless additional information is provided, there is no relation between the length and width of a rectangle other than that each must be a positive real number; NOT sufficient.

Taking (1) and (2) together, let L_F and L_G be the lengths, respectively, of F and G, and let W_F and W_G be the widths, respectively, of F and G. Suppose $L_F \leq L_G$. Multiplying both sides of this inequality by the positive quantity W_F gives $L_F W_F \leq L_G W_F$. From (2) it follows that $W_F < W_G$. Multiplying both sides of this last inequality by the positive quantity L_G gives $L_G W_F < L_G W_G$. From the inequalities $L_F W_F \leq L_G W_F$ and $L_G W_F < L_G W_G$ it follows that $L_F W_F < L_G W_G$, which contradicts (1). Therefore, $L_F \leq L_G$ is not possible, and it follows that $L_F > L_G$.

**The correct answer is C;
both statements together are sufficient.**

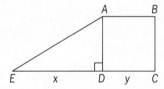

DS17502.01
251. In the figure above, is the area of triangular region ADE equal to the area of rectangular region $ABCD$?

(1) $x = 10$ and $y = 5$.

(2) $x = 2y$

Geometry Area

The area of triangle ADE is $\dfrac{1}{2} x (AD)$ and the area of rectangle $ABCD$ is $y(AD)$. Determine whether $\dfrac{1}{2} x (AD) = y(AD)$, or equivalently, determine whether $\dfrac{1}{2} x = y$.

(1)   Given that $x = 10$ and $y = 5$, it follows that $\dfrac{1}{2} x = y$; SUFFICIENT.

(2) Given that $x = 2y$, it follows that $\frac{1}{2}x = y$; SUFFICIENT.

The correct answer is D;
each statement alone is sufficient.

DS97502.01

252. Last year Publisher X published 1,100 books, consisting of first editions, revised editions, and reprints. How many first editions did Publisher X publish last year?

(1) The number of first editions published was 50 more than twice the number of reprints published.

(2) The number of revised editions published was half the number of reprints published.

Algebra Simultaneous Equations

Let A be the number of first editions, B be the number of revised editions, and C be the number of reprints. Then $A + B + C = 1{,}100$. Determine the value of A.

(1) Given that $A = 50 + 2C$, it is not possible to determine the value of A. This is because by choosing different values of C, different values of A can be obtained by using the equation $A = 50 + 2C$, and then the equation $A + B + C = 1{,}100$ can be used to determine whether acceptable values of B (nonnegative integers) exist for these values of A and C. For example, choosing $C = 100$ leads to $A = 250$ and $B = 750$, and choosing $C = 200$ leads to $A = 450$ and $B = 450$; NOT sufficient.

(2) Given that $B = \frac{1}{2}C$, or $C = 2B$, it is not possible to determine the value of A. This is because by choosing different values of B, different values of C can be obtained by using the equation $C = 2B$, and then the equation $A + B + C = 1{,}100$ can be used to determine different values of A. For example, choosing $B = 100$ leads to $C = 200$ and $A = 800$, and choosing $B = 200$ leads to $C = 400$ and $A = 500$; NOT sufficient.

Taking $A = 50 + 2C$ from (1) and $C = 2B$ from (2) together gives $A = 50 + 4B$. Thus, in the equation $A + B + C = 1{,}100$, A can be replaced with $50 + 4B$ and C can be replaced with $2B$ to

give $(50 + 4B) + B + 2B = 1{,}100$. Solving for B gives $B = 150$, and hence $C = 2B = 300$ and $A = 50 + 2C = 650$.

The correct answer is C;
both statements together are sufficient.

DS89502.01

253. How old is Jane?

(1) Ten years ago she was one-third as old as she is now.

(2) In 15 years, she will be twice as old as she is now.

Algebra First-Degree Equations

Determine the value of J, where J represents Jane's current age.

(1) In symbols, $J - 10$ represents Jane's age ten years ago and $\frac{1}{3}J$ represents one-third her current age. These expressions are equal by (1), so $J - 10 = \frac{1}{3}J$. This is a first-degree equation in the variable J and has a unique solution; SUFFICIENT.

(2) In symbols, $J + 15$ represents Jane's age 15 years from now and $2J$ represents twice her current age. These expressions are equal by (2), so $J + 15 = 2J$. This is a first-degree equation in the variable J and has a unique solution; SUFFICIENT.

The correct answer is D;
each statement alone is sufficient.

DS99502.01

254. What was the population of City X in 2002 ?

(1) X's population in 2002 increased by 2 percent, or 20,000 people, over 2001.

(2) In 2001, X's population was 1,000,000.

Algebra Percents

Letting P_1 and P_2 represent City X's population in 2001 and 2002, respectively, the percent increase in population from 2001 to 2002 is given as a decimal by $\frac{P_2 - P_1}{P_1}$.

(1) By (1) the percent increase was 2 percent, so $\dfrac{P_2 - P_1}{P_1} = 0.02$ or $P_2 - P_1 = 0.02P_1$. Also, by (1), $P_2 - P_1 = 20{,}000$, so $20{,}000 = 0.02P_1$ from which the value of P_1 can be uniquely determined. Then $P_1 + 20{,}000 = P_2$, which is the population of City X in 2002; SUFFICIENT.

(2) Even though (2) gives $P_1 = 1{,}000{,}000$, it gives no information about the population of City X in 2002 either by itself or in relation to the population in 2001; NOT sufficient.

The correct answer is A; statement 1 alone is sufficient.

DS79502.01

255. What is the perimeter of triangle *ABC*?

(1) *AB* = 16 inches

(2) △*ABC* is equilateral.

Geometry Triangles; Perimeter

(1) Given that *AB* = 16, it is not possible to determine the perimeter of △*ABC*. For example, *AB* = *BC* = *AC* = 16 is possible and gives a perimeter of 48. However, *AB* = *BC* = 16 and *AC* = 17 is possible and gives a perimeter of 49; NOT sufficient.

(2) Given that △*ABC* is equilateral, it is not possible to determine the perimeter of △*ABC*. For example, *AB* = *BC* = *AC* = 16 is possible and gives a perimeter of 48. However, *AB* = *BC* = *AC* = 20 is possible and gives a perimeter of 60; NOT sufficient.

Taking (1) and (2) together, it follows that *AB* = 16 and *AB* = *BC* = *AC*, and hence *AB* = *BC* = *AC* = 16. Therefore, the perimeter of △*ABC* is 48.

The correct answer is C; both statements together are sufficient.

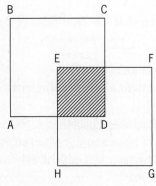

DS60602.01

256. In the figure above, is the shaded region a square region?

(1) *ABCD* and *EFGH* are squares.

(2) *BC* = *EF*

Geometry Quadrilaterals

(1) The left figure below shows that the overlap of two squares can be a square region, but the figure on the right shows that the overlap can also not be a square region; NOT sufficient.

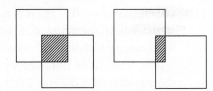

(2) In the figure above, the overlapping squares are the same size. The left figure shows that the overlap of two identically sized squares can be a square region, but the figure on the right shows that the overlap can also not be a square region; NOT sufficient.

Taking (1) and (2) together is also insufficient, because the same figures used to show that (1) is not sufficient also show that (2) is not sufficient.

The correct answer is E; both statements together still are not sufficient.

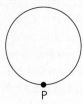

DS02602.01

257. *P* is a particle on the circle shown above. What is the length of the path traveled by *P* in one complete revolution around the circle?

(1)   The diameter of the circle is 1.5 meters.

(2)   The particle P moves in a clockwise direction at 0.5 meter per second.

Geometry Circles; Circumference

The length of the path traveled in one complete revolution is the circumference of the circle, which is equal to π times the diameter of the circle and hence can be determined if the diameter can be determined.

(1)   Given that the diameter of the circle is 1.5 meters, it follows from the preliminary comments above that the length of the path traveled in one complete revolution can be determined; SUFFICIENT.

(2)   Given that the particle moves clockwise at a speed of 0.5 meter per second, it is not possible to determine the length of the path traveled in one complete revolution, because no information about the size of the circle is provided; NOT sufficient.

The correct answer is A; statement 1 alone is sufficient.

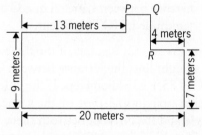

DS62602.01

258. The figure above shows the floor plan and inside dimensions of the ground level of a building. If all lines that intersect meet at right angles, what is the total floor area of this level of the building?

(1) $QR = 4$ meters

(2) PQ is less than QR.

Geometry Polygons

As shown in the figure below, the total floor area is equal to the area of the rectangle with sides $\overline{AC}$ and $\overline{AE}$ minus the sum of the areas of the two rectangles each shown with a pair of dashed sides, or $(AC)(20) - (AB)(13) - (QR)(4)$.

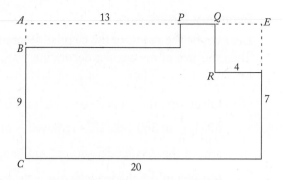

(1)   Given that $QR = 4$, it follows that $AC = 7 + 4 = 11$, and hence $AC = AB + BC$ becomes $11 = AB + 9$, which gives $AB = 2$. Therefore, from the preliminary comments above, the area of the floor is $(11)(20) - (2)(13) - (4)(4) = 178$; SUFFICIENT.

(2)   Given that PQ is less than QR, and $PQ = 3$ (this is from $AP + PQ + QE = 20$, or $13 + PQ + 4 = 20$), it follows that QR is greater than 3. In particular, $QR = 4$ is possible and $QR = 5$ is possible. If $QR = 4$, then from the result obtained when (1) alone is assumed, the area of the floor is 178. On the other hand, if $QR = 5$, then the same method can be used: $AC = 7 + 5 = 12$, and hence $AC = AB + BC$ becomes $12 = AB + 9$, which gives $AB = 3$, and so the area of the floor is $(12)(20) - (3)(13) - (5)(4) = 181$; NOT sufficient.

The correct answer is A; statement 1 alone is sufficient.

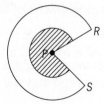

DS82602.01

259. The figure above shows the top of a circular cake with a slice removed. The shaded region on top of the cake is the remaining part of a circular decoration that was centered on the cake. What is the area of the shaded region?

(1)   P was the center of the top of the cake before the slice was removed and the angle of the slice, $\angle RPS$, is 60°.

(2) $PR = PS = 11$ centimeters

Geometry Circles; Area

Let r cm be the radius of the circular decoration. Then the area of the circular decoration was πr^2 cm^2.

(1) Given that the measure of $\angle RPS$ is 60° and 60° is $\frac{1}{6}$ of 360°, the slice removed $\frac{1}{6}$ of the area of the circular decoration, and hence the area of the shaded region is $\frac{5}{6}\pi r^2$ cm^2. However, because the value of r cannot be determined, the area of the shaded region cannot be determined; NOT sufficient.

(2) Given that $PR = PS = 11$ cm, the area of the shaded region cannot be determined because neither the radius of the circular decoration nor the fraction of the circular decoration that was removed can be determined; NOT sufficient.

Taking (1) and (2) together, the area of the shaded region is $\frac{5}{6}\pi r^2$ cm^2 and the radius of the cake is 11 cm. However, because the value of r cannot be determined, the area of the shaded region cannot be determined.

The correct answer is E; both statements together are still not sufficient.

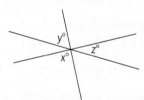

DS03602.01

260. If three straight lines intersect at a point as shown in the figure above, what is the value of x?

(1) $x = y = z$
(2) $z = 60$

Geometry Angles

The figure shows three pairs of vertical angles: one pair each with measure $x°$, a second pair each with measure $y°$, and a third pair each with measure $z°$. Therefore, x, y, and z are values for which $2x + 2y + 2z = 360$.

(1) Given $x = y = z$, it follows that, by substituting x for y and for z in

$2x + 2y + 2z = 360$ the equation becomes $2x + 2x + 2x = 360$, so $6x = 360$ and $x = 60$; SUFFICIENT.

(2) Given that $z = 60$, then $2x + 2y + 120 = 360$. It follows that $x + y = 120$ and this equation has infinitely many solutions for x and y; NOT sufficient.

The correct answer is A; statement 1 alone is sufficient.

DS23602.01

261. What is the distance between City A and City C?

(1) The distance between City A and City B is 75 kilometers.
(2) The distance between City B and City C is 135 kilometers.

Geometry Triangles

(1) Given only that the distance between Cities A and B is 75 kilometers, the distance between Cities A and C cannot be determined; NOT sufficient.

(2) Given only that the distance between Cities B and C is 135 kilometers, the distance between Cities A and C cannot be determined; NOT sufficient.

Taking (1) and (2) together, if the three cities are on a straight line, the distance between Cities A and C is 75 + 135 kilometers. If the cities are not on a straight line, they are the vertices of a triangle and the distance between them is less than 75 + 135 kilometers since the sum of the lengths of two sides of a triangle is greater than the length of the third side.

The correct answer is E; both statements together are still not sufficient.

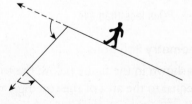

DS33602.01

262. A person walked completely around the edge of a park beginning at the midpoint of one edge and making the minimum number of turns, each with the minimum number of degrees necessary, as shown in the figure

above. What is the sum of the degrees of all the turns that the person made?

(1)   One of the turns is 80 degrees.

(2)   The number of sides of the park is 4, all of the sides are straight, and each interior angle is less than 180 degrees.

Geometry Quadrilaterals

(1)   Given that one of the turns is 80°, no information is given on the shape of the park and therefore no information is given on the number of other turns the person will make; NOT sufficient.

(2)   Given that the park has 4 straight sides and that each interior angle is less than 180°, it follows that the park is in the shape of a quadrilateral and the turns the person makes are the exterior angles of the 4 interior angles of the quadrilateral. If a, b, c, and d are the measures, in degrees, of the interior angles of the quadrilateral, where $a + b + c + d = 360$, then the sum of the measures, in degrees, of the turns the person will make is $(180 - a) + (180 - b) + (180 - c) + (180 - d) = 720 - (a + b + c + d) = 720 - 360 = 360$; SUFFICIENT.

The correct answer is B; statement 2 alone is sufficient.

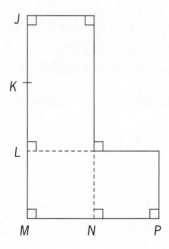

DS55602.01

263. What is the area, in square meters, of the building plot shown in the figure above?

(1) $KM = MP = 30$ meters

(2) $JK = KL = LM = MN = NP = 15$ meters

Geometry Quadrilaterals

(1)   Even with $KM = MP = 30$ meters given, it is not possible to determine the area of the plot without knowing JK as well as MN or NP; NOT sufficient.

(2)   Given $JK = KL = LM = MN = NP = 15$ meters, the area of the plot is $(4)(15)(15)$; SUFFICIENT.

The correct answer is B; statement 2 alone is sufficient.

DS90820.02

264. Yesterday Bookstore B sold twice as many softcover books as hardcover books. Was Bookstore B's revenue from the sale of softcover books yesterday greater than its revenue from the sale of hardcover books yesterday?

(1)   The average (arithmetic mean) price of the hardcover books sold at the store yesterday was $10 more than the average price of the softcover books sold at the store yesterday.

(2)   The average price of the softcover and hardcover books sold at the store yesterday was greater than $14.

Arithmetic Statistics

Letting s represent the number of softcover books sold; h, the number of hardcover books sold; S, the average price of the softcover books sold; and H, the average price of the hardcover books sold, determine whether the revenue from the sale of softcover books is greater than the revenue from the sale of hardcover books or if $sS > hH$, where $s = 2h$.

(1)   Given that $H = S + 10$, if $S = 10$, $H = 20$, $s = 10$, and $h = 5$, then $sS = 100$ and $hH = 100$, so $sS = hH$. On the other hand, if $S = 40$, $H = 50$, $s = 8$, and $h = 4$, then $sS = 320$ and $hH = 200$, so $sS > hH$; NOT sufficient.

(2)   Given that $\dfrac{sS + hH}{s + h} > 14$, if $s = 6$, $S = 10$, $h = 3$, and $H = 30$, $\dfrac{6(10) + 3(30)}{6 + 3} = \dfrac{150}{9} > 14$ and $6(10) < 3(30)$. On the other hand, if $s = 10$, $S = 15$, $h = 5$, and $H = 20$, $\dfrac{10(15) + 5(20)}{10 + 5} = \dfrac{250}{15} > 14$ and $10(15) > 5(20)$; NOT sufficient.

Taking (1) and (2) together,

$\dfrac{sS + hH}{s + h}$	>	14	from (2)
$\dfrac{2h(H - 10) + hH}{2h + h}$	>	14	$s = 2h$ (given) and $H = S + 10$ from (1)
$\dfrac{3H - 20}{3}$	>	14	cancel h and simplify
$3H - 20$	>	42	multiply both sides by 3
H	>	$\dfrac{62}{3}$	solve for H

To show that this leads to $sS > hH$, start with $sS > hH$ and then reverse the steps.

sS	>	hH	
$2h(H - 10)$	>	hH	$s = 2h$ and $S = H - 10$
$2hH - 20h$	>	hH	distributive property
$2hH$	>	$hH + 20h$	add $20h$ to both sides
hH	>	$20h$	subtract hH from both sides
H	>	20	divide both sides by $h > 0$

Now, reverse the steps.

H	>	$\dfrac{62}{3}$	derived earlier
H	>	20	$\dfrac{62}{3} > 20$
hH	>	$20h$	multiply both sides by $h > 0$
$2hH$	>	$hH + 20h$	add hH to both sides
$2hH - 20h$	>	hH	subtract $20h$ from both sides
$2h(H - 10)$	>	hH	factor
sS	>	hH	$s = 2h$ and $S = H - 10$

Thus, the revenue from the sale of softcover books was greater than the revenue from the sale of hardcover books.

The correct answer is C; both statements together are sufficient.

DS11820.02

265. What is the median of the nine consecutive even integers in a certain list?

(1) The median of the integers in the list is greater than 0.

(2) Of the integers in the list, the sum of the least of the negative integers and the least of the positive integers is −4.

Arithmetic Statistics

Determine the median of a list of 9 consecutive even integers.

(1) Given that the median of the integers in the list is greater than 0, the list could be 2, 4, 6, 8, 10, 12, 14, 16, and 18, in which case the median is 10. Or the list could be −4, −2, 0, 2, 4, 6, 8, 10, and 12, in which case the median is 4; NOT sufficient.

(2) Given that the sum of the least of the negative integers in the list and the least of the positive integers in the list is −4, it follows that $x + 2 = -4$, where x is the least of the negative integers and 2 is the least of the positive integers. Then $x = -6$ and the list is −6, −4, −2, 0, 2, 4, 6, 8, and 10 and the median is 2; SUFFICIENT.

The correct answer is B; statement 2 alone is sufficient.

Questions 266 to 306 - Difficulty: **Medium**

DS18502.01

266. The heart-shaped decoration shown in the figure above consists of a square and two semicircles. What is the radius of each semicircle?

(1)   The diagonal of the square is $10\sqrt{2}$ centimeters long.

(2)   The area of the square region minus the sum of the areas of the semicircular regions is $100 - 25\pi$ square centimeters.

Geometry Circles; Pythagorean Theorem

Let r cm be the radius of each semicircle. Then $2r$ cm is the side length of the square. Determine the value of r.

(1)   Given that the length of the diagonal of the square is $10\sqrt{2}$, it follows from the Pythagorean theorem that $(2r)^2 + (2r)^2 = (10\sqrt{2})^2$, or $8r^2 = 200$. Therefore, $r^2 = 25$ and $r = 5$; SUFFICIENT.

(2)   It is given that the area of the square, $(2r)^2 = 4r^2$, minus the total area of the two semicircular regions, πr^2, is equal to $100 - 25\pi$. That is, $4r^2 - \pi r^2 = 100 - 25\pi$, or $r^2(4 - \pi) = 25(4 - \pi)$. Dividing both sides of the last equation by $4 - \pi$ gives $r^2 = 25$ and $r = 5$; SUFFICIENT.

**The correct answer is D;
each statement alone is sufficient.**

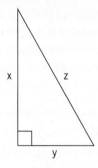

DS20602.01

267. If A is the area of a triangle with sides of lengths x, y, and z as shown above, what is the value of A?

(1) $z = 13$

(2) $A = \dfrac{5y}{2}$

Geometry Triangles; Area

(1)   By (1), $z = 13$, but the lengths of at least two sides of a right triangle must be known in order to find the area of the triangle; NOT sufficient.

(2)   Using the notation on the figure, $A = \dfrac{1}{2}xy$ and by (2), $A = \dfrac{5y}{2}$. It follows that $\dfrac{1}{2}xy = \dfrac{5y}{2}$, from which the value of x can be determined. However, the lengths of at least two sides of a right triangle must be known in order to find the area of the triangle; NOT sufficient.

Taking (1) and (2) together gives values for z and x from which the value of y, and, therefore, the area of the triangle, which is given by $\dfrac{1}{2}xy$, can be determined.

**The correct answer is C;
both statements together are sufficient.**

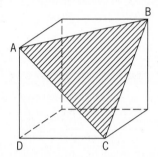

DS80602.01

268. The figure above shows a piece of cheese with a corner cut off to expose plane surface ABC. What is the area of surface ABC?

(1) $AD = 10$ centimeters

(2)   The shape of the cheese was a cube before the corner was cut off.

Geometry Rectangular Solids and Cylinders; Pythagorean Theorem

(1)   Given that $AD = 10$ cm, and assuming that the cheese is in the shape of a rectangular solid, then it is not possible to determine the area of surface ABC because, for example, it is clear that different areas arise when the two other dimensions of the cheese are 10 cm, and when the two other dimensions of the cheese are 100 cm; NOT sufficient.

(2)   Given that the shape of the cheese was a cube, it is not possible to determine the area of surface ABC because, for example, it is clear that different areas arise when the edge length of the cube is 10 cm, and when the edge length of the cube is 100 cm; NOT sufficient.

Taking (1) and (2) together, it follows that the cheese is in the shape of a cube with edge length 10 cm. Therefore, surface ABC is an equilateral triangle with side length equal to the length of a face diagonal of the cube. Since the length of a face diagonal can be determined, for example by applying the Pythagorean theorem to $\triangle ADC$ to get $(AD)^2 + (DC)^2 = (AC)^2$ and $10^2 + 10^2 = (AC)^2$, and the area of an equilateral triangle can be determined when its side length is known, it follows that the area of surface ABC can be determined.

The correct answer is C;
both statements together are sufficient.

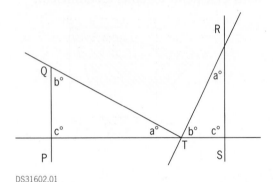

DS31602.01

269. The figure above shows a portion of a road map on which the measures of certain angles are indicated. If all lines shown are straight and intersect as shown, is road PQ parallel to road RS?

(1) $b = 2a$

(2) $c = 3a$

Geometry Triangles

Consider the following theorem: Two lines that are cut by a transversal are parallel if and only if the interior angles on the same side of the transversal are supplementary. In the figure, the two lines are $\overrightarrow{PQ}$ and $\overrightarrow{RS}$, the transversal is the line that goes through T and intersects $\overrightarrow{PQ}$ and $\overrightarrow{RS}$ at the points where angles of degree measure c are indicated, and those angles with degree measure c are the interior angles on the same side of the transversal. Restated using the notation of the figure, the theorem says $\overrightarrow{PQ}$ and $\overrightarrow{RS}$ are parallel if and only if $c + c = 180$ or if and only if $c = 90$. Equivalently, $\overrightarrow{PQ}$ and $\overrightarrow{RS}$ are not parallel if and only if $c \neq 90$. Also note that $a + b + c = 180$ since a, b, and c are the interior angles of a triangle.

(1)   Given that $b = 2a$, the values of a, b, and c could be 30, 60, and 90, respectively, (note that $60 = (2)(30)$ and $30 + 60 + 90 = 180$), in which case $\overrightarrow{PQ}$ and $\overrightarrow{RS}$ would be parallel. However, the values of a, b, and c could be 32, 64, and 84, respectively (note that $64 = (2)(32)$ and $32 + 64 + 84 = 180$), in which case $\overrightarrow{PQ}$ and $\overrightarrow{RS}$ would not be parallel; NOT sufficient.

(2)   Given $c = 3a$, the values of a, b, and c could be 30, 60, and 90, respectively, (note that $90 = 3(30)$ and $30 + 60 + 90 = 180$), in which case $\overrightarrow{PQ}$ and $\overrightarrow{RS}$ would be parallel. However, the values of a, b, and c could be 31, 56, and 93, respectively (note that $93 = (3)(31)$ and $31 + 56 + 93 = 180$), in which case $\overrightarrow{PQ}$ and $\overrightarrow{RS}$ would not be parallel; NOT sufficient.

Taking (1) and (2) together, $b = 2a$ and $c = 3a$ so $a + b + c = a + 2a + 3a = 6a = 180$, from which it follows that $a = 30$ and $c = (3)(30) = 90$. Therefore, $\overrightarrow{PQ}$ and $\overrightarrow{RS}$ are parallel as are the roads PQ and RS that they represent.

The correct answer is C;
both statements together are sufficient.

DS14602.01

270. It costs \$2,250 to fill right circular cylindrical Tank R with a certain industrial chemical. If the cost to fill any tank with this chemical is directly proportional to the volume of the chemical needed to fill the tank, how much does it cost to fill right circular cylindrical Tank S with the chemical?

(1)   The diameter of the interior of Tank R is twice the diameter of the interior of Tank S.

(2)   The interiors of Tanks R and S have the same height.

Geometry Volume

To find the cost of filling Tank S, which is directly proportional to the cost of filling Tank R, the ratio of the radii (or of the diameters) of the tanks and the ratio of their heights must be known.

(1)   This gives the ratio for the diameters of Tank R and Tank S, but not the ratio for the heights of Tank R and Tank S; NOT sufficient.

(2)   This gives the ratio for the heights of Tank R and Tank S, but not the ratio for the diameters of Tank R and Tank S; NOT sufficient.

Taking (1) and (2) together, the ratio of the diameter of Tank R to the diameter of Tank S is 2 (from which it follows that the ratio of the radius of Tank R to the radius of Tank S is 2) and the ratio of the height of Tank R to the height of Tank S is 1. If the radius of Tank R is r, then the radius of Tank S is $\dfrac{r}{2}$ and if the height of Tank R is h, then the height of Tank S is h. The volume of Tank R $= \pi r^2 h$ and the volume of Tank S $= \pi \left(\dfrac{r}{2}\right)^2 h = \dfrac{\pi r^2 h}{4}$. Therefore the cost of filling Tank S with the chemical is $\dfrac{1}{4}(\$2,250)$.

The correct answer is C; both statements together are sufficient.

	Yes	No	Don't Know
Program X	400	200	400
Program Y	300	350	350

DS17700.02

271.   The table shows the number of people who responded "yes" or "no" or "don't know" when asked whether their city council should implement environmental programs X and Y. If a total of 1,000 people responded to the question about both programs, what was the number of people who did not respond "yes" to implementing either of the two programs?

(1)   The number of people who responded "yes" to implementing only Program X was 300.

(2)   The number of people who responded "no" to implementing Program X and "no" to implementing Program Y was 100.

Arithmetic Interpretation of Tables; Sets (Venn Diagrams)

(1)   Given that 300 people responded "yes" to implementing only Program X, and because 400 people altogether responded "yes" to implementing Program X, it follows that 400 − 300 = 100 people responded "yes" to implementing both Program X and Program Y. Therefore, because 300 people altogether responded "yes" to implementing

Program Y, 300 − 100 = 200 people responded "yes" to implementing only Program Y. These results are shown in the Venn diagram below.

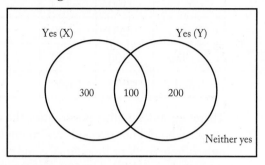

Since the Venn diagram above represents a total of 1,000 people, it follows that the number of people who did not respond "yes" to implementing either Program X or Program Y is 1,000 − (300 + 100 + 200) = 400; SUFFICIENT.

(2)   Given that 100 people responded "no" both to implementing Program X and to implementing Program Y, the table below shows a possibility whereby the number of people who did not respond "yes" to implementing either Program X or Program Y could be 400. Note that for each of the column headings "Yes," "No," and "Don't Know," the numbers under that column heading satisfy (X answered) + (Y answered) − (both answered) + (neither answered) = 1,000. Indeed, for each of these three columns a Venn diagram can be given that represents the numbers in that column.

	Yes	No	Don't Know
X	400	200	400
Y	300	350	350
Both	100	100	0
Neither	**400**	550	250
Total	1,000	1,000	1,000

However, the next table shows a possibility whereby the number of people who did not respond "yes" to implementing either Program X or Program Y could be 500.

	Yes	No	Don't Know
X	400	200	400
Y	300	350	350
Both	200	100	0
Neither	**500**	550	250
Total	1,000	1,000	1,000

Therefore, among other possibilities, the number of people who did not respond "yes" to implementing either Program X or Program Y could be 400, and this number could also be 500; NOT sufficient.

The correct answer is A; statement 1 alone is sufficient.

DS39510.02

272. An estimate of an actual data value has an error of p percent if $p = \dfrac{100|e-a|}{a}$, where e is the estimated value and a is the actual value. Emma's estimate for her total income last year had an error of less than 20 percent. Emma's estimate of her income from tutoring last year also had an error of less than 20 percent. Was Emma's actual income from tutoring last year at most 45 percent of her actual total income last year?

   (1)   Emma's estimated income last year from tutoring was 30 percent of her estimated total income last year.

   (2)   Emma's estimated total income last year was $40,000.

Arithmetic Estimation

Given that Emma's estimates for both her total income and her income from tutoring last year, E_I and E_T, respectively, were within 20 percent of her actual total income and her actual income from tutoring, A_I and A_T, respectively, it follows that $0.8E_I < A_I < 1.2E_I$ and $0.8E_T < A_T < 1.2E_T$.

Determine whether Emma's actual income from tutoring was at most 45 percent of her actual total income or if $\dfrac{A_T}{A_I} \le 0.45$.

   (1)   Given that $E_T = 0.3E_I$, it follows from $0.8E_T < A_T < 1.2E_T$ that $0.24E_I < A_T < 0.36E_I$. Then, since $0.8E_I < A_I < 1.2E_I$, it follows that

$\dfrac{1}{1.2E_I} < \dfrac{1}{A_I} < \dfrac{1}{0.8E_I}$. Multiplying the inequalities gives $\dfrac{0.24E_I}{1.2E_I} < \dfrac{A_T}{A_I} < \dfrac{0.36E_I}{0.8E_I}$ or $0.2 < \dfrac{A_T}{A_I} < 0.45$; SUFFICIENT.

   (2)   Given that Emma's estimated total income last year was $40,000, it is impossible to determine whether her actual income from tutoring was at most 45 percent of her actual total income because no information is given about her actual income from tutoring other than it was within 20 percent of her estimated income from tutoring. And there is no information from which her estimated income from tutoring can be determined; NOT sufficient.

The correct answer is A; statement 1 alone is sufficient.

DS97030.02

273. Was Store K's profit last month at least 10 percent greater than its profit the previous month?

   (1)   Store K's expenses last month were 5 percent greater than its expenses the previous month.

   (2)   Store K's revenues last month were 10 percent greater than its revenues the previous month.

Algebra Applied Problems

Let P_{last}, E_{last}, and R_{last} be, respectively, the profit, expenses, and revenues for last month. Also, let $P_{previous}$, $E_{previous}$, and $R_{previous}$ be, respectively, the profit, expenses, and revenues for the previous month. Then we have $P_{last} = R_{last} - E_{last}$ and $P_{previous} = R_{previous} - E_{previous}$. Determine whether $P_{last} \ge 1.1P_{previous}$ is true, or equivalently, determine whether $R_{last} - E_{last} \ge 1.1R_{previous} - 1.1E_{previous}$ is true.

   (1)   Given that $E_{last} = 1.05E_{previous}$, it follows that the inequality $R_{last} - E_{last} \ge 1.1R_{previous} - 1.1E_{previous}$ is equivalent to $R_{last} - 1.1R_{previous} \ge -0.05E_{previous}$. It is clear that, for suitable values of R_{last}, $R_{previous}$, and $E_{previous}$, this last inequality could be true and this last inequality could be false; NOT sufficient.

   (2)   Given that $R_{last} = 1.1R_{previous}$, it follows that the inequality $R_{last} - E_{last} \ge 1.1R_{previous} -$

$1.1E_{previous}$ is equivalent to $E_{last} \leq 1.1E_{previous}$. It is clear that, for suitable values of E_{last} and $E_{previous}$, this last inequality could be true and this last inequality could be false; NOT sufficient.

Taking (1) and (2) together, the following shows that $P_{last} \geq 1.1P_{previous}$ is true.

$$P_{last} = R_{last} - E_{last}$$
$$= 1.1R_{previous} - 1.05E_{previous}$$
$$\geq 1.1R_{previous} - 1.1E_{previous}$$

Therefore, $P_{last} \geq 1.1(R_{previous} - E_{previous})$, and hence $P_{last} \geq 1.1P_{previous}$ is true. (The reason for using $\geq$ above instead of $>$ is to allow for the possibility that $E_{previous} = 0$.)

**The correct answer is C;
both statements together are sufficient.**

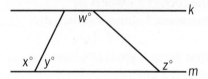

DS12862

274. In the figure shown, lines k and m are parallel to each other. Is $x = z$?

(1) $x = w$
(2) $y = 180 - w$

Geometry Angles

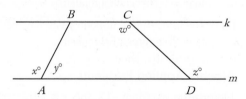

Since lines k and m are parallel, it follows from properties of parallel lines that in the diagram above x is the degree measure of $\angle ABC$ in quadrilateral $ABCD$. Therefore, because $y = 180 - x$, the four interior angles of quadrilateral $ABCD$ have degree measures $(180 - x)$, x, w, and $(180 - z)$.

(1)   Given that $x = w$, then because the sum of the degree measures of the angles of the quadrilateral $ABCD$ is 360, it follows that $(180 - x) + x + x + (180 - z) = 360$, or $x - z = 0$, or $x = z$; SUFFICIENT.

(2)   Given that $y = 180 - w$, then because $y = 180 - x$, it follows that $180 - w = 180 - x$, or $x = w$. However, it is shown in (1) that $x = w$ is sufficient; SUFFICIENT.

**The correct answer is D;
each statement alone is sufficient.**

DS13097

275. If k and ℓ are lines in the xy-plane, is the slope of k less than the slope of ℓ ?

(1)   The x-intercept of line k is positive, and the x-intercept of line ℓ is negative.

(2)   Lines k and ℓ intersect on the positive y-axis.

Geometry Simple Coordinate Geometry

Can we determine, for lines k and l in the xy plane, whether the slope of k is less than the slope of l ?

(1)   Given that the x-intercept of k is positive and the x-intercept of line l is negative, we cannot determine whether the slope of k is less than the slope of l. For example, in the case of line k, we have only been told where (within a certain range) line k intersects another line (the x-axis). Although a line with only a single x-intercept would not be horizontal, the line k could have any non-horizontal slope. Likewise in the case of line l. For example, the slope of k could be positive and the slope of l negative, or vice versa; NOT sufficient.

(2)   Given that k and l intersect on the positive y-axis, we cannot determine whether the slope of k is less than the slope of l. The point here is the same as the point with statement 1. With statement 2, we have only been given, for each of lines k and l, a condition on where the two lines intersect. And, given only that a line passes through a particular point (and regardless of whether another line happens to pass through this point), the line could have any slope. For example, again, the slope of k could be positive and the slope of l negative, or vice versa; NOT sufficient.

Considering statements 1 and 2 together, we have, for each of lines k and l, a condition on two of the points that the line passes through.

As illustrated in the diagram, the two conditions together are sufficient for determining the relationship in question.

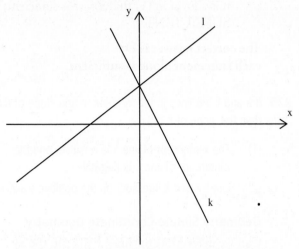

Because k intersects the positive y-axis and the positive x-axis, its slope must be downward (negative). And because l intersects the negative x-axis and the positive y-axis, its slope must be upward (positive). The slope of k is therefore less than the slope of l.

**The correct answer is C;
both statements together are sufficient.**

DS73340.02
276. Is n less than 1?

(1) n is less than 0.01 percent of 10,000.

(2) n is less than 0.1 percent of 1,200.

Arithmetic Percents

Determine whether n is less than 1.

(1) Given that n is less than 0.01% of 10,000, it follows that $n < 0.0001(10,000)$ or $n < 1$; SUFFICIENT.

(2) Given that n is less than 0.1% of 1,200, it follows that $n < 0.001(1,200)$ or $n < 1.2$, so n could be 0, in which case $n < 1$. On the other hand, n could be 1.1, in which case $n > 1$; NOT sufficient.

**The correct answer is A;
statement 1 alone is sufficient.**

DS18630.02
277. Gross profit is equal to selling price minus cost. A car dealer's gross profit on the sale of a certain car was what percent of the cost of the car?

(1) The selling price of the car was $\frac{11}{10}$ of the cost of the car.

(2) The cost of the car was $14,500.

Arithmetic Applied Problems

Determine the gross profit, P, on the sale of a car as a percent of the cost, C, of the car.

(1) Given that the selling price of the car was $\frac{11}{10}C$, $P = \frac{11}{10}C - C = \frac{1}{10}C$. Thus, the profit was 10% of the cost of the car; SUFFICIENT.

(2) Given that the cost of the car was $14,500, it is impossible to determine the profit because the selling price is not known nor is there enough information to determine it; NOT sufficient.

**The correct answer is A;
statement 1 alone is sufficient.**

DS09642
278. When the wind speed is 9 miles per hour, the wind-chill factor w is given by

$$w = -17.366 + 1.19t,$$

where t is the temperature in degrees Fahrenheit. If at noon yesterday the wind speed was 9 miles per hour, was the wind-chill factor greater than 0 ?

(1) The temperature at noon yesterday was greater than 10 degrees Fahrenheit.

(2) The temperature at noon yesterday was less than 20 degrees Fahrenheit.

Algebra Applied Problems

Determine whether $-17.366 + 1.19t$ is greater than 0.

(1) Given that $t > 10$, it follows that $-17.366 + 1.19t > -17.366 + 1.19(10)$, or $-17.366 + 1.19t > -5.466$. However, it is not possible to determine whether $-17.366 + 1.19t$ is greater than 0. For example, if $t = 19$, then $-17.366 + 1.19t = 5.244$ is greater than 0. However, if $t = 11$, then $-17.366 + 1.19t = -4.276$, which is not greater than 0; NOT sufficient.

(2) Given that $t < 20$, the same examples used in (1) show that it is not possible to determine whether $-17.366 + 1.19t$ is greater than 0; NOT sufficient.

Taking (1) and (2) together is of no more help than either (1) or (2) taken separately because the same examples were used in both (1) and (2).

The correct answer is E; both statements together are still not sufficient.

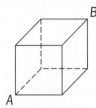

DS08852

279. What is the volume of the cube above?

(1) The surface area of the cube is 600 square inches.
(2) The length of diagonal AB is $10\sqrt{3}$ inches.

Geometry Volume

This problem can be solved by determining the side length, s, of the cube.

(1) This indicates that $6s^2 = 600$, from which it follows that $s^2 = 100$ and $s = 10$; SUFFICIENT.
(2) To determine diagonal AB, first determine diagonal AN by applying the Pythagorean theorem to $\triangle AMN$: $AN = \sqrt{s^2 + s^2} = \sqrt{2s^2}$. Now determine AB by applying the Pythagorean theorem to $\triangle ANB$: $AB = \sqrt{(AN)^2 + (NB)^2} = \sqrt{2s^2 + s^2} = \sqrt{3s^2} = s\sqrt{3}$. It is given that $AB = 10\sqrt{3}$, and so $s = 10$; SUFFICIENT.

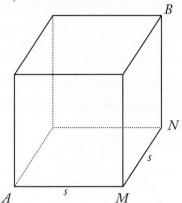

The correct answer is D; each statement alone is sufficient.

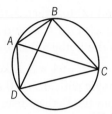

DS03989

280. In the figure shown, quadrilateral $ABCD$ is inscribed in a circle of radius 5. What is the perimeter of quadrilateral $ABCD$?

(1) The length of AB is 6 and the length of CD is 8.
(2) AC is a diameter of the circle.

Geometry Quadrilaterals; Perimeter; Pythagorean Theorem

Determine the perimeter of quadrilateral $ABCD$, which is given by $AB + BC + CD + DA$.

(1) This indicates that $AB = 6$ and $CD = 8$, but gives no information about BC or DA.

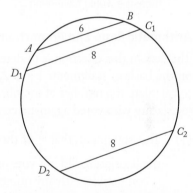

For example, the perimeter of ABC_1D_1 is clearly different than the perimeter of ABC_2D_2 and $\overline{CD}$ could be positioned where $\overline{C_1D_1}$ is on the diagram or it could be positioned where $\overline{C_2D_2}$ is on the diagram; NOT sufficient.

(2) This indicates that $AC = 2(5) = 10$ since AC is a diameter of the circle and the radius of the circle is 5. It also indicates that $\angle ABC$ and $\angle ADC$ are right angles since each is inscribed in a semicircle. However, there is no information about AB, BC, CD, or DA. For example, if $AB = CD = 6$, then $BC = DA = \sqrt{10^2 - 6^2} = \sqrt{64} = 8$ and the perimeter of $ABCD$ is $2(6 + 8) = 28$. However, if $AB = DA = 2$, then $BC = CD = \sqrt{10^2 - 2^2} = \sqrt{96}$ and the perimeter of $ABCD = 2(2 + \sqrt{96})$; NOT sufficient.

Taking (1) and (2) together, $\triangle ABC$ is a right triangle with $AC = 10$ and $AB = 6$. It follows from the Pythagorean theorem that $BC = \sqrt{10^2 - 6^2} = \sqrt{64} = 8$. Likewise, $\triangle ADC$ is a right triangle with $AC = 10$ and $CD = 8$. It follows from the Pythagorean theorem that $DA = \sqrt{10^2 - 8^2} = \sqrt{36} = 6$. Thus, the perimeter of quadrilateral $ABCD$ can be determined.

**The correct answer is C;
both statements together are sufficient.**

DS05766

281. How many members of a certain legislature voted against the measure to raise their salaries?

(1) $\frac{1}{4}$ of the members of the legislature did not vote on the measure.

(2) If 5 additional members of the legislature had voted against the measure, then the fraction of members of the legislature voting against the measure would have been $\frac{1}{3}$.

Arithmetic Ratio and Proportion

The task in this question is to determine whether, on the basis of statements 1 and 2, it is possible to calculate the number of members of the legislature who voted against a certain measure.

(1) This statement, that $\frac{1}{4}$ of the members of the legislature did not vote on the measure, is compatible with any number of members of the legislature voting against the measure. After all, any number among the $\frac{3}{4}$ of the remaining members could have voted against the measure. Furthermore, based on statement 1, we do not know the number of members of the legislature (although we do know, based on this statement, that the number of members of the legislature is divisible by 4); NOT sufficient.

(2) This statement describes a scenario, of 5 additional members of the legislature voting against the measure, and stipulates that $\frac{1}{3}$ of the members of the legislature would have voted against the measure in the scenario. Given this condition, we know that the number of members of the

legislature was divisible by 3, and that the legislature had at least 15 members (to allow for the "5 additional members of the legislature" that could have voted against the measure, for a total of $\frac{1}{3}$ of the members voting against it). However, beyond this we know essentially nothing from statement 2. In particular, depending on the number of members of the legislature (which we have not been given), any number of members could have voted against the measure. For example, exactly one member could have voted against the measure, in which case the legislature would have had $(1 + 5) \times 3 = 18$ members. Exactly two members could have voted against the measure, in which case the legislature would have had $(2 + 5) \times 3 = 21$ members, and so on for 3 members voting against, 4 members voting against, etc.; NOT sufficient.

Considering the statements 1 and 2 together, the reasoning is similar to the reasoning for statement 2, but with the further condition that the total number of members of the legislature is divisible by 12 (so as to allow that both exactly $\frac{1}{4}$ of the members did not vote on the measure while exactly $\frac{1}{3}$ could have voted against the measure). For example, it could have been the case that the legislature had 24 members. In this case, $\frac{1}{3}$ of the members would have been 8 members, and, consistent with statements 1 and 2, 3 of the members $(8 - 5)$ could have voted against the measure. Or the legislature could have had 36 members, in which case, consistent with statements 1 and 2, $\frac{1}{3}(36) - 5 = 12 - 5 = 7$ members could have voted against the measure.

**The correct answer is E;
both statements together are still not sufficient.**

DS05986

282. If $y \neq 0$, is $|x| = 1$?

(1) $x = \dfrac{y}{|y|}$

(2) $|x| = -x$

Algebra Absolute Value

Can we determine whether $|x| = 1$?

(1) Given that $x = \dfrac{y}{|y|}$, we consider two cases: $y > 0$ and $y < 0$. If $y > 0$, then $|y| = y$ and $\dfrac{y}{|y|} = \dfrac{y}{y} = 1$. So if $y > 0$, then $x = 1$ and, of course, $|x| = 1$. If $y < 0$, then $|y| = (-1)\,y$ and $x = \dfrac{y}{|y|} = \dfrac{y}{(-1)\,y} = (-1)\dfrac{y}{y} = (-1)(1) = -1$. So $|x| = 1$. If $y < 0$, then $|x| = 1$. In both of the two cases, $|x| = 1$; SUFFICIENT.

(2) Given that $|x| = -x$, all we know is that x is not positive. For example, both -4 and -5 satisfy this condition on x: $|-4| = 4 = -(-4)$ and $|-5| = 5 = -(-5)$; NOT sufficient.

The correct answer is A; statement 1 alone is sufficient.

DS08306

283. If x is a positive integer, what is the value of x ?

(1) $x^2 = \sqrt{x}$

(2) $\dfrac{n}{x} = n$ and $n \neq 0$.

Algebra Operations with Radicals

(1) It is given that x is a positive integer. Then,

$$
\begin{array}{ll}
x^2 = \sqrt{x} & \text{given} \\
x^4 = x & \text{square both sides} \\
x^4 - x = 0 & \text{subtract } x \text{ from both sides} \\
x(x-1)(x^2 + x + 1) = 0 & \text{factor left side}
\end{array}
$$

Thus, the positive integer value of x being sought will be a solution of this equation. One solution of this equation is $x = 0$, which is not a positive integer. Another solution is $x = 1$, which is a positive integer. Also, $x^2 + x + 1$ is a positive integer for all positive integer values of x, and so $x^2 + x + 1 = 0$ has no positive integer solutions. Thus, the only possible positive integer value of x is 1; SUFFICIENT.

(2) It is given that $n \neq 0$. Then,

$$
\begin{array}{ll}
\dfrac{n}{x} = n & \text{given} \\
n = nx & \text{multiply both sides by } x \\
1 = x & \text{divide both sides by } n, \text{ where } n \neq 0
\end{array}
$$

Thus, $x = 1$; SUFFICIENT.

The correct answer is D; each statement alone is sufficient.

DS07568

284. Is the median of the five numbers a, b, c, d, and e equal to d ?

(1) $a < c < e$

(2) $b < d < c$

Arithmetic Statistics

Determine if the median of the five numbers, a, b, c, d, and e, is equal to d.

(1) This indicates that $a < c < e$, but does not indicate a relationship of b and d with a, c, and e. For example, if $a = 5$, $b = 1$, $c = 10$, $d = 7$, and $e = 15$, then $a < c < e$, and d is the median. However, if $a = 5$, $b = 1$, $c = 10$, $d = 2$, and $e = 15$, then $a < c < e$, and a, not d, is the median; NOT sufficient.

(2) This indicates that $b < d < c$, but does not indicate a relationship of a and e with b, d, and c. For example, if $a = 5$, $b = 1$, $c = 10$, $d = 7$, and $e = 15$, then $b < d < c$, and d is the median. However, if $a = 5$, $b = 1$, $c = 10$, $d = 2$, and $e = 15$, then $b < d < c$, and a, not d, is the median; NOT sufficient.

Taking (1) and (2) together is of no more help than either (1) or (2) taken separately since the same examples used to show that (1) is not sufficient also show that (2) is not sufficient.

The correct answer is E; both statements together are still not sufficient.

DS10383

285. During a certain bicycle ride, was Sherry's average speed faster than 24 kilometers per hour? (1 kilometer = 1,000 meters)

(1) Sherry's average speed during the bicycle ride was faster than 7 meters per second.

(2) Sherry's average speed during the bicycle ride was slower than 8 meters per second.

Arithmetic Applied Problems

This problem can be solved by converting 24 kilometers per hour into meters per second. First, 24 kilometers is equivalent to 24,000 meters and 1 hour is equivalent to 3,600 seconds. Then, traveling 24 kilometers in 1 hour is equivalent to traveling 24,000 meters in 3,600 seconds, or $\frac{24,000}{3,600} = 6\frac{2}{3}$ meters per second.

(1) This indicates that Sherry's average speed was faster than 7 meters per second, which is faster than $6\frac{2}{3}$ meters per second and, therefore, faster than 24 kilometers per hour; SUFFICIENT.

(2) This indicates that Sherry's average speed was slower than 8 meters per second. Her average speed could have been 7 meters per second (since 7 < 8), in which case her average speed was faster than $6\frac{2}{3}$ meters per second and, therefore, faster than 24 kilometers per hour. Or her average speed could have been 5 meters per second (since 5 < 8), in which case her average speed was not faster than $6\frac{2}{3}$ meters per second and, therefore, not faster than 24 kilometers per hour; NOT sufficient.

**The correct answer is A;
statement 1 alone is sufficient.**

DS13907
286. Working together, Rafael and Salvador can tabulate a certain set of data in 2 hours. In how many hours can Rafael tabulate the data working alone?

(1) Working alone, Rafael can tabulate the data in 3 hours less time than Salvador, working alone, can tabulate the data.

(2) Working alone, Rafael can tabulate the data in $\frac{1}{2}$ the time that Salvador, working alone, can tabulate the data.

Algebra Simultaneous Equations

We are given that Rafael and Salvador, working together, can tabulate the set of data in two hours. That is, if Rafael tabulates data at the rate of R units of data per hour and Salvador tabulates the data at the rate of S units per hour, then, if the set of data is made up of D units, then $2R + 2S = D$. Can we determine how much time, in hours, it takes Rafael to tabulate the data if working alone?

(1) First of all, note that the choice of units used to measure the amounts of data doesn't

matter. In particular, we can define one unit of data to be D. Thus, $2R + 2S = 1$. With this in mind, consider the condition that Rafael, when working alone, can tabulate the data in 3 hours less time than Salvador can when working alone. Given that Rafael tabulates R units of data per unit time, he takes $\frac{1}{R}$ units of time to tabulate one unit of data. Similarly, Salvador takes $\frac{1}{S}$ units of time to tabulate one unit of data. This unit, as defined, is simply the entire set of data. Our given condition thus becomes $\frac{1}{R} = \frac{1}{S} - 3$, and we have the set of simultaneous equations made up of this equation and the equation $2R + 2S = 1$.

One way to determine the number of hours it would take Rafael to tabulate the data is to solve one of these equations for S and then substitute this solution into the other equation. Considering the first of these equations, we multiply both sides by RS and then manipulate the result as follows.

$$S = R - 3RS$$
$$S + 3RS = R$$
$$S(1 + 3R) = R$$
$$S = \frac{R}{1 + 3R}$$

Substituting into the equation $2R + 2S = 1$,

$$2R + \frac{2R}{1 + 3R} = 1$$

Multiplying both sides by $1 + 3R$ to eliminate the fraction,

$$2R(1 + 3R) + 2R = 1 + 3R$$
$$2R + 6R^2 = 1 + R$$
$$6R^2 + R - 1 = 0$$
$$(3R - 1)(2R + 1) = 0$$

This equation has two solutions, $-\frac{1}{2}$ and $\frac{1}{3}$. However, because the rate R cannot be negative, we find that Rafael tabulates $\frac{1}{3}$ of a unit of data every hour. Since one unit is the entire set, it takes Rafael 3 hours to tabulate the entire set; SUFFICIENT.

(2)   We are given that Rafael, working alone, can tabulate the data in $\frac{1}{2}$ the amount of time it takes Salvador, working alone, to tabulate the data. As in the discussion of statement 1, we have that Rafael tabulates R units of data every hour, and takes $\frac{1}{R}$ hours to tabulate one unit of data. Similarly, it takes Salvador $\frac{1}{S}$ hours to tabulate one unit of data. One unit of data has been defined to be the size of the entire set to be tabulated, so statement 2 becomes the expression

$$\frac{1}{R} = \frac{1}{2} \times \frac{1}{S} = \frac{1}{2S}$$

We thus have $2S = R$. Substituting this value for $2S$ in the equation $2R + 2S = 1$, we have $R + 2R = 1$, and $3R = 1$. Solving for R we get $\frac{1}{3}$; SUFFICIENT.

Note that, for both statements 1 and 2, it would have been possible to stop calculating once we had determined whether it was possible to find a unique value for R. The ability to make such judgments accurately is part of what the test has been designed to measure.

**The correct answer is D;
each statement alone is sufficient.**

DS04039
287. If x and y are integers, what is the value of x?

(1) $xy = 1$
(2) $x \neq -1$

Arithmetic Properties of Integers

Given that x and y are integers, determine the value of x.

(1)   If $x = y = -1$, then $xy = 1$, and if $x = y = 1$, then $xy = 1$; NOT sufficient.

(2)   Given that $x \neq -1$, the value of x could be any other integer; NOT sufficient.

Taking (1) and (2) together, since the two possibilities for the value of x are $x = -1$ or $x = 1$ by (1), and $x \neq -1$ by (2), then $x = 1$.

**The correct answer is C;
both statements together are sufficient.**

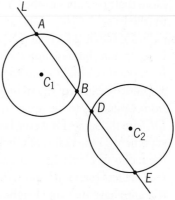

Note: Figure not drawn to scale.

DS18386
288. The figure above shows Line L, Circle 1 with center at C_1, and Circle 2 with center at C_2. Line L intersects Circle 1 at points A and B, Line L intersects Circle 2 at points D and E, and points C_1 and C_2 are equidistant from line L. Is the area of $\triangle ABC_1$ less than the area of $\triangle DEC_2$?

(1)   The radius of Circle 1 is less than the radius of Circle 2.

(2)   The length of chord $\overline{AB}$ is less than the length of chord $\overline{DE}$.

Geometry Triangles

We are given various elements of information that apply regardless of whether we assume that statements 1, 2, or both are true, and asked whether it is possible, when considering one or both of these statements, to determine if the area of triangle $\triangle ABC_1$ is less than the area of $\triangle DEC_2$.

(1)   Given the condition that the radius of Circle 1 is less than the radius of Circle 2, it may be useful to consider the following diagrams of the triangles, in which they have been rotated so as to have the sides AB and DE represented as horizontal and on the bottom. The diagrams are not drawn to scale.

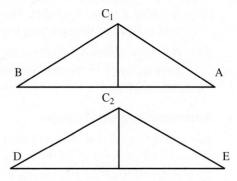

Note that the radius of the Circle 1 is equal to (the length) C_1B (= C_1A) and that the radius of Circle 2 is equal to C_2D (= C_2E). Furthermore, because line L is equidistant from points C_1 and C_2, we know that the respective heights of the triangles (distances from C_1 and C_2 to the respective bases BA and DE) are the same. However, because (with statement 1) the radius of Circle 1 is less than the radius of Circle 2, we know that C_1B and C_1A are less than C_2D and C_2E. Because the triangles have the same height, triangle ΔABC_1 must be less "wide" than ΔDEC_2 and must thus have a lesser base (length). And because the area of a triangle is always $\frac{1}{2} \times$ base $\times$ height, we can infer that the area of ΔABC_1 is less than the area of ΔDEC_2; SUFFICIENT.

(2) Given that AB is less than DE, we can infer that the area of ΔABC_1 is less than the area of ΔDEC_2. After all, we know that the heights of the two triangles are the same (because, as discussed in connection with statement 1, line L is equidistant from C_1 and C_2). The formula for the area of a triangle, $\frac{1}{2} \times$ base $\times$ height, thus allows us to make our inference; SUFFICIENT.

**The correct answer is D;
each statement alone is sufficient.**

DS15938
289. Yesterday between 9:00 a.m. and 6:00 p.m. at Airport X, all flights to Atlanta departed at equally spaced times and all flights to New York City departed at equally spaced times. A flight to Atlanta and a flight to New York City both departed from Airport X at 1:00 p.m. yesterday. Between 1:00 p.m. and 3:00 p.m. yesterday, did another pair of flights to these 2 cities depart from Airport X at the same time?

(1) Yesterday at Airport X, a flight to Atlanta and a flight to New York City both departed at 10:00 a.m.

(2) Yesterday at Airport X, flights to New York City departed every 15 minutes between 9:00 a.m. and 6:00 p.m.

Arithmetic Applied Problems

It is useful to note that although the departures discussed all lie between 9:00 a.m. and 6:00 p.m., there is no information concerning when the first departures took place during this time other than what is necessary for the information to be consistent. For example, since departures to both Atlanta and New York City took place at 1:00 p.m., the first departure to either of these cities could not have occurred after 1:00 p.m.

(1) Given that departures to both Atlanta and New York City took place at 10:00 a.m., it is not possible to determine whether simultaneous departures to these cities occurred between 1:00 p.m. and 3:00 p.m. For example, it is possible that departures to both Atlanta and New York City took place every 15 minutes beginning at 9:15 a.m., and thus it is possible that simultaneous departures to both these cities occurred between 1:00 p.m. and 3:00 p.m. However, it is also possible that departures to Atlanta took place every 3 hours beginning at 10:00 a.m. and departures to New York City took place every 15 minutes beginning at 9:15 a.m., and thus it is possible that no simultaneous departures to these cities occurred between 1:00 p.m. and 3:00 p.m.; NOT sufficient.

(2) Given that departures to New York City took place every 15 minutes, the same examples used in (1) can be used to show that it is not possible to determine whether simultaneous departures to these cities occurred between 1:00 p.m. and 3:00 p.m.; NOT sufficient.

Taking (1) and (2) together, it is still not possible to determine whether simultaneous departures to these cities occurred between 1:00 p.m. and 3:00 p.m. because both (1) and (2) are true for the examples above.

**The correct answer is E;
both statements together are still not sufficient.**

DS07206
290. Of the total number of copies of Magazine X sold last week, 40 percent were sold at full price. What was the total number of copies of the magazine sold last week?

(1) Last week, full price for a copy of Magazine X was $1.50 and the total revenue from full-price sales was $112,500.

(2) The total number of copies of Magazine X sold last week at full price was $75,000.

Algebra Applied Problems

For the copies of Magazine X sold last week, let n be the total number of copies sold and let $\$p$ be the full price of each copy. Then for Magazine X last week, a total of $0.4n$ copies were each sold at price $\$p$. What is the value of n ?

(1) Given that $\$p = 1.50$ and $(0.4n)(\$p) = \$112,500$, it follows that $(0.4n)(1.5) = 112,500$, or $0.6n = 112,500$, or

$$n = \frac{112,500}{0.6} ; \text{SUFFICIENT.}$$

(2) Given that $0.4n = 75,000$, it follows that

$$n = \frac{75,000}{0.4} ; \text{SUFFICIENT.}$$

**The correct answer is D;
each statement alone is sufficient.**

DS11614
291. If p, s, and t are positive, is $|ps - pt| > p(s - t)$?

(1) $p < s$
(2) $s < t$

Algebra Absolute Value

Since p is positive, it follows that $|p(s - t)| = |p||s - t| = p|s - t|$. Therefore, the task is to determine if $|s - t| > s - t$. Since $|s - t| = s - t$ if and only if $s - t \geq 0$, it follows that $|s - t| > s - t$ if and only if $s - t < 0$.

(1) This indicates that $p < s$ but does not provide information about the relationship between s and t. For example, if $p = 5$, $s = 10$, and $t = 15$, then $p < s$ and $s < t$, but if $p = 5$, $s = 10$, and $t = 3$, then $p < s$ and $s > t$; NOT sufficient.

(2) This indicates that $s < t$, or equivalently, $s - t < 0$; SUFFICIENT.

**The correct answer is B;
statement 2 alone is sufficient.**

DS04468
292. Is $x > y$?

(1) $x + y > x - y$
(2) $3x > 2y$

Algebra Inequalities

(1) Given that $x + y > x - y$, it follows that $y > -y$, or $2y > 0$, or $y > 0$. However, nothing is known about the value of x. If $x = 2$ and

$y = 1$, then $x + y > x - y$ and the answer to the question is yes. However, if $x = 1$ and $y = 1$, then $x + y > x - y$ and the answer to the question is no; NOT sufficient.

(2) Given that $3x > 2y$, then $x = 2$ and $y = 1$ is possible and the answer to the question is yes. However, if $3x > 2y$, then $x = 1$ and $y = 1$ is also possible and the answer to the question is no; NOT sufficient.

Taking (1) and (2) together is of no more help than either (1) or (2) taken separately because the same examples used to show that (1) is not sufficient also show that (2) is not sufficient.

**The correct answer is E;
both statements together are still not sufficient.**

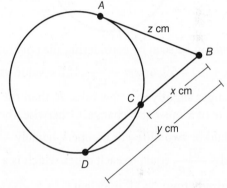

DS17588
293. In the figure above, $\overline{AB}$, which has length z cm, is tangent to the circle at point A, and $\overline{BD}$, which has length y cm, intersects the circle at point C. If $BC = x$ cm and $z = \sqrt{xy}$, what is the value of x ?

(1) $CD = x$ cm
(2) $z = 5\sqrt{2}$

Geometry Circles

(1) Given that $CD = x$ cm, it is not possible to determine the value of x because all the given information continues to hold when all the parts of the figure increase in length by any given nonzero factor; NOT sufficient.

(2) Given that $z = 5\sqrt{2}$, the value of x will vary when the radius of the circle varies and $\overline{CD}$ is a diameter and thus passes through the center of the circle. To see this, let r be the radius, in centimeters, of the circle and let O be the center of the circle, as shown in the figure below. Then, because $\overline{CD}$ is a

diameter, it follows that $CD = 2r$ and $y = x + CD = x + 2r$. Also, $\triangle OAB$ is a right triangle and the Pythagorean theorem gives $(OA)^2 + (AB)^2 = (OB)^2$, or $r^2 + (5\sqrt{2})^2 = (x + r)^2$, or $r^2 + 50 = x^2 + 2xr + r^2$, or $x(x + 2r) = 50$, which implies that $xy = z^2$ and $z = \sqrt{xy}$, since $y = x + 2r$ and $z = 5\sqrt{2}$. Therefore, if $z = 5\sqrt{2}$ and $\overline{CD}$ is a diameter, then $z = \sqrt{xy}$ holds, and the value of x can vary.

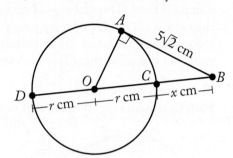

This can be seen by considering the equation $x(x + 2r) = 50$, or $x = \dfrac{50}{x + 2r}$. If the value of r changes slightly to a new value R, then the value of x must also change. Otherwise, there would be two different numbers, namely $\dfrac{50}{x + 2r}$ and $\dfrac{50}{x + 2R}$, equal to each other, which is a contradiction; NOT sufficient.

Taking (1) and (2) together, $y = x + CD = x + x = 2x$ and $z = 5\sqrt{2}$, so $z = \sqrt{xy}$ becomes $5\sqrt{2} = \sqrt{x(2x)}$, or $(5\sqrt{2})^2 = (\sqrt{x(2x)})^2$, or $50 = x(2x)$, or $x^2 = 25$, or $x = 5$.

**The correct answer is C;
both statements together are sufficient.**

DS15863

294. Is the integer n a prime number?

(1) $24 \leq n \leq 28$

(2) n is not divisible by 2 or 3.

Arithmetic Properties of Numbers

Determine if the integer n is a prime number.

(1) This indicates that n is between 24 and 28, inclusive. It follows that the value of n can be 24, 25, 26, 27, or 28. Each of these is NOT a prime number. Thus, it can be determined that n is NOT a prime number; SUFFICIENT.

(2) This indicates that n is not divisible by 2 or 3. If $n = 7$, then n is not divisible by 2 or 3 and is a prime number. However, if $n = 25$, then n is not divisible by 2 or 3 and is a not prime number since 25 has a factor, namely 5, other than 1 and itself; NOT sufficient.

**The correct answer is A;
statement 1 alone is sufficient.**

DS03615

295. What is the average (arithmetic mean) annual salary of the 6 employees of a toy company?

(1) If the 6 annual salaries were ordered from least to greatest, each annual salary would be $6,300 greater than the preceding annual salary.

(2) The range of the 6 annual salaries is $31,500.

Arithmetic Statistics

Can we determine the arithmetic mean of the annual salaries of the 6 employees?

(1) Given only that the 6 annual salaries can be put into a sequence from least to greatest, with a difference of $6,300 between adjacent members of the sequence, we can infer certain things about the mean of the salaries. For example, because none of the salaries would be negative, we know from statement 1 that the mean of the salaries is greater than or equal to

$$\frac{0 + \$6,300 + \$12,600 + \$18,900 + \$25,200 + \$31,500}{6}.$$

(It is not necessary to perform this calculation.) However, depending on what the least of the salaries is—that is, the value at which the sequence of salaries begins— the average of the salaries could, consistent with condition 1, take on any value greater than this quotient; NOT sufficient.

(2) Given the statement that the range of the salaries is $31,500, reasoning similar to the reasoning for statement 1 applies. A difference between least salary and greatest salary of $31,500 is consistent with any value for the least salary, so long as the greatest salary is $31,500 greater than the least salary. Furthermore, even if we knew what the least and the greatest salaries are, it would be impossible to determine the mean merely from the range; NOT sufficient.

As reflected in the numerator of the quotient in the discussion of statement 1, we can see that statement 1 implies statement 2. In the sequence of 6 salaries with a difference of $6,300 between adjacent members of the sequence, the difference between the least salary and the greatest salary is $5 \times \$6,300 = \$31,500$. Therefore, because statement 1 is insufficient for determining the mean of the salaries, the combination of statement 1 and statement 2 is also insufficient for determining the mean of the salaries.

The correct answer is E; both statements together are not sufficient.

DS17503

296. In a certain order, the pretax price of each regular pencil was $0.03, the pretax price of each deluxe pencil was $0.05, and there were 50% more deluxe pencils than regular pencils. All taxes on the order are a fixed percent of the pretax prices. The sum of the total pretax price of the order and the tax on the order was $44.10. What was the amount, in dollars, of the tax on the order?

(1) The tax on the order was 5% of the total pretax price of the order.

(2) The order contained exactly 400 regular pencils.

Arithmetic Percents

Let n be the number of regular pencils in the order and let $r\%$ be the tax rate on the order as a percent of the pretax price. Then the order contains $1.5n$ deluxe pencils, the total pretax price of the order is $(\$0.03)n + (\$0.05)(1.5n) = \$0.105n$, and the sum of the total pretax price of the order and the tax on the order is $\left(1+\dfrac{r}{100}\right)(\$0.105n)$. Given that $\left(1+\dfrac{r}{100}\right)(\$0.105n) = \$44.10$, what is the value of $\left(\dfrac{r}{100}\right)(\$0.105n)$?

(1) Given that $r = 5$, then $\left(1+\dfrac{r}{100}\right)(\$0.105n)$ $= \$44.10$ becomes $(1.05)(0.105n) = 44.10$, which is a first-degree equation that can be solved for n. Since the value of r is known and the value of n can be determined, it follows that the value of $\left(\dfrac{r}{100}\right)(\$0.105n)$ can be determined; SUFFICIENT.

(2) Given that $n = 400$, then

$$\left(1+\dfrac{r}{100}\right)(\$0.105n) = \$44.10 \text{ becomes}$$

$$\left(1+\dfrac{r}{100}\right)(0.105)(400) = 44.10, \text{ which is a}$$

first-degree equation that can be solved for r. Since the value of r can be determined and the value of n is known, it follows that the value of $\left(\dfrac{r}{100}\right)(\$0.105n)$ can be determined; SUFFICIENT.

The correct answer is D; each statement alone is sufficient.

DS06785

297. If m is an integer greater than 1, is m an even integer?

(1) 32 is a factor of m.

(2) m is a factor of 32.

Arithmetic Properties of Numbers

(1) Given that 32 is a factor of m, then each of the factors of 32, including 2, is a factor of m. Since 2 is a factor of m, it follows that m is an even integer; SUFFICIENT.

(2) Given that m is a factor of 32 and m is greater than 1, it follows that $m = 2, 4, 8, 16,$ or 32. Since each of these is an even integer, m must be an even integer; SUFFICIENT.

The correct answer is D; each statement alone is sufficient.

DS05657

298. If the set S consists of five consecutive positive integers, what is the sum of these five integers?

(1) The integer 11 is in S, but 10 is not in S.

(2) The sum of the even integers in S is 26.

Arithmetic Sequences

(1) This indicates that the least integer in S is 11 since S consists of consecutive integers and 11 is in S, but 10 is not in S. Thus, the integers in S are 11, 12, 13, 14, and 15, and their sum can be determined; SUFFICIENT.

(2) This indicates that the sum of the even integers in S is 26. In a set of 5 consecutive integers, either two of the integers or three of the integers are even. If there are three even

integers, then the first integer in S must be even. Also, since $\frac{26}{3} = 8\frac{2}{3}$, the three even integers must be around 8. The three even integers could be 6, 8, and 10, but are not because their sum is less than 26; or they could be 8, 10, and 12, but are not because their sum is greater than 26. Therefore, S cannot contain three even integers and must contain only two even integers. Those integers must be 12 and 14 since $12 + 14 = 26$. It follows that the integers in S are 11, 12, 13, 14, and 15, and their sum can be determined; SUFFICIENT.

Alternately, if n, $n + 1$, $n + 2$, $n + 3$, and $n + 4$ represent the five consecutive integers and three of them are even, then $n + (n + 2) + (n + 4) = 26$, or $3n = 20$, or $n = \frac{20}{3}$, which is not an integer. On the other hand, if two of the integers are even, then $(n + 1) + (n + 3) = 26$, or $2n = 22$, or $n = 11$. It follows that the integers are 11, 12, 13, 14, and 15, and their sum can be determined; SUFFICIENT.

**The correct answer is D;
each statement alone is sufficient.**

DS17543
299. If $x > 0$, what is the value of x?

(1) $x^3 - x = 0$
(2) $\sqrt[3]{x} - x = 0$

Algebra Factoring; Operations with Radical Expressions

(1) Given that $x^3 - x = 0$, factoring gives $x(x^2 - 1) = x(x - 1)(x + 1) = 0$. Hence, $x = 0$, $x = 1$, or $x = -1$. Since $x > 0$, the value of x cannot be 0 or -1, and so $x = 1$; SUFFICIENT.

(2) Given that $\sqrt[3]{x} - x = 0$, it follows that $\sqrt[3]{x} = x$, or $(\sqrt[3]{x})^3 = x^3$, or $x = x^3$. Therefore, $x^3 - x = 0$ and the discussion in (1) shows that the only positive value of x is $x = 1$; SUFFICIENT.

**The correct answer is D;
each statement alone is sufficient.**

DS08307
300. A total of 20 amounts are entered on a spreadsheet that has 5 rows and 4 columns; each of the 20 positions in the spreadsheet contains one amount. The average (arithmetic mean) of the amounts in row i is R_i ($1 \le i \le 5$). The average of the amounts in column j is C_j ($1 \le j \le 4$). What is the average of all 20 amounts on the spreadsheet?

(1) $R_1 + R_2 + R_3 + R_4 + R_5 = 550$
(2) $C_1 + C_2 + C_3 + C_4 = 440$

Arithmetic Statistics

It is given that R_i represents the average of the amounts in row i. Since there are four amounts in each row, $4R_i$ represents the total of the amounts in row i. Likewise, it is given that C_j represents the average of the amounts in column j. Since there are five amounts in each column, $5C_j$ represents the total of the amounts in column j.

(1) It is given that $R_1 + R_2 + R_3 + R_4 + R_5 = 550$, and so $4(R_1 + R_2 + R_3 + R_4 + R_5) = 4R_1 + 4R_2 + 4R_3 + 4R_4 + 4R_5 = 4(550) = 2{,}200$. Therefore, 2,200 is the sum of all 20 amounts (4 amounts in each of 5 rows), and the average of all 20 amounts is $\frac{2{,}200}{20} = 110$; SUFFICIENT.

(2) It is given that $C_1 + C_2 + C_3 + C_4 = 440$, and so $5(C_1 + C_2 + C_3 + C_4) = 5C_1 + 5C_2 + 5C_3 + 5C_4 = 5(440) = 2{,}200$. Therefore, 2,200 is the sum of all 20 amounts (5 amounts in each of 4 columns), and the average of all 20 amounts is $\frac{2{,}200}{20} = 110$; SUFFICIENT.

**The correct answer is D;
each statement alone is sufficient.**

DS13132
301. Was the range of the amounts of money that Company Y budgeted for its projects last year equal to the range of the amounts of money that it budgeted for its projects this year?

(1) Both last year and this year, Company Y budgeted money for 12 projects and the least amount of money that it budgeted for a project was $400.

(2) Both last year and this year, the average (arithmetic mean) amount of money that Company Y budgeted per project was $2,000.

Arithmetic Statistics

Let G_1 and L_1 represent the greatest and least amounts, respectively, of money that Company Y budgeted for its projects last year, and let G_2 and L_2 represent the greatest and least amounts, respectively, of money that Company Y budgeted for its projects this year. Determine if the range of the amounts of money Company Y budgeted for its projects last year is equal to the range of amounts budgeted for its projects this year; that is, determine if $G_1 - L_1 = G_2 - L_2$.

(1) This indicates that $L_1 = L_2 = \$400$, but does not give any information about G_1 or G_2; NOT sufficient.

(2) This indicates that the average amount Company Y budgeted for its projects both last year and this year was $2,000 per project, but does not give any information about the least and greatest amounts that it budgeted for its projects either year; NOT sufficient.

Taking (1) and (2) together, it is known that $L_1 = L_2 = \$400$ and that the average amount Company Y budgeted for its projects both last year and this year was $2,000 per project, but there is no information about G_1 or G_2. For example, if, for each year, Company Y budgeted $400 for each of 2 projects and $2,320 for each of the 10 others, then (1) and (2) are true and the range for each year was $2,320 − $400 = $1,920. However, if, last year, Company Y budgeted $400 for each of 2 projects and $2,320 for each of the 10 others, and, this year, budgeted $400 for each of 11 projects and $19,600 for 1 project, then (1) and (2) are true, but the range for last year was $1,920 and the range for this year was $19,600 − $400 = $19,200.

The correct answer is E;
both statements together are still not sufficient.

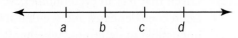

DS01633

302. If a, b, c, and d are numbers on the number line shown and if the tick marks are equally spaced, what is the value of $a + c$?

(1) $a + b = -8$

(2) $a + d = 0$

Algebra Sequences

It is given that the distance between a and b is the same as the distance between b and c, which is the same as the distance between c and d. Letting q represent this distance, then $b = a + q$, $c = a + 2q$, and $d = a + 3q$. The value of $a + c$ can be determined if the value of $a + (a + 2q) = 2a + 2q$ can be determined.

(1) It is given that $a + b = -8$. Then, $a + (a + q) = 2a + q = -8$. From this, the value of $2a + 2q$ cannot be determined. For example, the values of a and q could be −5 and 2, respectively, or they could be −6 and 4, respectively; NOT sufficient.

(2) It is given that $a + d = 0$. Then, $a + (a + 3q) = 2a + 3q = 0$. From this, the value of $2a + 2q$ cannot be determined. For example, the values of a and q could be −3 and 2, respectively, or they could be −6 and 4, respectively; NOT sufficient.

Taking (1) and (2) together, adding the equations, $2a + q = -8$ and $2a + 3q = 0$ gives $4a + 4q = -8$ and so $2a + 2q = \dfrac{-8}{2} = -4$.

The correct answer is C;
both statements together are sufficient.

DS06067

303. Is $xm < ym$?

(1) $x > y$

(2) $m < 0$

Algebra Inequalities

(1) Given that $x > y$, the inequality $xm < ym$ can be true (for example, if $m = -1$, then $xm < ym$ becomes $-x < -y$, or $x > y$, which is true by assumption) and it is possible that the inequality $xm < ym$ can be false (for example, if $m = 0$, then $xm < ym$ becomes $0 < 0$, which is false); NOT sufficient.

(2) Given that $m < 0$, the inequality $xm < ym$ can be true (for example, if $m = -1$, $x = 2$, and $y = 1$, then $xm < ym$ becomes $-2 < -1$, which is true) and it is possible that the inequality $xm < ym$ can be false (for example, if $m = -1$, $x = 1$, and $y = 2$, then $xm < ym$ becomes $-1 < -2$, which is false); NOT sufficient.

Taking (1) and (2) together, multiplying both sides of the inequality $x > y$ by m reverses the inequality sign (since $m < 0$), which gives $xm < ym$.

The correct answer is C;
both statements together are sufficient.

DS02899

304. If $y = x^2 - 6x + 9$, what is the value of x?

(1) $y = 0$

(2) $x + y = 3$

Algebra Second-Degree Equations

Given that $y = x^2 - 6x + 9 = (x - 3)^2$, what is the value of x?

(1) Given that $y = 0$, it follows that $(x - 3)^2 = 0$, or $x = 3$; SUFFICIENT.

(2) Given that $x + y = 3$, or $y = 3 - x$, then $x = 3$ and $y = 0$ are possible, since $y = (x - 3)^2$ becomes $0 = (3 - 3)^2$, which is true, and $y = 3 - x$ becomes $0 = 3 - 3$, which is true. However, $x = 2$ and $y = 1$ are also possible, since $y = (x - 3)^2$ becomes $1 = (2 - 3)^2$, which is true, and $y = 3 - x$ becomes $1 = 3 - 2$, which is true; NOT sufficient.

Note: The values for x and y used in (2) above can be found by solving $(x - 3)^2 = 3 - x$, which can be rewritten as $x^2 - 6x + 9 = 3 - x$, or $x^2 - 5x + 6 = 0$, or $(x - 3)(x - 2) = 0$.

The correct answer is A;
statement 1 alone is sufficient.

DS06810

305. What is the probability that Lee will make exactly 5 errors on a certain typing test?

(1) The probability that Lee will make 5 or more errors on the test is 0.27.

(2) The probability that Lee will make 5 or fewer errors on the test is 0.85.

Arithmetic Probability

(1) Given that 0.27 is the probability that Lee will make 5 or more errors on the test, it is clearly not possible to determine the probability that Lee will make exactly 5 errors on the test; NOT sufficient.

(2) Given that 0.85 is the probability that Lee will make 5 or fewer errors on the test, it is clearly not possible to determine the probability that Lee will make exactly 5 errors on the test; NOT sufficient.

Taking (1) and (2) together, let E be the event that Lee will make 5 or more errors on the test and let F be the event that Lee will make 5 or fewer errors on the test. Then $P(E \text{ or } F) = 1$, since it will always be the case that, when taking the test, Lee will make at least 5 errors or at most 5 errors. Also, (1) and (2) can be expressed as $P(E) = 0.27$ and $P(F) = 0.85$, and the question asks for the value of $P(E \text{ and } F)$. Using the identity $P(E \text{ or } F) = P(E) + P(F) - P(E \text{ and } F)$, it follows that $1 = 0.27 + 0.85 - P(E \text{ and } F)$, or $P(E \text{ and } F) = 0.27 + 0.85 - 1 = 0.12$. Therefore, the probability that Lee will make exactly 5 errors on the test is 0.12.

The correct answer is C;
both statements together are sufficient.

DS19208

306. If p is a positive integer, is $2^p + 1$ a prime number?

(1) p is a prime number.

(2) p is an even number.

Arithmetic Properties of Integers

Given that p is a positive integer, can we determine whether $2^p + 1$ is a prime number?

(1) Given that p is a prime number, we don't have enough information to determine whether $2^p + 1$ is a prime number. To see this, it best to consider some cases. If $p = 2$, then $2^p + 1 = 2^2 + 1 = 2 \times 2 + 1 = 4 + 1 = 5$, which is prime. And if $p = 3$, then $2^p + 1 = 2^3 + 1 = 2 \times 2 \times 2 + 1 = 8 + 1 = 9$, which is not prime (it is equal to 3×3); NOT sufficient.

(2) Given that p is an even number, we can again consider cases and see that it is impossible to determine whether $2^p + 1$ is a prime number. If $p = 2$ then $2^p + 1 = 2^2 + 1 = 4 + 1 = 5$, which, again, is prime. And if $p = 6$, then $2^p + 1 = 2^6 + 1 = 2 \times 2 \times 2 \times 2 \times 2 \times 2 + 1 = (2 \times 2 \times 2) \times (2 \times 2 \times 2) + 1 = 8 \times 8 + 1 = 64 + 1 = 65$, which is not prime (it is equal to 13×5); NOT sufficient.

Considering the two statements together, we have that p is both prime and even. The only even number that is not divisible by some other positive integer besides 1 is 2. That is, the only prime even integer is 2. $2^p + 1$ is therefore equal to $2^2 + 1 = 5$, which is prime.

The correct answer is C;
both statements together are sufficient.

Questions 307 to 373 - Difficulty: **Hard**

DS60130
307. What percent of the students at University X are enrolled in a science course but are not enrolled in a biology course?

(1) 28 percent of the students at University X are enrolled in a biology course.

(2) 70 percent of the students at University X who are enrolled in a science course are enrolled in a biology course.

Algebra Percents

Under the assumption that a biology course is a type of science course, determine the percent of University X students who are enrolled in a science course, but not in a biology course.

(1) Given that 28% of the students at University X are enrolled in a biology course, if 100% of the students are enrolled in a science course, then $(100 - 28)\% = 72\%$ are enrolled in a science course, but not in a biology course. On the other hand if 50% of the students at University X are enrolled in a science course, then $(50 - 28)\% = 22\%$ are enrolled in a science course, but not in a biology course; NOT sufficient.

(2) Given that 70% of the students at University X who are enrolled in a science course are enrolled in a biology course, if 100% of the students at University X are enrolled in a science course, then $(100 - 70)\% = 30\%$ are enrolled in a science course, but not in a biology course. On the other hand if 50% of the students at University X are enrolled in a science course, then 70% of 50% = 35% are enrolled in a biology course, $(50 - 35)\% = 15\%$ are enrolled in a science course, but not in a biology course; NOT sufficient.

Taking (1) and (2) together, $0.28 = 0.7x$ where x is the percent of the students at University X who are enrolled in a science course. It follows that $x = 0.4$ or 40%. Thus, $(40 - 28)\% = 12\%$ of the students at University X are enrolled in a science course, but not in a biology course.

The correct answer is C;
both statements together are sufficient.

DS02741
308. In the xy-plane, point (r,s) lies on a circle with center at the origin. What is the value of $r^2 + s^2$?

(1) The circle has radius 2.
(2) The point $\left(\sqrt{2}, -\sqrt{2}\right)$ lies on the circle.

Geometry Simple Coordinate Geometry

Let R be the radius of the circle. A right triangle with legs of lengths $|r|$ and $|s|$ can be formed so that the line segment with endpoints (r,s) and $(0,0)$ is the hypotenuse. Since the length of the hypotenuse is R, the Pythagorean theorem for this right triangle gives $R^2 = r^2 + s^2$. Therefore, to determine the value of $r^2 + s^2$, it is sufficient to determine the value of R.

(1) It is given that $R = 2$; SUFFICIENT.

(2) It is given that $\left(\sqrt{2}, -\sqrt{2}\right)$ lies on the circle. A right triangle with legs each of length $\sqrt{2}$ can be formed so that the line segment with endpoints $\left(\sqrt{2}, -\sqrt{2}\right)$ and $(0,0)$ is the hypotenuse. Since the length of the hypotenuse is the radius of the circle, which is R, where $R^2 = r^2 + s^2$, the Pythagorean theorem for this right triangle gives $R^2 = \left(\sqrt{2}\right)^2 + \left(\sqrt{2}\right)^2 = 2 + 2 = 4$. Therefore, $r^2 + s^2 = 4$; SUFFICIENT.

The correct answer is D;
each statement alone is sufficient.

DS06368
309. If r, s, and t are nonzero integers, is $r^5 s^3 t^4$ negative?

(1) rt is negative.
(2) s is negative.

Arithmetic Properties of Numbers

Since $r^5 s^3 t^4 = (rt)^4 rs^3$ and $(rt)^4$ is positive, $r^5 s^3 t^4$ will be negative if and only if rs^3 is negative, or if and only if r and s have opposite signs.

(1) It is given that rt is negative, but nothing can be determined about the sign of s. If the sign of s is the opposite of the sign of r, then $r^5s^3t^4 = (rt)^4rs^3$ will be negative. However, if the sign of s is the same as the sign of r, then $r^5s^3t^4 = (rt)^4rs^3$ will be positive; NOT sufficient.

(2) It is given that s is negative, but nothing can be determined about the sign of r. If r is positive, then $r^5s^3t^4 = (rt)^4rs^3$ will be negative. However, if r is negative, then $r^5s^3t^4 = (rt)^4rs^3$ will be positive; NOT sufficient.

Given (1) and (2), it is still not possible to determine whether r and s have opposite signs. For example, (1) and (2) hold if r is positive, s is negative, and t is negative, and in this case r and s have opposite signs. However, (1) and (2) hold if r is negative, s is negative, and t is positive, and in this case r and s have the same sign.

The correct answer is E;
both statements together are still not sufficient.

DS13706

310. Each Type A machine fills 400 cans per minute, each Type B machine fills 600 cans per minute, and each Type C machine installs 2,400 lids per minute. A lid is installed on each can that is filled and on no can that is not filled. For a particular minute, what is the total number of machines working?

   (1) A total of 4,800 cans are filled that minute.

   (2) For that minute, there are 2 Type B machines working for every Type C machine working.

Algebra Simultaneous Equations

(1) Given that 4,800 cans were filled that minute, it is possible that 12 Type A machines, no Type B machines, and 2 Type C machines were working, for a total of 14 machines, since $(12)(400) + (0)(600) = 4,800$ and $(2)(2,400) = 4,800$. However, it is also possible that no Type A machines, 8 Type B machines, and 2 Type C machines were working, for a total of 10 machines, since $(0)(400) + (8)(600) = 4,800$ and $(2)(2,400) = 4,800$; NOT sufficient.

(2) Given that there are 2 Type B machines working for every Type C machine working,

it is possible that there are 6 machines working—3 Type A machines, 2 Type B machines, and 1 Type C machine. This gives $3(400) + 2(600) = 2,400$ cans and $1(2,400) = 2,400$ lids. It is also possible that there are 12 machines working—6 Type A machines, 4 Type B machines, and 2 Type C machines. This gives $6(400) + 4(600) = 4,800$ cans and $2(2,400) = 4,800$ lids; NOT sufficient.

Taking (1) and (2) together, since there were 4,800 cans filled that minute, there were 4,800 lids installed that minute. It follows that 2 Type C machines were working that minute, since $(2)(2,400) = 4,800$. Since there were twice this number of Type B machines working that minute, it follows that 4 Type B machines were working that minute. These 4 Type B machines filled $(4)(600) = 2,400$ cans that minute, leaving $4,800 − 2,400 = 2,400$ cans to be filled by Type A machines. Therefore, the number of Type A machines working that minute was $\frac{2,400}{400} = 6$, and it follows that the total number of machines working that minute was $2 + 4 + 6 = 12$.

The correct answer is C;
both statements together are sufficient.

DS08660

311. If a and b are constants, what is the value of a?

   (1) $a < b$

   (2) $(t - a)(t - b) = t^2 + t - 12$, for all values of t.

Algebra Second-Degree Equations

(1) Given that $a < b$, it is not possible to determine the value of a. For example, $a < b$ is true when $a = 1$ and $b = 2$, and $a < b$ is true when $a = 2$ and $b = 3$; NOT sufficient.

(2) By factoring, what is given can be expressed as $(t - a)(t - b) = (t + 4)(t - 3)$, so either $a = −4$ and $b = 3$, or $a = 3$ and $b = −4$; NOT sufficient.

Taking (1) and (2) together, the relation $a < b$ is satisfied by only one of the two possibilities given in the discussion of (2) above, namely $a = −4$ and $b = 3$. Therefore, the value of a is −4.

The correct answer is C;
both statements together are sufficient.

DS04474
312. If x is a positive integer, is $\sqrt{x}$ an integer?

   (1) $\sqrt{4x}$ is an integer.

   (2) $\sqrt{3x}$ is not an integer.

Algebra Radicals

(1) It is given that $\sqrt{4x} = n$, or $4x = n^2$, for some positive integer n. Since $4x$ is the square of an integer, it follows that in the prime factorization of $4x$, each distinct prime factor is repeated an even number of times. Therefore, the same must be true for the prime factorization of x, since the prime factorization of x only differs from the prime factorization of $4x$ by two factors of 2, and hence by an even number of factors of 2; SUFFICIENT.

(2) Given that $\sqrt{3x}$ is not an integer, it is possible for $\sqrt{x}$ to be an integer (for example, $x = 1$) and it is possible for $\sqrt{x}$ to not be an integer (for example, $x = 2$); NOT sufficient.

**The correct answer is A;
statement 1 alone is sufficient.**

DS16456
313. If p, q, x, y, and z are different positive integers, which of the five integers is the median?

   (1) $p + x < q$

   (2) $y < z$

Arithmetic Statistics

Since there are five different integers, there are two integers greater and two integers less than the median, which is the middle number.

(1) No information is given about the order of y and z with respect to the other three numbers; NOT sufficient.

(2) This statement does not relate y and z to the other three integers; NOT sufficient.

Because (1) and (2) taken together do not relate p, x, and q to y and z, it is impossible to tell which is the median. For example, if $p = 3$, $x = 4$, $q = 8$, $y = 9$, and $z = 10$, then the median is 8, but if $p = 3$, $x = 4$, $q = 8$, $y = 1$, and $z = 2$, then the median is 3.

**The correct answer is E;
both statements together are still not sufficient.**

DS16277
314. If $w + z = 28$, what is the value of wz?

   (1) w and z are positive integers.

   (2) w and z are consecutive odd integers.

Arithmetic Arithmetic Operations

(1) The fact that w and z are both positive integers does not allow the values of w and z to be determined because, for example, if $w = 20$ and $z = 8$, then $wz = 160$, and if $w = 10$ and $z = 18$, then $wz = 180$; NOT sufficient.

(2) Since w and z are consecutive odd integers whose sum is 28, it is reasonable to consider the possibilities for the sum of consecutive odd integers: $\ldots, (-5) + (-3) = -8$, $(-3) + (-1) = -4$, $(-1) + 1 = 0$, $1 + 3 = 4,\ldots$, $9 + 11 = 20$, $11 + 13 = 24$, $13 + 15 = 28$, $15 + 17 = 32, \ldots$. From this list it follows that only one pair of consecutive odd integers has 28 for its sum, and hence there is exactly one possible value for wz.

This problem can also be solved algebraically by letting the consecutive odd integers w and z be represented by $2n + 1$ and $2n + 3$, where n can be any integer. Since $28 = w + z$, it follows that

$$28 = (2n+1)+(2n+3)$$

$28 = 4n + 4$	simplify
$24 = 4n$	subtract 4 from both sides
$6 = n$	divide both sides by 4

Thus, $w = 2(6) + 1 = 13$, $z = 2(6) + 3 = 15$, and hence exactly one value can be determined for wz; SUFFICIENT.

**The correct answer is B;
statement 2 alone is sufficient.**

DS02474
315. If $abc \neq 0$, is $\dfrac{\frac{a}{b}}{c} = \dfrac{a}{\frac{b}{c}}$?

   (1) $a = 1$

   (2) $c = 1$

Algebra Fractions

Since $\dfrac{\dfrac{a}{b}}{c} = \dfrac{a}{b} \div c = \dfrac{a}{b} \times \dfrac{1}{c} = \dfrac{a}{bc}$ and

$\dfrac{\dfrac{a}{b}}{c} = a \div \dfrac{b}{c} = a \times \dfrac{c}{b} = \dfrac{ac}{b}$, it is to be

determined whether $\dfrac{a}{bc} = \dfrac{ac}{b}$.

(1) Given that $a = 1$, the equation to be investigated, $\dfrac{a}{bc} = \dfrac{ac}{b}$, is $\dfrac{1}{bc} = \dfrac{c}{b}$. This equation can be true for some nonzero values of b and c (for example, $b = c = 1$) and false for other nonzero values of b and c (for example, $b = 1$ and $c = 2$); NOT sufficient.

(2) Given that $c = 1$, the equation to be investigated, $\dfrac{a}{bc} = \dfrac{ac}{b}$, is $\dfrac{a}{b} = \dfrac{a}{b}$. This equation is true for all nonzero values of a and b; SUFFICIENT.

**The correct answer is B;
statement 2 alone is sufficient.**

DS14471
316. The arithmetic mean of a collection of 5 positive integers, not necessarily distinct, is 9. One additional positive integer is included in the collection and the arithmetic mean of the 6 integers is computed. Is the arithmetic mean of the 6 integers at least 10 ?

(1) The additional integer is at least 14.
(2) The additional integer is a multiple of 5.

Arithmetic Statistics

Since the arithmetic mean of the 5 integers is 9, the sum of the 5 integers divided by 5 is equal to 9, and hence the sum of the 5 integers is equal to $(5)(9) = 45$. Let x be the additional positive integer. Then the sum of the 6 integers is $45 + x$, and the arithmetic mean of the 6 integers is $\dfrac{45+x}{6}$. Determine whether $\dfrac{45+x}{6} \geq 10$, or equivalently, whether $45 + x \geq 60$, or equivalently, whether $x \geq 15$.

(1) Given that $x \geq 14$, then x could equal 14 and $x \geq 15$ is not true, or x could equal 15 and $x \geq 15$ is true; NOT sufficient.

(2) Given that x is a multiple of 5, then x could equal 10 and $x \geq 15$ is not true, or x could equal 15 and $x \geq 15$ is true; NOT sufficient.

Taking (1) and (2) together, then x is a multiple of 5 that is greater than or equal to 14, and so x could equal one of the numbers 15, 20, 25, 30, …. Each of these numbers is greater than or equal to 15.

**The correct answer is C;
both statements together are sufficient.**

DS11003
317. A certain list consists of 400 different numbers. Is the average (arithmetic mean) of the numbers in the list greater than the median of the numbers in the list?

(1) Of the numbers in the list, 280 are less than the average.
(2) Of the numbers in the list, 30 percent are greater than or equal to the average.

Arithmetic Statistics

In a list of 400 numbers, the median will be halfway between the 200th and the 201st numbers in the list when the numbers are ordered from least to greatest.

(1) This indicates that 280 of the 400 numbers in the list are less than the average of the 400 numbers. This means that both the 200th and the 201st numbers, as well as the median, are less than the average and, therefore, that the average is greater than the median; SUFFICIENT.

(2) This indicates that $(0.3)(400) = 120$ of the numbers are greater than or equal to the average. This means that the other $400 - 120 = 280$ numbers are less than the average, which is the same as the information in (1); SUFFICIENT.

**The correct answer is D;
each statement alone is sufficient.**

DS03678
318. In a two-month survey of shoppers, each shopper bought one of two brands of detergent, X or Y, in the first month and again bought one of these brands in the second month. In the survey, 90 percent of the shoppers who bought Brand X in the first month bought Brand X again in the second month, while 60 percent of the shoppers who bought Brand Y in the first month bought

Brand Y again in the second month. What percent of the shoppers bought Brand Y in the second month?

(1) In the first month, 50 percent of the shoppers bought Brand X.

(2) The total number of shoppers surveyed was 5,000.

Arithmetic Percents

This problem can be solved by using the following contingency table where A and B represent, respectively, the number of shoppers who bought Brand X and the number of shoppers who bought Brand Y in the first month; C and D represent, respectively, the number of shoppers who bought Brand X and the number of shoppers who bought Brand Y in the second month; and T represents the total number of shoppers in the survey. Also in the table, $0.9A$ represents the 90% of the shoppers who bought Brand X in the first month and also bought it in the second month, and $0.1A$ represents the $(100 - 90)\% = 10\%$ of the shoppers who bought Brand X in the first month and Brand Y in the second month. Similarly, $0.6B$ represents the 60% of the shoppers who bought Brand Y in the first month and also bought it in the second month, and $0.4B$ represents the $(100 - 60)\% = 40\%$ of the shoppers who bought Brand Y in the first month and Brand X in the second month.

		Second Month		
		X	**Y**	**Total**
First Month	**X**	$0.9A$	$0.1A$	A
	Y	$0.4B$	$0.6B$	B
	Total	C	D	T

Determine the value of $\dfrac{D}{T}$ as a percentage.

(1) This indicates that 50% of the shoppers bought Brand X in the first month, so $A = 0.5T$. It follows that the other 50% of the shoppers bought Brand Y in the first month, so $B = 0.5T$. Then, $D = 0.1A + 0.6B = 0.1(0.5T) + 0.6(0.5T) = 0.05T + 0.30T = 0.35T$. It follows that $\dfrac{D}{T} = \dfrac{0.35T}{T} = 0.35$, which is 35%; SUFFICIENT.

(2) This indicates that $T = 5,000$, as shown in the following table:

		Second Month		
		X	**Y**	**Total**
First Month	**X**	$0.9A$	$0.1A$	A
	Y	$0.4B$	$0.6B$	B
	Total	C	D	5,000

But not enough information is given to be able to determine D or D as a percentage of 5,000; NOT sufficient.

The correct answer is A; statement 1 alone is sufficient.

DS15902

319. If m and n are positive integers, is $m + n$ divisible by 4 ?

(1) m and n are each divisible by 2.

(2) Neither m nor n is divisible by 4.

Arithmetic Properties of Numbers

Determine whether the sum of the positive integers m and n is divisible by 4.

(1) It is given that m is divisible by 2 and n is divisible by 2. If, for example, $m = 2$ and $n = 2$, then each of m and n is divisible by 2 and $m + n = 2 + 2 = 4$, which is divisible by 4. However, if $m = 2$ and $n = 4$, then each of m and n is divisible by 2 and $m + n = 2 + 4 = 6$, which is not divisible by 4; NOT sufficient.

(2) It is given that neither m nor n is divisible by 4. If, for example, $m = 3$ and $n = 5$, then neither m nor n is divisible by 4 and $m + n = 3 + 5 = 8$, which is divisible by 4. On the other hand, if $m = 3$ and $n = 6$, then neither m nor n is divisible by 4 and $m + n = 3 + 6 = 9$, which is not divisible by 4; NOT sufficient.

Taking (1) and (2) together, m is not divisible by 4, so $m = 4q + r$, where q is a positive integer and $0 < r < 4$. However, m is divisible by 2, so r must be even. Since the only positive even integer less than 4 is 2, then $r = 2$ and $m = 4q + 2$. Similarly, since n is divisible by 2 but not by 4, $n = 4s + 2$. It follows that $m + n = (4q + 2) + (4s + 2) = 4q + 4s + 4 = 4(q + s + 1)$, and $m + n$ is divisible by 4.

The correct answer is C; both statements together are sufficient.

DS02940
320. What is the area of rectangular region R?

    (1)   Each diagonal of R has length 5.

    (2)   The perimeter of R is 14.

Geometry Rectangles

Let L and W be the length and width of the rectangle, respectively. Determine the value of LW.

    (1)   It is given that a diagonal's length is 5. Thus, by the Pythagorean theorem, it follows that $L^2 + W^2 = 5^2 = 25$. The value of LW cannot be determined, however, because $L = \sqrt{15}$ and $W = \sqrt{10}$ satisfy $L^2 + W^2 = 25$ with $LW = \sqrt{150}$, and $L = \sqrt{5}$ and $W = \sqrt{20}$ satisfy $L^2 + W^2 = 25$ with $LW = \sqrt{100}$; NOT sufficient.

    (2)   It is given that $2L + 2W = 14$, or $L + W = 7$, or $L = 7 - W$. Therefore, $LW = (7 - W)W$, which can vary in value. For example, if $L = 3$ and $W = 4$, then $L + W = 7$ and $LW = 12$. However, if $L = 2$ and $W = 5$, then $L + W = 7$ and $LW = 10$; NOT sufficient.

Given (1) and (2) together, it follows from (2) that $(L + W)^2 = 7^2 = 49$, or $L^2 + W^2 + 2LW = 49$. Using (1), 25 can be substituted for $L^2 + W^2$ to obtain $25 + 2LW = 49$, or $2LW = 24$, or $LW = 12$. Alternatively, $7 - W$ can be substituted for L in $L^2 + W^2 = 25$ to obtain the quadratic equation $(7 - W)^2 + W^2 = 25$, or $49 - 14W + W^2 + W^2 = 25$, or $2W^2 - 14W + 24 = 0$, or $W^2 - 7W + 12 = 0$. The left side of the last equation can be factored to give $(W - 4)(W - 3) = 0$. Therefore, $W = 4$, which gives $L = 7 - W = 7 - 4 = 3$ and $LW = (3)(4) = 12$, or $W = 3$, which gives $L = 7 - W = 7 - 3 = 4$ and $LW = (4)(3) = 12$. Since $LW = 12$ in either case, a unique value for LW can be determined.

**The correct answer is C;
both statements together are sufficient.**

DS17137
321. How many integers n are there such that $r < n < s$?

    (1) $s - r = 5$

    (2) r and s are not integers.

Arithmetic Properties of Numbers

    (1)   The difference between s and r is 5. If r and s are integers (e.g., 7 and 12), the number of integers between them (i.e., n could be 8,

9, 10, or 11) is 4. If r and s are not integers (e.g., 6.5 and 11.5), then the number of integers between them (i.e., n could be 7, 8, 9, 10, or 11) is 5. No information is given that allows a determination of whether s and r are integers; NOT sufficient.

    (2)   No information is given about the difference between r and s. If $r = 0.4$ and $s = 0.5$, then r and s have no integers between them. However, if $r = 0.4$ and $s = 3.5$, then r and s have 3 integers between them; NOT sufficient.

Using the information from both (1) and (2), it can be determined that, because r and s are not integers, there are 5 integers between them.

**The correct answer is C;
both statements together are sufficient.**

DS17147
322. If the total price of n equally priced shares of a certain stock was \$12,000, what was the price per share of the stock?

    (1)   If the price per share of the stock had been \$1 more, the total price of the n shares would have been \$300 more.

    (2)   If the price per share of the stock had been \$2 less, the total price of the n shares would have been 5 percent less.

Arithmetic Arithmetic Operations; Percents

Since the price per share of the stock can be expressed as $\dfrac{\$12{,}000}{n}$, determining the value of n is sufficient to answer this question.

    (1)   A per-share increase of \$1 and a total increase of \$300 for n shares of stock mean together that $n(\$1) = \$300$. It follows that $n = 300$; SUFFICIENT.

    (2)   If the price of each of the n shares had been reduced by \$2, the total reduction in price would have been 5 percent less or 0.05(\$12,000). The equation $2n = 0.05(\$12{,}000)$ expresses this relationship. The value of n can be determined to be 300 from this equation; SUFFICIENT.

**The correct answer is D;
each statement alone is sufficient.**

DS02865
323. If n is positive, is $\sqrt{n} > 100$?

   (1) $\sqrt{n-1} > 99$
   (2) $\sqrt{n+1} > 101$

Algebra Radicals

Determine if $\sqrt{n} > 100$ or equivalently, if $n > (100)(100) = 10{,}000$.

   (1) Given that $\sqrt{n-1} > 99$, or equivalently, $n - 1 > (99)(99)$, it follows from

$$
\begin{aligned}
(99)(99) &= 99(100 - 1) \\
&= 9{,}900 - 99 \\
&= 9{,}801
\end{aligned}
$$

   that $\sqrt{n-1} > 99$ is equivalent to $n - 1 > 9{,}801$, or $n > 9{,}802$. Since $n > 9{,}802$ allows for values of n that are greater than $10{,}000$ and $n > 9{,}802$ allows for values of n that are not greater than $10{,}000$, it cannot be determined if $n > 10{,}000$; NOT sufficient.

   (2) Given that $\sqrt{n+1} > 101$, or equivalently, $n + 1 > (101)(101)$, it follows from

$$
\begin{aligned}
(101)(101) &= 101(100 + 1) \\
&= 10{,}100 + 101 \\
&= 10{,}201
\end{aligned}
$$

   that $\sqrt{n+1} > 101$ is equivalent to $n + 1 > 10{,}201$, or $n > 10{,}200$. Since $10{,}200 > 10{,}000$, it can be determined that $n > 10{,}000$; SUFFICIENT.

**The correct answer is B;
statement 2 alone is sufficient.**

DS17150
324. Is $xy > 5$?

   (1) $1 \le x \le 3$ and $2 \le y \le 4$.
   (2) $x + y = 5$

Algebra Inequalities

   (1) While it is known that $1 \le x \le 3$ and $2 \le y \le 4$, xy could be $(3)(4) = 12$, which is greater than 5, or xy could be $(1)(2) = 2$, which is not greater than 5; NOT sufficient.

   (2) Given that $x + y = 5$, xy could be 6 (when $x = 2$ and $y = 3$), which is greater than 5, and

xy could be 4 (when $x = 1$ and $y = 4$), which is not greater than 5; NOT sufficient.

Both (1) and (2) together are not sufficient since the two examples given in (2) are consistent with both statements.

**The correct answer is E;
both statements together are still not sufficient.**

DS17151
325. In Year X, 8.7 percent of the men in the labor force were unemployed in June compared with 8.4 percent in May. If the number of men in the labor force was the same for both months, how many men were unemployed in June of that year?

   (1) In May of Year X, the number of unemployed men in the labor force was 3.36 million.
   (2) In Year X, 120,000 more men in the labor force were unemployed in June than in May.

Arithmetic Percents

Since 8.7 percent of the men in the labor force were unemployed in June, the number of unemployed men could be calculated if the total number of men in the labor force was known. Let t represent the total number of men in the labor force.

   (1) This implies that for May $(8.4\%)t = 3{,}360{,}000$, from which the value of t can be determined; SUFFICIENT.

   (2) This implies that $(8.7\% - 8.4\%)t = 120{,}000$ or $(0.3\%)t = 120{,}000$. This equation can be solved for t; SUFFICIENT.

**The correct answer is D;
each statement alone is sufficient.**

DS17112
326. If $x \ne 0$, what is the value of $\left(\dfrac{x^p}{x^q}\right)^4$?

   (1) $p = q$
   (2) $x = 3$

Arithmetic; Algebra Arithmetic Operations;
Simplifying Expressions

   (1) Since $p = q$, it follows that

$$\left(\frac{x^p}{x^q}\right)^4 = \left(\frac{x^p}{x^p}\right)^4 = (1)^4;\ \text{SUFFICIENT.}$$

(2) Since $x = 3$ (and, therefore, $x \neq 1$) and the values of p or q are unknown, the value of the expression $\left(\dfrac{x^p}{x^q}\right)^4$ cannot be determined; NOT sufficient.

The correct answer is A; statement 1 alone is sufficient.

DS17153

327. On Monday morning a certain machine ran continuously at a uniform rate to fill a production order. At what time did it completely fill the order that morning?

(1) The machine began filling the order at 9:30 a.m.

(2) The machine had filled $\dfrac{1}{2}$ of the order by 10:30 a.m. and $\dfrac{5}{6}$ of the order by 11:10 a.m.

Arithmetic Arithmetic Operations

(1) This merely states what time the machine began filling the order; NOT sufficient.

(2) In the 40 minutes between 10:30 a.m. and 11:10 a.m., $\dfrac{5}{6} - \dfrac{1}{2} = \dfrac{1}{3}$ of the order was filled. Therefore, the entire order was completely filled in $3 \times 40 = 120$ minutes, or 2 hours. Since half the order took 1 hour and was filled by 10:30 a.m., the second half of the order, and thus the entire order, was filled by 11:30 a.m.; SUFFICIENT.

The correct answer is B; statement 2 alone is sufficient.

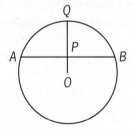

DS17107

328. What is the radius of the circle above with center O?

(1) The ratio of OP to PQ is 1 to 2.

(2) P is the midpoint of chord AB.

Geometry Circles

(1) It can be concluded only that the radius is 3 times the length of OP, which is unknown; NOT sufficient.

(2) It can be concluded only that $AP = PB$, and the chord is irrelevant to the radius; NOT sufficient.

Together, (1) and (2) do not give the length of any line segment shown in the circle. In fact, if the circle and all the line segments were uniformly expanded by a factor of, say, 5, the resulting circle and line segments would still satisfy both (1) and (2). Therefore, the radius of the circle cannot be determined from (1) and (2) together.

The correct answer is E; both statements together are still not sufficient.

DS15618

329. If a and b are positive integers, what is the value of the product ab?

(1) The least common multiple of a and b is 48.

(2) The greatest common factor of a and b is 4.

Arithmetic Properties of Numbers

Determine the value of the product of positive integers a and b.

(1) This indicates that the least common multiple (lcm) of a and b is 48, which means that 48 is the least integer that is a multiple of both a and b. If $a = 24$ and $b = 16$, then the multiples of a are 24, 48, 72, ..., and the multiples of b are 16, 32, 48, 64, ... So, 48 is the lcm of 24 and 16, and $ab = (24)(16)$. However, if $a = 48$ and $b = 16$, then the multiples of a are 48, 96, ..., and the multiples of b are 16, 32, 48, 64, ... So, 48 is the lcm of 48 and 16, and $ab = (48)(16)$; NOT sufficient.

(2) This indicates that 4 is the greatest common factor (gcf) of a and b, which means that 4 is the greatest integer that is a factor of both a and b. If $a = 4$ and $b = 4$, then 4 is the gcf a and b, and $ab = (4)(4)$. However, if $a = 4$ and $b = 16$, then 4 is the gcf of a and b, and $ab = (4)(16)$; NOT sufficient.

Taking (1) and (2) together, each of a and b is a multiple of 4 (which means that each of a and b is divisible by 4) and 48 is a multiple of each of a and b (which means that 48 is divisible by each of a and b). It follows that the only possible values for a and b are 4, 8, 12, 16, 24, and 48. The following table shows all possible pairs of these values and that only 4 of them ($a = 4$ and $b = 48$,

$a = 12$ and $b = 16$, $a = 16$ and $b = 12$, $a = 48$ and $b = 4$), satisfy both (1) and (2).

		b					
		4	**8**	**12**	**16**	**24**	**48**
a	**4**	lcm is 4, not 48	lcm is 8, not 48	lcm is 12, not 48	lcm is 16, not 48	lcm is 24, not 48	lcm is 48, gcf is 4
	8	lcm is 8, not 48	lcm is 8, not 48	lcm is 24, not 48	gcf is 8, not 4	gcf is 8, not 4	gcf is 8, not 4
	12	lcm is 12, not 48	lcm is 24, not 48	gcf is 12, not 4	lcm is 48, gcf is 4	gcf is 12, not 4	gcf is 12, not 4
	16	lcm is 16, not 48	gcf is 8, not 4	lcm is 48, gcf is 4	gcf is 16, not 4	gcf is 8, not 4	gcf is 16, not 4
	24	lcm is 24, not 48	gcf is 8, not 4	gcf is 12, not 4	gcf is 8, not 4	gcf is 24, not 4	gcf is 24, not 4
	48	lcm is 48, gcf is 4	gcf is 8, not 4	gcf is 12, not 4	gcf is 16, not 4	gcf is 24, not 4	gcf is 48, not 4

In each case where both (1) and (2) are satisfied, $ab = 192$.

Alternatively,

(1) Using prime factorizations, since the least common multiple of a and b is 48 and $48 = 2^4 \cdot 3^1$, it follows that $a = 2^p \cdot 3^q$, where $p \le 4$ and $q \le 1$, and $b = 2^r \cdot 3^s$, where $r \le 4$ and $s \le 1$. Since the least common multiple of two positive integers is the product of the highest power of each prime in the prime factorizations of the two integers, one of p or r must be 4 and one of q or s must be 1. If, for example, $p = 4$, $q = 1$, and $r = s = 0$, then $a = 2^4 \cdot 3^1 = 48$, $b = 2^0 \cdot 3^0 = 1$, and $ab = (48)(1) = 48$. However, if $p = 4$, $q = 1$, $r = 4$, and $s = 1$, then $a = 2^4 \cdot 3^1 = 48$, $b = 2^4 \cdot 3^1 = 48$, and $ab = (48)(48) = 2{,}304$; NOT sufficient.

(2) If $a = 4$ and $b = 4$, then the greatest common factor of a and b is 4 and $ab = (4)(4) = 16$. However, if $a = 4$ and $b = 12$, then the greatest common factor of a and b is 4 and $ab = (4)(12) = 48$; NOT sufficient.

Taking (1) and (2) together, by (1), $a = 2^p \cdot 3^q$, where $p \le 4$ and $q \le 1$, and $b = 2^r \cdot 3^s$, where $r \le 4$ and $s \le 1$. Since the least common multiple of two positive integers is the product of the highest power of each prime in the prime factorizations of the two integers, exactly one of p or r must be 4 and the other one must be 2. Otherwise, either the least common multiple of a and b would not be 48 or the greatest common factor would not be 4. Likewise, exactly one of q or s must be 1 and the other one must be 0. The following table gives all possible combinations of values for p, q, r, and s along with corresponding values of a, b, and ab.

p	q	r	s	$a = 2^p \cdot 3^q$	$b = 2^r \cdot 3^s$	ab
2	0	4	1	$2^2 \cdot 3^0 = 4$	$2^4 \cdot 3^1 = 48$	192
2	1	4	0	$2^2 \cdot 3^1 = 12$	$2^4 \cdot 3^0 = 16$	192
4	0	2	1	$2^4 \cdot 3^0 = 16$	$2^2 \cdot 3^1 = 12$	192
4	1	2	0	$2^4 \cdot 3^1 = 48$	$2^2 \cdot 3^0 = 4$	192

In each case, $ab = 192$.

The correct answer is C;
both statements together are sufficient.

DS17095

330. What is the number of 360-degree rotations that a bicycle wheel made while rolling 100 meters in a straight line without slipping?

(1) The diameter of the bicycle wheel, including the tire, was 0.5 meter.

(2) The wheel made twenty 360-degree rotations per minute.

Geometry Circles

For each 360-degree rotation, the wheel has traveled a distance equal to its circumference. Given either the circumference of the wheel or the means to calculate its circumference, it is thus possible to determine the number of times the circumference of the wheel was laid out along the straight-line path of 100 meters.

(1) The circumference of the bicycle wheel can be determined from the given diameter using the equation $C = \pi d$, where d = the diameter; SUFFICIENT.

(2) The speed of the rotations is irrelevant, and no dimensions of the wheel are given; NOT sufficient.

The correct answer is A; statement 1 alone is sufficient.

DS17168

331. In the equation $x^2 + bx + 12 = 0$, x is a variable and b is a constant. What is the value of b ?

(1) $x - 3$ is a factor of $x^2 + bx + 12$.

(2) 4 is a root of the equation $x^2 + bx + 12 = 0$.

Algebra First- and Second-Degree Equations

(1) Method 1: If $x - 3$ is a factor, then $x^2 + bx + 12 = (x - 3)(x + c)$ for some constant c. Equating the constant terms (or substituting $x = 0$), it follows that $12 = -3c$, or $c = -4$. Therefore, the quadratic polynomial is $(x - 3)(x - 4)$, which is equal to $x^2 - 7x + 12$, and hence $b = -7$.

Method 2: If $x - 3$ is a factor of $x^2 + bx + 12$, then 3 is a root of $x^2 + bx + 12 = 0$. Therefore, $3^2 + 3b + 12 = 0$, which can be solved to get $b = -7$.

Method 3: The value of b can be found by long division:

$$x - 3 \overline{\smash{\big)}\ x^2 + bx + 12}$$
$$\ \underline{x^2 - 3x}$$
$$(b + 3)x + 12$$
$$\underline{(b + 3)x - 3b - 9}$$
$$3b + 21$$

with quotient $x + (b + 3)$.

These calculations show that the remainder is $3b + 21$. Since the remainder must be 0, it follows that $3b + 21 = 0$, or $b = -7$; SUFFICIENT.

(2) If 4 is a root of the equation, then 4 can be substituted for x in the equation $x^2 + bx + 12 = 0$, yielding $4^2 + 4b + 12 = 0$. This last equation can be solved to obtain a unique value for b; SUFFICIENT.

The correct answer is D; each statement alone is sufficient.

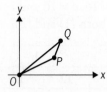

DS07715

332. In the figure above, line segment OP has slope $\frac{1}{2}$ and line segment PQ has slope 2. What is the slope of line segment OQ ?

(1) Line segment OP has length $2\sqrt{5}$.

(2) The coordinates of point Q are (5,4).

Geometry Coordinate Geometry

Let P have coordinates (a,b) and Q have coordinates (x,y). Since the slope of $\overline{OP}$ is $\frac{1}{2}$, it follows that $\frac{b - 0}{a - 0} = \frac{1}{2}$, or $a = 2b$. What is the slope of $\overline{OQ}$?

(1) Given that $\overline{OP}$ has length $2\sqrt{5}$, it follows from the Pythagorean theorem that $a^2 + b^2 = \left(2\sqrt{5}\right)^2$, or $(2b)^2 + b^2 = 20$, or $5b^2 = 20$. The only positive solution of this equation is $b = 2$, and therefore $a = 2b = 4$ and the coordinates of P are $(a,b) = (4,2)$. However, nothing is known about how far Q is from P. If Q is close to P, then the slope of $\overline{OQ}$ will be close to $\frac{1}{2}$ (the slope of $\overline{OP}$), and if Q is far from P, then the slope of $\overline{OQ}$ will be close to 2 (the slope of $\overline{PQ}$). To be explicit, since the slope of $\overline{PQ}$ is 2, it follows that $\frac{y - 2}{x - 4} = 2$, or $y = 2x - 6$. Choosing $x = 4.1$ and $y = 2(4.1) - 6 = 2.2$ gives $(x,y) = (4.1,2.2)$, and the slope of $\overline{OQ}$ is $\frac{2.2}{4.1}$, which is close to $\frac{1}{2}$. On the other hand, choosing $x = 100$ and $y = 2(100) - 6 = 194$ gives $(x,y) = (100,194)$, and the slope of $\overline{OQ}$ is $\frac{194}{100}$, which is close to 2; NOT sufficient.

(2) Given that the coordinates of point Q are (5,4), it follows that the slope of $\overline{OQ}$ is $\frac{4 - 0}{5 - 0} = \frac{4}{5}$; SUFFICIENT.

The correct answer is B; statement 2 alone is sufficient.

DS17164

333. In $\triangle XYZ$, what is the length of YZ?

(1) The length of XY is 3.

(2) The length of XZ is 5.

Geometry Triangles

Given the length of one side of a triangle, it is known that the sum of the lengths of the other two sides is greater than that given length. The length of either of the other two sides, however, can be any positive number.

(1) Only the length of one side, XY, is given, and that is not enough to determine the length of YZ; NOT sufficient.

(2) Again, only the length of one side, XZ, is given and that is not enough to determine the length of YZ; NOT sufficient.

Even by using the triangle inequality stated above, only a range of values for YZ can be determined from (1) and (2). If the length of side YZ is represented by k, then it is known both that $3 + 5 > k$ and that $3 + k > 5$, or $k > 2$. Combining these inequalities to determine the length of k yields only that $8 > k > 2$.

The correct answer is E; both statements together are still not sufficient.

DS07217

334. If the average (arithmetic mean) of n consecutive odd integers is 10, what is the least of the integers?

(1) The range of the n integers is 14.

(2) The greatest of the n integers is 17.

Arithmetic Statistics

Let k be the least of the n consecutive odd integers. Then the n consecutive odd integers are $k, k + 2, k + 4, \ldots, k + 2(n - 1)$, where $k + 2(n - 1)$ is the greatest of the n consecutive odd integers and $[k + 2(n - 1)] - k = 2(n - 1)$ is the range of the n consecutive odd integers. Determine the value of k.

(1) Given that the range of the odd integers is 14, it follows that $2(n - 1) = 14$, or $n - 1 = 7$, or $n = 8$. It is also given that the average of the 8 consecutive odd integers is 10, and so, $\dfrac{k + (k + 2) + (k + 4) + \ldots + (k + 14)}{8} = 10$

from which a unique value for k can be determined; SUFFICIENT.

(2) Given that the greatest of the odd integers is 17, it follows that the n consecutive odd integers can be expressed as $17, 17 - 2$, $17 - 4, \ldots, 17 - 2(n - 1)$. Since the average of the n consecutive odd integers is 10, then

$$\frac{17 + (17 - 2) + (17 - 4) + \ldots + [17 - 2(n - 1)]}{n} = 10,$$

or

$$17 + (17 - 2) + (17 - 4) + \ldots + [17 - 2(n - 1)] = 10n \text{ (i)}$$

The n consecutive odd integers can also be expressed as $k, k + 2, k + 4, \ldots, k + 2(n - 1)$.

Since the average of the n consecutive odd integers is 10, then

$$\frac{k + (k + 2) + (k + 4) + \ldots + [k + 2(n - 1)]}{n} = 10,$$

or

$$k + (k + 2) + (k + 4) + \ldots + [k + 2(n - 1)] = 10n \text{ (ii)}$$

Adding equations (i) and (ii) gives
$$(17 + k) + (17 + k) + (17 + k) + \ldots + (17 + k) = 20n$$
$$n(17 + k) = 20n$$
$$17 + k = 20$$
$$k = 3$$

Alternatively, because the numbers are consecutive odd integers, they form a data set that is symmetric about its average, and so the average of the numbers is the average of the least and greatest numbers. Therefore, $10 = \dfrac{k + 17}{2}$, from which a unique value for k can be determined; SUFFICIENT.

The correct answer is D; each statement alone is sufficient.

DS16044

335. If x, y, and z are positive numbers, is $x > y > z$?

(1) $xz > yz$

(2) $yx > yz$

Algebra Inequalities

(1) Dividing both sides of the inequality by z yields $x > y$. However, there is no information relating z to either x or y; NOT sufficient.

(2) Dividing both sides of the inequality by
 y yields only that $x > z$, with no further
 information relating y to either x or z; NOT
 sufficient.

From (1) and (2) it can be determined that x is
greater than both y and z. Since it still cannot be
determined which of y or z is the least, the correct
ordering of the three numbers also cannot be
determined.

**The correct answer is E;
both statements together are still not sufficient.**

DS06644
336. K is a set of numbers such that

(i)   if x is in K, then $-x$ is in K, and

(ii) if each of x and y is in K, then xy is in K.

Is 12 in K?

(1) 2 is in K.
(2) 3 is in K.

Arithmetic Properties of Numbers

(1) Given that 2 is in K, it follows that K
 could be the set of all real numbers,
 which contains 12. However, if K is the set
 $\{\ldots, -16, -8, -4, -2, 2, 4, 8, 16, \ldots\}$, then K
 contains 2 and K satisfies both (i) and (ii), but
 K does not contain 12. To see that K satisfies
 (ii), note that K can be written as $\{\ldots, -2^4,$
 $-2^3, -2^2, -2^1, 2^1, 2^2, 2^3, 2^4, \ldots\}$, and thus a
 verification of (ii) can reduce to verifying that
 the sum of two positive integer exponents is a
 positive integer exponent; NOT sufficient.

(2) Given that 3 is in K, it follows that K could
 be the set of all real numbers, which contains
 12. However, if K is the set $\{\ldots, -81, -27, -9,$
 $-3, 3, 9, 27, 81, \ldots\}$, then K contains 3 and
 K satisfies both (i) and (ii), but K does not
 contain 12. To see that K satisfies (ii), note
 that K can be written as $\{\ldots, -3^4, -3^3, -3^2,$
 $-3^1, 3^1, 3^2, 3^3, 3^4, \ldots\}$, and thus a verification
 of (ii) can reduce to verifying that the sum of
 two positive integer exponents is a positive
 integer exponent; NOT sufficient.

Given (1) and (2), it follows that both 2 and 3 are
in K. Thus, by (ii), (2)(3) = 6 is in K. Therefore,
by (ii), (2)(6) = 12 is in K.

**The correct answer is C;
both statements together are sufficient.**

DS05637
337. If $x^2 + y^2 = 29$, what is the value of $(x - y)^2$?

(1) $xy = 10$
(2) $x = 5$

Algebra Simplifying Algebraic Expressions
Since $(x - y)^2 = (x^2 + y^2) - 2xy$ and it is given that
$x^2 + y^2 = 29$, it follows that $(x - y)^2 = 29 - 2xy$.
Therefore, the value of $(x - y)^2$ can be determined
if and only if the value of xy can be determined.

(1) Since the value of xy is given, the value of
 $(x - y)^2$ can be determined; SUFFICIENT.

(2) Given only that $x = 5$, it is not possible to
 determine the value of xy. Therefore, the
 value of $(x - y)^2$ cannot be determined;
 NOT sufficient.

**The correct answer is A;
statement 1 alone is sufficient.**

DS16470
338. After winning 50 percent of the first 20 games it played,
Team A won all of the remaining games it played. What
was the total number of games that Team A won?

(1) Team A played 25 games altogether.
(2) Team A won 60 percent of all the games it played.

Arithmetic Percents
Let r be the number of the remaining games
played, all of which the team won. Since the team
won (50%)(20) = 10 of the first 20 games and the
r remaining games, the total number of games the
team won is $10 + r$. Also, the total number of games
the team played is $20 + r$. Determine the value of r.

(1) Given that the total number of games
 played is 25, it follows that $20 + r = 25$, or
 $r = 5$; SUFFICIENT.

(2) It is given that the total number of
 games won is (60%)(20 + r), which can
 be expanded as $12 + 0.6r$. Since it is also
 known that the number of games won is
 $10 + r$, it follows that $12 + 0.6r = 10 + r$.
 Solving this equation gives $12 - 10 = r - 0.6r$,
 or $2 = 0.4r$, or $r = 5$; SUFFICIENT.

**The correct answer is D;
each statement alone is sufficient.**

DS17181

339. Is x between 0 and 1 ?

(1) x^2 is less than x.

(2) x^3 is positive.

Arithmetic Arithmetic Operations

(1) Since x^2 is always nonnegative, it follows that here x must also be nonnegative, that is, greater than or equal to 0. If $x = 0$ or 1, then $x^2 = x$. Furthermore, if x is greater than 1, then x^2 is greater than x. Therefore, x must be between 0 and 1; SUFFICIENT.

(2) If x^3 is positive, then x is positive, but x can be any positive number; NOT sufficient.

The correct answer is A; statement 1 alone is sufficient.

DS04083

340. If m and n are nonzero integers, is m^n an integer?

(1) n^m is positive.

(2) n^m is an integer.

Arithmetic Properties of Numbers

It is useful to note that if $m > 1$ and $n < 0$, then $0 < m^n < 1$, and therefore m^n will not be an integer. For example, if $m = 3$ and $n = -2$, then $m^n = 3^{-2} = \dfrac{1}{3^2} = \dfrac{1}{9}$.

(1) Although it is given that n^m is positive, m^n can be an integer or m^n can fail to be an integer. For example, if $m = 2$ and $n = 2$, then $n^m = 2^2 = 4$ is positive and $m^n = 2^2 = 4$ is an integer. However, if $m = 2$ and $n = -2$, then $n^m = (-2)^2 = 4$ is positive and $m^n = 2^{-2} = \dfrac{1}{2^2} = \dfrac{1}{4}$ is not an integer; NOT sufficient.

(2) Although it is given that n^m is an integer, m^n can be an integer or m^n can fail to be an integer. For example, if $m = 2$ and $n = 2$, then $n^m = 2^2 = 4$ is an integer and $m^n = 2^2 = 4$ is an integer. However, if $m = 2$ and $n = -2$, then $n^m = (-2)^2 = 4$ is an integer and $m^n = 2^{-2} = \dfrac{1}{2^2} = \dfrac{1}{4}$ is not an integer; NOT sufficient.

Taking (1) and (2) together, it is still not possible to determine if m^n is an integer, since the same examples are used in both (1) and (2) above.

The correct answer is E; both statements together are still not sufficient.

DS16034

341. What is the value of xy ?

(1) $x + y = 10$

(2) $x - y = 6$

Algebra First- and Second-Degree Equations; Simultaneous Equations

(1) Given $x + y = 10$, or $y = 10 - x$, it follows that $xy = x(10 - x)$, which does not have a unique value. For example, if $x = 0$, then $xy = (0)(10) = 0$, but if $x = 1$, then $xy = (1)(9) = 9$; NOT sufficient.

(2) Given $x - y = 6$, or $y = x - 6$, it follows that $xy = x(x - 6)$, which does not have a unique value. For example, if $x = 0$, then $xy = (0)(-6) = 0$, but if $x = 1$, then $xy = (1)(-5) = -5$; NOT sufficient.

Using (1) and (2) together, the two equations can be solved simultaneously for x and y. One way to do this is by adding the two equations, $x + y = 10$ and $x - y = 6$, to get $2x = 16$, or $x = 8$. Then substitute into either of the equations to obtain an equation that can be solved to get $y = 2$. Thus, xy can be determined to have the value $(8)(2) = 16$. Alternatively, the two equations correspond to a pair of nonparallel lines in the (x, y) coordinate plane, which have a unique point in common.

The correct answer is C; both statements together are sufficient.

DS13189

342. If n is the least of three different integers greater than 1, what is the value of n ?

(1) The product of the three integers is 90.

(2) One of the integers is twice one of the other two integers.

Arithmetic Operations with Integers

Given that n is the least of three different integers n, p, and q, where $1 < n < p < q$, determine the value of n.

(1) This indicates that the product of the three integers is 90. The integers could be 2, 5, and 9 since $(2)(5)(9) = 90$, and n would be 2.

However, the integers could be 3, 5, and 6 since $(3)(5)(6) = 90$, and n would be 3; NOT sufficient.

(2) This indicates that one of the integers is twice one of the others. It could be that $p = 2n$, or $q = 2n$, or $q = 2p$. For example, if $n = 2$, $p = 4$, and $q = 5$, then $p = 2n$, and the value of n would be 2. If $n = 3$, $p = 4$, and $q = 6$, then $q = 2n$, and the value of n would be 3; NOT sufficient.

Taking (1) and (2) together, if $p = 2n$, then $npq = (n)(2n)(q) = 90$, or $n^2q = 45$. It follows that $n = 3$, $p = (2)(3) = 6$, and $q = 5$. The value of n is 3. If $q = 2n$, then $npq = (n)(p)(2n) = 90$ or $n^2p = 45$. It follows that $n = 3$, $p = 5$, and $q = (2)(3) = 6$. The value of n is 3. If $q = 2p$, then $npq = (n)(p)(2p) = 90$ or $np^2 = 45$. It follows that $n = 5$, $p = 3$, and $q = (2)(3) = 6$, and this case can be eliminated because n is not the least of the three integers. Therefore, the value of n is 3.

Alternatively, taking (1) and (2) together, the integers n, p, and q are among 2, 3, 5, 6, 9, 10, 15, 18, 30, and 45 since they are factors of 90 from (1). Because all three integers are different and $90 = (2)(3)(15) = (2)(3^2)(5)$, n, p, and q must be among the integers 2, 3, 5, 9, 10, and 15. Only two pairs of these integers satisfy (2): 3 and 6 since $6 = (2)(3)$ and 5 and 10 since $10 = (2)(5)$. However, for each possible value for n, $(n)(5)(10) > 90$. Therefore, the only pair that satisfies both (1) and (2) is 3 and 6, and the third integer is then $\dfrac{90}{(3)(6)} = 5$. Thus, the value of n is 3.

The correct answer is C; both statements together are sufficient.

DS16461

343. Is x^2 greater than x ?

(1) x^2 is greater than 1.

(2) x is greater than -1.

Arithmetic; Algebra Exponents; Inequalities

(1) Given $x^2 > 1$, it follows that either $x > 1$ or $x < -1$. If $x > 1$, then multiplying both sides of the inequality by the positive number x gives $x^2 > x$. On the other hand, if $x < -1$, then x is negative and x^2 is positive

(because $x^2 > 1$), which also gives $x^2 > x$; SUFFICIENT.

(2) Given $x > -1$, x^2 can be greater than x (for example, $x = 2$) and x^2 can fail to be greater than x (for example, $x = 0$); NOT sufficient.

The correct answer is A; statement 1 alone is sufficient.

DS03503

344. Michael arranged all his books in a bookcase with 10 books on each shelf and no books left over. After Michael acquired 10 additional books, he arranged all his books in a new bookcase with 12 books on each shelf and no books left over. How many books did Michael have before he acquired the 10 additional books?

(1) Before Michael acquired the 10 additional books, he had fewer than 96 books.

(2) Before Michael acquired the 10 additional books, he had more than 24 books.

Arithmetic Properties of Numbers

If x is the number of books Michael had before he acquired the 10 additional books, then x is a multiple of 10. After Michael acquired the 10 additional books, he had $x + 10$ books and $x + 10$ is a multiple of 12.

(1) If $x < 96$, where x is a multiple of 10, then $x = 10, 20, 30, 40, 50, 60, 70, 80$, or 90 and $x + 10 = 20, 30, 40, 50, 60, 70, 80, 90$, or 100. Since $x + 10$ is a multiple of 12, then $x + 10 = 60$ and $x = 50$; SUFFICIENT.

(2) If $x > 24$, where x is a multiple of 10, then x must be one of the numbers 30, 40, 50, 60, 70, 80, 90, 100, 110, …, and $x + 10$ must be one of the numbers 40, 50, 60, 70, 80, 90, 100, 110, 120, …. Since there is more than one multiple of 12 among these numbers (for example, 60 and 120), the value of $x + 10$, and therefore the value of x, cannot be determined; NOT sufficient.

The correct answer is A; statement 1 alone is sufficient.

DS16469

345. If $xy > 0$, does $(x - 1)(y - 1) = 1$?

(1) $x + y = xy$

(2) $x = y$

Algebra First- and Second-Degree Equations

By expanding the product $(x-1)(y-1)$, the question is equivalent to whether $xy - y - x + 1 = 1$, or $xy - y - x = 0$, when $xy > 0$.

(1) If $x + y = xy$, then $xy - y - x = 0$, and hence by the remarks above, $(x-1)(y-1) = 1$; SUFFICIENT.

(2) If $x = y$, then $(x-1)(y-1) = 1$ can be true ($x = y = 2$) and $(x-1)(y-1) = 1$ can be false ($x = y = 1$); NOT sufficient.

The correct answer is A; statement 1 alone is sufficient.

DS06842
346. Last year in a group of 30 businesses, 21 reported a net profit and 15 had investments in foreign markets. How many of the businesses did not report a net profit nor invest in foreign markets last year?

(1) Last year 12 of the 30 businesses reported a net profit and had investments in foreign markets.

(2) Last year 24 of the 30 businesses reported a net profit or invested in foreign markets, or both.

Arithmetic Concepts of Sets

Consider the Venn diagram below in which x represents the number of businesses that reported a net profit and had investments in foreign markets. Since 21 businesses reported a net profit, $21 - x$ businesses reported a net profit only. Since 15 businesses had investments in foreign markets, $15 - x$ businesses had investments in foreign markets only. Finally, since there is a total of 30 businesses, the number of businesses that did not report a net profit and did not invest in foreign markets is $30 - (21 - x + x + 15 - x) = x - 6$.

Determine the value of $x - 6$, or equivalently, the value of x.

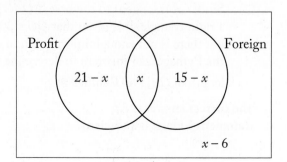

(1) It is given that $12 = x$; SUFFICIENT.

(2) It is given that $24 = (21 - x) + x + (15 - x)$. Therefore, $24 = 36 - x$, or $x = 12$.

Alternatively, the information given is exactly the number of businesses that are not among those to be counted in answering the question posed in the problem, and therefore the number of businesses that are to be counted is $30 - 24 = 6$; SUFFICIENT.

The correct answer is D; each statement alone is sufficient.

DS17110
347. Is the perimeter of square S greater than the perimeter of equilateral triangle T?

(1) The ratio of the length of a side of S to the length of a side of T is 4:5.

(2) The sum of the lengths of a side of S and a side of T is 18.

Geometry Perimeter

Letting s and t be the side lengths of square S and triangle T, respectively, the task is to determine if $4s > 3t$, which is equivalent (divide both sides by $4t$) to determining if $\frac{s}{t} > \frac{3}{4}$.

(1) It is given that $\frac{s}{t} = \frac{4}{5}$. Since $\frac{4}{5} > \frac{3}{4}$, it follows that $\frac{s}{t} > \frac{3}{4}$; SUFFICIENT.

(2) Many possible pairs of numbers have the sum of 18. For some of these (s,t) pairs it is the case that $\frac{s}{t} > \frac{3}{4}$ (for example, $s = t = 9$), and for others of these pairs it is not the case that $\frac{s}{t} > \frac{3}{4}$ (for example, $s = 1$ and $t = 17$); NOT sufficient.

The correct answer is A; statement 1 alone is sufficient.

DS17136
348. If $x + y + z > 0$, is $z > 1$?

(1) $z > x + y + 1$

(2) $x + y + 1 < 0$

Algebra Inequalities

(1) The inequality $x + y + z > 0$ gives $z > -x - y$. Adding this last inequality to the given inequality, $z > x + y + 1$, gives $2z > 1$, or $z > \dfrac{1}{2}$, which suggests that (1) is not sufficient. Indeed, z could be 2 ($x = y = 0$ and $z = 2$ satisfy both $x + y + z > 0$ and $z > x + y + 1$), which is greater than 1, and z could be $\dfrac{3}{4}$ ($x = y = -\dfrac{1}{4}$ and $z = \dfrac{3}{4}$ satisfy both $x + y + z > 0$ and $z > x + y + 1$), which is not greater than 1; NOT sufficient.

(2) It follows from the inequality $x + y + z > 0$ that $z > -(x + y)$. It is given that $x + y + 1 < 0$, or $(x + y) < -1$, or $-(x + y) > 1$. Therefore, $z > -(x + y)$ and $-(x + y) > 1$, from which it follows that $z > 1$; SUFFICIENT.

The correct answer is B; statement 2 alone is sufficient.

DS07832

349. For all z, $\lceil z \rceil$ denotes the least integer greater than or equal to z. Is $\lceil x \rceil = 0$?

(1) $-1 < x < -0.1$

(2) $\lceil x + 0.5 \rceil = 1$

Algebra Operations with Real Numbers

Determining if $\lceil x \rceil = 0$ is equivalent to determining if $-1 < x \le 0$. This can be inferred by examining a few representative examples, such as $\lceil -1.1 \rceil = -1, \lceil -1 \rceil = -1, \lceil -0.9 \rceil = 0, \lceil -0.1 \rceil = 0, \lceil 0 \rceil = 0$, and $\lceil 0.1 \rceil = 1$.

(1) Given $-1 < x < -0.1$, it follows that $-1 < x \le 0$, since $-1 < x \le 0$ represents all numbers x that satisfy $-1 < x < -0.1$ along with all numbers x that satisfy $-0.1 \le x \le 0$; SUFFICIENT.

(2) Given $\lceil x + 0.5 \rceil = 1$, it follows from the same reasoning used just before (1) above that this equality is equivalent to $0 < x + 0.5 \le 1$, which in turn is equivalent to $-0.5 < x \le 0.5$. Since from among these values of x it is possible for $-1 < x \le 0$ to be true (for example, $x = -0.1$) and it is possible for $-1 < x \le 0$ to be false (for example, $x = 0.1$), it cannot be determined if $\lceil x \rceil = 0$; NOT sufficient.

The correct answer is A; statement 1 alone is sufficient.

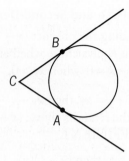

DS16464

350. The circular base of an above-ground swimming pool lies in a level yard and just touches two straight sides of a fence at points A and B, as shown in the figure above. Point C is on the ground where the two sides of the fence meet. How far from the center of the pool's base is point A?

(1) The base has area 250 square feet.

(2) The center of the base is 20 feet from point C.

Geometry Circles

Let Q be the center of the pool's base and r be the distance from Q to A, as shown in the figure below.

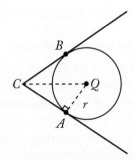

Since A is a point on the circular base, QA is a radius (r) of the base.

(1) Since the formula for the area of a circle is area $= \pi r^2$, this information can be stated as $250 = \pi r^2$ or $\sqrt{\dfrac{250}{\pi}} = r$; SUFFICIENT.

(2) Since $\overline{CA}$ is tangent to the base, $\triangle QAC$ is a right triangle. It is given that $QC = 20$, but there is not enough information to use the Pythagorean theorem to determine the length of $\overline{QA}$; NOT sufficient.

The correct answer is A; statement 1 alone is sufficient.

DS16050
351. If $xy = -6$, what is the value of $xy(x + y)$?

 (1) $x - y = 5$

 (2) $xy^2 = 18$

Algebra First- and Second-Degree Equations

By substituting -6 as the value of xy, the question can be simplified to "What is the value of $-6(x + y)$?"

 (1) Adding y to both sides of $x - y = 5$ gives $x = y + 5$. When $y + 5$ is substituted for x in the equation $xy = -6$, the equation yields $(y + 5)y = -6$, or $y^2 + 5y + 6 = 0$. Factoring the left side of this equation gives $(y + 2)(y + 3) = 0$. Thus, y may have a value of -2 or -3. Since a unique value of y is not determined, neither the value of x nor the value of xy can be determined; NOT sufficient.

 (2) Since $xy^2 = (xy)y$ and $xy^2 = 18$, it follows that $(xy)y = 18$. When -6 is substituted for xy, this equation yields $-6y = 18$, and hence $y = -3$. Since $y = -3$ and $xy = -6$, it follows that $-3x = -6$, or $x = 2$. Therefore, the value of $x + y$, and hence the value of $xy(x + y) = -6(x + y)$ can be determined; SUFFICIENT.

The correct answer is B; statement 2 alone is sufficient.

DS05519
352. $[y]$ denotes the greatest integer less than or equal to y. Is $d < 1$?

 (1) $d = y - [y]$

 (2) $[d] = 0$

Algebra Operations with Real Numbers

 (1) It is given $d = y - [y]$. If y is an integer, then $y = [y]$, and thus $y - [y] = 0$, which is less than 1. If y is not an integer, then y lies between two consecutive integers, the smaller of which is equal to $[y]$. Since each of these two consecutive integers is at a distance of less than 1 from y, it follows that $[y]$ is at a distance of less than 1 from y, or $y - [y] < 1$. Thus, regardless of whether y is an integer or y is not an integer, it can be determined that $d < 1$; SUFFICIENT.

 (2) It is given that $[d] = 0$, which is equivalent to $0 \le d < 1$. This can be inferred by

examining a few representative examples, such as $[-0.1] = -1, [0] = 0, [0.1] = 0, [0.9] = 0$, and $[1.1] = 1$. From $0 \le d < 1$, it follows that $d < 1$; SUFFICIENT.

The correct answer is D; each statement alone is sufficient.

DS14052
353. If N is a positive odd integer, is N prime?

 (1) $N = 2^k + 1$ for some positive integer k.

 (2) $N + 2$ and $N + 4$ are both prime.

Arithmetic Properties of Numbers

Determine whether the positive odd integer N is prime.

 (1) This indicates that $N = 2^k + 1$ for some positive integer k. If $k = 1$, then $N = 2^1 + 1 = 3$ and N is prime. However, if $k = 3$, then $N = 2^3 + 1 = 9$ and N is not prime; NOT sufficient.

 (2) This indicates that both $N + 2$ and $N + 4$ are prime. If $N = 3$, then $N + 2 = 5$ and $N + 4 = 7$ are both prime and N is prime. However, if $N = 9$, then $N + 2 = 11$ and $N + 4 = 13$ are both prime and N is not prime; NOT sufficient.

Taking (1) and (2) together is of no more help than (1) and (2) taken separately since the same examples were used to show that neither (1) nor (2) is sufficient.

The correct answer is E; both statements together are still not sufficient.

DS01140
354. If m is a positive integer, then m^3 has how many digits?

 (1) m has 3 digits.

 (2) m^2 has 5 digits.

Arithmetic Properties of Numbers

 (1) Given that m has 3 digits, then m could be 100 and $m^3 = 1,000,000$ would have 7 digits, or m could be 300 and $m^3 = 27,000,000$ would have 8 digits; NOT sufficient.

 (2) Given that m^2 has 5 digits, then m could be 100 (because $100^2 = 10,000$ has 5 digits) or m could be 300 (because $300^2 = 90,000$ has 5 digits). In the former case, $m^3 = 1,000,000$ has 7 digits and in the latter case, $m^3 = 27,000,000$ has 8 digits; NOT sufficient.

Given (1) and (2), it is still possible for m to be 100 or for m to be 300, and thus m^3 could have 7 digits or m^3 could have 8 digits.

The correct answer is E; both statements together are still not sufficient.

DS03308

355. What is the value of $x^2 - y^2$?

(1) $(x - y)^2 = 9$

(2) $x + y = 6$

Algebra Second-Degree Equations

Determine the value of $x^2 - y^2$.

(1) This indicates that $(x - y)^2 = 9$. It follows that $x - y = -3$ or $x - y = 3$, which gives information about the value of $x - y$ but not specific information about the value of x, y, or $x^2 - y^2$. For example, if $x = \dfrac{9}{2}$ and $y = \dfrac{3}{2}$, then $(x - y)^2 = \left(\dfrac{9}{2} - \dfrac{3}{2}\right)^2 = 9$ and $x^2 - y^2 = \dfrac{81}{4} - \dfrac{9}{4} = 18$. But if $x = \dfrac{3}{2}$ and $y = \dfrac{9}{2}$, then $(x - y)^2 = \left(\dfrac{3}{2} - \dfrac{9}{2}\right)^2 = 9$ and $x^2 - y^2 = \dfrac{9}{4} - \dfrac{81}{4} = -18$; NOT sufficient.

(2) This indicates that $x + y = 6$ but does not give specific information about the value of x, y, or $x^2 - y^2$. For example, if $x = \dfrac{9}{2}$ and $y = \dfrac{3}{2}$, then $x + y = \dfrac{9}{2} + \dfrac{3}{2} = 6$ and $x^2 - y^2 = \dfrac{81}{4} - \dfrac{9}{4} = 18$. But if $x = \dfrac{3}{2}$ and $y = \dfrac{9}{2}$, then $x + y = \dfrac{3}{2} + \dfrac{9}{2} = 6$ and $x^2 - y^2 = \dfrac{9}{4} - \dfrac{81}{4} = -18$; NOT sufficient.

Taking (1) and (2) together is of no more help than (1) and (2) taken separately since the same examples were used to show that neither (1) nor (2) is sufficient.

Alternatively, note that $x^2 - y^2 = (x - y)(x + y)$. From (1), $x - y = \pm 3$, and from (2), $x + y = 6$. Therefore, taking (1) and (2) together allows for both $x^2 - y^2 = (3)(6) = 18$ and $x^2 - y^2 = (-3)(6) = -18$.

The correct answer is E; both statements together are still not sufficient.

DS01267

356. For each landscaping job that takes more than 4 hours, a certain contractor charges a total of r dollars for the first 4 hours plus $0.2r$ dollars for each additional hour or fraction of an hour, where $r > 100$. Did a particular landscaping job take more than 10 hours?

(1) The contractor charged a total of \$288 for the job.

(2) The contractor charged a total of $2.4r$ dollars for the job.

Algebra Applied Problems

If y represents the total number of hours the particular landscaping job took, determine if $y > 10$.

(1) This indicates that the total charge for the job was \$288, which means that $r + 0.2r(y - 4) = 288$. From this it cannot be determined if $y > 10$. For example, if $r = 120$ and $y = 11$, then $120 + 0.2(120)(7) = 288$, and the job took more than 10 hours. However, if $r = 160$ and $y = 8$, then $160 + 0.2(160)(4) = 288$, and the job took less than 10 hours; NOT sufficient.

(2) This indicates that $r + 0.2r(y - 4) = 2.4r$, from which it follows that

$r + 0.2ry - 0.8r = 2.4r$	use distributive property
$0.2ry = 2.2r$	subtract $(r - 0.8r)$ from both sides
$y = 11$	divide both sides by $0.2r$

Therefore, the job took more than 10 hours; SUFFICIENT.

The correct answer is B; statement 2 alone is sufficient.

DS17600

357. If $x^2 = 2^x$, what is the value of x ?

(1) $2x = \left(\dfrac{x}{2}\right)^3$

(2) $x = 2^{x-2}$

Algebra Exponents

Given $x^2 = 2^x$, determine the value of x. Note that $x \neq 0$ because $0^2 = 0$ and $2^0 = 1$.

(1) This indicates that $2x = \left(\dfrac{x}{2}\right)^3$, so $2x = \dfrac{x^3}{8}$ and $16x = x^3$. Since $x \neq 0$, then $16 = x^2$, so $x = -4$ or $x = 4$. However, $(-4)^2 = 16$ and $2^{-4} = \dfrac{1}{16}$, so $x \neq -4$. Therefore, $x = 4$; SUFFICIENT.

(2) This indicates that $x = 2^{x-2}$, so $x = \dfrac{2^x}{2^2}$ and $4x = 2^x$. Since it is given that $x^2 = 2^x$, then $4x = x^2$ and, because $x \neq 0$, it follows that $x = 4$; SUFFICIENT.

The correct answer is D;
each statement alone is sufficient.

DS01169

358. The sequence s_1, s_2, s_3, ..., s_n, ... is such that $s_n = \dfrac{1}{n} - \dfrac{1}{n+1}$ for all integers $n \geq 1$. If k is a positive integer, is the sum of the first k terms of the sequence greater than $\dfrac{9}{10}$?

(1) $k > 10$

(2) $k < 19$

Arithmetic Sequences

The sum of the first k terms can be written as

$$\left(\dfrac{1}{1} - \dfrac{1}{2}\right) + \left(\dfrac{1}{2} - \dfrac{1}{3}\right) + \ldots + \left(\dfrac{1}{k-1} - \dfrac{1}{k}\right) + \left(\dfrac{1}{k} - \dfrac{1}{k+1}\right)$$

$$= 1 + \left(-\dfrac{1}{2} + \dfrac{1}{2}\right) + \left(-\dfrac{1}{3} + \dfrac{1}{3}\right) + \ldots + \left(-\dfrac{1}{k} + \dfrac{1}{k}\right) - \dfrac{1}{k+1}$$

$$= 1 - \dfrac{1}{k+1}.$$

Therefore, the sum of the first k terms is greater than $\dfrac{9}{10}$ if and only if $1 - \dfrac{1}{k+1} > \dfrac{9}{10}$, or $1 - \dfrac{9}{10} > \dfrac{1}{k+1}$, or $\dfrac{1}{10} > \dfrac{1}{k+1}$. Multiplying both sides of the last inequality by $10(k+1)$ gives the equivalent condition $k + 1 > 10$, or $k > 9$.

(1) Given that $k > 10$, then it follows that $k > 9$; SUFFICIENT.

(2) Given that $k < 19$, it is possible to have $k > 9$ (for example, $k = 15$) and it is possible to not have $k > 9$ (for example, $k = 5$); NOT sufficient.

The correct answer is A;
statement 1 alone is sufficient.

DS05518

359. In the sequence S of numbers, each term after the first two terms is the sum of the two immediately preceding terms. What is the 5th term of S?

(1) The 6th term of S minus the 4th term equals 5.

(2) The 6th term of S plus the 7th term equals 21.

Arithmetic Sequences

If the first two terms of sequence S are a and b, then the remaining terms of sequence S can be expressed in terms of a and b as follows.

n	nth term of sequence S
1	a
2	b
3	$a + b$
4	$a + 2b$
5	$2a + 3b$
6	$3a + 5b$
7	$5a + 8b$

For example, the 6th term of sequence S is $3a + 5b$ because $(a + 2b) + (2a + 3b) = 3a + 5b$. Determine the value of the 5th term of sequence S, that is, the value of $2a + 3b$.

(1) Given that the 6th term of S minus the 4th term of S is 5, it follows that $(3a + 5b) - (a + 2b) = 5$. Combining like terms, this equation can be rewritten as $2a + 3b = 5$, and thus the 5th term of sequence S is 5; SUFFICIENT.

(2) Given that the 6th term of S plus the 7th term of S is 21, it follows that $(3a + 5b) + (5a + 8b) = 21$. Combining like terms, this equation can be rewritten as $8a + 13b = 21$. Letting e represent the 5th term of sequence S, this last equation is equivalent to $4(2a + 3b) + b = 21$, or $4e + b = 21$, which gives a direct correspondence between the 5th term of sequence S and the 2nd term of sequence S. Therefore, the 5th term of sequence S can be determined

if and only if the 2nd term of sequence S can be determined. Since the 2nd term of sequence S cannot be determined, the 5th term of sequence S cannot be determined. For example, if $a = 1$ and $b = 1$, then $8a + 13b = 8(1) + 13(1) = 21$ and the 5th term of sequence S is $2a + 3b = 2(1) + 3(1) = 5$. However, if $a = 0$ and $b = \frac{21}{13}$, then

$$8a + 13b = 8(0) + 13\left(\frac{21}{13}\right) = 21$$

and the 5th term of sequence S is

$$2a + 3b = 2(0) + 3\left(\frac{21}{13}\right) = \frac{63}{13}; \text{ NOT}$$

sufficient.

**The correct answer is A;
statement 1 alone is sufficient.**

DS01121

360. If 75 percent of the guests at a certain banquet ordered dessert, what percent of the guests ordered coffee?

(1) 60 percent of the guests who ordered dessert also ordered coffee.

(2) 90 percent of the guests who ordered coffee also ordered dessert.

Arithmetic Concepts of Sets; Percents

Consider the Venn diagram below that displays the various percentages of 4 groups of the guests. Thus, x percent of the guests ordered both dessert and coffee and y percent of the guests ordered coffee only. Since 75 percent of the guests ordered dessert, $(75 − x)\%$ of the guests ordered dessert only. Also, because the 4 percentages represented in the Venn diagram have a total sum of 100 percent, the percentage of guests who did not order either dessert or coffee is $100 − [(75 − x) + x + y] = 25 − y$. Determine the percentage of guests who ordered coffee, or equivalently, the value of $x + y$.

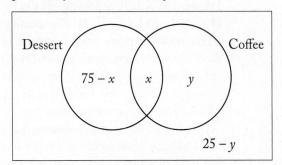

(1) Given that x is equal to 60 percent of 75, or 45, the value of $x + y$ cannot be determined; NOT sufficient.

(2) Given that 90 percent of $x + y$ is equal to x, it follows that $0.9(x + y) = x$, or $9(x + y) = 10x$. Therefore, $9x + 9y = 10x$, or $9y = x$. From this the value of $x + y$ cannot be determined. For example, if $x = 9$ and $y = 1$, then all 4 percentages in the Venn diagram are between 0 and 100, $9y = x$, and $x + y = 10$. However, if $x = 18$ and $y = 2$, then all 4 percentages in the Venn diagram are between 0 and 100, $9y = x$, and $x + y = 20$; NOT sufficient.

Given both (1) and (2), it follows that $x = 45$ and $9y = x$. Therefore, $9y = 45$, or $y = 5$, and hence $x + y = 45 + 5 = 50$.

**The correct answer is C;
both statements together are sufficient.**

DS05302

361. A tank containing water started to leak. Did the tank contain more than 30 gallons of water when it started to leak? (Note: 1 gallon = 128 ounces)

(1) The water leaked from the tank at a constant rate of 6.4 ounces per minute.

(2) The tank became empty less than 12 hours after it started to leak.

Arithmetic Rate Problems

(1) Given that the water leaked from the tank at a constant rate of 6.4 ounces per minute, it is not possible to determine if the tank leaked more than 30 gallons of water. In fact, any nonzero amount of water leaking from the tank is consistent with a leakage rate of 6.4 ounces per minute, since nothing can be determined about the amount of time the water was leaking from the tank; NOT sufficient.

(2) Given that the tank became empty in less than 12 hours, it is not possible to determine if the tank leaked more than 30 gallons of water because the rate at which water leaked from the tank is unknown. For example, the tank could have originally contained 1 gallon of water that emptied in exactly 10 hours or the tank could have originally contained 31 gallons

of water that emptied in exactly 10 hours; NOT sufficient.

Given (1) and (2) together, the tank emptied at a constant rate of

$$\left(6.4\,\frac{oz}{min}\right)\left(60\,\frac{min}{hr}\right)\left(\frac{1}{128}\,\frac{gal}{oz}\right)=\frac{(64)(6)}{128}\,\frac{gal}{hr}=$$

$$\frac{(64)(6)}{(64)(2)}\,\frac{gal}{hr}=3\,\frac{gal}{hr}\text{ for less than 12 hours.}$$

If t is the total number of hours the water leaked from the tank, then the total amount of water emptied from the tank, in gallons, is $3t$, which is therefore less than $(3)(12) = 36$. From this it is not possible to determine if the tank originally contained more than 30 gallons of water. For example, if the tank leaked water for a total of 11 hours, then the tank originally contained $(3)(11)$ gallons of water, which is more than 30 gallons of water. However, if the tank leaked water for a total of 2 hours, then the tank originally contained $(3)(2)$ gallons of water, which is not more than 30 gallons of water.

**The correct answer is E;
both statements together are still not sufficient.**

DS12752

362. In the xy-plane, lines k and ℓ intersect at the point $(1,1)$. Is the y-intercept of k greater than the y-intercept of ℓ?

(1)   The slope of k is less than the slope of ℓ.

(2)   The slope of ℓ is positive.

Algebra Coordinate Geometry

Let m_1 and m_2 represent the slopes of lines k and ℓ, respectively. Then, using the point-slope form for the equation of a line, an equation of line k can be determined: $y - 1 = m_1(x - 1)$, or $y = m_1 x + (1 - m_1)$. Similarly, an equation for line ℓ is $y = m_2 x + (1 - m_2)$. Determine if $(1 - m_1) > (1 - m_2)$, or equivalently if $m_1 < m_2$.

(1)   This indicates that $m_1 < m_2$; SUFFICIENT.

(2)   This indicates that $m_2 > 0$. If $m_1 = -1$, for example, then $m_1 < m_2$, but if $m_2 = 4$ and $m_1 = 5$, then $m_1 > m_2$; NOT sufficient.

**The correct answer is A;
statement 1 alone is sufficient.**

DS14588

363. A triangle has side lengths of a, b, and c centimeters. Does each angle in the triangle measure less than 90 degrees?

(1)   The 3 semicircles whose diameters are the sides of the triangle have areas that are equal to 3 cm², 4 cm², and 6 cm², respectively.

(2) $c < a + b < c + 2$

Geometry Triangles; Pythagorean Theorem

Given a triangle with sides of lengths a, b, and c centimeters, determine whether each angle of the triangle measures less than 90°. Assume that the vertices of the triangle are A, B, and C and that a is the side length of the side opposite $\angle A$, b is the side length of the side opposite $\angle B$, and c is the side length of the side opposite $\angle C$, where $a \le b \le c$.

Note that for a right triangle, $a^2 + b^2 = c^2$. However, if $a^2 + b^2 > c^2$, then the triangle is acute (i.e., a triangle with each angle measuring less than 90°). This is illustrated by the following figures.

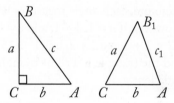

ΔBCA on the left is a right triangle with sides $BC = a$, $CA = b$, and $AB = c$, where $a^2 + b^2 = c^2$ by the Pythagorean theorem. The triangle on the right, $\Delta B_1 CA$, has sides $B_1 C = a$, $CA = b$, and $AB_1 = c_1$. Clearly $AB = c > AB_1 = c_1$, so $c^2 > c_1^2$. Since $a^2 + b^2 = c^2$ and $c^2 > c_1^2$, it follows that $a^2 + b^2 > c_1^2$, and $\Delta B_1 CA$ is clearly an acute triangle.

(1)   This indicates that the areas of the 3 semicircles whose diameters are the sides of the triangle are 3 cm², 4 cm², and 6 cm², respectively. Then, because "respectively" implies that a is the diameter of the semicircle with area 3 cm², b is the diameter of the semicircle with area 4 cm², and c is the diameter of the semicircle with area 6 cm², as shown below, then $3 = \frac{1}{2}\pi\left(\frac{a}{2}\right)^2$ from which it follows that $a^2 = \frac{24}{\pi}$. Similarly, $b^2 = \frac{32}{\pi}$, and $c^2 = \frac{48}{\pi}$.

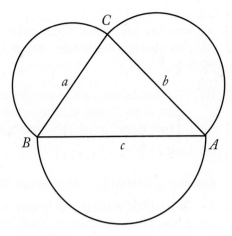

Because $a^2 + b^2 = \dfrac{24}{\pi} + \dfrac{32}{\pi} = \dfrac{56}{\pi} > \dfrac{48}{\pi} = c^2$, the angle with greatest measure (i.e., the angle at C) is an acute angle, which implies that each angle in the triangle is acute and measures less than 90°; SUFFICIENT.

(2)　This indicates that $c < a + b < c + 2$. If $a = 1$, $b = 1$, and $c = 1$, then $1 < 1 + 1 < 1 + 2$. It follows that the triangle is equilateral; therefore, each angle measures less than 90°. However, if $a = 1$, $b = 1$, and $c = \sqrt{2}$, then $\sqrt{2} < 1 + 1 < \sqrt{2} + 2$, but $1^2 + 1^2 = (\sqrt{2})^2$ and the triangle is a right triangle; NOT sufficient.

The correct answer is A; statement 1 alone is sufficient.

DS00890

364.　Each of the 45 books on a shelf is written either in English or in Spanish, and each of the books is either a hardcover book or a paperback. If a book is to be selected at random from the books on the shelf, is the probability less than $\dfrac{1}{2}$ that the book selected will be a paperback written in Spanish?

(1)　Of the books on the shelf, 30 are paperbacks.

(2)　Of the books on the shelf, 15 are written in Spanish.

Arithmetic Probability

(1)　This indicates that 30 of the 45 books are paperbacks. Of the 30 paperbacks, 25 could be written in Spanish. In this case, the probability of randomly selecting a paperback book written in Spanish is $\dfrac{25}{45} > \dfrac{1}{2}$. On the other hand, it

is possible that only 5 of the paperback books are written in Spanish. In this case, the probability of randomly selecting a paperback book written in Spanish is $\dfrac{5}{45} < \dfrac{1}{2}$; NOT sufficient.

(2)　This indicates that 15 of the books are written in Spanish. Then, at most 15 of the 45 books on the shelf are paperbacks written in Spanish, and the probability of randomly selecting a paperback book written in Spanish is at most $\dfrac{15}{45} < \dfrac{1}{2}$; SUFFICIENT.

The correct answer is B; statement 2 alone is sufficient.

DS06683

365.　A small school has three foreign language classes, one in French, one in Spanish, and one in German. How many of the 34 students enrolled in the Spanish class are also enrolled in the French class?

(1)　There are 27 students enrolled in the French class, and 49 students enrolled in either the French class, the Spanish class, or both of these classes.

(2)　One-half of the students enrolled in the Spanish class are enrolled in more than one foreign language class.

Arithmetic Sets

Given that 34 students are enrolled in the Spanish class, how many students are enrolled in both the Spanish and French classes? In other words, given that $x + y = 34$ in the diagram below, what is the value of y?

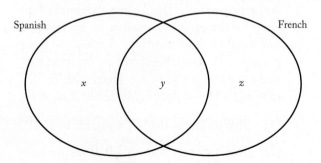

(1)　It is given that $y + z = 27$ and $x + y + z = 49$. Adding the equations $x + y = 34$ and $y + z = 27$ gives $x + 2y + z = 34 + 27 = 61$, or $y + (x + y + z) = 61$. Since $x + y + z = 49$, it follows that $y + 49 = 61$, or $y = 12$; SUFFICIENT.

(2) Given that half the students enrolled in the Spanish class are enrolled in more than one foreign language class, then it is possible that no students are enrolled in the French and German classes only and 17 students are enrolled in both the Spanish and French classes. On the other hand, it is also possible that there are 17 students enrolled in the French and German classes only and no students enrolled in both the Spanish and French classes; NOT sufficient.

**The correct answer is A;
statement 1 alone is sufficient.**

DS04910
366. If S is a set of four numbers w, x, y, and z, is the range of the numbers in S greater than 2 ?

(1) $w - z > 2$

(2) z is the least number in S.

Arithmetic Statistics

The range of the numbers w, x, y, and z is equal to the greatest of those numbers minus the least of those numbers.

(1) This reveals that the difference between two of the numbers in the set is greater than 2, which means that the range of the four numbers must also be greater than 2; SUFFICIENT.

(2) The information that z is the least number gives no information regarding the other numbers or their range; NOT sufficient.

**The correct answer is A;
statement 1 alone is sufficient.**

DS12187
367. Last year $\frac{3}{5}$ of the members of a certain club were males. This year the members of the club include all the members from last year plus some new members. Is the fraction of the members of the club who are males greater this year than last year?

(1) More than half of the new members are male.

(2) The number of members of the club this year is $\frac{6}{5}$ the number of members last year.

Arithmetic Operations with Fractions

Let L represent the number of members last year; N the number of new members added this year; and x the number of members added

this year who are males. It is given that $\frac{3}{5}$ of the members last year were males. It follows that the number of members who are male this year is $\frac{3}{5}L + x$. Also, the total number of members this year is $L + N$. Determine if $\dfrac{\frac{3}{5}L + x}{L + N} > \frac{3}{5}$, or equivalently, determine if $3L + 5x > 3L + 3N$ or simply if $x > \frac{3}{5}N$.

(1) This indicates that $x > \frac{1}{2}N$. If, for example,

   $N = 20$ and $x = 11$, then $11 > \frac{1}{2}(20) = 10$,

   but $11 \not> \frac{3}{5}(20) = 12$. On the other hand,

   if $N = 20$ and $x = 16$, then $16 > \frac{1}{2}(20) = 10$,

   and $16 > \frac{3}{5}(20) = 12$; NOT sufficient.

(2) This indicates that $L + N = \frac{6}{5}L$. It follows

   that $N = \frac{1}{5}L$. If, for example, $L = 100$, then

   $N = \frac{1}{5}(100) = 20$. If $x = 11$, then $11 \not> \frac{3}{5}$

   $(20) = 12$. On the other hand, if $x = 16$, then

   $16 > \frac{1}{2}(20) = 10$, and $16 > \frac{3}{5}(20) = 12$;

   NOT sufficient.

Taking (1) and (2) together is of no more help than (1) and (2) taken separately since the same examples were used to show that neither (1) nor (2) is sufficient.

**The correct answer is E;
both statements together are still not sufficient.**

DS13640
368. If a, b, and c are consecutive integers and $0 < a < b < c$, is the product abc a multiple of 8 ?

(1) The product ac is even.

(2) The product bc is a multiple of 4.

Arithmetic Operations with Integers

Determine whether the product of three consecutive positive integers, a, b and c, where $a < b < c$, is a multiple of 8.

Since a, b, and c are consecutive integers, then either both a and c are even and b is odd, or both a and c are odd and b is even.

(1) This indicates that at least one of *a* or *c* is even, so both *a* and *c* are even. Since, when counting from 1, every fourth integer is a multiple of 4, one integer of the pair of consecutive even integers *a* and *c* is a multiple of 4. Since the other integer of the pair is even, the product *ac* is a multiple of 8, and, therefore, *abc* is a multiple of 8; SUFFICIENT.

(2) This indicates that *bc* is a multiple of 4. If *b* = 3 and *c* = 4, then *a* = 2 and *bc* = 12, which is a multiple of 4. In this case, *abc* = (2)(3)(4) = 24, which is a multiple of 8. However, if *b* = 4 and *c* = 5, then *a* = 3 and *bc* = 20, which is a multiple of 4. In this case, *abc* = (3)(4)(5) = 60, which is not a multiple of 8; NOT sufficient.

**The correct answer is A;
statement 1 alone is sufficient.**

DS13837

369. *M* and *N* are integers such that 6 < *M* < *N*. What is the value of *N*?

(1) The greatest common divisor of *M* and *N* is 6.

(2) The least common multiple of *M* and *N* is 36.

Arithmetic Properties of Numbers

(1) Given that the greatest common divisor (GCD) of *M* and *N* is 6 and 6 < *M* < *N*, then it is possible that *M* = (6)(5) = 30 and *N* = (6)(7) = 42. However, it is also possible that *M* = (6)(7) = 42 and *N* = (6)(11) = 66; NOT sufficient.

(2) Given that the least common multiple (LCM) of *M* and *N* is 36 and 6 < *M* < *N*, then it is possible that *M* = (4)(3) = 12 and *N* = (9)(2) = 18. However, it is also possible that *M* = (4)(3) = 12 and *N* = (9)(4) = 36; NOT sufficient.

Taking (1) and (2) together, it follows that 6 is a divisor of *M* and *M* is a divisor of 36. Therefore, *M* is among the numbers 6, 12, 18, and 36. For the same reason, *N* is among the numbers 6, 12, 18, and 36. Since 6 < *M* < *N*, it follows that *M* cannot be 6 or 36 and *N* cannot be 6. Thus, there are three choices for *M* and *N* such that *M* < *N*. These three choices are displayed in the table below, which indicates why only one of the choices, namely *M* = 12 and *N* = 18, satisfies both (1) and (2).

M	N	GCD	LCM
12	18	6	36
12	36	12	36
18	36	18	36

**The correct answer is C;
both statements together are sufficient.**

DS98530.02

370. Machines K, M, and N, each working alone at its constant rate, produce 1 widget in *x*, *y*, and 2 minutes, respectively. If Machines K, M, and N work simultaneously at their respective constant rates, does it take them less than 1 hour to produce a total of 50 widgets?

(1) *x* < 1.5

(2) *y* < 1.2

Algebra Work Problem

Because Machine N produces 1 widget every 2 minutes, Machine N produces $\frac{60}{2} = 30$ widgets in 1 hour = 60 minutes.

(1) Given that *x* < 1.5, it follows that Machine K, which produces $\frac{60}{x}$ = widgets in 60 minutes, produces more than $\frac{60}{1.5} = 40$ widgets in 1 hour = 60 minutes. Thus, regardless of the number of widgets produced by Machine M, when all three machines are working simultaneously at their respective constant rates, more than 30 + 40 = 70 widgets will be produced in 1 hour. Therefore, the three machines will together have produced 50 widgets in less than 1 hour; SUFFICIENT.

(2) Given that *y* < 1.2, it follows that Machine M, which produces $\frac{60}{y}$ = widgets in 60 minutes, produces more than $\frac{60}{1.2} = 50$ widgets in 1 hour = 60 minutes. Thus, regardless of the number of widgets produced by Machine K, when all three machines are working simultaneously at their respective constant rates, more than 30 + 50 = 80 widgets will be produced in 1 hour. Therefore, the three machines will

together have produced 50 widgets in less than 1 hour; SUFFICIENT.

The correct answer is D; each statement alone is sufficient.

DS07575

371. Stations X and Y are connected by two separate, straight, parallel rail lines that are 250 miles long. Train P and train Q simultaneously left Station X and Station Y, respectively, and each train traveled to the other's point of departure. The two trains passed each other after traveling for 2 hours. When the two trains passed, which train was nearer to its destination?

    (1) At the time when the two trains passed, train P had averaged a speed of 70 miles per hour.

    (2) Train Q averaged a speed of 55 miles per hour for the entire trip.

Arithmetic Applied Problems; Rates

(1) This indicates that Train P had traveled $2(70) = 140$ miles when it passed Train Q. It follows that Train P was $250 - 140 = 110$ miles from its destination and Train Q was 140 miles from its destination, which means that Train P was nearer to its destination when the trains passed each other; SUFFICIENT.

(2) This indicates that Train Q averaged a speed of 55 miles per hour for the entire trip, but no information is given about the speed of Train P. If Train Q traveled for 2 hours at an average speed of 55 miles per hour and Train P traveled for 2 hours at an average speed of 70 miles per hour, then Train P was nearer to its destination when the trains passed. However, if Train Q traveled for 2 hours at an average speed of 65 miles per hour and Train P traveled for 2 hours at an average speed of 60 miles per hour, then Train Q was nearer to its destination when the trains passed. Note that if Train Q traveled at $\frac{(120)(55)}{140} = 47\frac{1}{7}$ miles per hour for the remainder of the trip, then its average speed for the whole trip was 55 miles per hour; NOT sufficient.

The correct answer is A; statement 1 alone is sufficient.

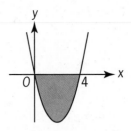

DS01613

372. In the xy-plane shown, the shaded region consists of all points that lie above the graph of $y = x^2 - 4x$ and below the x-axis. Does the point (a,b) (not shown) lie in the shaded region if $b < 0$?

    (1) $0 < a < 4$

    (2) $a^2 - 4a < b$

Algebra Coordinate Geometry

In order for (a,b) to lie in the shaded region, it must lie above the graph of $y = x^2 - 4x$ and below the x-axis. Since $b < 0$, the point (a,b) lies below the x-axis. In order for (a,b) to lie above the graph of $y = x^2 - 4x$, it must be true that $b > a^2 - 4a$.

(1) This indicates that $0 < a < 4$. If $a = 2$, then $a^2 - 4a = 2^2 - 4(2) = -4$, so if $b = -1$, then $b > a^2 - 4a$ and (a,b) is in the shaded region. But if $b = -5$, then $b < a^2 - 4a$ and (a,b) is not in the shaded region; NOT sufficient.

(2) This indicates that $b > a^2 - 4a$, and thus, (a,b) is in the shaded region; SUFFICIENT.

The correct answer is B; statement 2 alone is sufficient.

DS01685

373. If a and b are positive integers, is $\sqrt[3]{ab}$ an integer?

    (1) $\sqrt{a}$ is an integer.

    (2) $b = \sqrt{a}$

Arithmetic Properties of Numbers

(1) Given that $\sqrt{a}$ is an integer, then $a = 4$ is possible. If, in addition $b = 1$, then $\sqrt[3]{ab} = \sqrt[3]{4}$ is not an integer. However, if, in addition $b = 2$, then $\sqrt[3]{ab} = \sqrt[3]{8} = 2$ is an integer; NOT sufficient.

(2) Given that $b = \sqrt{a}$, then $\sqrt[3]{ab} = \sqrt[3]{a\sqrt{a}} = \sqrt[3]{\sqrt{a^3}} = \sqrt{\sqrt[3]{a^3}} = \sqrt{a} = b$ is an integer; SUFFICIENT.

The correct answer is B; statement 2 alone is sufficient.

6.0 GMAT™ Official Guide Quantitative Review Question Index

6.0 GMAT™ Official Guide Quantitative Review Question Index

The Quantitative Review Question Index is organized by GMAT™ section, difficulty level, and then by mathematical concept. The question number, page number, and answer explanation page number are listed so that questions within the book can be quickly located.

To locate a question from the online question bank in the book—Every question in the online question bank has a unique ID, called the Practice Question Identifier, or PQID, which appears above the question number. Look up the PQID in the table to find its problem number and page number in the book.

Math Review

Difficulty	Concept	Question #	Page	Answer Explanation Page	PQID
Easy	Algebra Applied Problems	11	51	52	PS51061.03
Easy	Algebra Ratio and Proportion	7	37	39	DS71210.03
Easy	Algebra; Arithmetic Simplifying Algebraic Expressions; Percents	14	51	53	PS23461.03
Easy	Arithmetic Percents	12	51	52	DS15161.03
Easy	Arithmetic Rate Problem	13	51	53	DS07061.03
Easy	Arithmetic Statistics	16	67	69	PS07310.03
Easy	Arithmetic Statistics	17	67	69	PS57720.03
Easy	Arithmetic; Algebra Interpretation of Tables; Applied Problems	6	37	38	PS21840.03
Easy	Geometry Angle Measure in Degrees	21	87	88	PS22061.03
Easy	Geometry Volume	22	87	89	DS17061.03
Easy	Geometry; Arithmetic Percents; Interpretation of Graphs	23	87	90	PS29261.03
Medium	Algebra Exponents	8	38	39	DS84820.03
Medium	Algebra Inequalities	2	24	26	DS38350.03
Medium	Algebra Inequalities	10	38	40	DS53060.02
Medium	Algebra Order	3	25	26	DS75160.03
Medium	Algebra Simultaneous Equations	9	38	40	DS67730.03
Medium	Algebra; Geometry Quadrilaterals	24	87	90	DS48061.03
Medium	Arithmetic Applied Problems; Operations with Decimals	4	25	27	PS10241.03
Medium	Arithmetic Measurement Conversion	1	24	25	PS87710.03
Medium	Arithmetic Statistics	18	68	70	PS97920.03
Medium	Geometry Circles; Area	25	88	91	DS39161.03

(Continued)

Difficulty	Concept	Question #	Page	Answer Explanation Page	PQID
Hard	Algebra Applied Problems	15	52	54	PS61361.03
Hard	Arithmetic Probability	20	68	71	DS11040.03
Hard	Arithmetic Properties of Numbers	5	25	27	DS10680.03
Hard	Arithmetic Sets	19	68	71	DS22030.03

Problem Solving

Difficulty	Concept	Question #	Page	Answer Explanation Page	PQID
Easy	Absolute Value	38	117	159	PS04362
Easy	Applied Problems	8	113	149	PS11468
Easy	Applied Problems	13	113	151	PS03036
Easy	Applied Problems	14	114	151	PS02019
Easy	Applied Problems	21	115	153	PS01949
Easy	Applied Problems	39	117	159	PS12934
Easy	Applied Problems	44	118	161	PS06726
Easy	Applied Problems	47	118	161	PS01099
Easy	Applied Problems	50	119	163	PS14063
Easy	Applied Problems	53	119	164	PS02498
Easy	Applied Problems	54	119	164	PS04971
Easy	Applied Problems	68	121	168	PS10174
Easy	Applied Problems	78	123	172	PS03831
Easy	Applied Problems; Operation with Fractions	52	119	163	PS15753
Easy	Applied Problems; Percents	63	120	167	PS02256
Easy	Applied Problems; Proportions	11	113	150	PS00812
Easy	Applied Problems; Substitution	19	114	152	PS10862
Easy	Area	17	114	152	PS14037
Easy	Area	23	115	154	PS09983
Easy	Area; Pythagorean Theorem	61	120	166	PS13205
Easy	Coordinate Geometry	4	112	148	PS08375
Easy	Coordinate Geometry	34	116	158	PS05109
Easy	Estimation	60	120	166	PS10921
Easy	Exponents	43	117	160	PS01650
Easy	Exponents	46	118	161	PS13426
Easy	Factoring	3	112	147	PS02978

Difficulty	Concept	Question #	Page	Answer Explanation Page	PQID
Easy	Factors, Multiples, and Divisibility	5	112	148	PS03887
Easy	First-Degree Equations	10	113	150	PS12926
Easy	First-Degree Equations	16	114	151	PS08011
Easy	First-Degree Equations	31	116	157	PS07380
Easy	First-Degree Equations	42	117	160	PS14237
Easy	First-Degree Equations	45	118	161	PS07080
Easy	First-Degree Equations	55	119	164	PS25440.02
Easy	Formulas	59	120	166	PS89821.02
Easy	Formulas	73	122	170	PS21080.02
Easy	Fractions	27	115	155	PS15994
Easy	Inequalities	9	113	149	PS06937
Easy	Inequalities	40	117	160	PS15469
Easy	Interpretation of Graphs	70	122	169	PS13841
Easy	Lines and Segments	6	113	148	PS13800
Easy	Operations on Integers	7	113	149	PS05292
Easy	Operations on Integers	22	115	153	PS06555
Easy	Operations on Integers	72	122	169	PS05916
Easy	Operations on Integers	75	122	171	PS04765
Easy	Operations on Rational Numbers	15	114	151	PS13583
Easy	Operations on Rational Numbers	25	115	154	PS05129
Easy	Operations with Fractions	66	121	167	PS11738
Easy	Operations with Fractions	67	121	168	PS14293
Easy	Operations with Fractions	71	122	169	PS05775
Easy	Operations with Integers	65	121	167	PS10422
Easy	Operations with Integers	69	121	168	PS00111
Easy	Operations with Integers	80	123	173	PS80871.02
Easy	Order	18	114	152	PS03918
Easy	Percents	12	113	150	PS07793
Easy	Percents	24	115	154	PS07659
Easy	Percents	33	116	158	PS00335
Easy	Percents	41	117	160	PS09322
Easy	Percents	56	120	165	PS12657
Easy	Percents	64	121	167	PS10339
Easy	Percents	77	123	172	PS06180
Easy	Perimeter and Area	35	117	158	PS05008
Easy	Place Value	36	117	159	PS00918
Easy	Place Value	81	123	173	PS12759

(Continued)

Difficulty	Concept	Question #	Page	Answer Explanation Page	PQID
Easy	Properties of Integers	29	116	156	PS01466
Easy	Properties of Numbers	32	116	157	PS01120
Easy	Properties of Numbers	49	118	162	PS13829
Easy	Properties of Numbers	62	120	166	PS00817
Easy	Properties of Numbers	79	123	172	PS12857
Easy	Rate	1	112	147	PS03439
Easy	Rate Problems	20	115	153	PS06719
Easy	Rate Problems	48	118	162	PS01443
Easy	Ratio and Proportion	57	120	165	PS07394
Easy	Second-Degree Equations	2	112	147	PS11042
Easy	Second-Degree Equations	26	115	155	PS13917
Easy	Second-Degree Equations	58	120	165	PS13882
Easy	Sequences	74	122	171	PS00777
Easy	Series and Sequences	30	116	156	PS01867
Easy	Series and Sequences	51	119	163	PS01656
Easy	Simplifying Algebraic Expressions; Substitution	28	116	156	PS13686
Easy	Simultaneous Equations	37	117	159	PS57330.02
Easy	Statistics	76	123	171	PS10810
Medium	Absolute Value	131	132	189	PS12785
Medium	Angle Measure in Degrees	100	127	179	PS85602.01
Medium	Angles	97	126	178	PS15602.01
Medium	Applied Problems	84	124	174	PS78502.01
Medium	Applied Problems	87	124	175	PS68502.01
Medium	Applied Problems	112	129	183	PS27680.02
Medium	Applied Problems	119	130	186	PS97190.02
Medium	Applied Problems	126	131	188	PS01875
Medium	Applied Problems	130	132	189	PS03614
Medium	Applied Problems	142	134	193	PS09294
Medium	Applied Problems	144	134	194	PS05413
Medium	Applied Problems	153	135	197	PS07058
Medium	Circles	94	126	178	PS44602.01
Medium	Circles	105	128	181	PS36602.01
Medium	Coordinate Geometry	145	134	194	PS11454
Medium	Decimals	127	131	188	PS00774
Medium	Equations; Inequalities	110	129	182	PS22680.02
Medium	Estimation	154	136	197	PS09439
Medium	Estimation; Area	151	135	196	PS11692

Difficulty	Concept	Question #	Page	Answer Explanation Page	PQID
Medium	Factoring	116	130	185	PS16980.02
Medium	First-Degree Equations	82	124	173	PS67502.01
Medium	First-Degree Equations	111	129	183	PS17680.02
Medium	First-Degree Equations	113	130	184	PS39680.02
Medium	Formulas	115	130	184	PS34880.02
Medium	Formulas	122	131	187	PS67941.02
Medium	Functions; Absolute Value	109	129	182	PS29580.02
Medium	Inequalities	123	131	187	PS00986
Medium	Inequalities	125	131	187	PS07001
Medium	Inequalities	136	133	191	PS06913
Medium	Inequalities	147	135	195	PS30421.02
Medium	Inequalities; Absolute Value	140	133	193	PS08598
Medium	Measurement Conversion	118	130	185	PS08090.02
Medium	Measurement Conversion	152	135	197	PS03623
Medium	Operations with Integers	91	125	176	PS91602.01
Medium	Order	86	124	174	PS09502.01
Medium	Percents	148	135	195	PS05924
Medium	Percents	155	136	198	PS17708
Medium	Percents; Estimation	132	132	190	PS04160
Medium	Percents; Estimation	146	134	195	PS05470
Medium	Perimeter	99	127	179	PS35602.01
Medium	Place Value	133	132	190	PS09820
Medium	Place Value	157	136	198	PS34550.02
Medium	Properties of Integers	107	129	181	PS56602.01
Medium	Properties of Integers	156	136	198	PS18180.02
Medium	Properties of Numbers	124	131	187	PS14087
Medium	Properties of Numbers	137	133	191	PS11647
Medium	Properties of Numbers	138	133	192	PS02378
Medium	Properties of Numbers	149	135	196	PS01285
Medium	Quadrilaterals	90	125	176	PS50602.01
Medium	Ratio and Proportion	143	134	194	PS09050
Medium	Ratios	85	124	174	PS87502.01
Medium	Rectangles	89	125	176	PS88502.01
Medium	Rectangles; Perimeter	139	133	192	PS17806
Medium	Rectangular Solids and Cylinders	93	126	177	PS93602.01
Medium	Rectangular Solids and Cylinders	101	127	180	PS95602.01
Medium	Second-Degree Equations	117	130	185	PS29980.02

(Continued)

Difficulty	Concept	Question #	Page	Answer Explanation Page	PQID
Medium	Second-Degree Equations	121	131	186	PS16731.02
Medium	Series and Sequences	158	136	198	PS19941.02
Medium	Sets (Venn Diagrams)	88	125	175	PS29502.01
Medium	Simple Coordinate Geometry	83	124	173	PS48502.01
Medium	Simple Coordinate Geometry	134	133	190	PS14060
Medium	Simultaneous Equations	114	130	184	PS84780.02
Medium	Simultaneous Equations	120	131	186	PS90731.02
Medium	Simultaneous Equations	135	133	191	PS89670.02
Medium	Simultaneous Equations	150	135	196	PS16620.02
Medium	Statistics	108	129	182	PS28580.02
Medium	Statistics	128	132	188	PS08407
Medium	Statistics	141	134	193	PS12450
Medium	Surface Area	129	132	189	PS08051
Medium	Triangles	96	126	178	PS05602.01
Medium	Triangles	104	128	181	PS26602.01
Medium	Triangles; Area; Measurement Conversion	95	126	178	PS54602.01
Medium	Triangles; Pythagorean Theorem	92	125	177	PS73602.01
Medium	Triangles; Pythagorean Theorem	102	128	180	PS06602.01
Medium	Volume	98	127	179	PS25602.01
Medium	Volume	103	128	180	PS16602.01
Medium	Volume	106	128	181	PS46602.01
Hard	Absolute Value	178	139	206	PS03356
Hard	Angles	199	142	215	PS16967
Hard	Applied Problems	163	137	200	PS76841.02
Hard	Applied Problems	192	141	211	PS06959
Hard	Applied Problems	195	142	213	PS05972
Hard	Applied Problems	205	143	217	PS12151.02
Hard	Applied Problems	210	144	220	PS79981.02
Hard	Applied Problems	212	144	220	PS67381.02
Hard	Applied Problems; Percents	169	138	202	PS11755
Hard	Applied Problems; Percents	198	142	214	PS02389
Hard	Area	206	143	218	PS07117
Hard	Arithmetic Operations	161	136	199	PS24000.02
Hard	Circles; Triangles; Area	160	136	199	PS00904
Hard	Circles; Triangles; Circumference	180	140	207	PS08859
Hard	Elementary Combinatorics	181	140	208	PS02955
Hard	Elementary Combinatorics	184	140	209	PS10309

Difficulty	Concept	Question #	Page	Answer Explanation Page	PQID
Hard	Elementary Combinatorics	186	140	209	PS01334
Hard	Estimation	172	138	203	PS11024
Hard	Exponents	171	138	203	PS03696
Hard	First-Degree Equations	159	136	199	PS19062
Hard	First-Degree Equations; Percents	182	140	208	PS06189
Hard	First-Degree Equations; Percents	190	141	211	PS09056
Hard	First-Degree Equations; Percents	191	141	211	PS14267
Hard	Inequalities	193	141	212	PS08654
Hard	Operations on Radical Expressions	185	140	209	PS17461
Hard	Operations on Rational Numbers	200	142	215	PS07426
Hard	Operations on Rational Numbers	211	144	220	PS16963
Hard	Operations with Integers	162	137	200	PS02053
Hard	Operations with Integers	179	139	207	PS39160.02
Hard	Percents	170	138	202	PS05146
Hard	Place Value	188	141	210	PS04254
Hard	Place Value	209	144	219	PS65741.02
Hard	Polygons	167	137	201	PS03779
Hard	Polygons	168	137	202	PS03695
Hard	Polygons; Triangles	174	138	204	PS08572
Hard	Probability	197	142	214	PS01564
Hard	Probability; Concepts of Sets	187	140	210	PS03774
Hard	Properties of Integers	207	143	219	PS66661.02
Hard	Properties of Integers	208	144	219	PS62451.02
Hard	Properties of Numbers	164	137	200	PS08485
Hard	Properties of Numbers	173	138	203	PS08729
Hard	Properties of Numbers	189	141	210	PS06312
Hard	Properties of Numbers	196	142	213	PS04780
Hard	Properties of Numbers	201	143	216	PS16977
Hard	Properties of Numbers	203	143	216	PS08416
Hard	Properties of Numbers	204	143	217	PS14051.02
Hard	Sequences and Series	165	137	200	PS11430
Hard	Sequences and Series	166	137	201	PS09901
Hard	Sets	183	140	208	PS02528
Hard	Simplifying Algebraic Expressions; Applied Problems	202	143	216	PS16990
Hard	Solids	177	139	206	PS15538

(Continued)

Difficulty	Concept	Question #	Page	Answer Explanation Page	PQID
Hard	Statistics	175	139	205	PS07771
Hard	Statistics	176	139	205	PS04987
Hard	Triangles; Area; Inequalities	194	141	212	PS14397

Data Sufficiency

Difficulty	Concept	Question #	Page	Answer Explanation Page	PQID
Easy	Angles	260	231	262	DS03602.01
Easy	Applied Problems	217	227	245	DS15510
Easy	Applied Problems	225	228	248	DS04510
Easy	Applied Problems	229	228	249	DS02589
Easy	Applied Problems	230	228	250	DS15349
Easy	Applied Problems	236	229	252	DS07258
Easy	Applied Problems	240	229	253	DS14170
Easy	Area	251	230	258	DS17502.01
Easy	Arithmetic Operations	244	229	255	DS08352
Easy	Circles; Area	259	231	261	DS82602.01
Easy	Circles; Circumference	257	231	260	DS02602.01
Easy	Coordinate Geometry	239	229	253	DS01130
Easy	Coordinate Geometry; Triangles	235	229	251	DS03939
Easy	Equations	245	229	256	DS05989
Easy	Exponents	227	228	249	DS05172
Easy	First-Degree Equations	213	227	244	DS05149
Easy	First-Degree Equations	218	227	245	DS37130.02
Easy	First-Degree Equations	247	230	256	DS15099
Easy	First-Degree Equations	253	230	259	DS89502.01
Easy	Inequalities	220	227	246	DS04644
Easy	Inequalities	231	228	250	DS04573
Easy	Linear Equations	242	229	255	DS09385
Easy	Percents	237	229	252	DS06650
Easy	Percents	254	230	259	DS99502.01
Easy	Polygons	258	231	261	DS62602.01
Easy	Probability	216	227	245	DS35330.02
Easy	Properties of Integers	226	228	248	DS01104
Easy	Properties of Numbers	222	227	247	DS04636
Easy	Properties of Numbers	232	228	250	DS12033
Easy	Properties of Numbers	238	229	253	DS17319

Difficulty	Concept	Question #	Page	Answer Explanation Page	PQID
Easy	Properties of Numbers	243	229	255	DS09260
Easy	Quadrilaterals	256	230	260	DS60602.01
Easy	Quadrilaterals	262	231	262	DS33602.01
Easy	Quadrilaterals	263	232	263	DS55602.01
Easy	Rate Problems	234	228	251	DS23820.02
Easy	Ratio and Proportion	233	228	250	DS03006
Easy	Ratio and Proportion	246	229	256	DS13457
Easy	Rectangles	250	230	258	DS96502.01
Easy	Rounding	219	227	246	DS13384
Easy	Series and Sequences	215	227	245	DS01503
Easy	Simultaneous Equations	252	230	259	DS97502.01
Easy	Statistics	214	227	244	DS96720.02
Easy	Statistics	221	227	246	DS38720.02
Easy	Statistics	223	227	247	DS02779
Easy	Statistics	224	227	247	DS69610.02
Easy	Statistics	241	229	254	DS87910.02
Easy	Statistics	248	230	257	DS40410.02
Easy	Statistics	249	230	257	DS93510.02
Easy	Statistics	264	232	263	DS90820.02
Easy	Statistics	265	232	264	DS11820.02
Easy	Triangles	261	231	262	DS23602.01
Easy	Triangles; Perimeter	255	230	260	DS79502.01
Easy	Triangles; Pythagorean Theorem	228	228	249	DS17640
Medium	Absolute Value	282	234	272	DS05986
Medium	Absolute Value	291	235	277	DS11614
Medium	Angles	274	233	269	DS12862
Medium	Applied Problems	273	233	268	DS97030.02
Medium	Applied Problems	277	234	270	DS18630.02
Medium	Applied Problems	278	234	270	DS09642
Medium	Applied Problems	285	234	273	DS10383
Medium	Applied Problems	289	235	276	DS15938
Medium	Applied Problems	290	235	276	DS07206
Medium	Circles	293	235	277	DS17588
Medium	Circles; Pythagorean Theorem	266	232	264	DS18502.01
Medium	Estimation	272	233	268	DS39510.02
Medium	Factoring; Operations with Radical Expressions	299	236	280	DS17543
Medium	Inequalities	292	235	277	DS04468

(Continued)

Difficulty	Concept	Question #	Page	Answer Explanation Page	PQID
Medium	Inequalities	303	236	281	DS06067
Medium	Interpretation of Tables; Sets (Venn Diagrams)	271	233	267	DS17700.02
Medium	Operations with Radicals	283	234	273	DS08306
Medium	Percents	276	233	270	DS73340.02
Medium	Percents	296	236	279	DS17503
Medium	Probability	305	236	282	DS06810
Medium	Properties of Integers	287	235	275	DS04039
Medium	Properties of Integers	306	236	282	DS19208
Medium	Properties of Numbers	294	235	278	DS15863
Medium	Properties of Numbers	297	236	279	DS06785
Medium	Quadrilaterals; Perimeter; Pythagorean Theorem	280	234	271	DS03989
Medium	Ratio and Proportion	281	234	272	DS05766
Medium	Rectangular Solids and Cylinders; Pythagorean Theorem	268	232	265	DS80602.01
Medium	Second-Degree Equations	304	236	282	DS02899
Medium	Sequences	298	236	279	DS05657
Medium	Sequences	302	236	281	DS01633
Medium	Simple Coordinate Geometry	275	233	269	DS13097
Medium	Simultaneous Equations	286	234	274	DS13907
Medium	Statistics	284	234	273	DS07568
Medium	Statistics	295	235	278	DS03615
Medium	Statistics	300	236	280	DS08307
Medium	Statistics	301	236	280	DS13132
Medium	Triangles	267	232	265	DS20602.01
Medium	Triangles	269	233	266	DS31602.01
Medium	Triangles	288	235	275	DS18386
Medium	Volume	270	233	266	DS14602.01
Medium	Volume	279	234	271	DS08852
Hard	Applied Problems	356	240	300	DS01267
Hard	Applied Problems	370	241	306	DS98530.02
Hard	Applied Problems; Rates	371	241	307	DS07575
Hard	Arithmetic Operations	314	237	285	DS16277
Hard	Arithmetic Operations	326	238	289	DS17112
Hard	Arithmetic Operations	327	238	290	DS17153
Hard	Arithmetic Operations	339	239	295	DS17181
Hard	Arithmetic Operations; Percents	322	237	288	DS17147
Hard	Circles	328	238	290	DS17107

Difficulty	Concept	Question #	Page	Answer Explanation Page	PQID
Hard	Circles	330	238	291	DS17095
Hard	Circles	350	240	298	DS16464
Hard	Concepts of Sets	346	239	297	DS06842
Hard	Concepts of Sets; Percents	360	240	302	DS01121
Hard	Coordinate Geometry	332	238	292	DS07715
Hard	Coordinate Geometry	362	241	303	DS12752
Hard	Coordinate Geometry	372	242	307	DS01613
Hard	Exponents	357	240	300	DS17600
Hard	Exponents; Inequalities	343	239	296	DS16461
Hard	First- and Second-Degree Equations	331	238	292	DS17168
Hard	First- and Second-Degree Equations	345	239	296	DS16469
Hard	First- and Second-Degree Equations	351	240	299	DS16050
Hard	First- and Second-Degree Equations; Simultaneous Equations	341	239	295	DS16034
Hard	Fractions	315	237	285	DS02474
Hard	Inequalities	324	238	289	DS17150
Hard	Inequalities	335	238	293	DS16044
Hard	Inequalities	348	239	297	DS17136
Hard	Operations with Fractions	367	241	305	DS12187
Hard	Operations with Integers	342	239	295	DS13189
Hard	Operations with Integers	368	241	305	DS13640
Hard	Operations with Real Numbers	349	239	298	DS07832
Hard	Operations with Real Numbers	352	240	299	DS05519
Hard	Percents	307	236	283	DS60130
Hard	Percents	318	237	286	DS03678
Hard	Percents	325	238	289	DS17151
Hard	Percents	338	239	294	DS16470
Hard	Perimeter	347	239	297	DS17110
Hard	Probability	364	241	304	DS00890
Hard	Properties of Numbers	309	237	283	DS06368
Hard	Properties of Numbers	319	237	287	DS15902
Hard	Properties of Numbers	321	237	288	DS17137
Hard	Properties of Numbers	329	238	290	DS15618
Hard	Properties of Numbers	336	239	294	DS06644
Hard	Properties of Numbers	340	239	295	DS04083
Hard	Properties of Numbers	344	239	296	DS03503

(*Continued*)

Difficulty	Concept	Question #	Page	Answer Explanation Page	PQID
Hard	Properties of Numbers	353	240	299	DS14052
Hard	Properties of Numbers	354	240	299	DS01140
Hard	Properties of Numbers	369	241	306	DS13837
Hard	Properties of Numbers	373	242	307	DS01685
Hard	Radicals	312	237	285	DS04474
Hard	Radicals	323	238	289	DS02865
Hard	Rate Problems	361	240	302	DS05302
Hard	Rectangles	320	237	288	DS02940
Hard	Second-Degree Equations	311	237	284	DS08660
Hard	Second-Degree Equations	355	240	300	DS03308
Hard	Sequences	358	240	301	DS01169
Hard	Sequences	359	240	301	DS05518
Hard	Sets	365	241	304	DS06683
Hard	Simple Coordinate Geometry	308	236	283	DS02741
Hard	Simplifying Algebraic Expressions	337	239	294	DS05637
Hard	Simultaneous Equations	310	237	284	DS13706
Hard	Statistics	313	237	285	DS16456
Hard	Statistics	316	237	286	DS14471
Hard	Statistics	317	237	286	DS11003
Hard	Statistics	334	238	293	DS07217
Hard	Statistics	366	241	305	DS04910
Hard	Triangles	333	238	293	DS17164
Hard	Triangles; Pythagorean Theorem	363	241	303	DS14588

Appendix A   Answer Sheets

Problem Solving Answer Sheet

1.	35.	69.	103.	137.
2.	36.	70.	104.	138.
3.	37.	71.	105.	139.
4.	38.	72.	106.	140.
5.	39.	73.	107.	141.
6.	40.	74.	108.	142.
7.	41.	75.	109.	143.
8.	42.	76.	110.	144.
9.	43.	77.	111.	145.
10.	44.	78.	112.	146.
11.	45.	79.	113.	147.
12.	46.	80.	114.	148.
13.	47.	81.	115.	149.
14.	48.	82.	116.	150.
15.	49.	83.	117.	151.
16.	50.	84.	118.	152.
17.	51.	85.	119.	153.
18.	52.	86.	120.	154.
19.	53.	87.	121.	155.
20.	54.	88.	122.	156.
21.	55.	89.	123.	157.
22.	56.	90.	124.	158.
23.	57.	91.	125.	159.
24.	58.	92.	126.	160.
25.	59.	93.	127.	161.
26.	60.	94.	128.	162.
27.	61.	95.	129.	163.
28.	62.	96.	130.	164.
29.	63.	97.	131.	165.
30.	64.	98.	132.	166.
31.	65.	99.	133.	167.
32.	66.	100.	134.	168.
33.	67.	101.	135.	169.
34.	68.	102.	136.	170.

171.	180.	189.	198.	207.
172.	181.	190.	199.	208.
173.	182.	191.	200.	209.
174.	183.	192.	201.	210.
175.	184.	193.	202.	211.
176.	185.	194.	203.	212.
177.	186.	195.	204.	
178.	187.	196.	205.	
179.	188.	197.	206.	

Data Sufficiency Answer Sheet

213.	249.	285.	321.	357.
214.	250.	286.	322.	358.
215.	251.	287.	323.	359.
216.	252.	288.	324.	360.
217.	253.	289.	325.	361.
218.	254.	290.	326.	362.
219.	255.	291.	327.	363.
220.	256.	292.	328.	364.
221.	257.	293.	329.	365.
222.	258.	294.	330.	366.
223.	259.	295.	331.	367.
224.	260.	296.	332.	368.
225.	261.	297.	333.	369.
226.	262.	298.	334.	370.
227.	263.	299.	335.	371.
228.	264.	300.	336.	372.
229.	265.	301.	337.	373.
230.	266.	302.	338.	
231.	267.	303.	339.	
232.	268.	304.	340.	
233.	269.	305.	341.	
234.	270.	306.	342.	
235.	271.	307.	343.	
236.	272.	308.	344.	
237.	273.	309.	345.	
238.	274.	310.	346.	
239.	275.	311.	347.	
240.	276.	312.	348.	
241.	277.	313.	349.	
242.	278.	314.	350.	
243.	279.	315.	351.	
244.	280.	316.	352.	
245.	281.	317.	353.	
246.	282.	318.	354.	
247.	283.	319.	355.	
248.	284.	320.	356.	

Notes

Notes